On Tyranny

Leo Strauss   Alexandre Kojève

ON TYRANNY

Leo Strauss

REVISED AND EXPANDED EDITION
Including the Strauss-Kojève Correspondence

Edited by Victor Gourevitch
and Michael S. Roth

THE FREE PRESS
A Division of Macmillan, Inc.
NEW YORK
Maxwell Macmillan Canada
TORONTO
Maxwell Macmillan International
NEW YORK OXFORD SINGAPORE SYDNEY

The Free Press
A Division of Macmillan, Inc.
866 Third Avenue, New York, N. Y. 10022

Maxwell Macmillan Canada, Inc.
1200 Eglinton Avenue East
Suite 200
Don Mills, Ontario M3C 3N1

Macmillan, Inc. is part of the Maxwell Communication
Group of Companies.

Printed in the United States of America

printing number

  2 3 4 5 6 7 8 9 10

Library of Congress Cataloging-in-Publication Data

Strauss, Leo.
  On tyranny / Leo Strauss.—Rev. and expanded ed.,
  including the Strauss-Kojève correspondence / edited by Victor
  Gourevitch and Michael S. Roth.
     p.   cm.
  Includes index.
  ISBN 0-02-912735-1 (paper).—ISBN 0-02-912736-X (cloth):
  1. Xenophon. Hiero. 2. Kojève, Alexandre, 1902-1968. Tyranny
  and wisdom. 3. Political science—Philosophy. 4. Despotism.
  I. Kojève, Alexandre, 1902-1968.   II. Gourevitch, Victor.
  III. Roth Michael S.   IV. Title.
  PA4494.H6S8   1991
  321.9—dc20   90-49377
                                                    CIP

Contents

Preface and Acknowledgments

On Tyranny, Leo Strauss's critical study of Xenophon's *Hiero*, was first published in 1948. A French edition appeared in 1954, which, in addition to Strauss's original study, included a French version of the *Hiero*, a slightly edited version of Alexandre Kojève's important review of Strauss's study, and a "Restatement" by Strauss that briefly replies to a review by Professor Eric Voegelin and goes on to challenge Kojève's review point by point. A volume containing essentially the same texts appeared in English in 1963. We are happy to be able to bring out a new edition of this now classic volume, enlarged by the full surviving correspondence between Strauss and Kojève.

We have taken the opportunity provided by this re-publication to correct various errors in the earlier edition, and to revise the translations. We are particularly grateful to Professor Seth Benardete for his careful review of the translation of the *Hiero*. The earlier version of Kojève's "Tyranny and Wisdom" required such extensive revisions, that we for all intents and purposes re-translated it.

We have restored the important concluding paragraph of Strauss's "Restatement" which appeared in the original French edition but was omitted from the subsequent American edition. Unfortunately we did not find a copy of Strauss's English-language original, and we therefore had to translate the published French translation of that paragraph.

In our Introduction we chose to concentrate on the issues raised in the texts that are included in the present volume, and in particular on the debate between Strauss and Kojève. Readers interested in the broader context of that debate will find it discussed more fully in Victor Gourevitch, "Philosophy and Politics," I–II, *The Review of Metaphysics*, 1968, *32*: 58–84, 281–328; and in "The Problem of Natural Right and the Fundamental Alternatives in *Natural Right and History*," in *The Crisis of Liberal Democracy*, K. Deutsch and W. Soffer eds., SUNY Press, 1987, pp. 30–47; as well as in Michael Roth's *Knowing and History: Appropriations of Hegel in Twentieth Century France* (Cornell 1988); and in "The Problem of Recognition: Alexandre Kojève and the End of History," *History and Theory*, 1985, *24*: 293–306.

We have been reluctant to come between the reader and the texts, and have therefore kept editorial intrusions to a minimum. Unless otherwise indicated, they are placed between wedge-brackets: < >.

Michael Roth found the Strauss letters among Kojève's papers in the course of research for his *Knowing and History*. Kojève's surviving letters to Strauss are preserved in the Strauss Archive of the University of Chicago Library. We wish to thank Nina Ivanoff, Kojève's legatee, for permission to publish the Strauss letters, and Professor Joseph Cropsey, Executor of the Literary Estate of Leo Strauss, as well as the University of Chicago Archives, for permission to publish the Kojève letters. We are also grateful to Mr. Laurence Berns for placing the photograph of Strauss at our disposal and to Nina Ivanoff for placing the photograph of Kojève at our disposal.

Victor Gourevitch transcribed, translated, and annotated the Correspondence, and wrote the Prefatory Note to it. We collaborated on the Introduction. .

V.G., M.S.R.
June 1990

Introduction

Over the last decade there has been a lively debate about the nature of modernity. Can it be that we have passed from a modern to a post-modern age? And, if we have made this transition, how can we evaluate the history that has led to it? Or is it the case that the transition is marked by our inability to make such evaluations? This new edition of *On Tyranny* recalls two earlier positions about modernity: those of Leo Strauss and Alexandre Kojève. In their debate about tyranny, and in their correspondence, we see articulated the fundamental alternatives regarding the possibility and the responsibilities of philosophy now.

The debate between them is most unusual. It ranges from comparatively superficial political differences to basic disagreements about first principles. As a rule, when disagreement is this deep and this passionate, there is little serious discussion. Here, the parties' desire to understand the issues is greater than their attachment to their own position. That is one reason why they state their positions so radically. They know perfectly well that, for the most part, it is not sensible to reduce the philosophical or the political alternatives to only two. But the exercise does help to bring the issues into crisp focus.

The advantages in presenting these various related texts together are obvious. The major drawback in doing so is perhaps less immediately apparent: by being made part of a larger whole, Strauss's original *On Tyranny* becomes difficult to see on its own terms. Yet it is worth the effort. *On Tyranny* is a close reading of Xenophon's short dialogue between Hiero, tyrant of Syracuse, and Simonides, the wise poet, about the burdens of tyranny and about how these burdens might be lightened. Strauss was an exemplary reader. He read with respect and an open mind. Because he read in order to learn, he read critically. But nothing was more alien to him than to use texts as pretexts for displays of his own ingenuity. *On Tyranny* was his first published full-length analysis of a single classical work, and it remains the most accessible of his close readings. It seems fitting that it should have been devoted to a dialogue. He very reasonably assumes that careful writers choose the form in which they present their thought, and that the difference between a dialogue and a treatise is therefore of philosophic import. Accordingly, he attends as closely to a dialogue's setting, characters, and actions, as he does to its speeches. *On Tyranny* illustrates how much one's understanding of a dialogue's argument can be enriched by such close attention to its dramatic features. Strauss's way of reading goes directly counter to Hegel's view that the dramatic features of the dialogue are mere embellishments. The difference between the two approaches is vividly illustrated by the contrast between Kojève's Hegelian reading of Plato, and Strauss's reading of the same dialogues. In discussing these differences Strauss succinctly states his principles of interpretation, and he goes on to comment briefly but interestingly on a number of dialogues which he never discussed in print. This series of letters about Plato—beginning with Kojève's letter of 11 April 1957, and ending with Strauss's letter of 11 September 1957—might usefully be read in conjunction with Strauss's interpretation of the *Hiero*. It is altogether one of the high points of this correspondence.

Strauss opens *On Tyranny* defiantly: modern political science is so lacking in understanding of the most massive political phenomena, that it cannot even recognize the worst tyrannies for what they are.

> . . . when we were brought face to face with tyranny—with a kind of tyranny that surpassed the boldest imagination of the most powerful thinkers of the past—our political science failed to recognize it. (23; 177).

In view of the failure of "our political science," he invites us to reconsider how classical political philosophy or science understood tyranny. The invitation immediately raises the question of how classical thought could possibly do justice to political phenomena so radically different from those of which it had direct experience. The question presupposes the truth of Hegel's claim that "philosophy is its own time grasped in thought." One of the aims of *On Tyranny* is to challenge that claim. The basic premise of classical political philosophy which Strauss invites us to reconsider is that the fundamental problems—and in particular the fundamental problems of political life—are, at least in principle, always and everywhere accessible. Now, "[t]yranny is a danger coeval with political life" (22), and reflection on political life suggests that "society will always try to tyrannize thought" (27). Reflection on tyranny thus leads to reflection on the relation between thought or philosophy and society. Strauss therefore gradually shifts the focus of his inquiry from tyranny proper to the relation between philosophy and society. In his view, the *Hiero* enacts the classical, Socratic understanding of that relation: Simonides represents the philosophic life, and Hiero the political life. Now, the relation of philosophy and society is as central to the understanding of modern tyranny as it is to the understanding of ancient tyranny. For while modern tyranny owes its distinctive character to ideology and to technology, ideology and technology are products or by-products of the specifically modern understanding of the relationship between philosophy and society (23). Strauss makes himself the spokesman for the classical understanding of this relationship, and Kojève makes himself the spokesman for the modern understanding of it.

The two fully agree that there is a tension, indeed a conflict, between philosophy and society (195, 205, cp. 27); and they agree that philosophy or wisdom ranks highest in the order of ends, that it is the architectonic end or principle (*Introduction* 303:4, 95, 273–275, 397f; 15 September 1950). They disagree about whether the conflict between philosophy and society can—and should—be resolved. In other words, they disagree about the possibility of a fully rational society. The choice is clear: to try as far as possible to elude the conflict between philosophy and society by maintaining as great a distance as possible between them; or to try as far as possible to resolve the conflict between philosophy and society by working for a reconciliation between them. Strauss opts for the first alternative; Kojève for the second.

For Strauss the conflict between philosophy and society is inevitable because society rests on a shared trust in shared beliefs, and philosophy questions every trust and authority. He sides with Plato against Kojève's Hegel in holding that philosophy cannot cease to be a quest and become wisdom simply.

Philosophy as such is nothing but genuine awareness of the problems, i.e., of the fundamental and comprehensive problems. It is impossible to think about these problems without becoming inclined toward a solution, toward one or the other of the very few solutions. Yet as long as there is no wisdom but only quest for wisdom, the evidence of all solutions is necessarily smaller than the evidence of the problems. (196; 16 January 1934, 28 May 1957).

Philosophy is inherently skeptical or "zetetic" (196). It therefore threatens to undermine society's self-confidence and to sap its will. It must therefore take account of society's requirements. But the moment it yields to them, it ceases to be philosophy and becomes dogmatism. It must therefore go its own way. The human problem does not admit of a political solution (182).

Kojève rejects that conclusion. In his view, the philosopher who finds himself faced by inconsistencies—"contradictions"—in the practices and beliefs of his society or of his age, cannot leave it at resolving them "merely" in thought. He must resolve them in deed as well. The only effective way to resolve "contradictions"—the only effective way to resolve any differences among men or between men and nature—is by laboring and struggling to change the reality that exhibited them in the first place: to change men's attitudes, beliefs, ways of life, through enlightenmenn or ideology; and to change their material conditions of life through the mastery and control of nature or technology (178). All significant theoretical disagreements are at the same time practical. It follows that they can also not be resolved by oneself alone, but can only be resolved together, by the combined efforts of each and all. Philosophy is necessarily political, and politics philosophical. Or, as Kojève puts it, anyone seriously intent on knowing, in the strong sense of the term, will be driven to "verify" his merely "subjective certainties" (152, 163f, 166).

> Now, as long as a man is alone in knowing something, he can never be sure that he truly *knows* it. If, as a consistent atheist, one replaces God (taken as consciousness and will surpassing human consciousness and will) by Society (the State) and History, one must say that whatever is, in fact, outside of the range of social and historical verification is forever relegated to the domain of *opinion* (*doxa*). (p. 161).

The only way to "verify" our opinions is to have them "recognized." Recognition "verifies" our "subjective certainty" that what is "for us" is also "for others." It thus establishes an "intersubjective consensus." Recognition is necessarily mutual. There is therefore always also a moral dimension to recognition. At a minimum, recognition is always also recognition of others as free and equal. It follows that philosophical progress is possible only hand in hand with moral and political progress (174f). "History," in the strong sense Kojève attaches to the term, is, then, the history of successive "verifications" "recognized." "Recognition" makes for "satisfaction." Kojève prefers to speak of "satisfaction" rather than of "happiness" because, once again, "satisfaction" is a more public, and hence a more "objective" criterion than "happiness," which tends to be private or "subjective." Recognition makes for satisfaction; whether it also makes for happiness is another question entirely (22 June 1946, 8 June 1956; Hegel, e.g *Vernunft in der Geschichte*, Lasson ed., Meiner, 1930, pp. 70, 78). History in the strong sense of the term, men's millennial labor and struggle to achieve satisfaction through recognition, is, then, the successive actualization and "verification" of harmony among men, and conformity between them and their world. In short, history is the progressive recognition of the proposition that all men are free and equal.

Kojève argues that, in the final analysis, the quest for mutual recognition can only be satisfied in what he calls the "universal and homogeneous state." Anything short of "homogeneity," that is to say of equality, would leave open the possibility of arbitrary distinctions of class, status, gender. Anything short of "universality" would leave open the possibility of sectarian, religious, or national rivalries, and of continuing civil and foreign wars. In the universal and homogenous state everyone "knows" and lives in the "knowledge" that everyone enjoys equal dignity, and that knowledge is embedded in the state's practices and institutions (e.g., *Introduction*, 184f). Once all recognize that all are free, there is no further collective dis-satisfaction, hence no further collective seeking or striving, and in particular no further collective labor and struggle for new modes and orders or for a new understanding. Once men are free and universally recognize that they are, history, in the strong sense of the term, is at an end. And in so far as political and philosophical progress go hand in hand, so does their fulfillment. The end of history therefore also marks the end of philosophy or of the quest for wisdom, and the beginning of the reign of wisdom simply (e.g., *Introduction*, 435n).

For Kojève's Hegel, history was the revelation of truth, and this truth was revealed primarily through the various turns taken by the master-slave dialectic. The master-slave dialectic was the motor of history, and the desire for recognition its fuel. Why did the central role which Kojève assigned to the master-slave dialectic prove so powerful? Kojève's Hegel was certainly a dramatic pragmatist. Truth and successful action were tied together, and progress was accomplished through labor and bloody battles for recognition. Kojève claimed that he was able to make sense of the totality of history and of the structure of human desire by looking at them through lenses ground against the texts of Marx and Heidegger. History and desire became understandable when their ends, their goals, became clear. Kojève claimed to provide this clarity, and he couched his interpretation in the form of a political propaganda which would further the revolution that would confirm the interpretation itself. In the 1930s Kojève thought that Hegel's philosophy promoted the self-consciousness that is appropriate to the final stage of history, a stage which would be characterized by satisfaction of the fundamental human desire for mutual and equal recognition. Kojève—and everybody else—could also see who the enemies of equality were, and thus the battle lines for the final struggle for recognition were clear. Philosophy and revolution were linked in what would be the culmination of world history.

After the War, perhaps in response to Strauss's sharp criticisms of his views, especially in his letter of 22 August 1948, and perhaps also in response to what he may have perceived as an increasingly congealed political environment, Kojève abandoned his "heroic Hegelianism," his confidence in the meaning and direction of history. His late work no longer took the form of propaganda aimed at stimulating a revolutionary self-consciousness. It took the form, instead, of a commentary on a history that had already run its course. The change in the place of revolution entailed a change in the form of his philosophy: he shifts from being a dramatic pragmatist to being an ironic culture critic. He continued to believe that the culmination of world history would define the truth of all previous events, and he continued to write of Hegelian philosophy as providing this truth. Instead of situating this philosophy at the onset of the culmination, however, in his late work Kojève claims that the end of history has already occurred. Once it became clear that revolution was not just about to occur, the only *political* rhetoric possible for Kojève's Hegelianism was in the mode of irony. The ironic edge of much of his late work results from his valorization of self-consciousness even when progress is not possible.

The expressions "the end of history" and "the end of philosophy" have become fashionable and hence virtually empty slogans. In our time, Kojève was the first seriously to think what such expressions might mean.

With a certain rhetorical flourish, he maintained that history "ended" in 1806 with Napoleon's victory over Prussia in the battle of Jena, a victory which opened the rest of Europe and, in the long run, the rest of the world to the principles of the French Revolution.

> What has happened since then has been nothing but an extension in space of the universal revolutionary force actualized in France by Robespierre-Napoleon. From the genuinely historical perspective, the two World Wars with their train of small and large revolutions have only had the effect of bringing the backward civilizations of the outlying provinces into line with the (really or virtually) most advanced European historical stages. If the sovietization of Russia and the communization of China are anything more and other than the democratization of Imperial Germany (by way of Hitlerism) or of the accession of Togo to independence or even of the self-determination of the Papuans, they are so only because the Sino-Soviet actualization of Robespierran Bonapartism compels post-Napoleonic Europe to accelerate the elimination of the numerous more or less anachronistic remainders of its pre-revolutionary past. This process of elimination is already more advanced in the North-American extensions of Europe than it is in Europe itself. It might even be said that, from a certain point of view, the United States has already reached the final stage of Marxist "communism," since all the members of a "classless society" can, for all practical purposes, acquire whatever they please, whenever they please, without having to work for it any more thall they are inclined to do. *(Introduction,* 2nd ed., p. 436n; J. H. Nichols Jr. translation, pp. 160f, somewhat altered.)

Clearly, if the Russian and the Chinese Revolutions, the two World Wars, Stalinism and Hiterlism merely confirm—"verify"—it, then "the end of history" cannot possibly mean that nothing more happens. It can only mean that nothing *radically* new can be achieved, nothing comparable in magnitude to the recognition, at all levels of life and over the entire face of the earth, that, in Hegel's phrase, all men are free; or, as Kojève's phrase "universal and homogeneous state" suggests, that all are free and equal. But that does not by any means, entail an end to politics. As Strauss notes, Kojève holds out no prospect of the state's ever withering away (210).

Kojève argues that if history is the millennial struggle to achieve freedom and equality, then the end of history also marks the end of "historical man," of man striving and struggling, in short of man as we have so far known him. (19 September 1950, *Introduction,* 387 n. 1, 434, 64). He does not share Marx's vision of an end of history that opens to "the realm of true freedom," in which men might hunt in the morning, fish in the afternoon, farm in the evening, and engage in criticism after dinner, without needing to become hunters, fishermen, farmers, or critics (*Kapital*, III, 48, iii; *German Ideology*, I A). Nor does he expect that once men have achieved freedom and equality, they will go on and seek to achieve the noble or the good. He envisages, rather, that most men, satisfied with one another's mutual recognition, doing whatever they do without purpose or constraints, and free to acquire and consume to their hearts' content, would do what is right and avoid doing what is wrong because nothing would constrain them to do otherwise. They would not be heroes; but, he appears to think, neither would they be villains. They will be mere "automata" that might assert a remnant of humanity by such utterly formal rituals of pure snobbishness as tea-ceremonies, flower arrangements, or Noh plays. As for the few who remain dissatisfied with their aimless existence in the universal and homogenous state, they will seek wisdom. Since they live in an essentially rational order, they no longer need to change it in order to understand. They can now "merely" contemplate (September 19, 1950; *Introduction*, 440n; second edition, 436n). "The owl of Minerva takes flight at dusk."

It is a constant of Kojève's thought that the end, so understood, is good and desirable. Kojèvian philosophers will therefore do what they can to embed freedom and equality in practices and institutions, or "at least *accept* and 'justify' such action if someone somewhere engages in it." (*Introduction* 291, 29 October 1953 i.f.) One cannot help wondering how Kojève reconciles arguing for universal recognition with "accepting" and "justifying" the worst tyrants of the age. It is true that in "Tyranny and Wisdom" his advice to tyrants is to work for mutual recognition in the universal homogeneous state, in other words for "liberalization" and, at least in the long run, for some form of democracy. He, of course, knew that if his advice were to have reached the tyrant, the tyrant would, at best, have turned a deaf ear to it. But Kojève also knew that deeds carry more weight than speeches, and regardless of what he may have said, his actions were designed to put as much pressure as he could on the tyrant. He quite rightly thought that the European Economic Community which he was helping to establish, could become an economic power capable of standing up to the Soviet Union, and hence of forcing it to liberalize (19 September 1950). He evidently also came to think of the European Economic Community and of the Soviet Union as the most plausible alternative models for the "universal and homogeneous state," and he spent the last twenty-five years of his life trying to tip the balance in favor of the European model. He did not turn his back on the horrors of the age and, "like a man in a storm, seek shelter behind a wall."

The end of history, as Kojève understands it, also marks "the end of philosophy." Indeed, he regards the universal and homogeneous state as the goal and fulfillment of history only because he regards it as the necessary condition for the comprehensive, coherent, hence definitive, hence true account; in short, for wisdom (19 September 1950; *Introduction*, 288f, 291). Wisdom is the architectonic principle. The comprehensive and coherent account is "circular": it explains and resolves the conflicts between "all" alternative, provisional—earlier—accounts, at the same time as it accounts for itself. Provisional accounts, that is to say philosophy or philosophies in the strict sense of the term, are inevitably shadowed by skepticism. The comprehensive and coherent account would overcome that skepticism.

Skepticism is one thing; relativism is another thing entirely. Skepticism leaves open the possibility of a definitive account. Relativism categorically denies that possibility. The most typical and influential versions of relativism accept Hegel's argument that, up to "now," being, life, and thought have been through and through historical, but reject his conclusion, that history has "now" ended. They hold that history cannot "end," and that therefore there cannot "ever" be a definitive account. Kojève and Strauss are at one in categorically rejecting this decapitated Hegelianism (e.g., 19 September 1950, 1 August 1957 i.f.) Kojève rejects it in the name of the comprehensive and coherent account, and Strauss in the name of skepticism or, as he prefers to call it, zeteticism.

Kojève does not think that "the end of philosophy" leaves nothing to think about, or that men would cease to think. Rather, as far as we can tell, or, as he says, as far as he can tell, there would henceforth be no occasion for thinking which, in the language of the long Note quoted above, makes a difference from "the genuinely historical perspective." Henceforth men think "merely" in order to understand. Henceforth to think is to re-think or to re-collect (*erinnern*) and to re-construct history, and most particularly the history of philosophy, and re-confirm its end. It is in this spirit that Kojève thought his later studies in ancient philosophy about which he speaks at such length in his correspondence with Strauss.

Strauss rejects Kojève's reconciliation of philosophy and society root and branch. It is not necessary, it is not desirable, it is not even possible. One aim—perhaps the main aim—of his study of the *Hiero* is to present the alternative to the arguments in support of their reconciliation, and he seizes the opportunity to restate that alternative in his reply to Kojève's review. In his judgment, that review only confirms that the effort to reconcile philosophy and society is bound to be destructive of both. It thus once again confirms the need to sort out—to "de-construct"—their entanglement, and to restore their classical separation.

Strauss grants, indeed he stresses, that the philosophic life, as he envisages it, is essentially a life apart. It is as self-sufficient as is humanly possible. The philosophers' "self-admiration or self-satisfaction does not have to be confirmed by others to be reasonable" (204). He does not protest when Kojève calls this account of the philosophic life "Epicurean." Nor is he deterred by Kojève's "verificationist" argument. Subjective certainty is regrettable; it may be inescapable. Philosophers have always tended to cluster in rival sects. But, he adds in a clear allusion to the life-long friendly disagreements between Kojève and himself, "recognition" among philosophers can also transcend sectarian allegiances. *Amicus Plato*. However, while "recognition" need not remain restricted to members of the same sect, it cannot be universal. Universal recognition slights or altogether ignores the difference between the competent and the incompetent, or between knowledge and opinion. As a matter of fact, the desire for recognition is not a desire for knowledge at all. The desire for recognition is nothing but vanity by another name: *Recognitio recognitiorum* (209). Kojève had sought to ward off this criticism by speaking of "earned recognition" (156). But earned recognition, the recognition we have earned from those who have earned ours, simply cannot be reconciled with the equal and universal recognition Kojève calls for. "Recognition" can, then, not solve the problem of philosophic isolation. Kojève's argument for verification by recognition—that philosophers must change the world as well as themselves in order to bring it and their otherwise merely subjective certainties into harmony—is therefore without force. So, therefore, is the conclusion that philosophy is necessarily political (207f, 195f, 202f).

More precisely, Strauss fully grants, indeed he stresses that philosophy is inevitably political, if only because philosophers live in political communities. But he denies that philosophy needs to contribute to the improvement of any given political order. It does not need to do so for its own good, and it is not obligated to do so for the common good. For the contradictions in men's beliefs and practices cannot be resolved in deed. What is more, philosophy does not require a just, or even a coherent political order. Philosophy and philosophical education thrive in the most diverse regimes, and they necessarily come into conflict with all regimes. Philosophy will therefore always and everywhere have to protect itself against the suspicion or even the outright accusation of corrupting the young, and of propagating skepticism and atheism. To that end it engages in what Strauss calls "philosophic politics," the effort by philosophers always and everywhere to win their society's tolerance and even approval by persuading it that philosophers cherish what it cherishes and abhor what it abhors (205f). Whereas Kojève assigns the task of mediating between philosophy and the political community to intellectuals who try to bring philosophy to the community and to enlighten it (173), Strauss assigns the task of mediating between them to rhetoricians who, like Prospero's art, try to protect philosophy and the community from one another (205f):

> I do not believe in the possibility of a conversation of Socrates with the *people* (it is not clear to me what you think about this); the relation of the philosopher to the people is mediated by a certain kind of rhetoricians who arouse fear of punishment after death; the philosophers can guide these rhetoricians but can not do their work (this is the meaning of the *Gorgias*). (22 April 1957)

For Strauss it is primarily the manner of philosophy that is political. For Kojève it is just as much its matter.

Kojève's argument stands or falls with his claim that the reconciliation of philosophy and society makes it possible to put an end to philosophy as quest, and provides the conditions for wisdom understood as the definitive, comprehensive, and coherent account. Such an account would, in Kojève's terse formula, deduce everything we (can) say from the mere fact that we speak (29 October 1953). He evidently does not think it necessary—or possible—also to deduce "the fact that we speak." Yet wisdom as he conceives of it, the comprehensive and coherent, i.e. "circular" account, would require him to deduce it: man is not simply self-caused. The comprehensive and coherent account would therefore require a deductive account of man, hence of living beings, hence of nature. Hegel attempted such a deduction. Kojève consistently denies that such a deduction or, indeed, any discursive account of nature is possible (*Introduction* 166–168, 378). The question therefore arises whether his account can, even if only in principle, be comprehensive and coherent. The same question arises in an only slightly different guise as soon as one pauses to reflect on Kojève's claim that the reconciliation between philosophy and society required for his comprehensive and coherent account presupposes the mastery and control of nature; and thus presupposes that nature yields to man's will and reason (*Introduction*, 301). In other words, as Strauss points out, it presupposes an anthropocentric teleology or providence. If one rejects that presupposition, as Kojève explicitly does and as Strauss does tacitly, then philosophy cannot overcome skepticism. "Nature" places limits on our capacity to give a comprehensive account. Strauss therefore calls into question the claim that philosophy and society are or can be fully reconciled. The problem of nature can no more be set aside, than it can be disposed of by "recognition" (28 May 1957, 279; cp. 22 August 1948, 237; see also *Natural Right and History*, p. 173 n. 9).

As for the moral dimension of "recognition," Strauss rejects out of hand the proposition that people can or should be satisfied with everyone's recognition of everyone's equal freedom of opportunity and dignity. (207f, 209.) He frequently leaves the reader with the distinct impression that, in his view, freedom and equality are not so much goals as they are concessions to weakness and passion. He challenges Kojève to show how the citizens of his universal and homogeneous end-state differ from Nietzsche's "last men." (208; 22 August 1948, i.f.; 11 Sept. 1957: *Thus Spake Zarathustra*, I, 3–5.) The last men are self-absorbed and self-satisfied. They know neither wonder nor awe, neither fear nor shame. Their souls are atrophied. They are utterly repugnant. The mere fact that we cannot help recoiling from them clearly shows that we aspire to more than the satisfaction of being recognized as free and equal. In particular, a political society that does not allow adequate scope for the soul's aspiration to greatness might succeed in destroying or subjugating man's humanity for a time, but it is most likely to lead to its own destruction in the long run. When souls driven by great ambition are denied scope to seek what is noble and beautiful, they will become bent on destruction. If they cannot be heroes, they will become villains. With these few terse references to the soul, Strauss returns to the problem of nature, and most specifically to the problem of human nature: any adequate ethics and politics has to take the nature of the soul into account. Kojève grants that if there is a human nature, Strauss is right. But he rejects human nature as a standard, and he most particularly rejects it as the standard for morals or politics:

. . . the question arises whether there is not a *contradiction* between speaking about "ethics" and "ought" on the one hand, and about conforming to a "given" or "innate" human *nature* on the other. For animals, which unquestionably have such a *nature*, are not morally "good" or "evil," but at most *healthy* or *sick*, and *wild* or *trained*. One might therefore conclude that it is precisely *ancient* anthropology that would lead to mass-*training* and *eugenics*. (29 October 1953).

For once Kojève's language takes on a very sharp edge: Massen*dressur* or mass-*training*, and Volks*hygiene* or *eugenics*, inevitably call to mind Nazi language and practice. Still, regardless of what one thinks of such charges of "biologism," the problem is not resolved by ignoring nature, or by invoking *Geist* or *esprit*. For Kojève the struggles and bloody battles by which *Geist* conquers nature are not just figures of speech. Earlier in the same letter, he had defended Stalin's and Mao's collectivizations. The term he chose, *Kollektivierungsaktion*, clearly acknowledges the ruthless brutality of these collectivizations. He appears to have shared Hegel's chilling judgment that "the wounds of the Spirit heal without scars."

On Tyranny is dedicated to the effort to restore classical political philosophy. The reader may therefore be somewhat startled to find Strauss assert that

[i]t would not be difficult to show that . . . liberal or constitutional democracy comes closer to what the classics demanded than any alternative that is viable in our age. (194).

He does not say what alternatives to liberal or constitutional democracy he considers viable in our age. Nor does he show the affinity between the political orders which the classics favored—or even those which they found merely acceptable—and modern liberal democracy. Aristotle's mixed regime is sometimes said to come close to our liberal democracy. But no one ever derived modern liberal democracy from Aristotle's principles (cp. e.g. *Politics* III, ix, 8). It may, of course, seem that, to paraphrase a remark of Strauss's about the relation between natural right and divine revelation, once the idea of liberal democracy has emerged and become a matter of course, it can easily be accommodated to classical political philosophy. But to judge by the efforts of thoughtful and patriotic scholars who have tried to reconcile classical

political philosophy with modern liberal democracy, all such attempts
end either in admissions of failure, or in concessions to the moderns—
regarding, for example, natural rights, commercial republicanism, or
technology—which Strauss consistently refused to make (205; 223,
190, 22, 207). His suggestion that liberal democracy be justified in
terms of the classics is, therefore, perhaps best understood as a suggestion for a radical revision of our conception of liberal democracy.

with~

The correspondence confirms what attentive readers had noticed
long ago, that although Heidegger is never mentioned in the published
debate, he is present throughout it. It is not surprising that he should
be. Both Strauss and Kojève had been deeply impressed by him in their
formative years. And besides, how could they, how could anyone
reflect on the relations between tyranny and philosophy during the
years when the full horror of Nazism was being uncovered, without
being constantly mindful of the only significant thinker who joined the
Nazis and, what is more, who did so in the name of his teaching?
Perhaps no major thinker in the history of philosophy ever so compro-
mised the good name of philosophy or so radically challenged in deed
the Socratic dictum that knowledge is virtue, and its correlate, that the
soul insensibly conforms to the objects to which it attends. He would
seem to be the target of the concluding lines in Strauss's original
"Restatement:" *et humiliter serviebant et superbe dominabantur*—"either
humbly slavish, or ruling haughtily"—a slight paraphrase of what Livy
says about the nature of the mob as he recounts how it behaved during
and immediately after the tyranny of another, later Hiero of Syracuse
(XXIV, xxv, 8). We can only speculate about Strauss's reasons for
omitting this passage from the subsequently published English versions
of this text. It seems plausible that by the time he did so, he had
decided to speak out about Heidegger explicitly and at length, and that
he wished his public comments to be suitably modulated. But there is
no reason at all to doubt that reflection on Heidegger's political career
only confirmed him—as well as Kojève—in the conviction that the
thinking of what is first in itself or of Being has to remain continuous
with what is first for us, the political life.

The dialogue between Strauss and Kojève does not end in reconciliation. Both are willing to accept the full consequences of their
respective positions. At the same time, precisely because it does not
end in reconciliation, their dialogue helps us to see more clearly the
temptations and the risks of the most basic alternatives before us.

I

On Tyranny

Xenophon

Hiero or Tyrannicus

1

(1) Simonides the poet came once upon a time to Hiero the tyrant. After both had found leisure, Simonides said,

"Would you be willing, Hiero, to explain what you probably know better than I?"

"And just what sort are they," said Hiero, "which I myself would know better than so wise a man as you?"

(2) "I know for my part," he said, "that you have been a private man and are now a tyrant. It is likely, then, that since you have experienced both, you also know better than I how the tyrannical and the private life differ in human joys and pains."

(3) "Then why don't you remind me of the things in private life," said Hiero, "since, at present at least, you are still a private man? For in this way I think I would best be able to show you the difference in each."

(4) So Simonides spoke in this way: "Well then, Hiero, I seem to have observed that private men feel pleasure and distress at sights through the eyes; at sounds through the ears, at smells through the nose, at foods and drinks through the mouth, and as to sex through what, of course, we all know. (5) As to what is cold and hot, hard and soft, light and heavy, when we distinguish between them, we

---

Translated by Marvin Kendrick; revised by Seth Bernardete.

3

seem to me to be pleased and pained by them with our entire body. And we seem to me to enjoy and be pained by what is good and bad sometimes through the soul alone, and at other times through the soul and through the body. (6) That we are pleased by sleep I imagine I'm aware but how, by what, and when—of this I believe I am somehow more ignorant," he said. "And perhaps it is not to be wondered that things in waking give us clearer perceptions than do things in sleep."

(7) Now to this Hiero replied: "Then I for one, Simonides," he said, "would certainly be unable to say how the tyrant can perceive anything other than these things you yourself have mentioned. So that up to this point at least I do not know whether the tyrannical life differs in any respect from the private life."

(8) Simonides spoke. "But in this way it does differ," he said, "[the tyrant's] pleasure is multiplied many times over through each of these means, and he has the painful things for less.

"That is not so, Simonides," Hiero said. "Know well tyrants have much fewer pleasures than private men who live on modest means, and they have far more and greater pains."

(9) "What you say is incredible," said Simonides. "For if this were the case, why would many desire to be tyrants, and what's more many who are reputed to be most able men? And why would all be jealous of the tyrants?"

(10) "By Zeus," said Hiero, "because they speculate about it, although they are inexperienced in the deeds of both lives. I will try to teach you that I speak the truth, beginning with sight; for I seem to recall you also began speaking there.

(11) "In the first place, when I reason on it, I find that tyrants are at a disadvantage in the spectacles which impress us through vision. For one thing, there are different things in different countries worth seeing. Private men go to each of these places, and to whatever cities they please, for the sake of spectacles. And they go to the common festivals, where the things which human beings hold most worth seeing are brought together. (12) But tyrants have little share in viewing these, for it is not safe for them to go where they are not going to be stronger than those who will be present. Nor is what they possess at home secure enough for them to entrust it to others and go abroad. For there is the fear that they will at the same time be deprived of their rule and become powerless to take vengeance on those who have committed the injustice.

(13) "Perhaps, then, you may say, 'But after all [sights] of this kind come to them, even when they remain at home.' By Zeus, yes, Simonides, but only few of many; and these, being of such a kind, are sold to tyrants at such a price that those who display anything at all expect to leave, receiving from the tyrant in a moment an amount multiplied many times over what they acquire from all human beings besides in their entire lifetime."

(14) And Simonides said, "But if you are worse off with respect to spectacles, you at least gain the advantage through hearing; since you never lack praise, the sweetest sound. For all who are in your presence praise everything you say and everything you do. You in turn are out of the range of abuse, the harshest of things to hear; for no one is willing to accuse a tyrant to his face."

(15) Hiero spoke. "What pleasure," he said, "do you think a tyrant gets from those who say nothing bad, when he knows clearly every thought these silent men have is bad for him? Or what pleasure do you think he gets from those who praise him, when he suspects them of bestowing their praise for the sake of flattery?"

(16) And Simonides said, "By Zeus, this I certainly grant you, Hiero: the sweetest praise comes from those who are free in the highest degree. But, you see, you still would not persuade any human being that you do not get much more pleasure from that which nourishes us humans."

(17) "I know, at least, Simonides," he said, "that the majority judge we drink and eat with more pleasure than private men, believing they themselves would dine more pleasantly on the dish served to us than the one served to them; for what surpasses the ordinary causes the pleasures. (18) For this reason all human beings save tyrants anticipate feasts with delight. For [tyrants'] tables are always prepared for them in such abundance that they admit no possibility of increase at feasts. So, first in this pleasure of hope [tyrants] are worse off than private men." (19) "Next," he said, "I know well that you too have experience of this, that the more someone is served with an amount beyond what is sufficient, the more quickly he is struck with satiety of eating. So in the duration of pleasure too, one who is served many dishes fares worse than those who live in a moderate way."

(20) "But, by Zeus," Simonides said, "for as long as the soul is attracted, is the time that those who are nourished by richer dishes have much more pleasure than those served cheaper fare."

(21) "Then do you think, Simonides," said Hiero, "that the man who gets the most pleasure from each act also has the most love for it?"

"Certainly," he said.

"Well, then, do you see tyrants going to their fare with any more pleasure than private men to theirs?"

"No, by Zeus," he said, "I certainly do not, but, as it would seem to many, even more sourly."

(22) "For why else," said Hiero, "do you see so many contrived dishes served to tyrants: sharp, bitter, sour, and the like?"

"Certainly," Simonides said, "and they seem to me very unnatural for human beings."

(23) "Do you think these foods," said Hiero, "anything else but objects of desire to a soft and sick soul? Since I myself know well, and presumably you know too, that those who eat with pleasure need none of these sophistries."

(24) "Well, and what is more," said Simonides, "as for these expensive scents you anoint yourself with, I suppose those near you enjoy them more than you yourselves do; just as a man who has eaten does not himself perceive graceless odors as much as those near him."

(25) "Moreover," said Hiero, "so with respect to food, the one who always has all kinds takes none of it with longing. But the one who lacks something takes his fill with delight whenever it comes to sight before him."

(26) "It is probable that the enjoyment of sex," said Simonides, "comes dangerously close to producing desires for tyranny. For there it is possible for you to have intercourse with the fairest you see."

(27) "But now," said Hiero, "you have mentioned the very thing—know well—in which, if at all, we are at a greater disadvantage than private men. For as regards marriage, first there is marriage with those superior in wealth and power, which I presume is held to be the noblest, and to confer a certain pleasurable distinction on the bridegroom. Secondly, there is marriage with equals. But marriage with those who are lower is considered very dishonorable and useless. (28) Well then, unless the tyrant marries a foreign woman, necessity compels him to marry an inferior, so that what would content him is not readily accessible to him. Furthermore, it is attentions from the proudest women which give the most pleasure, whereas attentions from slaves, even when they are available, do not content at all, and rather occasion fits of terrible anger and pain if anything is neglected.

(29) "But in the pleasures of sex with boys the tyrant comes off still much worse than in those with women for begetting offspring. For I presume we all know these pleasures of sex give much greater enjoyment when accompanied with love. (30) But love in turn is least of all willing to arise in the tyrant, for love takes pleasure in longing not for what is at hand, but for what is hoped for. Then, just as a man without experience of thirst would not enjoy drinking, so too the man without experience of love is without experience of the sweetest pleasures of sex." So Hiero spoke.

(31) Simonides laughed at this and said, "What do you mean, Hiero? So you deny that love of boys arises naturally in a tyrant? How could you, in that case, love Dailochus, the one they call the fairest?"

(32) "By Zeus, Simonides," he said, "it is not because I particularly desire to get what seems available in him, but to win what is very ill-suited for a tyrant. (33) Because I love Dailochus for that very thing which nature perhaps compels a human being to want from the fair, and it is this I love to win; but I desire very deeply to win it with love* and from one who is willing; and I think I desire less to take it from him by force than to do myself an injury. (34) I believe myself that to take from an unwilling enemy is the most pleasant of all things, but I think the favors are most pleasant from willing boys. (35) For instance, the glances of one who loves back are pleasant; the questions are pleasant and pleasant the answers; but fights and quarrels are the most sexually provocative. (36) It certainly seems to me," he said, "that pleasure taken from unwilling boys is more an act of robbery than of sex. Although the profit and vexation to his private enemy give certain pleasures to the robber, yet to take pleasure in the pain of whomever one loves, to kiss and be hated, to touch and be loathed—must this not by now be a distressing and pitiful affliction? (37) To the private man it is immediately a sign that the beloved grants favors from love when he renders some service, because the private man knows his beloved serves under no compulsion. But it is never possible for the tyrant to trust that he is loved. (38) For we know as a matter of course that those who serve through fear try by every means in their power to make themselves appear to be like friends by the services of friends.

** <Here φιλία, love returned on the part of the beloved. Hiero maintains a distinction throughout this passage (29—end) between the ἔρως (erotic or passionate love) which is not engendered on his part and the φιλία (love, liking, friendship) which is not returned by the beloved. The parallel to μετὰ φιλίας is μετ' ἔρωτος in 29 *supra*. Note by M.K. >*

And what is more, plots against tyrants spring from none more than from those who pretend to love them most.''

2

(1) To this Simonides said, "Well, these disadvantages you mention seem to me at least to be very trivial. For I see many," he said, "of those who are reputed to be real men, willingly suffer disadvantages in food, drink, and delicacies, and even refrain from sex. (2) But you tyrants far surpass private men surely in the following. You devise great enterprises; you execute them swiftly; you have the greatest amount of superfluous things; you own horses surpassing in virtue, arms surpassing in beauty, superior adornment for your women, the most magnificent houses, and these furnished with what is of the most value; moreoever, the servants you possess are the best in their numbers and their knowledge; and you are the ones most capable of harming your private enemies and benefiting your friends."

(3) To this Hiero said, "I do not wonder at all that the multitude of human beings are utterly deceived by tyranny, Simonides. For the crowd seems to me to form the opinion that some men are happy and wretched by seeing. (4) Now tyranny displays openly, evident for all to see, the possessions which are held to be of much value. But it keeps what is harsh hidden in the tyrants' souls, where human happiness and unhappiness are stored up. (5) That this escapes the notice of the multitude is, as I said, not a wonder to me. But that you too are unaware of this, you who are reputed to get a finer view of most matters through your understanding than through your eyes, this I do hold to be a wonder. (6) But I myself know clearly from experience, Simonides, and I tell you that the tyrant has the least share of the greatest goods, and possesses the largest share of the greatest evils. (7) Take this for example: if peace is held to be a great good for human beings, for tyrants there is the least share in it; and if war is a great evil, in this tyrants get the largest share. (8) For, to begin with, it is possible for private men, unless their city is engaged in fighting a common war, to take a journey wherever they wish, without being afraid that someone will kill them. But the tyrants, all of them, proceed everywhere as through hostile territory. They themselves at least think it necessary to go armed and always to be surrounded by an armed bodyguard. (9) Moreover, if private men go on an expedition somewhere into enemy

country, they believe they are safe at least after they have returned home. But the tyrants know that when they reach their own city they are then in the midst of the largest number of their enemies. (10) Again, if others who are stronger attack the city, and those outside the wall, being weaker, think they are in danger, all believe they have been rendered safe, at least after they have come within the fortifications. The tyrant, however, not even when he passes inside his house is free from danger; he thinks it is there that he must be particularly on his guard. (11) Furthermore, for private men, relief from war is brought about both by treaties and by peace. Whereas for tyrants peace is never made with those subject to their tyranny; nor could the tyrant be confident trusting for a moment to a treaty.

(12) "There are wars of course which cities wage and war which tyrants wage against those they have subjected to force. Now in these wars, everything hard which the man in the cities undergoes, the tyrant too undergoes. (13) For both must be armed, must be on their guard, and run risks; and if, being beaten, they suffer some harm, each suffers pain from these wars. (14) Up to this point, then, the wars of both are equal. But when it comes to the pleasures which the men in the cities get from fighting the cities, these the tyrants cease to have. (15) For surely when the cities overpower their opponents in a battle, it is not easy to express how much pleasure [the men] get from routing the enemy; how much from the pursuit; how much from killing their enemies; how they exult in the deed; how they receive a brilliant reputation for themselves; and how they take delight in believing they have augmented their city. (16) Each one pretends that he shared in the planning and killed the most; and it is hard to find where they do not make some false additions, claiming they killed more than all who really died. So noble a thing does a great victory seem to them.

(17) "But when the tyrant suspects certain men of plotting against him, and, perceiving that they are in fact plotting, puts them to death, he knows that he does not augment the whole city; he knows without a doubt that he will rule fewer men, and he cannot be glad; he does not pride himself on the deed, but rather minimizes what has happened as much as he can, and while he does it he makes the apology that he has done it without committing injustice. Thus what he has done does not seem noble even to him. (18) And when they whom he feared are dead he is not any bolder, but is still more on his guard than before. So, then, the tyrant spends his life fighting the kind of war which I myself am showing you."

3

(1) "Now consider friendship in its turn, and how the tyrants partake of it. First let us reflect whether friendship is a great good for human beings. (2) For surely it is the case with a man who is loved by someone that the one who loves him gladly sees him present; gladly benefits him; longs for him if he is absent; welcomes him returning again; takes pleasure with him in the goods which are his; and comes to his aid if he sees him fallen into any trouble.

(3) "Moreover, it has not even escaped the notice of the cities that friendship is a very great good and very pleasant to human beings. At any rate, many cities have established a law that only adulterers may be killed with impunity, evidently for this reason, because they believe adulterers are destroyers of the wives' friendship for their husbands. (4) Since whenever a woman submits to intercourse by way of some misfortune, her husband honors her no less, as far as this goes, provided he is of the opinion that her friendship continues uncorrupted.

(5) "I myself judge being loved a good so great that I believe benefits actually come of themselves to the one who is loved, both from gods and men. (6) Yet in this kind of possession too, tyrants are at a disadvantage beyond all others.

"But if you wish to know, Simonides, that I speak the truth, reflect on this consideration. (7) For surely the firmest friendships are held to be those of parents for children, and children for their parents, brothers for their brothers, wives for their husbands, and comrades for comrades. (8) If, then, you are willing to reflect thoughtfully on it, you will find that private men are loved chiefly by these, whereas many tyrants have killed their own children, and many have themselves perished at the hands of their children; that many brothers in tyrannies have become one another's murderers; and that many tyrants have been brought to ruin both by their wives and by comrades who they thought were most their friends. (9) How should they believe they are loved by anyone else, inasmuch as they are so hated by such as are inclined by nature and compelled by law to love them?

4

(1) "Again, take trust also, who can share least in this and not suffer disadvantage in a great good? For what kind of companionship is

sweet without mutual trust? What kind of intimacy is delightful to man and wife without trust? Or what kind of servant is pleasing if he is not trusted? (2) Now of this trusting someone, a tyrant has the least share; inasmuch as he not only spends his life without trusting his food and drink, but it is even a practice tyrants have, before they begin sacrifice to the gods, to first bid the attendants taste it, because of their distrust that even in that they may eat or drink something bad.

(3) "Fatherlands in their turn, are worth very much to other human beings. For citizens act as a bodyguard to one another against slaves, and against evil-doers, without pay, so that no citizen will meet a violent death. (4) And they have advanced so far in watchfulness that many have made a law that even the accomplice of a slayer is not free from taint. Thus, because of the fatherlands, each of the citizens lives his life in safety. (5) But in this too it is the reverse for the tyrants. For instead of avenging them, the cities magnificently honor the tyrannicide; and instead of excluding the killer from sacred rites, as they do the murderers of private men, the cities erect in their temples statues of those who have committed such an act.

(6) "And if you think that because the tyrant has more possessions than private men he gets more pleasure from them, this is not the case either, Simonides. But just as athletes do not enjoy proving stronger than private men, but are annoyed when they prove weaker than their opponents, so the tyrant gets no pleasure when he evidently has more than private men, but suffers pain when he has less than other tyrants. For these he regards as rivals for his own wealth.

(7) "Nor does something of what he desires come more quickly to the tyrant than to the private man. For the private man desires a house, or a field, or a domestic slave; but the tyrant desires cities, extensive territory, harbors, or mightly citadels, which are things much harder and more dangerous to win than the objects desired by private men.

(8) "And, furthermore, you will see but few private men as poor as many tyrants. For what is a large and sufficient amount is not judged by an enumeration, but with a view to its use. Accordingly, an amount which exceeds what is sufficient is large, but what falls short of sufficiency is small. (9) Now for the tyrant a multiplicity of possessions is less adequate for his necessary expenditures than for the private man. For private men can cut their daily expenditure in any way they wish, but the tyrants cannot, because their largest and most necessary expenses go to guard their lives. And to curtail these is thought to be ruinous.

(10) "Next, why would someone pity as poor all those who can get what they need by just means? And who would not justly call wretched and poor all those who are compelled by their need to live by contriving something bad and base? (11) Now the tyrants are compelled most of the time to plunder unjustly both temples and human beings, because they always need additional money to meet their necessary expenses. For, as if there were a perpetual war on, [tyrants] are compelled to support an army or perish."

5

(1) "I will tell you of another harsh affliction, Simonides, which the tyrants have. For although they are acquainted with the decent, the wise, and the just, no less than private men [the tyrants] fear rather than admire them. They fear the brave because they might dare something for the sake of freedom; the wise, because they might contrive something; and the just, because the multitude might desire to be ruled by them. (2) When, because of their fear, they do away secretly with such men, who is left for them to use save the unjust, the incontinent, and the slavish? The unjust are trusted because they are afraid, just as the tyrants are, that some day the cities, becoming free, will become their masters. The incontinent are trusted because they are at liberty for the present, and the slavish because not even they deem themselves worthy to be free. This affliction, then, seems harsh to me: to think some are good men, and yet to be compelled to make use of the others.

(3) "Moreover, the tyrant also is compelled to be a lover of the city; for without the city he would not be able either to preserve himself or to be happy. Yet tyranny compels to give trouble to even their own fatherlands. For they do not rejoice in making the citizens either brave or well-armed. Rather they take pleasure in making strangers more formidable than the citizens, and these strangers they use as bodyguards. (4) Furthermore, when good seasons come and there is an abundance of good things, not even then does the tyrant rejoice with them. For [tyrants] think that as men are more in want, they are more submissive for being used."

6

(1) "I wish, Simonides," he said, "to make clear to you those pleasures which I enjoyed when I was a private man; now, since I

became a tyrant, I perceive that I am deprived of them. (2) I was together with companions of my own age, taking pleasure in them, and they in me; I was a companion to myself when I desired peace and tranquility; I lived amid banquets, often until I forgot everything harsh in human life, and often until my soul was completely absorbed in song, festivity, and dancing, and often until there was desire for intercourse between me and those who were present. (3) Now I am deprived of those who take pleasure in me, because I have slaves instead of friends for comrades. I myself am deprived of pleasant intimacy with them, because I see in them no good will for me. And I guard against strong drink and sleep as if I were in an ambush. (4) To fear the crowd, yet to fear solitude; to fear being without a guard, and to fear the very men who are guarding; to be unwilling to have unarmed men about me, yet not gladly to see them armed—how could this fail to be a painful condition? (5) Furthermore, to trust strangers more than citizens, barbarians more than Greeks; to desire to keep the free slaves, and be compelled to make the slaves free—do not all these things seem to you signs of a soul distracted by fears?

(6) "Fear, you know, when in the soul is not only painful itself, it also becomes the spoiler of all the pleasures it accompanies. (7) If you too have experience of war, Simonides, and have ever before now been posted near the enemy line, recall what sort of food you took at that time, and what sort of sleep you had. (8) The kind of pain you suffered then is the kind the tyrants have, and that more terrible. For the tyrants believe they see enemies not only in front of them, but on every side."

(9) After he heard this, Simonides interrupted and said, "I think you put some things extremely well. For war is a fearful thing. But nevertheless, Hiero, we at any rate post guards, when we are on a campaign, and take our share of food and sleep with confidence.

(10) And Hiero said, "Yes, by Zeus, Simonides, for the laws stand watch over the guards, so that they fear for themselves and in your behalf. But the tyrants hire guards, like harvesters, for pay. (11) And surely the guards, if they ought to be capable of doing anything, ought to be faithful. Yet one faithful man is much harder to find than a great many workers for whatever kind of task you wish, especially when those doing the guarding are only present for the sake of money, and when they may get in a moment much more by killing the tyrant than all they earn from him being his guards for a long time.

(12) "As to why you were jealous of us, because we are most able to benefit out friends, and because we, above all men, master our private enemies, this is not the case either. (13) For as to friends, how

would you believe that you ever confer a benefit, when you know well that the one who receives the most from you would the most gladly get out of your sight as quickly as possible? For whatever it is he receives from a tyrant, no one believes it his own until he is beyond the tyrant's power to command. (14) As for private enemies in their turn, how would you say the tyrants have the most ability to master them, when they know well that all their subjects are their enemies, and when it is not possible either to kill all these outright or to put them in chains? For who then would be left for [the tyrant] to rule? But knowing that they are his enemies, he must at the same time guard against, and be compelled to make use of, these very men.

(15) "Know well, Simonides, that those whom they fear among the citizens they find it hard to see alive, and yet hard to kill. It is just as if there were a good horse who yet gives rise to the fear that he might do some irreparable harm; a man would find it hard to kill him because of his virtue, yet hard to manage him alive, being constantly alert against his working irreparable harm in the midst of danger. (16) So too with respect to as many other possessions as are hard to manage but useful; all alike give pain to their possessors, and to those who are rid of them."

7

(1) When he heard these things from [Hiero], Simonides spoke. "Honor," he said "seems to be something great, and human beings undergo all toil and endure all danger striving for it. (2) You too, apparently, although tyranny has as many difficulties as you say, nevertheless rush into it headlong in order that you may be honored, and in order that all—all who are present—may serve you in all your commands without excuses, admire you, rise from their seats, give way in the streets, and always honor you both in speeches and deeds. For these are of course the kinds of things that subjects do for tyrants and for anyone else they happen to honor at the moment.

(3) "I myself think, Hiero, that a real man differs from the other animals in this striving for honor. Since, after all, all animals alike seem to take pleasure in food, drink, sleep, and sex. But ambition does not arise naturally either in the irrational animals or in all human beings. Those in whom love of honor and praise arises by nature differ the most from, and who are also believed to be no longer human beings merely, but real men. (4) Accordingly, it seems to me that you probably endure all these things you bear in the tyranny because you are

honored above all other human beings. For no human pleasure seems to come closer to what is divine than the joy connected with honors."

(5) To this Hiero said, "But, Simonides, even the honors of the tyrants appear to me of a kind similar to that which I demonstrated their sexual pleasures to be. (6) For services from those who do not love in return we did not think to be favors, anymore than sex which is forced appears pleasant. In the same way, services from those under fear are not honors. (7) For must we say that those who are forced to rise from their chairs stand up to honor those who are treating them unjustly, or that those who give way in the streets to the stronger yield to honor those who are treating them unjustly?

(8) "And further, the many offer gifts to those they hate, and what is more, particularly when they fear they may suffer some harm from them. But this, I think, would probably be considered deeds of slavery. Whereas I believe for my part that honors derive from acts the opposite of this. (9) For when human beings, considering a real man able to be their benefactor, and believing that they enjoy his goods, for this reason have him on their lips in praise; when each one sees him as his own private good; when they willingly give way to him in the streets and rise from their chairs out of liking and not fear; when they crown him for his public virtue and beneficence, and willingly bestow gifts on him; these men who serve him in this way, I believe, honor him truly; and the one deemed worthy of these things I believe to be honored in reality. I myself count blessed the one so honored. (10) For I perceive that he is not plotted against, but rather that he causes anxiety lest he suffer harm, and that he lives his life—happy, without fear, without envy, and without danger. But the tyrant, Simonides, knows well, lives night and day as one condemned by all human beings to die for his injustice."

(11) When Simonides heard all this through to the end, he said, "But why, Hiero, if being a tyrant is so wretched, and you realize this, do you not rid yourself of so great an evil, and why did no one else ever willingly let a tyranny go, who once acquired it?"

(12) "Because," he said, "in this too is tyranny most miserable, Simonides: it is not possible to be rid of it either. For how would some tyrant ever be able to repay in full the money of those he has dispossessed, or suffer in turn the chains he has loaded on them, or how supply in requital enough lives to die for those he has put to death? (13) Rather, if it profit any man, Simonides, to hang himself, know," he said, "that I myself find this most profits the tyrant. He alone, whether he keeps his troubles or lays them aside, gains no advantage."

8

(1) Simonides took him up and said, "Well, Hiero, I do not wonder that you are for the moment out of heart with tyranny; since, desiring to be loved by human beings, you believe that tyranny is an obstacle in the way of your attaining this. However, I think myself able to teach you that ruling does not at all prevent your being loved, and that it even has the advantage of private life in this respect. (2) While examining whether this is of itself the case, let us not yet inquire whether because of his greater power the ruler also would be able to grant more favors; but rather, if the private man and the tyrant do similar things, consider which of the two wins more gratitude by means of equal favors. I will begin with the smallest examples. (3) First, suppose the ruler and the private man, when they see someone, address him in a friendly way. In this case, from which man do you believe the greeting gives the hearer more pleasure? Again, suppose both praise the same man; from which of them do you think the praise brings greater pleasure? Suppose each, when he offer sacrifice, honors the same man; from which of the two do you think the honor would obtain more gratitude? (4) Suppose they alike attend a sick person; is it not obvious that attentions from the most powerful produce the greatest cheer? Suppose, then, they make equal gifts; is it not clear, in this case too, that favors of half the value from the most powerful are worth more than the whole of a grant from the private man? (5) Indeed, I myself hold that even from gods a certain honor and grace attend a man who rules. For not only does ruling make a real man nobler, but we behold with greater pleasure the same man when he is ruling than when he lives privately; and we delight more in discoursing with those preeminent in honor than with those equal to us.

(6) "As for boys, with regard to whom you found the most fault with tyranny, they are least offended at the old age of one who rules, and they pay least attention to a beloved's ugliness. For his being honored itself helps most to dignify him, so that his offensiveness disappears, and what is noble appears more resplendent.

(7) "Since, then, you obtain greater thanks by means of equal services, must it not be fitting, when you are able to confer benefits by accomplishing many times more things and are able to make many times more gifts, that you also be loved far more than the private men?"

(8) Hiero answered at once, "No, by Zeus, Simonides," he said,

"because we are compelled to do the things on the basis of which men incur enmity, more than private men. (9) We must exact money if we are to have the means to spend on our needs; we must compel [men] to guard the things which need guarding; we must punish the unjust; we must restrain those who wish to be insolent; and when the moment comes to set out with all speed on an expedition by land or sea, we must not entrust the business to the sluggards. (10) Moreover, the man who is a tyrant needs mercenaries. And no burden weighs heavier on the citizens than that. For the citizens believe that tyrants keep these mercenaries not to share equal honors with themselves, but to get the advantage by supporting them."

9

(1) To this in its turn Simonides said, "Well, I do not deny that all these matters require attention, Hiero. Some cares seem to me, however, to lead to much hatred, whereas others seem to be mutually very gratifying. (2) For to teach what is best, and to praise and honor the man who achieves this in the noblest way, is a concern which itself gives rise to mutual regard; whereas to rebuke the one who is slack in doing something, to coerce, to punish, to correct—these things necessarily give rise more to mutual enmity. (3) Accordingly I say that the man who rules ought to command others to punish the one who requires coercion, but that he ought to award the prizes himself. What occurs at present confirms that this is a good arrangement. (4) For whenever we wish our choruses to compete, the *Archon* offers the prizes, but he orders the managers of each chorus to assemble them, and others to instruct them and to apply coercion to those who are at all slack in performing. Accordingly, what gives rise to gratitude in these contests comes about at once through the *Archon*, and what is repulsive comes about through others. (5) Now what prevents all other political things from also being managed in this way? For all the cities are apportioned up, some according to tribes, some according to divisions, others according to companies, and rulers are put in charge of each section. (6) If someone should offer prizes to these sections, like choruses, for good arms, good discipline, horsemanship, prowess in war, and justice in contractual relations, it is likely that all these things, through emulation, would be practiced intently. (7) Yes, and, by Zeus, they would set out on an expedition with more speed

wherever required, striving for honor; they would contribute money more promptly when the moment for this came; and farming, certainly the most useful thing of all, but the least accustomed to being managed by emulation, would itself greatly improve, if someone should offer prizes by fields or villages to those who best cultivate the ground; and many good things would be accomplished by those among the citizens who turn to it vigorously. (8) For the revenues would increase, and moderation would follow much more closely upon the absence of leisure. And as for evil doings, they arise less naturally in those who are busy.

(9) "If imports are of any benefit to a city, the one honored the most for engaging in this would also bring together more importers. And if it should become apparent that the man who invents some painless revenue for the city will be honored, not even this kind of reflection would be left uncultivated. (10) To sum it up, if it should become clear with respect to all matters that the man who introduces something beneficial will not go unhonored, he would stimulate many to engage in reflecting on something good. And whenever many are concerned with what is useful, this is necessarily discovered and perfected all the more.

(11) "But if you are afraid, Hiero, that when prizes are offered among many, correspondingly many expenses will arise, keep in mind that no articles of commerce are cheaper than what human beings purchase by means of prizes. Do you see that in contests of horsemanship, gymnastic, and choruses small prizes bring forth great expenditures, much toil, and much care from human beings?"

10

(1) And Hiero said, "Well, Simonides, you seem to me to speak well as far as these matters go; but have you anything to say regarding the mercenaries, so that I may not incur hatred because of them? Or do you mean that once a ruler wins friendship he will no longer need a bodyguard at all?"

(2) "By Zeus, certainly he will need it," said Simonides. "For I know that it is inbred in some human beings, just as in horses, to be insolent in proportion as the needs they have are more fully satisfied. (3) The fear inspired by the bodyguard would make such men more moderate. And as for the gentlemen, there is nothing, it seems to me, by means of which you would confer so great services on them as by the

mercenaries. (4) For surely you support them as guards for yourself; but before now many masters have died violently at the hands of their slaves. If, then, one—and this the first—of the mercenaries' orders should be, that as the bodyguard of all the citizens they were, whenever they perceived a thing of this kind, to go to the aid of all—and if they were ordered to guard against the evil-doers we all know arise in cities—the citizens would know they were helped by them. (5) In addition to this, these [mercenaries] would probably best be able to provide confidence and safety for the husband-men and property of herds and flocks in the country, alike for your own privately and for those throughout the country. They are capable, moreover, of providing the citizens with leisure to concern themselves with their private property, by guarding the positions of advantage. (6) Furthermore, as regards the secret and surprise attacks of enemies, who would be readier either to perceive them in advance or to prevent them than those who are always under arms and disciplined? Surely on a campaign, what is more useful to citizens than mercenaries? For [mercenaries] are likely to be readier to toil, run risks, and stand guard for the citizens. (7) As for the neighboring cities, is there not a necessity, brought about by those who are constantly under arms, for them especially to desire peace? For being disciplined the mercenaries would best be able to preserve what belongs to their friends and to destroy what belongs to their enemies. (8) Surely when the citizens realize that these mercenaries do no harm at all to one who commits no injustice; that they restrain those who wish to do evil; that they come to the aid of those who are unjustly wronged; and that they take counsel for and incur danger in behalf of the citizens—must they not necessarily spend very gladly for their upkeep? After all, men support guards privately, and for lesser objects than these. "

11

(1) "You must not, Hiero, shrink from spending from your private possessions for the common good. For it seems to me that what a man as tyrant lays out for the city is spent more on what is necessary than what he lays out for his private [estate]. Let us examine each detail point by point. (2) First, which do you think would dignify you more, a house embellished at tremendous cost, or the whole city furnished with walls, temples, colonnades, market places, and harbors? (3) As for arms, which of the two would appear more formidable to your en-

emies, yourself fitted out in the most splendid arms, or your entire city well armed? (4) Take revenues; in which way do you think they would become greater, if you should keep your private property alone productive, or if you should contrive to make the property of all the citizens so? (5) And regarding the pursuit believed to be the most noble and magnificent of all, the raising of chariot horses, in which way do you think there would be greater dignity, if you yourself should raise the most teams among the Greeks and send them to the games, or if the most breeders, and the most in competition, should be from your city? And as for winning victories, which do you hold the nobler way, by the virtue of your chariot horses, or by the happiness of the city which you rule? (6) I myself say that it is not fitting for a man who is a tyrant even to compete against private men. For, should you win, you would not be admired, but envied, as meeting the cost by means of many estates, and should you lose, you would be ridiculed most of all.

(7) "But I tell you, Hiero, your contest is against others who rule cities; if you make the city you rule the happiest of these, know well that you will be declared by herald the victor in the most noble and magnificent contest among human beings. (8) First, you would at once secure the love of your subjects, which is the very thing you happen to desire. Further, the herald of your victory would not be one, but all human beings would sing of your virtue. (9) Being an object of attention you would be cherished not only by private men, but by many cities; marveled at not only in private, but in public among all as well; (10) it would be possible for you, as far as safety is concerned, to travel wherever you wish, for the sake of viewing the sights; and it would be possible for you to do this remaining here. For there would be a continual festival by you of those wishing to display whatever wise, beautiful, or good thing they had, and of those desiring to serve you as well. (11) Every man present would be your ally, and every man absent would desire to see you. Therefore, you would not only be liked, you would be loved by human beings; as for the fair, you would not have to seduce them, but submit to being seduced by them; as for fear, that you might suffer some harm; (12) you would have willing men obeying you, and you would see them willingly take thought for you; if there should be some danger, you would see not only allies, but also champions, and those eager; being deemed worthy of many gifts, you will not be at a loss for someone well disposed with whom to share them, with all men rejoicing at your good things and all fighting for those which are yours just as if they were their own. (13) For treasuries, furthermore, you would have all the wealth of your friends.

"But enrich your friends with confidence, Hiero; for you will enrich yourself. Augment the city, for you will attach power to yourself. Acquire allies for it. (14) Consider the fatherland to be your estate, the citizens your comrades, friends your own children, your sons the same as your life, and try to surpass all these in benefactions. (15) For you prove superior to your friends in beneficence, your enemies will be utterly unable to resist you. And if you do all these things, know well, of all things you will acquire the most noble and most blessed possessions to be met with among human beings, for while being happy, you will not be envied for being happy."

Leo Strauss

On Tyranny

The habit of writing against the government had, of itself, an unfavorable effect on the character. For whoever was in the habit of writing against the government was in the habit of breaking the law; and the habit of breaking even an unreasonable law tends to make men altogether lawless. . . .

From the day on which the emancipation of our literature was accomplished, the purification of our literature began. . . . During a hundred and sixty years the liberty of our press has been constantly becoming more and more entire; and during those hundred and sixty years the restraint imposed on writers by the general feeling of readers has been constantly becoming more and more strict. . . . At this day foreigners, who dare not print a word reflecting on the government under which they live, are at a loss to understand how it happens that the freest press in Europe is the most prudish.

MACAULAY

INTRODUCTION

It is proper that I should indicate my reasons for submitting this detailed analysis of a forgotten dialogue on tyranny to the consideration of political scientists.

Tyranny is a danger coeval with political life. The analysis of tyranny is therefore as old as political science itself. The analysis of tyranny that was made by the first political scientists was so clear, so comprehensive, and so unforgettably expressed that it was remembered and understood by generations which did not have any direct experience of actual tyranny. On the other hand, when we were brought face to face with tyranny—with a kind of tyranny that surpassed the boldest imagination of the most powerful thinkers of the past—our political science failed to recognize it. It is not surprising then that many of our contemporaries, disappointed or repelled by present-day analyses of present-day tyranny, were relieved when they rediscovered the pages in which Plato and other classical thinkers seemed to have interpreted for us the horrors of the twentieth century. What is surprising is that the renewed general interest in authentic interpretation of the phenomenon of tyranny did not lead to renewed interest, general or scholarly, in the only writing of the classical period which is explicitly devoted to the discussion of tyranny and its implications, and to nothing else, and which has never been subjected to comprehensive analysis: Xenophon's *Hiero*.

Not much observation and reflection is needed to realize that there is an essential difference between the tyranny analyzed by the classics and that of our age. In contradistinction to classical tyranny, present-day tyranny has at its disposal "technology" as well as "ideologies"; more generally expressed, it presupposes the existence of "science," i.e., of a particular interpretation, or kind, of science. Conversely, classical tyranny, unlike modern tyranny, was confronted, actually or potentially, by a science which was not meant to be applied to "the conquest of nature" or to be popularized and diffused. But in noting this one implicitly grants that one cannot understand modern tyranny in its specific character before one has understood the elementary and in a sense natural form of tyranny which is premodern tyranny. This basic stratum of modern tyranny remains, for all practical purposes, unintelligible to us if we do not have recourse to the political science of the classics.

It is no accident that present-day political science has failed to grasp tyranny as what it really is. Our political science is haunted by the belief that "value judgments" are inadmissible in scientific considerations, and to call a regime tyrannical clearly amounts to pronouncing a "value judgment." The political scientist who accepts this view of science will speak of the mass-state, of dictatorship, of totalitarianism, of authoritarianism, and so on, and as a citizen he may wholeheartedly condemn these things; but as a political scientist he is forced to reject the notion of tyranny as "mythical." One cannot overcome this limitation without reflecting on the basis, or the origin, of present-day political science. Present-day political science often traces its origin to

Machiavelli. There is truth in this contention. To say nothing of broader considerations, Machiavelli's *Prince* (as distinguished from his *Discourses on Livy*) is characterized by the deliberate indifference to the distinction between king and tyrant; the *Prince* presupposes the tacit rejection of that traditional distinction.[1] Machiavelli was fully aware that by conceiving the view expounded in the *Prince* he was breaking away from the whole tradition of political science; or, to apply to the *Prince* an expression which he uses when speaking of his *Discourses*, that he was taking a road which had not yet been followed by anyone.[2] To understand the basic premise of present-day political science, one would have to understand the meaning of the epoch-making change effected by Machiavelli; for that change consisted in the discovery of the continent on which all specifically modern political thought, and hence especially present-day political science, is at home.

It is precisely when trying to bring to light the deepest roots of modern political thought that one will find it to be very useful, not to say indispensable, to devote some attention to the *Hiero*. One cannot understand the meaning of Machiavelli's achievement if one does not confront his teaching with the traditional teaching he rejects. As regards the *Prince* in particular, which is deservedly his most famous work, one has to confront its teaching with that of the traditional mirrors of princes. But in doing this one must beware of the temptation to try to be wiser, or rather more learned, than Machiavelli wants his readers to be, by attaching undue importance to medieval and early modern mirrors of princes which Machiavelli never stoops to mention by name. Instead one should concentrate on the only mirror of princes to which he emphatically refers and which is, as one would expect, the classic and the fountainhead of this whole genre: Xenophon's *Education of Cyrus*.[3] This work has never been studied by modern historians with even a small fraction of the care and concentration it merits and which is needed if it is to disclose its meaning. The *Education of Cyrus* may be said to be devoted to the perfect king in contradistinction to the tyrant, whereas the *Prince* is characterized by the deliberate disregard of the difference between king and tyrant. There is only one earlier work on tyranny to which Machiavelli emphatically refers: Xenophon's *Hiero*.[4] The analysis of the *Hiero* leads to the conclusion that the teaching of that dialogue comes as near to the teaching of the *Prince* as the teaching of any Socratic could possibly come. By confronting the teaching of the *Prince* with that transmitted through the *Hiero*, one can grasp most clearly the subtlest and indeed the decisive difference between Socratic political science and Machiavellian political science. If it is true that all premodern political science rests on the foundations laid by Socrates, whereas all specifically modern political science rests on the foundations laid by Machiavelli, one may also say that the *Hiero* marks the point of closest contact between premodern and modern political science.[5]

As regards the manner in which I have treated my subject, I have been mindful that there are two opposed ways in which one can study the thought of the past. Many present-day scholars start from the historicist assumption, namely, that all human thought is "historical" or that the foundations of human thought are laid by specific experiences which are not, as a matter of principle, coeval with human thought as such. Yet there is a fatal disproportion betwen historicism and true historical understanding. The goal of the historian of thought is to understand the thought of the past "as it really has been," i.e., to understand it as exactly as possible as it was actually understood by its authors. But the historicist approaches the thought of the past on the basis of the historicist assumption which was wholly alien to the thought of the past. He is therefore compelled to attempt to understand the thought of the past better than it understood itself before he has understood it exactly as it understood itself. In one way or the other, his presentation will be a questionable mixture of interpretation and critique. It is the beginning of historical understanding, its necessary and, one is tempted to add, its sufficient condition that one realizes the problematic character of historicism. For one cannot realize it without becoming seriously interested in an impartial confrontation of the historicist approach that prevails today with the nonhistoricist approach of the past. And such a confrontation in its turn requires that the nonhistoricist thought of the past be understood on its own terms, and not in the way in which it presents itself within the horizon of historicism.

In accordance with this principle, I have tried to understand Xenophon's thought as exactly as I could. I have not tried to relate his thought to his "historical situation" because this is not the natural way of reading the work of a wise man; and, in addition, Xenophon never indicated that he wanted to be understood that way. I assumed that Xenophon, being an able writer, gave us to the best of his powers the information required for understanding his work. I have relied therefore as much as possible on what he himself says, directly or indirectly, and as little as possible on extraneous information, to say nothing of modern hypotheses. Distrustful of all conventions, however trivial, which are likely to do harm to matters of importance, I went so far as to omit the angular brackets with which modern scholars are in the habit of adorning their citations of certain ancient writings. It goes without saying that I never believed that my mind was moving in a larger "circle of ideas" than Xenophon's mind.

The neglect of the *Hiero* (as well as of the *Education of Cyrus*) is no doubt partly due to the fashionable underestimation and even contempt of Xenophon's intellectual powers. Until the end of the eighteenth century, he was generally considered a wise man and a classic in the precise sense. In the nineteenth and twentieth centuries, he is compared as a philosopher to Plato, and found wanting; he is compared as a historian to Thucydides, and found wanting. One need not, as well one might, take issue with the views of philosophy and of history which are presupposed in these comparisons. One merely has to raise the question whether Xenophon wanted to be understood primarily as a philosopher or as a historian. In the manuscripts of his works, he is frequently designated as "the orator Xenophon." It is reasonable to assume that the temporary eclipse of Xenophon—just as the temporary eclipse of Livy and of Cicero—has been due to a decline in the understanding of the significance of rhetoric: both the peculiar "idealism" and the peculiar "realism" of the nineteenth century were guided by the modern concept of "Art" and for that reason were unable to understand the crucial significance of the lowly art of rhetoric. While they could thus find a place for Plato and Thucydides, they completely failed duly to appreciate Xenophon.

Xenophon's rhetoric is not ordinary rhetoric; it is Socratic rhetoric. The character of Socratic rhetoric does not become sufficiently clear from the judiciously scattered remarks on the subject that occur in Plato's and Xenophon's writings, but only from detailed analyses of its products. The most perfect product of Socratic rhetoric is the dialogue. The form of Plato's dialogues has been discussed frequently, but no one would claim that the problem of the Platonic dialogue has been solved. Modern analyses are, as a rule, vitiated by the estheticist prejudice of the interpreters. Yet Plato's expulsion of the poets from his best city should have sufficed for discouraging any estheticist approach. It would seeem that the attempt to clarify the meaning of the dialogue should start from an analysis of Xenophon's dialogue. Xenophon uses far fewer devices than Plato uses even in his simplest works. By understanding the art of Xenophon, one will realize certain minimum requirements that one must fulfill when interpreting any Platonic dialogue, requirements which today are so little fulfilled that they are hardly known.

The dialogue that deserves the name communicates the thought of the author in an indirect or oblique way. Thus the danger of arbitrary interpretation might well seem to be overwhelming. The danger can be overcome only if the greatest possible attention is paid to every detail, and especially to the unthematic details, and if the function of Socratic rhetoric is never lost sight of.

Socratic rhetoric is meant to be an indispensable instrument of philosophy. Its purpose is to lead potential philosophers to philosophy both by training them and by liberating them from the charms which obstruct the philosophic effort, as well as to prevent the access to philosophy of those who are not fit for it. Socratic rhetoric is emphatically just. It is animated by the spirit of social responsibility. It is based on the premise that there is a disproportion between the intransigent quest for truth and the requirements of society, or that not all truths are always harmless. Society will always try to tyrannize thought. Socratic rhetoric is the classic means for ever again frustrating these attempts. This highest kind of rhetoric did not die with the immediate pupils of Socrates. Many monographs bear witness to the fact that great thinkers of later times have used a kind of caution or thrift in communicating their thought to posterity which is no longer appreciated: it ceased to be appreciated at about the same time at which historicism emerged, at about the end of the eighteenth century.

The experience of the present generation has taught us to read the great political literature of the past with different eyes and with different expectations. The lesson may not be without value for our political orientation. We are now brought face to face with a tyranny which holds out the threat of becoming, thanks to "the conquest of nature" and in particular of human nature, what no earlier tyranny ever became: perpetual and universal. Confronted by the appalling alternative that man, or human thought, must be collectivized either by one stroke and without mercy or else by slow and gentle processes, we are forced to wonder how we could escape from this dilemma. We reconsider therefore the elementary and unobtrusive conditions of human freedom.

The historical form in which this reflection is here presented is perhaps not inappropriate. The manifest and deliberate collectivization or coordination of thought is being prepared in a hidden and frequently quite unconscious way by the spread of the teaching that all human thought is collective independently of any human effort directed to this end, because all human thought is historical. There seems to be no more appropriate way of combating this teaching than the study of history.

As has been indicated, one must have some patience if one wants to grasp the meaning of the *Hiero*. The patience of the interpreter does not make superfluous the patience of the reader of the interpretation. In explaining writings like the *Hiero*, one has to engage in long-winded and sometimes repetitious considerations which can arrest attention only if one sees their purpose, and it is necessary that this purpose should reveal itself in its proper place, which cannot be at the beginning. If one wants to establish the precise meaning of a subtle hint, one must proceed in a way which comes dangerously close to the loathsome business of explaining a joke. The charm produced by Xenophon's unobtrusive art is destroyed, at least for a moment, if that art is made obtrusive by the interpretation. Still, I believe that I have not dotted all the *i*'s. One can only hope that the time will again come when Xenophon's art will be understood by a generation which, properly trained in their youth, will no longer need cumbersome introductions like the present study.

I

The Problem

The intention of the *Hiero* is nowhere stated by the author. Being an account of a conversation between the poet Simonides and the tyrant Hiero, the work consists almost exclusively of the utterances, recorded in direct speech, of these two characters. The author limits himself to describing at the beginning in sixteen words the circumstances in which the conversation took place, and to linking with each other, or separating from each other, the statements of the two interlocutors by such expressions as "Simonides said" and "Hiero answered."

The intention of the work does not become manifest at once from the content. The work consists of two main parts of very unequal length, the first part making up about five sevenths of the whole. In the first part (ch. 1–7), Hiero proves to Simonides that the life of a tyrant, as compared with the life of a private man, is so unhappy that the tyrant can hardly do better than to hang himself. In the second part (ch. 8–11), Simonides proves to Hiero that the tyrant could be the happiest of men. The first part seems to be directed against the popular prejudice that the life of a tyrant is more pleasant than private life. The second part, however, seems to establish the view that the life of a beneficent tyrant is superior, in the most important respect, to private life.[1] At first glance, the work as a whole clearly conveys the message that the life of a beneficent tyrant is highly desirable. But it is not clear what that message means since we do not know to what type of men it is addressed. If we assume that the work is addressed to tyrants, its intention is to exhort them to exercise their rule in a spirit of shrewd benevolence. Yet only a very small part of its readers can be supposed to be actual tyrants. The work as a whole may therefore have to be taken as a recommendation addressed to properly equipped young men who are pondering what way of life they should choose—a recommendation to strive for tyrannical power, not indeed to gratify their desires, but to gain the love and admiration of all men by deeds of benevolence on the greatest possible scale.[2] Socrates, the teacher of Xenophon, was suspected of teaching his companions to be "tyrannical":[3] Xenophon lays himself open to the same suspicion.

Yet it is not Xenophon but Simonides who proves that a beneficent tyrant will reach the summit of happiness, and one cannot identify without further consideration the author's views with those of one of his characters. The fact that Simonides is called "wise" by Hiero[4] does not prove anything, since we do not know what Xenophon thought of Hiero's competence. But even if we assume that Simonides is simply the mouthpiece of Xenophon, great difficulties remain, for Simonides' thesis is ambiguous. It is addressed to a tyrant who is out of heart with tyranny, who has just declared that a tyrant can hardly do better than to hang himself. Does it not serve the purpose of comforting the sad tyrant, and does not the intention to comfort detract from the sincerity of a speech?[5] Is any speech addressed to a tyrant by a man who is in the tyrant's power likely to be a sincere speech?[6]

II

The Title and the Form

While practically everything said in the *Hiero* is said by Xenophon's characters, Xenophon himself takes full responsibility for the title of the work.[1] The title is Ἱέρων ἢ Τυραννικός. No other work contained in the *Corpus Xenophonteum* has a title consisting of both a proper name and an adjective referring to the subject. The first part of the title is reminiscent of the title of the *Agesilaus*. The *Agesilaus* deals with an outstanding Greek king, just as the *Hiero* deals with an outstanding Greek tyrant. Proper names of individuals also occur in the titles of the *Cyri Institutio*, the *Cyri Expeditio*, and the *Apologia Socratis*. Agesilaus, the two Cyruses, and Socrates seem to be the men Xenophon admired most. But the two Cyruses were not Greek, and Socrates was not a ruler: the *Agesilaus* and the *Hiero*, the only writings of Xenophon the titles of which contain proper names of individuals in the nominative, are the only writings of Xenophon which may be said to be devoted to Greek rulers.

The second part of the title reminds one of the titles of the *Hipparchicus*, the *Oeconomicus*, and the *Cynegeticus*. These three writings serve the purpose of teaching skills befitting gentlemen: the skill of a commander of cavalry, the skill of managing one's estate, and the skill of hunting.[2] Accordingly, one should expect that the purpose of the *Tyrannicus* is to teach the skill of the tyrant, the σοφία (or τέχνη) τυραννική;[3] and in fact Simonides does therein teach Hiero how best to exercise tyrannical rule.

There is only one work of Xenophon apart from the *Hiero* which has an alternative title: the Πόροι ἢ περὶ προσόδων (*Ways and Means*). The purpose of that work is to show the (democratic) rulers of Athens how they could become more just by showing them how they could

31

overcome the necessity under which they found themselves of acting unjustly.[4] That is to say, its purpose is to show how the democratic order of Athens could be improved without being fundamentally changed. Similarly, Simonides shows the tyrannical ruler of Syracuse how he could overcome the necessity of acting unjustly under which he found himself without abandoning tyrannical rule as such.[5] Xenophon, the pupil of Socrates, seems to have considered both democracy and tyranny faulty regimes.[6] The *Ways and Means* and the *Hiero* are the only works of Xenophon which are devoted to the question of how a given political order ($\pi o\lambda\iota\tau\epsilon\iota\alpha$) of a faulty character could be corrected without being transformed into a good political order.

Xenophon could easily have explained in direct terms the conditional character of the policy recommended in the *Hiero*. Had he done so, however, he might have conveyed the impression that he was not absolutely opposed to tyranny. But "the cities," and especially Athens, were absolutely opposed to tyranny.[7] Besides, one of the charges brought against Socrates was that he taught his pupils to be "tyrannical." Reasons such as these explain why Xenophon presented his reflections on the improvement of tyrannical rule (and therewith on the stabilization of such rule), as distinguished from his reflections on the improvement of the Athenian regime, in the form of a dialogue in which he does not participate in any way: the *Hiero* is the only work of Xenophon in which the author, when speaking in his own name, never uses the first person, whereas the *Ways and Means* is the only work of Xenophon whose very opening word is an emphatic *I*. The reasons indicated explain besides why the fairly brief suggestions for the improvement of tyrannical rule are prefaced by a considerably more extensive discourse which expounds the undesirable character of tyranny in the strongest possible terms.

The *Hiero* consists almost exclusively of utterances of men other than the author. There is only one other work of Xenophon which has that character: the *Oeconomicus*. In the *Oeconomicus*, too, the author "hides himself"[8] almost completely. The *Oeconomicus* is a dialogue between Socrates and another Athenian on the management of the household. According to Socrates, there does not seem to be an essential difference between the art of managing the household and that of managing the affairs of the city: both are called by him "the royal art."[9] Hence it can only be due to secondary considerations that the dialogue which is destined to teach that art is called *Oeconomicus*, and not *Politicus* or *Basilicus*. There is ample evidence to show that the *Oeconomicus*, while apparently devoted to the economic art only, actually deals with the royal art as such.[10] It is then permissible to describe the relation of Xenophon's two dialogues as that of a *Basilicus* to a *Tyrannicus*: the two dialogues deal with *the* two types of monarchic rule.[11] Since the economist is a ruler, the *Oeconomicus* is, just as the *Hiero*, a dialogue between a wise man (Socrates)[12] and a ruler (the potential economist Critobulus and the actual economist Ischomachus). But whereas the wise man and the rulers of the *Oeconomicus* are Athenians, the wise man and the ruler of the *Hiero* are not. And whereas the wise man and the potential ruler of the *Oeconomicus* were friends of Xenophon, and Xenophon himself was present at their conversation, the wise man and the ruler of the *Hiero* were dead long before Xenophon's time. It was evidently impossible to assign the "tyrannical" teaching to Socrates. But the reason was not that there was any scarcity of actual or potential tyrants in the entourage of Socrates. Rather the reverse. Nothing would have been easier for Xenophon than to arrange a conversation on how to rule well as a tyrant between Socrates and Charmides or Critias[13] or Alcibiades. So doing, though—giving Socrates such a role in such a context—he would have destroyed the basis of his own defense of Socrates. It is for this reason that the place occupied in the *Oeconomicus* by Socrates is occupied in the *Hiero* by another wise man. After having chosen Simonides, Xenophon was free to present him as engaged in a conversation with the Athenian tyrant Hipparchus;[14] but he apparently wished to avoid any connection between the topics "tyranny" and "Athens."

One cannot help wondering why Xenophon chose Simonides as a chief character in preference to certain other wise men who were known to have conversed with tyrants.[15] A clue is offered by the parallelism between the *Hiero* and the *Oeconomicus*. The royal art is morally superior to the tyrannical art. Socrates, who teaches the royal or economic art, has perfect self-control as regards the pleasures deriving from wealth.[16] Simonides, who teaches the tyrannical art, was famous for his greed.[17] Socrates, who teaches the economic or royal art, was not himself an economist because he was not interested in increasing his property; accordingly, his teaching consists largely of giving to a potential economist an account of a conversation which he once had with an actual economist.[18] Simonides, who teaches the tyrannical art, and therewith at least some rudiments of the economic art as well,[19] without any assistance, *was* an "economist."

In the light of the parallelism between the *Oeconomicus* and the *Hiero*, our previous explanation of the fact that Xenophon presented the "tyrannical" teaching in the form of a dialogue proves to be insufficient. With a view to that parallelism, we have to raise the more comprehensive question as to why the *Oeconomicus* and the *Hiero*, as distinguished from Xenophon's two other technical writings, the *Hipparchicus* and the *Cynegticus*, are written in the form not of treatises, nor even of stories, but of dialogues. The subjects of the two former works, we shall venture to say, are of a higher order, or are more philosophic than those of the two latter. Accordingly, their treatment too should be more philosophic. From Xenophon's point of view, philosophic treatment is conversational treatment. Conversational teaching of the skill of ruling has these two particular advantages. First, it necessitates the confrontation of a wise man (the teacher) and a ruler (the pupil). Besides, it compels the reader to wonder whether the lessons given by the wise man to the ruler bore fruit, because it compels the author to leave unanswered that question which is nothing less than a special form of the fundamental question of the relation of theory and practice, or of knowledge and virtue.

The second advantage of conversational teaching is particularly striking in the *Hiero*. Whereas the proof of the unhappiness of the unjust tyrant is emphatically based on experience,[20] the proof of the happiness of the beneficent tyrant is not: that happiness is merely promised—by a poet. The reader is left wondering whether experience offered a single instance of a tyrant who was happy because he was virtuous.[21] The corresponding question forced upon the reader of the *Oeconomicus* is answered, if not by the *Oeconomicus* itself, by the *Cyropaedia* and the *Agesilaus*. But the question of the actual happiness of the virtuous tyrant is left open by the *Corpus Xenophonteum* as a whole. And whereas the *Cyropaedia* and the *Agesilaus* set the happiness of the virtuous kings Cyrus and Agesilaus beyond any imaginable doubt by showing or at least intimating how they died, the *Hiero*, owing to its form, cannot throw any light on the end of the tyrant Hiero.[22]

We hope to have explained why Xenophon presents the "tyrannical" teaching in the form of a conversation between Simonides and a non-Athenian tyrant. An adequate understanding of that teaching requires more than an understanding of its content. One must also consider the form in which it is presented, for otherwise one cannot realize the place which it occupies, according to the author, within the whole of wisdom. The form in which it is presented characterizes it as a philosophic teaching of the sort that a truly wise man would not care to present in his own name. Moreover, by throwing some light on the procedure of the wise man who stoops to present the "tyrannical" teaching in his own name, i.e., of Simonides, the author shows us how that teaching should be presented to its ultimate addressee, the tyrant.

III

The Setting

A. THE CHARACTERS AND THEIR INTENTIONS

"Simonides the poet came once upon a time to Hiero the tyrant. After both had found leisure, Simonides said. . . ." This is all that Xenophon says thematically and explicitly about the situation in which the conversation took place. "Simonides came to Hiero": Hiero did not come to Simonides. Tyrants do not like to travel to foreign parts,[1] and, as Simonides seems to have said to Hiero's wife, the wise are spending their time at the doors of the rich and not *vice versa*.[2] Simonides came to Hiero "once upon a time": he was merely visiting Hiero; those coming to display before the tyrant something wise or beautiful or good prefer to go away as soon as they have received their reward.[3] The conversation opens "after both had found leisure" and, we may add, when they were alone: it does not open immediately on Simonides' arrival. It appears in the course of the conversation that prior to the conversation Hiero had acquired a definite opinion of Simonides' qualities, and Simonides had made some observations about Hiero. It is not impossible that the business which each had before both found leisure was a business which they had with each other. At any rate, they were not complete strangers to each other at the moment when the conversation starts. Their knowledge of, or their opinions about, each other might even explain why they engage in a leisurely conversation at all, as well as how they behave during their conversation from its very beginning.

It is Simonides who opens the conversation. What is his purpose? He starts with the question whether Hiero would be willing to explain to him something which he is likely to know better than the poet. The polite question which he addresses to a tyrant who is not his ruler keeps in the appropriate middle between the informal request, so frequently used by Socrates in particular, "Tell me," or the polite request, "I want very much to learn," on the one hand, and the deferential question addressed by Socrates to tyrants who were his rulers (the "legislators" Critias and Charicles), "Is it permitted to inquire. . .?" on the other.[4] By his question, Simonides presents himself as a wise man who, always desirous to learn, wishes to avail himself of the opportunity of learning something from Hiero. He thus assigns Hiero the position of a man who is, in a certain respect, wiser, a greater authority than he is himself. Hiero, fully aware of how wise Simonides is, has not the slightest notion as to what sort of thing he could know better than a man of Simonides' wisdom. Simonides explains to him that since he, Hiero, was born a private man and is now a tyrant, he is, on the basis of his experience of both conditions, likely to know better than Simonides in what way the life of a tyrant and that of private men differ with regard to human enjoyments and pains.[5] The choice of the topic is perfect. A comparison of a tyrant's life and private life is the only comprehensive, or "wise," topic in the discussion of which a wise man can with some plausibility be presented as inferior to a tyrant who once had been a private man and who is not wise. Moreover, the point of view which, as Simonides suggests, should guide the comparison— pleasure–pain as distinguished from virtue–vice—seems to be charac- teristic of tyrants as distinguished from kings.[6] Simonides seems then to open the conversation with the intention of learning something from Hiero, or of getting some first-hand information from an au- thority on the subject which he proposes.

Yet the reason with which he justifies his question in the eyes of Hiero is only a probable one. It leaves out of consideration the decisive contribution of judgment, or wisdom, to the correct evaluation of experiences.[7] Moreover, the question itself is not of such a nature that peculiar experiences which a wise man may or may not have had (such as those which only an actual tyrant can have had) could contribute significantly to its complete answer. It rather belongs to the kind of question to which the wise man as such (and only the wise man as such) necessarily possesses the complete answer. Simonides' question concerning the manner of difference between the tyrant's life and private life in regard to pleasures and pains is identical, in the context, with the question as to which of the two ways of life is more desirable; for "pleasure-pain" is the only ultimate criterion of preference which is thematically considered. The initial question is rendered more specific by the assertion which Simonides makes soon afterward that the tyrant's life knows many more pleasures of all kinds and many fewer pains of all kinds than private life, in other words, that tyrannical life is more desirable than private life.[8] Even Hiero states that Simonides' assertion is surprising in the mouth of a reputedly wise man: a wise man should be able to judge of the happiness or misery of the tyrant's life without ever having had the actual experience of tyrannical life.[9] The question as to whether, or how far, tyrannical life is more desirable than private life, and in particular whether, or how far, it is more desirable from the point of view of pleasure, is no longer a question for a man who has acquired wisdom.[10] If Simonides was a wise man, he must then have had a motive other than eagerness to learn for inquiring with Hiero about that subject.

Hiero expresses the view that Simonides is a wise man, a man much wiser than he himself is. This assertion is borne out to a certain extent by the action of the dialogue, by which Simonides is shown to be able to teach Hiero the art of ruling as a tyrant. While Simonides is thus shown to be wiser than Hiero, it is by no means certain that Xenophon considered him simply wise. What Xenophon thought of Simonides' wisdom can be definitely established only by a comparison of Simonides with Socrates, whom Xenophon certainly considered wise. It is possible, however, to reach a provisional conclusion on the basis of the parallelism of the *Hiero* and the *Oeconomicus* as well as of the following consideration: If Simonides was wise, he had conversation skill; i.e., he could do what he liked with any interlocutor,[11] or he could lead any conversation to the end which he desired. His conversation with Hiero leads up to such suggestions about the improvement of tyrannical rule as a wise man could be expected to make to a tyrant toward whom he is well disposed. We shall then assume that the wise Simonides opens the conversation intending to be of some benefit to Hiero, perhaps in order to be benefited in turn or to benefit the tyrant's subjects. During his stay with Hiero, Simonides had observed several things about the ruler—some concerning his appetite, some concerning his amours;[12] and Simonides knew that Hiero was making certain grave mistakes, such as his participating at the Olympic and Pythian games.[13] To express this more generally, Simonides knew that Hiero was not a perfect ruler. He decided to teach him how to rule well as a tyrant. More specifically, he considered it advisable to warn him against certain grave mistakes. But, to say nothing of common politeness, no one wishes to rebuke, or to speak against, a tyrant in his presence.[14] Simonides had, then, by the least offensive means to reduce the tyrant to a mood in which the latter would be pleased to listen attentively to, and even to ask for, the poet's advice. He had at the same time, or by the same action, to convince Hiero of his competence to give sound advice to a tyrant.

Before Simonides can teach Hiero how to rule as a tyrant, he has to make him aware, or to remind him, of the difficulties with which he is beset and which he cannot overcome, of the shortcomings of his rule, and indeed of his whole life. To be made aware by someone else of one's own shortcomings means, for most people to be humbled by the censor. Simonides has to humble the tyrant; he has to reduce him to a condition of inferiority; or, to describe Simonides' intention in the light of the aim apparently achieved by him, he has to dishearten the tyrant. Moreover, if he intends to use Hiero's recognition of his shortcomings as the starting point for his teaching, he has to induce Hiero expressly to grant all the relevant unpleasant facts about his life. The least he can do, in order to avoid unnecessary offense, is to talk, not about Hiero's life, but about a more general, a less offensive, subject. To begin with, we shall assume that when starting a conversation with Hiero about the relative desirability of the life of the tyrant and private life, he is guided by the intention to dishearten the tyrant by a comparison of the life of the tyrant, and therewith of Hiero's own life, with private life.

To reach this immediate aim in the least offensive manner, Simonides has to create a situation in which not he, but the tyrant himself, explains the shortcomings of his life, or of tyrannical life in general, and a situation in which, moreover, the tyrant does this normally unpleasant work not only spontaneously but even gladly. The artifice by means of which Simonides brings about this result consists in his giving to Hiero an opportunity of vindicating his superiority while demonstrating his inferiority. He starts the conversation by presenting himself explicitly as a man who has to learn from Hiero, or who is, in a certain respect, less wise than Hiero, or by assuming the role of the pupil. Thereafter, he makes himself the spokesman of the opinion that tyrannical life is more desirable than private life, i.e., of the crude opinion about tyranny which is characteristic of the unwise, of the multitude, or the vulgar.[15] He thus presents himself tacitly, and therefore all the more effectively, as a man who is absolutely less wise than Hiero. He thus tempts Hiero to assume the role of the teacher.[16] He succeeds in seducing him into refuting the vulgar opinion, and thus into proving that tyrannical life, and hence his own life, is extremely unhappy. Hiero vindicates his superiority by winning his argument, which, so far as its content is concerned, would be merely depressing for him: by proving that he is extremely unhappy, he proves that he is wiser than the wise Simonides. Yet his victory is his defeat. By appealing to the tyrant's interest in superiority, or desire for victory, Simonides brings about the tyrant's spontaneous and almost joyful recognition of all the shortcomings of his life and therewith a situation in which the offering of advice is the act, not of an awkward schoolmaster, but of a humane poet. And besides, in the moment that Hiero becomes aware of his having walked straight into the trap which Simonides had so ingeniously and so charmingly set for him, he will be more convinced than ever before of Simonides' wisdom.

Before Simonides starts teaching Hiero, in other words, in the largest part of the *Hiero* (ch. 1–7), he presents himself to Hiero as less wise than he really is. In the first part of the *Hiero,* Simonides hides his wisdom. He does not merely report the vulgar opinion about tyranny, he does not merely hand it over to Hiero for its refutation by asking him what he thinks about it; he actually adopts it. Hiero is justifiably under the impression that Simonides is ignorant of or deceived about the nature of tyrannical life.[17] Thus the question arises as to why Simonides' artifice does not defeat his purpose: why can Hiero still take him seriously? Why does he not consider him a fool, a foolish follower of the opinions of the vulgar? The situation in which the conversation takes place remains wholly obscure as long as this difficulty is not satisfactorily explained.

The difficulty would be insoluble if to be vulgar merely meant to be simply foolish or unwise. The vulgar opinion about tyranny can be summarized as follows: Tyranny is bad for the city but good for the tyrant, for the tyrannical life is the most enjoyable and desirable way of life.[18] This opinion is founded on the basic premise of the vulgar mind that bodily pleasures and wealth or power are more important than virtue. The vulgar opinion is contested, not only by the wise, but above all by the gentlemen. According to the opinion of the perfect gentleman, tyranny is bad, not only for the city, but above all for the tyrant himself.[19] By adopting the vulgar view, Simonides tacitly rejects the gentleman's view. Could he not be a gentleman? Could he lack the moderation, the self-restraint of the gentleman? Could he be dangerous? Whether this suspicion arises evidently depends on what opinion is held by Hiero about the relation of "wise" and "gentlemen." But if it arises, the theoretical and somewhat playful discussion will transform itself into a conflict.

The ironic element of Simonides' procedure would endanger the achievement of his serious purpose if it did not arouse a deeper emotion in the soul of the tyrant than the somewhat whimsical desire to win a dialectical victory. The manner in which he understands, and reacts to, Simonides' question and assertion is bound to be determined by his view of Simonides' qualities and of his intention. He considers Simonides a wise man. His attitude toward Simonides will then be a special case of his attitude toward wise men in general. He says that tyrants fear the wise. His attitude toward Simonides must be understood accordingly: "Instead of admiring" him, he fears him.[20] Considering the fact that Simonides is a stranger in Hiero's city, and therefore not likely to be really dangerous to Hiero's rule,[21] we prefer to say that his admiration for Simonides is mitigated by some fear, by some fear *in statu nascendi*, i.e., by distrust. He does not trust people in any case; he will be particularly distrustful in his dealings with a man of unusually great abilities. Hence he is not likely to be perfectly frank. He is likely to be as reserved as Simonides, although for somewhat different reasons.[22] Their conversation is likely to take place in an atmosphere of limited straightforwardness.

The tyrant's fear of the wise is a specific one. This crucial fact is explained by Hiero in what is even literally the central passage of the *Hiero*.[23] He fears the brave because they might take risks for the sake of freedom. He fears the just because the multitude might desire to be ruled by them. As regards the wise, he fears that "they might contrive something." He fears, then, the brave and the just because their virtues or virtuous actions might bring about the restoration of freedom or at least of nontyrannical government. This much, and not more, is explained by Hiero in unequivocal terms. He does not say explicitly what kind of danger he apprehends from the wise: Does he fear that they might contrive something for the sake of freedom or of just government, or does he fear that they might contrive something for some other purpose?[24] Hiero's explicit statement leaves unanswered the crucial question, Why does the tyrant fear the wise?

The most cautious explanation of Hiero's silence would be the suggestion that he does not know what the wise intend. Having once been a private man, a private citizen, a subject of a tyrant, he knows and understands the goals of the brave and the just as well as they themselves do. But he has never been a wise man: he does not know wisdom from his own experience. He realizes that wisdom is a virtue, a power, hence a limit to the tyrant's power, and therefore a danger to the tyrant's rule. He realizes, besides, that wisdom is something different from courage and justice. But he does not clearly grasp the specific and positive character of wisdom: wisdom is more elusive than courage and justice. Perhaps it would not be too much to say that for the tyrant wisdom, as distinguished from courage and justice, is something uncanny. At any rate, his fear of the wise is an indeterminate fear, in some cases (as in the case of Hiero's fear of Simonides) hardly more than a vague, but strong, uneasiness.

This attitude toward the wise is characteristic not only of tyrants. The fate of Socrates must be presumed always to have been present to Xenophon's mind. It confirmed the view that wise men are apt to be envied by men who are less wise or altogether unwise, and that they are exposed to all sorts of vague suspicion on the part of "the many." Xenophon himself suggested that the same experience which Socrates had had under a democracy would have been had by him under a monarchy: wise men are apt to be envied, or suspected, by monarchs as well as by ordinary citizens.[25] The distrust of the wise, which proceeds from lack of understanding of wisdom, is characteristic of the vulgar, of tyrants and nontyrants alike. Hiero's attitude toward the wise bears at least some resemblance to the vulgar attitude.

The fate of Socrates showed that those who do not understand the nature of wisdom are apt to mistake the wise man for the sophist. Both the wise man and the sophist are in a sense possessors of wisdom. But whereas the sophist prostitutes wisdom for base purposes, and especially for money, the wise man makes the most noble or moral use of wisdom.[26] The wise man is a gentleman, whereas the sophist is servile. The error of mistaking the wise man for the sophist is made possible by the ambiguity of "gentlemanliness." In common parlance, "gentleman" designates a just and brave man, a good citizen, who as such is not necessarily a wise man. Ischomachus, that perfectly respectable man whom Xenophon confronts with Socrates, is called a gentleman by everyone, by men and women, by strangers and citizens. In the Socratic meaning of the term, the gentleman is identical with the wise man.[27] The essence of wisdom, or what distinguishes wisdom from ordinary gentlemanliness, escapes the vulgar, who may thus be led to believe in an opposition between wisdom and the only gentlemanliness known to them: they may doubt the gentlemanliness of the wise. They will see this much, that wisdom is the ability to contrive the acquisition of that possession which is most valuable and therefore most difficult to obtain. But believing that the tyrannical life is the most enjoyable and therefore the most desirable possession, they will be inclined to identify wisdom with the ability to become a tyrant or to remain a tyrant. Those who succeeded in acquiring tyrannical power, and in preserving it for ever so short a time, are admired as wise and lucky men: the specific ability which enables a man to become, and to remain, a tyrant is popularly identified with wisdom. On the other hand, if a wise man manifestly abstains from striving for tyrannical power, he may still be suspected of teaching his friends to be "tyrannical."[28] On the basis of the vulgar notion of wisdom, the conclusion is plausible that a wise man would aspire to tyranny or, if he is already a tyrant, that he would attempt to preserve his position.

Let us now return to Hiero's statement about the various types of human excellence. The brave would take risks for the sake of freedom; the just would be desired as rulers by the multitude. The brave as brave would not be desired as rulers, and the just as just would not rebel. As clearly as the brave as brave are distinguished from the just as just, the wise as wise are distinguished from both the brave and the just. Would the wise take risks for the sake of freedom? Did Socrates, as distinguished from Thrasybulus, take such risks? While blaming "somewhere" the practices of Critias and his fellows, and while refusing to obey their unjust commands, he did not work for their overthrow.[29] Would the wise be desired as rulers by the multitude? Was Socrates desired as a ruler by the multitude? One has no right to assume that Hiero's view of wisdom and justice is identical with Xenophon's. The context suggests that, according to Hiero, the wise as wise have a purpose different from those of the brave and of the just, or, if courage and justice combined are the essence of gentlemanliness, that the wise man is not necessarily a gentleman. The context suggests that the wise have another goal than the typical enemies of tyranny, who are concerned with restoring freedom and "possession of good laws."[30] This suggestion is far from being contradicted by Simonides, who avoids in his teaching the very terms "freedom" and "law." There is only one reasonable alternative: the tyrant fears the wise man because he might attempt to overthrow the tyrant, not in order to restore nontyrannical government, but to become a tyrant himself or because he might advise a pupil or friend of his as to how he could become a tyrant by overthrowing the actual tyrant. Hiero's central statement does not exclude but rather suggests the vulgar view of wisdom;[31] it does not exclude but rather suggests the view that the wise man is a potential tyrant.[32]

Hiero is somehow aware of the fact that wise men do not judge of happiness or misery on the basis of outward appearance because they know that the seat of happiness and misery is in the souls of men. It therefore seems surprising to him that Simonides should identify, for all practical purposes, happiness with wealth and power, and ultimately with the tyrannical life. He does not say, however, that Simonides, being a wise man, cannot possibly mean what he says, or that he must be joking. On the contrary, he takes Simonides' assertion most seriously. He does not consider it incredible or impossible that a wise man should hold the view adopted by Simonides.[33] He does not consider it impossible because he believes that only the experience of a tyrant can establish with final certainty whether tyrannical life is, or is not, more desirable than private life.[34] He does not really know the purpose of the wise. He is then not convinced that the wise man is a potential tyrant. Nor is he convinced of the contrary. He oscillates between two diametrically opposed views, between the vulgar view and the wise view of wisdom. Which of the two opposed views he will take in a given case will depend on the behavior of the wise individual with whom he converses. Regarding Simonides, the question is decided by the fact that he adopts the vulgar opinion according to which the tyrannical life is more desirable than private life. At least in his conversation with Simonides, Hiero will be disturbed by the suspicion that the wise man may be a potential tyrant, or a potential adviser of possible rivals of Hiero.[35]

Hiero's fear or distrust of Simonides originates in his attitude toward wise men and would exist regardless of the topic of their conversation. But if there were any one topic which could aggravate Hiero's suspicion of Simonides, it is that topic which the wise man in fact proposed—a topic relating to the object with regard to which the tyrants fear the wise. In addition, Simonides explicitly says that all men regard tyrants with a mixture of admiration and envy, or that they are jealous of tyrants, and Hiero understands the bearing of this statement sufficiently to apply it to Simonides by speaking of Simonides himself being jealous of tyrants.[36] Hiero does not possess that true understanding of the nature of wisdom which alone could protect him from being suspicious of Simonides' question about the relative desirability of tyrannical and private life. Lacking such understanding, Hiero cannot be certain that the question might not serve the very practical purpose of eliciting some first-hand information from the tyrant about a condition of which the poet is jealous or to which he is aspiring for himself or someone else. His fear or distrust of Simonides will be a fear or distrust strengthened and rendered definite by Simonides' apparently believing that the tyrannical life is more desirable than private life. Simonides' apparently frank confession of his preference will seem to Hiero to supply him with an opportunity of getting rid of his uneasiness. His whole answer will serve the very practical purpose of dissuading Simonides from looking at tyrants with a mixture of admiration and envy.

By playing upon this intention of Hiero,[37] Simonides compels him to use the strongest possible language against tyranny and thus finally to declare his bankruptcy, therewith handing over the leadership in the conversation to Simonides. Simonides' intention to dishearten Hiero and Hiero's intention to dissuade Simonides from admiring or envying tyrants produce by their cooperation the result primarily intended by Simonides, viz., a situation in which Hiero has no choice but to listen to Simonides' advice.

In order to provoke Hiero's passionate reaction, Simonides has to overstate the case for tyranny. When reading all his statements by themselves, one is struck by the fact that there are indeed some passages in which he, more or less compelled by Hiero's arguments, grants that tyranny has its drawbacks, whereas one finds more passages in which he spontaneously and strongly asserts its advantages. The statements of Simonides on tyranny would justify Hiero in thinking that Simonides is envious of tyrants. Yet the ironic character of Simonides' praise of tyranny as such (as distinguished from his praise of beneficent tyranny in the second part of the *Hiero*) can hardly escape the notice of any reader. For instance, when he asserts that tyrants derive greater pleasure from sounds than private men because they constantly hear the most pleasant kind of sound—viz., praise—he is not ignorant of the fact that the praise bestowed upon tyrants by their entourage is not genuine praise.[38] On the other hand, Hiero is interested in overstating the case against tyranny. This point requires some discussion since the explicit indictment of tyranny in the *Hiero* is entrusted exclusively to Hiero, and therefore the understanding of the tendency of the *Hiero* as a whole depends decisively on the correct appreciation of Hiero's utterances on the subject.

It is certainly inadmissible to take for granted that Hiero simply voices Xenophon's considered judgment on tyranny: Hiero is not Xenophon. Besides, there is some specific evidence which goes to show that Hiero's indictment of tyranny is, according to Xenophon's view, exaggerated. Hiero asserts that "*the* cities magnificently honor the tyrannicide"; Xenophon, however, tells us that those murderers of Jason who survived were honored "in *most* of the Greek cities" to which they came.[39] Hiero asserts that the tyrants "know well that *all* their subjects are their enemies"; Xenophon, however, tells us that the *beyond this you Xenophon* [handwritten marginal note]

subjects of the tyrant Euphron considered him their benefactor and revered him highly.[40] Hiero describes the tyrant as deprived of all pleasures of gay companionship; Xenophon, however, describes the tyrant Astyages as securely enjoying those pleasures to the full.[41] Yet Hiero may have said more against tyranny than Xenophon would grant; he may still have said exactly what he himself thought about the subject on the basis of his bitter experiences. Now, no reader however careful of the speeches of Hiero can possibly know anything of the expression of Hiero's face, of his gestures, and of the inflections of his voice. He is then not in the best position to detect which words of Hiero's rang true and which rang false. One of the many advantages of a dialogue one character of which is a wise man is that it puts at the disposal of the reader the wise man's discriminating observations concerning the different degree of reliability of the various utterances which flow with an equal ease, but not necessarily with an equal degree of conviction, from his companion's mouth. When reading the *Hiero* cursorily, one is bound to feel that Hiero is worried particularly by the tyrant's lack of friendship, confidence, patriotism, and true honor as well as by the constant danger of assassination. Yet Xenophon's Simonides, who is our sole authority for the adequate interpretation of the speeches of Xenophon's Hiero, was definitely not under the impression that Hiero's greatest sorrow was caused by the lack of the noble things mentioned, or by those agonies of perpetual and limitless fear which he describes in so edifying a manner. He has not the slightest doubt that Hiero has blamed tyranny most of all with a view to the fact that the tyrant is deprived of the sweetest pleasures of homosexual love, i.e., of pleasures which Simonides himself declares to be of minor importance.[42] Simonides is then not greatly impressed by Hiero's indictment of tyranny. That indictment, however touching or eloquent, has therefore to be read with a great deal of reasonable distrust.

When proving that private men derive greater pleasure from victory than tyrants, Hiero compares the victory of the citizens over their foreign enemies with the victory of the tyrant over his subjects: the citizens consider their victory something noble, and they are proud of it and boast of it, whereas the tyrant cannot be proud of his victory, or boast of it, or consider it noble.[43] Hiero fails to mention not only the victory of a party in a civil war but above all the victory of the citizens governed or led by their tyrannical ruler over their foreign enemies: he forgets his own victory in the battle of Cumae. He fails to consider the obvious possibility that a tyrant, who takes the chief responsibility for the outcome of a war, might be more gratified by victory than might the ordinary citizen; for it was the prudent counsel and efficient leadership of the tyrant that brought about the happy issue, while the ordinary citizen never can have had more than a small share in the deliberations concerning the war. Hiero fails to consider that this great pleasure might fully compensate the tyrant for the lack of many lesser pleasures.

We may speak of a twofold meaning of the indictment of tyranny, which forms the first and by far the largest part of the *Hiero*. According to its obvious meaning, it amounts to the strongest possible indictment of tyranny: the greatest possible authority on the subject, a tyrant who as such speaks from experience, shows that tyranny is bad even from the point of view of tyrants, even from the point of view of the pleasures of the tyrant.[44] This meaning is obvious; one merely has to read the first part of the *Hiero,* which consists chiefly of speeches of Hiero to this effect, in order to grasp it. A less obvious meaning of the first part of the *Hiero* comes into sight as soon as one considers its conversational setting—the fact that the distrustful tyrant is speaking *pro domo*—and, going one step further in the same direction, when one considers the facts recorded in Xenophon's historical work (the *Hellenica*). These considerations lead one to a more qualified indictment of tyranny, or to a more truthful account of tyranny, or to the wise view of tyranny. This means that in order to grasp Xenophon's view of tyranny as distinguished from Hiero's utterances about tyranny, one has to consider Hiero's "speeches" in the light of the more trustworthy "deeds" or "actions" or "facts,"[45] and in particular that most important of "facts," the conversational setting of the *Hiero*. To the two meanings correspond then two types of reading, and ultimately two types of men. It was with a view to this difference between types of men and a corresponding difference between types of speaking that Socrates liked to quote the verses from the *Iliad* in which Odysseus is described as using different language when speaking to outstanding men on the one hand, and when speaking to the common people on the other;[46] and that he distinguished the superficial understanding of Homer on the part of the rhapsodes from that understanding which grasps the poet's "insinuations."[47] The superficial understanding is not simply wrong, since it grasps the obvious meaning which is as much intended by the author as is the deeper meaning. To describe in one sentence the art employed by Xenophon in the first part of the *Hiero,* we may say that by choosing a conversational setting in which the strongest possible indictment of tyranny becomes necessary, he intimates the limited validity of that indictment.[48]

B. THE ACTION OF THE DIALOGUE

No genuine communication could develop if Hiero were animated exclusively by distrust of Simonides, or if Simonides did not succeed in gaining the tyrant's confidence to some extent. At the beginning of the conversation he reassures Hiero by declaring his willingness to learn from Hiero, i.e., to trust him in what he is going to say about the relative desirability of tyrannical and private life. The first section of the dialogue (ch. 1) is characterized by the interplay of Simonides' intention to reassure Hiero with his intention to dishearten him. That interplay ceases as soon as Hiero is completely committed to the continuance of the conversation. From that moment Simonides limits himself to provoking Hiero to express his unqualified indictment of tyranny.

Hiero, perhaps offended by Simonides' inevitable reference to his pretyrannical past and at the same time desirous to know more about Simonides' intentions and his preferences, emphasizes how remote he considers that past by asking Simonides to remind him of the pleasures and pains of private men: he pretends to have forgotten them.[1] In this context he mentions the fact that Simonides is "at present still a private man." Simonides seems to accept the challenge for a moment. At any rate, he makes to begin with a distinction between himself and private men ("I seem to have observed that private men enjoy . . . ."); but he soon drops that odious distinction by identifying himself unreservedly with the private men ("We seem to enjoy . . . .").[2] In complying with Hiero's request, Simonides enumerates various groups of pleasurable and painful things. The enumeration is in a sense complete: it covers the pleasures and pains of the body, those of the soul, and those common to body and soul. Otherwise, it is most surprising. While it is unnecessarily detailed as regards the pleasures and pains of the body, it does not give any details whatsoever as regards the other kinds of pleasure and pain mentioned. It is reasonable to assume that the selection is made, at least partly, *ad hominem,* or that it is meant to prepare a discussion which serves a specific practical purpose. Simonides enumerates seven groups of things which are sometimes pleasant and sometimes painful for private men, and one which is always pleasant for them: that which is always pleasant for them is sleep—which the tyrant, haunted by fears of all kinds, must strive to avoid.[3] This example seems to show that the purpose of Simonides' enumeration is to remind the tyrant of the pleasures of which he is supposed to be deprived, and thus to induce him to make clear to himself the misery of tyrannical life. It is for this reason, one might surmise to begin with, that the enumeration puts the emphasis on the pleasures of the body,[4] i.e., on those pleasures the enjoyment of which is not characteristic of actual or potential tyrants. However, if Simonides' chief intention had been to remind Hiero of the pleasures of which he is actually or supposedly deprived, he would not have dropped the topic "sleep" in the discussion which immediately follows (in ch. 1). Furthermore, Simonides' initial enumeration fails to have any depressing effect on Hiero. It seems therefore preferable to say that his emphasizing the pleasures of the body in the initial enumeration is chiefly due to his intention to reassure Hiero. Emphasizing these pleasures, he creates the impression that he is himself chiefly interested in them. But men chiefly interested in bodily pleasures are not likely to aspire to any ruling position.[5]

Hiero is satisfied with Simonides' enumeration. He gives Simonides to understand that it exhausts the types of pleasure and pain experienced by tyrants as well as by private men. Simonides strikes the first obvious note of dissonance by asserting that the life of a tyrant contains many more pleasures of all kinds and many fewer pains of all kinds than private life. Hiero's immediate answer is still restrained. He does not assert that tyrannical life is inferior to private life as such; he merely says that tyrannical life is inferior to the life of private men of moderate means.[6] He admits by implication that the condition of tyrants is preferable to that of poor men. Yet poverty and wealth are to be measured, not by number, but with a view to use, or to need.[7] At least from this point of view, Simonides may be poor and hence justified in being jealous of tyrants. At any rate, he now reveals that he looks at tyrants with a mixture of admiration and envy and that he might belong to the "many who are reputed to be most able men" who desire to be tyrants. The tension increases. Hiero strengthens his reply, which is more emphatic than any previous utterance of his, by an oath, and he expresses his intention to teach Simonides the truth about the relative desirability of tyrannical and private life.[8] Speaking as a teacher, he embarks upon a discussion of the various kinds of bodily pleasure which keeps in the main to the order followed by Simonides in his initial enumeration.[9] Hiero now tries to prove the thesis that tyrannical life is inferior, not merely to a specific private life, but to private life as such.[10]

The discussion of bodily pleasures (1.10–38) reveals the preferences of the two interlocutors in an indirect way.[11] According to Hiero, the inferiority of tyranny shows itself most clearly with regard to the pleasures of sex, and especially of homosexuality.[12] The only proper name occurring in the *Hiero* (apart from those of Simonides, Hiero, Zeus, and the Greeks), i.e., the only concrete reference to Hiero's life, as well as Hiero's second emphatic oath (which is his last emphatic oath), occurs in the passage dealing with homosexual love.[13] Simonides is particularly vocal regarding the pleasures of hearing, i.e., the pleasures of hearing praise, and, above all, regarding the pleasures of food. His most emphatic assertion, occurring in the discussion of bodily pleasures, concerns food.[14] Two of his five "by Zeus" occur in the passage dealing with food.[15] That passage is the only part of the *Hiero* where the conversation takes on the character of a lively discussion, and in fact of a Socratic elenchus (with Hiero in the role of Socrates): Hiero is compelled, point by point, to refute Simonides' assertion that tyrants derive greater pleasure from food than private men.[16] Only in reading the discussion concerning food does one get the impression that Hiero has to overcome a serious resistance on the part of Simonides: four times he appeals from Simonides' assertion to Simonides' experience, observation, or knowledge. How much Hiero is aware of this state of things is shown by the fact that after Simonides had already abandoned the subject, Hiero once more returns to it in order to leave no doubt whatsoever in Simonides' mind as to the inferiority of tyrannical life in the matter of the pleasures of the table: he does not rest until Simonides has granted that, as regards these pleasures, tyrants are worse off than private men.[17] As an explanation we suggest that Simonides wants to reassure Hiero by presenting himself as a man chiefly interested in food, or in "good living" in general, or by ironically overstating his actual liking for "good living."[18]

At the end of the discussion of the bodily pleasures, we seem to have reached the end of the whole conversation. Simonides had originally enumerated eight groups of pleasurable or painful things: (1) sights, (2) sounds, (3) odors, (4) food and drink, (5) sex, (6) objects perceived by the whole body, (7) good and bad things, and (8) sleep. After four of them (sights, sounds, food and drink, odors) have been discussed, he says that the pleasures of sex seem to be the only motive which excites in tyrants the desire for tyrannical rule.[19] By implication, he thus dismisses as irrelevant three of the four groups of pleasant or painful things which had not thereto been discussed (objects perceived by the whole body, good and bad things, sleep). Hence, he narrows down the whole question of the relative desirability of tyrannical and private life to the question, Do tyrants or private men enjoy to a higher degree the pleasures of sex? So doing, he completely reassures Hiero: he practically capitulates. For of nothing is Hiero more convinced than of this, that precisely as regards the pleasures of sex, tyrants are most evidently worse off than private men. He is so much convinced of the truth of his thesis and of the decisive character of the argument by which he upholds it that he can speak later on of his having "demonstrated" to Simonides the true character of a tyrant's amatory pleasures.[20] At the end of the discussion of sex, i.e., at the end of the discussion of the bodily pleasures, Hiero has proved to Simonides what the latter had admitted to be the only point which still needed proof if Hiero's general thesis were to be established securely. On the level of the surface argument the discussion has reached its end. The discussion would have reached its end as well if Simonides had no other intention than to find out what Hiero's greatest worries are, or to remind him of the pleasures from the lack of which he suffers most, or to give him an opportunity of speaking freely of what disturbs him most. All these aims have been reached at the end of the discussion of sex: Hiero is concerned most of all with the tyrant's lack of the sweetest pleasures of homosexual love,[21] and the later discussion is devoted to entirely different subjects. On the other hand, the continuation of the conversation is evidently necessary if Simonides' intention is to defeat Hiero by playing upon the tyrant's fear of the wise.

The first round ends, so it seems, with a complete victory for Hiero. He has proved his thesis without saying too much against tyranny and therewith against himself. Now the struggle begins in earnest. In the preceding part of the conversation, Simonides' expressions of jealousy of the tyrants had been mitigated, if not altogether retracted, by his emphasis on the pleasures of the body. Now he declares in glaring contrast to all that has gone before, and in particular to what he has said about the unique significance of the pleasures of sex, that the whole preceding discussion is irrelevant, because it dealt only with what he believes to be very minor matters: many of those who are reputed to be (real) men ($\check{\alpha}\nu\delta\rho\epsilon\varsigma$)[22] just despise the bodily pleasures; they aspire to greater things, namely, to power and wealth; it is in relation to wealth and power that tyrannical life is manifestly superior to private life. In the preceding part of the conversation,

Simonides had tacitly identified himself with the vulgar; now he tacitly makes a distinction between himself and the vulgar. But the nonvulgar type to which he tacitly claims to belong is not the type of the "gentleman" but of the "real man."[23] While elaborating the thesis that tyrannical life brings greater wealth and power than private life, he supplements his initial enumeration of pleasurable and painful things (in which the "good and bad" things have almost disappeared amid the throng of objects of bodily pleasure) by an enumeration of the elements of power and wealth. In doing this he seems to imply that power and wealth are unambiguously "good" and in fact the only things that matter.[24] Since Simonides knows that Hiero considers him a real man, and since he declares explicitly that he himself considers the bodily pleasures as of very minor importance, Simonides thus intimates[25] an unequivocal taste for tyranny. In enumerating the various elements of power and wealth, he reveals his taste more specifically, and more subtly, by what he mentions and by what he fails to mention.[26]

From this moment the conversation changes its character in a surprising manner. Whereas Simonides had been fairly vocal during the rather short discussion of the bodily pleasures (his contribution consisting of about 218 words out of 1058), he is almost completely silent during the much more extensive discussion of the good or bad things (his contribution consisting of 28 words out of about 2000). Besides, the discussion of the bodily pleasures had kept, in the main, to the items and the sequence suggested in Simonides' initial enumeration, and this had been due largely to Simonides' almost continuous interference with Hiero's exposition. But now, in the discussion of the good or bad things, Hiero deviates considerably, not to say completely, from Simonides' enumeration of these things and their sequence by introducing topics which had barely been hinted at by Simonides.[27] The purpose of Hiero's procedure is evident. In the first place, he can refute only with difficulty the cautious assertion to which the wise Simonides had limited himself,[28] that the tyrant possesses greater power and wealth than private men. Above all, he is very anxious to push "wealth" into the background in favor of the other good things because wealth is so highly desired by "real men" of the type of Simonides as well as by the actual tyrant himself.[29] The topics not mentioned by Simonides but introduced by Hiero are: peace and war, friendship,[30] confidence, fatherland, good men, city and citizens, fear and protection. Simonides' declaration asserting the superiority of tyrants as regards power and wealth provokes Hiero to an eloquent indictment of tyranny which surpasses in scope everything said in the first section: the tyrant is cut off from such good things as peace, the pleasant aspects of war, friendship, confidence, fatherland, and the company of good men; he is hated and conspired against by his nearest relatives and friends; he cannot enjoy the greatness of his own father-land; he lives in perpetual fear for his life; he is compelled to commit grave crimes against gods and men; those who kill him, far from being punished, are greatly honored. Simonides has succeeded in increasing Hiero's tenseness far beyond the limits which it had reached during the discussion of the bodily pleasures. This shows itself particularly in those passages where the tyrant speaks of subjects already mentioned in the first section.[31] And this increase of tension is due, not only to the declaration with which the poet had opened the second round, but, above all, to the ambiguous silence with which he listens to Hiero's tirade. Is he overawed by Hiero's indictment of tyranny? Does he doubt Hiero's sincerity? Or is he just bored by Hiero's speech because his chief concern is with "food," with the pleasures of the body, the discussion of which had interested him sufficiently to make him talk? Hiero cannot know.

The meaning of Simonides' silence is partly revealed by its immediate consequence. It leads to the consequence that the topics introduced by Hiero are hardly as much as mentioned, and certainly not discussed by Simonides in the first two sections of the dialogue. His silence thus brings out in full relief the contrast between the topics introduced in the first two sections by Hiero on the one hand and by Simonides on the other. Simonides introduces the pleasures of the body as well as wealth and power; Hiero introduces the loftier things. Simonides, who has to convince Hiero of his competence to give sound advice to tyrants, must guard by all means against appearing in Hiero's eyes as a poet: he limits himself to speaking about the more pedestrian things.[32] Hiero, who tries to dissuade Simonides from being jealous of tyrants or from aspiring to tyranny, has to appeal from Simonides' craving for low things to his more noble aspirations. The lesson which Xenophon ironically conveys by this element of the conversational setting seems to be this: a teacher of tyrants has to appear as a hardboiled man; it does not do any harm if he makes his pupil suspect that he cannot be impressed by considerations of a more noble character.

The poet interrupts his silence only once. The circumstances of that interruption call for some attention. Hiero had given Simonides more than one opportunity to say something, especially by addressing him by name.[33] This applies especially to his discussion of friendship. Therein one can almost see Hiero urging him toward at least some visible reaction.[34] After all his efforts to make Simonides talk have failed, he turns to what he considers the characteristic pleasures of private men: drink, song, and sleep, which he, having become a tyrant, cannot enjoy any longer because he is perpetually harassed by fear, the spoiler of all pleasures.[35] Simonides remains silent. Hiero makes a last attempt, this one more successful. Reminding himself of the fact that Simonides had been most vocal while food was being discussed, he replaces ''strong drink and sleep'' by ''food and sleep.''[36] Referring to the poet's possible experience of fear in battle, he asserts that tyrants can enjoy food and sleep as little as, or less than, soldiers who have the enemy's phalanx close in front of them. Simonides replies that his military experience proves to him the possibility of combining ''living dangerously'' with a healthy appetite and a sound sleep.[37] Saying this, he tacitly denies more strongly than by his statement at the beginning of the second section the reassuring implications of his previous emphasis on the pleasures of the body.[38]

We must now step back and look again at the picture as a whole. Taken as a whole, the second section consists of Hiero's sweeping indictment of tyranny, to which Simonides listens in silence. The meaning of this silence is finally revealed by what happens in the third section (ch. 7). The third section, the shortest section of the *Hiero,* contains, or immediately prepares for, the peripeteia. It culminates in Hiero's declaration that the tyrant can hardly do better than to hang himself. By making this declaration, Hiero abdicates the leadership in the conversation in favor of Simonides, who keeps it throughout the fourth and last section (ch. 8–11).[39] We contend that this crucial event—Hiero's breakdown or the change from Hiero's leadership to Simonides' leadership—is consciously and decisively prepared by Simonides' remaining silent in the second section.

The third section opens again with a surprising move of Simonides.[40] He grants to Hiero that tyranny is as toilsome and as dangerous as the latter had asserted; yet, he says, those toils and dangers are reasonably borne because they lead to the pleasure deriving from honors, and no other human pleasure comes nearer to divinity than this kind of pleasure: tyrants are honored more than any other men. In the parallel at the beginning of the second section Simonides had spoken only of what ''*many* of those who are *reputed* to be (real) men'' desire, and had merely implied that what they desire is power and wealth. Now he openly declares that the desire for honor is characteristic of real men as such, i.e., as distinguished from ordinary "human beings."[41] There seems to be no longer any doubt that Simonides, who is admittedly a real man, longs for tyrannical power.

Hiero's immediate reply reveals that he is more alarmed than ever before. He had mentioned before the facts that the tyrant is in perpetual danger of being assassinated and that tyrants commit acts of injustice. But never before had he mentioned these two facts within one and the same sentence. Still less had he explicitly established a connection between them. Only now, while trying to prove that the tyrant does not derive any pleasure from the honors shown to him, does he declare that the tyrant spends night and day like one condemned by all men to die for his injustice.[42] One might think for a moment that this increase in the vehemence of Hiero's indictment of tyranny is due to the subject matter so unexpectedly introduced by Simonides: Hiero might seem to suffer most of all from the fact that the tyrant is deprived of genuine honor. But if this is the case, why does he not protest against Simonides' later remark that Hiero had depreciated tyranny most because it frustrated the tyrant's homosexual desires? Why did he not bring up the subject of "honor" himself instead of waiting until Simonides did it? Why did he not find fault with Simonides' misleading initial enumeration of pleasures? Last but not least, why did the earlier discussion of a similar subject—praise[43]—fail to make any noticeable impression on his mood? It is not so much the intrinsic significance of Simonides' statement on honor as its conversational significance which accounts for its conspicuous and indeed decisive effect.

At the beginning of his statement on honor, Simonides alludes to Hiero's description of the toils and dangers which attend the life of a tyrant. But Hiero had described not merely those toils and dangers, but also the moral depravity to which the tyrant is condemned: he is compelled to live "by contriving something bad and base"; he is compelled to commit the crime of robbing temples and men; he cannot be a true patriot; he desires to enslave his fellow citizens; only the consideration that a tyrant must have living subjects who walk around seems to prevent him from killing or imprisoning all his subjects. After Hiero has finished his long speech, Simonides declares that in spite of everything that the tyrant has said, tyranny is highly desirable because it leads to supreme honor. As regards the toils and dangers pointed out by Hiero, Simonides pauses to allude to them; as regards the moral flaws deplored by Hiero, he simply ignores them. That is to say, the poet is not at all impressed by the immorality, or the injustice, characteristic of the tyrannical life; certainly its inevitable immorality would not prevent him for a moment from aspiring to tyranny for the sake of honor. No wonder then that Hiero collapses shortly afterward: what overwhelms him is not Simonides' statement on honor itself, but the poet's making it in this particular context. Because it is made in that context, and merely because it is made in that context, does it make Hiero realize to what lengths a man of Simonides' exceptional "wisdom" could go in "contriving something" and in particular in "contriving something bad and base." It is by thus silently, i.e., most astutely, revealing a complete lack of scruple that the poet both overwhelms Hiero and convinces him of his competence to give sound advice to a tyrant.[44]

The lesson which Xenophon conveys by making Simonides listen silently to Hiero's long speech, as well as by his answer to that speech, can now be stated as follows. Even a perfectly just man who wants to give advice to a tyrant has to present himself to his pupil as an utterly unscrupulous man. The greatest man who ever imitated the *Hiero* was Machiavelli. I should not be surprised if a sufficiently attentive study of Machiavelli's work would lead to the conclusion that it is precisely Machiavelli's perfect understanding of Xenophon's chief pedagogic lesson which accounts for the most shocking sentences occurring in the *Prince.* But if Machiavelli understood Xenophon's lesson, he certainly did not apply it in the spirit of its originator. For, according to Xenophon, the teacher of tyrants has to appear as an utterly unscrupulous man, not by protesting that he does not fear hell nor devil, nor by expressing immoral principles, but by simply failing to take notice of the moral principles. He has to reveal his alleged or real freedom from morality, not by speech but by silence. For by doing so— by disregarding morality "by deed" rather than by attacking it "by speech"—he reveals at the same time his understanding of political things. Xenophon, or his Simonides, is more "politic" than Machiavelli; he refuses to separate "moderation" (prudence) from "wisdom" (insight).

By replying to Hiero's long speech in the manner described, Simonides compels him to use still stronger language against tyranny than he had done before. Now Hiero declares that a tyrant, as distinguished from a man who is a benefactor of his fellows and therefore genuinely honored, lives like one condemned by all men to die for his injustice. Arrived at this point, Simonides could have replied in the most natural manner that, this being the case, the tyrant ought to rule as beneficently as possible. He could have begun at once to teach

Hiero how to rule well as a tyrant. But he apparently felt that he needed some further information for sizing Hiero up, or that Hiero needed a further shock before he would be prepared to listen. Therefore he asks Hiero why, if tyranny is really such a great evil for the tyrant, neither he nor any other tyrant ever yet gave up his position voluntarily. Hiero answers that no tyrant can abdicate because he cannot make amends for the robbing, imprisoning, and killing of his subjects; (just as it does not profit him to live as a tyrant, it does not profit him to live again as a private man); if it profits any man (to cease living), to hang himself, it profits the tyrant most of all.[45] This answer puts the finishing touch to the preparation for Simonides' instruction. Simonides' final attack had amounted to a veiled suggestion addressed to the tyrant to return to private life. That suggestion is the necessary conclusion which a reasonable man would draw from Hiero's comparison between tyrannical and private life. Hiero defends himself against that suggestion by revealing what might seem to be some rudimentary sense of justice: he cannot return to private life because he cannot make amends for the many acts of injustice which he has committed. This defense is manifestly hypocritical: if tyranny is what he has asserted it to be, he prefers heaping new crimes on the untold number of crimes which he has already committed rather than stop his criminal career and suffer the consequences of his former misdeeds. His real motive for not abdicating seems then to be fear of punishment. But could he not escape punishment by simply fleeing? This is indeed the crucial implication of Hiero's last word against tyranny: as if there never had been a tryant who, after having been expelled from his city, lived quietly thereafter in exile, and although he himself had said on a former occasion[46] that while making a journey abroad, the tyrant might easily be deposed, Hiero refuses to consider the possibility of escape from his city. He thus reveals himself as a man who is unable to live as a stranger.[47] It is this citizen spirit of his—the fact that he cannot help being absolutely attached to his city—to which the wandering poet silently appeals when teaching him how to be a good ruler.

Hiero has finally been rendered incapable of any further move. He has been reduced to a condition in which he has to fetter himself by a sincere or insincere assertion, or in which he has to use the language of a man who is despondent. He uses entirely different language in the two fairly brief utterances which he makes in the fourth or last section. Whereas his indictment of tyranny in the first part of the *Hiero* had presented the tyrant as the companion of the unjust and had culminated in the description of the tryant as injustice incarnate, he describes him in the last part of the dialogue—i.e., a few minutes later—as a man who punishes the unjust,[48] as a defender of justice. This quick change of language, or of attitude, is most astonishing. As we have seen, the vehemence of Hiero's indictment had been increasing from section to section because Simonides had not been deterred from praising tyranny by the shortcomings of tyranny pointed out by Hiero. Now, Hiero had spoken against tyranny in the third section more violently than ever before, and in the fourth section Simonides continues praising tyranny.[49] Hence one should expect that Hiero will continue still increasing the vehemence of his indictment of tyranny. Yet he takes the opposite course. What has happened? Why does Simonides' praise of tyranny in the fourth section, and especially in the early part of that section (8.1–7), fail to arouse Hiero's violent reaction? We suggest the following answer: Simonides' praise of tyranny in the fourth section—as distinguished from his praise of tyranny in the preceding sections—is not considered by Hiero an expression of the poet's jealousy of tyrants. More precisely, Simonides' immediate reaction to Hiero's statement that a tyrant can hardly do better than to hang himself, or the use which Simonides makes of his newly acquired leadership, convinces Hiero that the poet is not concerned with "contriving something" of an undesirable character. The action by which Simonides breaks down the walls of Hiero's distrust, is the peripeteia of the dialogue.

The difficult position into which Hiero has been forced is not without its advantages. Hiero had been on the defensive because he did not know what Simonides might be contriving. By his defeat, by his declaration of bankruptcy, he succeeds in stopping Simonides to the extent that he forces him to show his hand. He presents himself as a man who knows that neither of the two ways of life—the tyrannical and the private life—profits him, but who does not know whether it would profit him to cease living by hanging himself ("*if* it profits any man . . .").[50] Simonides could have taken up in a fairly natural manner the question implicitly raised by Hiero as to whether suicide is an advisable course of action, and in particular whether there are not other forms of death preferable to, or easier than, hanging.[51] In other words, the poet could conceivably have tried to persuade the tyrant to commit suicide, or to commit suicide in the easiest manner. To exaggerate grossly for purposes of clarification: the victory of the wise man over the tyrant, achieved solely by means of speech prudently interspersed with silence, is so complete that the wise man could kill the tyrant without lifting a finger, employing only speech, only persuasion. But he does nothing of the kind: he who has the power of persuasion, he who can do what he likes with any interlocutor, prefers to make use of the obedience of a living man rather than to kill him.[52] After having made Hiero realize fully that a wise man has the power of going to any length in contriving anything, Simonides gives him to understand that the wise man would not make use of this power. Simonides' refraining from acting like a man who wants to do away with a tyrant, or to deprive him of his power, is the decisive reason for the change in Hiero's attitude.

But silence is not enough: Simonides has to say something. What he says is determined by his intention to advise Hiero, and by the impossibility of advising a man who is despondent. It is immaterial in this respect that Hiero's complaints about his situation are of questionable sincerity; for Simonides is not in a position openly to question their sincerity. He has then to comfort Hiero while advising him or prior to advising him. Accordingly, his teaching of the tyrannical art is presented in the following form: Tyranny is most desirable ("comfort") if you will only do such and such things ("advice"). The comfort element of Simonides' teaching—the praise of (beneficent) tyranny—is due to the conversational situation and cannot be presumed to be an integral part of Xenophon's teaching concerning tyranny until it has been proved to be so. On the other hand, Simonides' advice can be presumed from the outset to be identical with Xenophon's suggestions about the improvement of tyrannical rule as a radically faulty political order.

It would not have been impossible for Simonides to refute Hiero by showing that the latter's account of tyranny is exaggerated, i.e., by discussing Hiero's indictment of tyranny point by point. But such a detailed discussion would merely have led to the conclusion that tyranny is not quite as bad as Hiero had asserted. That dreary result would not have sufficed for restoring Hiero's courage or for counteracting the crushing effect of his final verdict on tyranny. Or, to disregard for one moment the conversational setting, an exact examination of Hiero's arguments would have destroyed completely the edifying effect of the indictment of tyranny in the first part of the *Hiero*. Xenophon had then to burden his Simonides with the task of drawing a picture of tyranny which would be at least as bright as the one drawn by Hiero had been dark. The abundant use of the *modus potentialis* in Simonides' speech as well as the silence of the *Hiero* and indeed of the whole *Corpus Xenophonteum* about happy tyrants who actually existed anywhere in Greece make it certain that Simonides' praise of tyranny in the second part of the *Hiero* was considered by Xenophon even more rhetorical than Hiero's indictment of tyranny in the first part.

Hiero had tried to show that tyrannical life is inferior to private life from the point of view of pleasure. In the existing situation, Simonides cannot appeal directly from the pleasant to the noble, for Hiero had just declared in the most emphatic manner that, as a matter of fact, a tyrant is a man who has committed an untold number of crimes. Simonides is therefore compelled to show (what in the first part he had hardly more than asserted) that tyrannical life is superior to private life from the point of view of pleasure. Being compelled to accept the tyrant's end, he must show that Hiero used the wrong means. In other words, he must trace Hiero's being out of heart with tyranny not to a wrong intention but to an error of judgment, to an erroneous belief.[53]

Simonides discovers the specific error which he ascribes to Hiero by reflecting on the latter's reply to the poet's statement concerning honor. Hiero had compared the honors enjoyed by tyrants with their sexual pleasures: just as services rendered by those who do not love in turn, or who act under compulsion, are no favors, services rendered by those who fear, are no honors. The *tertium comparationis* between the pleasures of sex and those of honor is that both must be granted by people who are prompted by love ($\phi\iota\lambda\iota\alpha$) and not by fear. Now Hiero is worried most by his being deprived of the genuine pleasures of sex. But Simonides might offend him by emphasizing this fact and thus asserting that Hiero is more concerned with sex than with honor and hence perhaps not a "real man." He elegantly avoids this embarrassment by escaping into something more general, viz., into that which is common to "honor" and "sex."[54] For whether Hiero is chiefly concerned with the one or the other, he is in both cases in need of love ($\phi\iota\lambda\iota\alpha$). And in both cases his misery is due to his belief that being a tyrant and being loved are mutually exclusive.[55] This is then the diagnosis of Hiero's illness from which Simonides starts: Hiero is out of heart with tyranny because, desiring to be loved by human beings, he believes that tyrannical rule prevents him from being so loved.[56] Simonides does not limit himself to rejecting this belief. He asserts that tyrants are more likely to gain affection than private men. For whatever might have to be said against tyranny, the tyrant is certainly a ruler, hence a man of high standing among his fellows, and "we" naturally admire men of high social standing. Above all, the prestige attending ruling positions adds an unbought grace to any act of kindness performed by rulers in general and hence by tyrants in particular.[57] It is by means of this assertion that Simonides surreptitiously suggests his cure for Hiero's illness, a cure discovered, just as the illness itself was, by reflecting on Hiero's comparison of "honor" and "sex." Hiero had granted as a matter of course that in order to receive favors, to be loved in return, one must first love: the misery of the tyrant consists in the very fact that he loves and is not loved in turn.[58] Simonides tacitly applies what Hiero had granted as regards sexual love to love in general: he who wants to be loved must love first; he who wants to be loved by his subjects in order to be genuinely honored by them must love them first; to gain favors he must first show favors. He does not state this lesson in so many words, but he transmits it implicitly by comparing the effects of a tyrant's acts of kindness with the effects of a private man's acts of kindness. He thus shifts the emphasis almost insensibly from the pleasant feelings primarily desired to the noble or praiseworthy actions which directly or indirectly bring about those pleasant feelings. He tacitly advises the tyrant to think not of his own pleasures but of the pleasures of others; not of his being served and receiving gifts, but of his doing services and making gifts.[59] That is to say, he tacitly gives the tyrant exactly the same advice which Socrates explicitly gives his companions, nay, which Virtue herself explicitly gives to Heracles.[60]

Simonides' virtuous advice does not spoil the effect of his previous indifference to moral principles because the virtuous character of his advice is sufficiently qualified by the context in which it is given. Socrates and Virtue shout their advice from the housetops to men who are of normal decency, and even potential paragons of virtue. Simonides, on the other hand, suggests substantially the same advice in the most subdued language to a tyrant who has just confessed having committed an untold number of crimes. It is true, Simonides' language becomes considerably less restrained toward the end of the conversation. But it is also true that throughout the conversation he presents the pleasant effects of a tyrant's kind actions as wholly independent of the manner in which the tyrant had come to power and of any of his previous misdeeds. Simonides' alleged or real freedom from scruple is preserved in, and operates in, his very recommendation of virtue.[61]

Hiero answers "straightway," "at once." This is the only occasion on which either of the two interlocutors says something "straightway."[62] It is Simonides' reaction to Hiero's statement that the tyrant can hardly do better than to hang himself, which induces the tyrant to

answer "at once," i.e., to proceed without that slowness, or circum-
spection, which characterizes all other utterances of the two men.
Dropping his habitual reserve, Hiero gives a sincere, not exaggerated
account of the difficulties confronting the tyrant. He no longer denies
that tyrants have greater power than private men to do things by
means of which men gain affection; he merely denies that they are for
this reason more likely to be loved than private men, because they are
also compelled to do very many things by which men incur hatred.
Thus, e.g., they have to exact money and to punish the unjust; and,
above all, they are in need of mercenaries.[63] Simonides does not say
that one should not take care of all these matters.[64] But, he believes,
there are ways of taking care of things which lead to hatred and other
ways which lead to gratification: a ruler should himself do the gratifying things (such as the awarding of prizes) while entrusting to others
the hateful things (such as the inflicting of punishment). The implication of this advice as well as of all other advice given to Hiero by
Simonides is, of course, that Hiero needs such advice, or that he is
actually doing the opposite of what Simonides is advising him to do,
i.e., that he is at present a most imperfect ruler. Imitating in his speech
by anticipation the hoped-for behavior of his pupil Hiero, or rather
giving him by his own action an example of the behavior proper to a
tyrant, Simonides soon drops all explicit mention of the hateful things
inseparable from tyranny, if not from government as such, while he
praises the enormous usefulness of offering prizes: the hateful aspects
of tyranny are not indeed annihilated, but banished from sight.[65]
Simonides' praise of beneficent tyranny thus serves the purpose not
merely of comforting Hiero (who is certainly much less in need of
comfort than his utterances might induce the unwary reader to believe), but above all of teaching him in what light the tyrant should
appear to his subjects: far from being a naïve expression of a naïve belief
in virtuous tyrants, it is rather a prudently presented lesson in political
prudence.[66] Simonides goes so far as to avoid in this context the very
term "tyrant."[67] On the other hand, he now uses the terms "noble"
as well as "good" and "useful" much more frequently than ever
before, while speaking considerably less of the "pleasant." With a view
to the difficulty of appealing directly from the pleasant to the noble,
however, he stresses for the time being the "good" (with its "util-
itarian" implications) considerably more than the "noble" or "fair."[68]
Furthermore, he shows that striving for honor is perfectly compatible
with being the subject of a tyrant, thus blotting out completely the
odious implications of his previous statement about honor. He shows,

too, that honoring subjects by means of prizes is an excellent bargain.[69] And what is most important, he strongly (but by implication) advises against disarming the citizens when he suggests that prizes be offered them for certain achievements of a military nature.[70]

Only after all these steps have been taken does there appear some agreement between Hiero and Simonides on the subject of tyranny. Only now is Hiero prepared not only to listen to Simonides' advice but to address to him a question, his only question, concerning the proper conduct of tyrannical government. The formulation of the question shows that he has learned something: he does not speak any longer of "tyrant," but of "ruler." The purport of the question is established by these facts: First, that Simonides had not said anything about the mercenaries whom Hiero had described in his preceding statement as an oppressive burden on the citizens;[71] and second, that Simonides' speech might seem to imply a suggestion that the mercenaries be replaced by citizens. Accordingly, Hiero's question consists of two parts. First, he asks Simonides to advise him how he could avoid incurring hatred on account of his employing mercenaries. Then he asks him whether he means that a ruler who has gained affection is no longer in need of a bodyguard.[72] Simonides answers emphatically that a bodyguard is indispensable:[73] the improvement of tyrannical government should not go to the extreme of undermining the very pillar of tyrannical rule. Thus Simonides' answer to Hiero's only question is tantamount to strong counsel against the abdication which he had tentatively suggested earlier. Besides, Hiero's question as to whether a bodyguard might not be dispensed with might have been prompted by his desire to save the enormous expenses involved. With a view to this possibility, Simonides' statement implies the answer that such expenses are indeed inevitable, but that the proper use of the mercenaries will dispose the subjects to pay the cost of them most cheerfully.[74] Yet, Simonides says, adding a word of advice for which he had not been asked, while the ample use of prizes and the proper use of the mercenaries will help greatly in the solution of the tyrant's financial problems, a tyrant ought not to hesitate to spend his own money for the common good.[75] Nay, a tyrant's interests are better served if he spends money for public affairs rather than for his own affairs. In this context Simonides gives the more specific advice—the giving of which may have been the only purpose of Simonides' starting a conversation with Hiero—that a tyrant should not compete with private men in chariot races and the like, but rather should take care that the greatest number of competitors should come from his city.[76] He should compete with other leaders of cities for victory in the noblest and grandest contest—viz., in making his city as happy as possible. By winning that contest, Simonides promises him, he will gain the love of all his subjects, the regard of many cities, the admiration of all men, and many other good things; by surpassing his friends in acts of kindness he will be possessed of the noblest and most blessed possession among men: he will not be envied while being happy.[77] With this outlook the dialogue ends. Any answer of the tyrant to the poet's almost boundless promise would have been an anticlimax, and, what would have been worse, it would have prevented the reader from reasonably enjoying the polite silence in which a Greek tyrant, old in crime and martial glory, could listen to a siren-song of virtue.[78]

C. THE USE OF CHARACTERISTIC TERMS

One may say that "the gist of Xenophon's counsel to despots is that a despot should endeavour to rule like a good king."[1] It is therefore all the more striking that he avoids consistently the very term "king." By avoiding the term "king" in a work destined to teach the art of a tyrant, he complies with the rule of tact which requires that one should not embarrass people by mentioning things from the lack of which they can be presumed to suffer: a tyrant must be presumed to suffer from the lack of a valid title to his position. Xenophon's procedure may have been the model for the apparently opposite but fundamentally identical device of Machiavelli, who in his *Prince* avoids the term "tiranno": individuals who are called "tiranni" in the *Discourses* and elsewhere are called "principi" in the *Prince*.[2] We may also note the absence of the terms *demos* and *politeia*[3] from the *Hiero*.

As for Simonides in particular, he never uses the term "law." He mentions justice only once, making it clear that he is speaking of that justice only which is required of subjects rather than rulers: justice in business dealings.[4] He never speaks of truth or of falsehood or of deceiving. While laughing is never mentioned by Simonides or by Hiero, Simonides speaks once of καταγελᾶν. This is not insignificant because in the only remark of that kind which occurs in the *Hiero*, Xenophon notes that Simonides made a certain statement—it concerns Hiero's love affairs—"laughingly"; Hiero is always serious.[5] Simonides, who never mentions courage (ἀνδρεία),[6] once mentions moderation (σωφροσύνη) which is never mentioned by Hiero. On the other hand, Hiero uses the terms μέτριος, κόσμιος, and ἀκρατής which are never used by Simonides.[7]

Some consideration should also be given the distribution of characteristic terms between the two main parts of the dialogue, namely, the indictment of tyranny on the one hand, the suggestions concerning the improvement of tyrannical rule on the other. Terms which are avoided in the second part are: law, free (freedom), nature, courage, misery. On the other hand, moderation is mentioned only in the second part. "Tyrant" (and derivatives) occurs relatively much more frequently in the first part (83 times) than in the second part (7 times); on the other hand, "ruling" (and derivatives) occurs much more frequently in the much shorter second part (12 times) than in the much more extensive first part (4 times): Simonides wants to induce Hiero to think of his position in terms of "ruling" rather than in terms of "tyranny"; for it is not good for any man to think of his activity in odious terms. How well Simonides succeeds is shown by the fact that in his last remark[8] Hiero speaks of "ruler" and no longer of "tyrant." Terms designating pleasure and pain occur relatively much more frequently in the first part (93 times) than in the second part (6 times). On the other hand, "noble" ("fair") and "base" ("ugly") occur relatively much more frequently in the second part (15 times) than in the first part (9 times). The reason is obvious: Simonides wants to educate Hiero to take his bearings by the fair rather than by the pleasant. Χάρις (and derivates) occurs relatively much more frequently in the second part (9 times) than in the first part (4 times). 'Ανάγκη (and derivatives) occurs relatively less frequently in the second part (9 times) than in the first part (16 times).

IV

The Teaching Concerning Tyranny

Since tyranny is essentially a faulty political order, the teaching concerning tyranny necessarily consists of two parts. The first part has to make manifest the specific shortcomings of tyranny ("pathology"), and the second part has to show how these shortcomings can be mitigated ("therapeutics"). The bipartition of the *Hiero* reflects the bipartition of the "tyrannical" teaching itself. Now, Xenophon chose to present that teaching in the form of a dialogue, and he had therefore to choose a particular conversational setting. However sound, and even compelling, his reasons may have been, they certainly lead to the result that he has not given us his "tyrannical" teaching in its pure, scientific form, in the form of a treatise. The reader has to add to and to subtract from Hiero's and Simonides' speeches in order to lay hold of Xenophon's teaching. That addition and subtraction is not left to the reader's arbitrary decision. It is guided by the author's indications, some of which have been discussed in the preceding chapters. Nevertheless, a certain ambiguity remains, an ambiguity ultimately due not to the unsolved riddles implied in many individual passages of the *Hiero* but to the fact that a perfectly lucid and unambiguous connection between content and form, between a general teaching and a contingent event (e.g., a conversation between two individuals) is impossible.

Considering the primarily practical character of the "tyrannical" teaching as a political teaching, it is necessary that one interlocutor, the pupil, should be a tyrant. It is equally necessary that he should be an

66

actual tyrant, not a potential tyrant. If the pupil were only a potential tyrant, the teacher would have to show him how to become a tyrant, and in so doing he would have to teach him injustice, whereas in the case of an actual tyrant the teacher has the much less odious task of showing him a way toward lesser injustice. Seeing that a tyrant (Periander of Corinth) was said to have instituted most of the common devices for preserving tyranny,[1] one might think that the natural teacher of the tyrannical art would be a great tyrant; but preservation of tyranny and correction of tyranny are two different things. Xenophon evidently felt that only a wise man could teach what he considered the tyrannical art, i.e., the art of ruling well as a tyrant, and that a tyrant would not be wise. This leads to the consequence that the wise man who teaches the tyrannical art cannot have learned that art from a tyrant as Socrates, who teaches the economic art, has learned it from an economist. In other words, the wise teacher of the tyrannical art has to teach it by himself, without any assistance, or he has to discover it by himself.[2] Now, the wise man might transmit to his pupil the whole "tyrannical" teaching, i.e., both the indictment of tyranny and the correction of tyranny; but Xenophon apparently thought that a tyrant's indictment of tyranny would be more impressive for the average reader.[3] Finally, the tyrant might start the conversation by complaining to a wise man about a tyrant's sad lot, in order to elicit his advice. This, however, would presuppose that the tyrant would have a wise friend whom he trusts, and that he would consider himself in need of advice.[4] To sum up, the more one considers alternatives to the conversational setting chosen by Xenophon, the more one becomes convinced that his choice was sound.

Yet this choice, however sound and even necessary, leads to the result that Xenophon's indictment of tyranny is presented by a man who is not wise and who has a selfish interest in disparaging tyranny, whereas his praise of tyranny is presented by a wise man who argues in favor of tyranny without an apparent selfish interest. Besides, since the indictment of tyranny precedes the praise of tyranny, the indictment is presented on the basis of insufficient evidence—for Hiero does not take into account the facts or possibilities set forth by Simonides in the latter part of the *Hiero*—whereas the praise of tyranny seems to be voiced *en pleine connaissance de cause*. That is to say, Xenophon could not help being led to giving a greater weight, at least apparently, to the praise of tyranny than to the indictment of tyranny. The question arises whether this is merely the inevitable result of considerations such as those sketched before, or whether it is directly intended.

One might think for a moment that the ambiguity under consideration was caused merely by Xenophon's decision to treat at all in a dialogue the question of the improvement of tyrannical rule: every ambiguity would have been avoided if he had limited himself to indicting tyranny. A comparison of his conversational treatment of tyranny with Plato's, however, shows that this suggestion does not go to the root of the matter. Plato refrained from teaching the tyrannical art and he entrusted his indictment of tyranny to Socrates. The price which he had to pay for this choice was that he had to entrust his praise of tyranny to men who were not wise (Polos, Callicles, and Thrasymachus) and who therefore were openly praising the very injustice of tyranny. To avoid the latter inconvenience, Xenophon had to pay the price of burdening a wise man with the task of praising tyranny. An effective conversational treatment of tyranny which is free from inconveniences is impossible. For there are only two possibilities apart from those chosen by Xenophon and Plato: the praise of tyranny by the wise might be succeeded by the indictment of tyranny by the unwise, and the indictment of tyranny by the wise might be succeeded by the praise of tyranny by the unwise; these alternatives are ruled out by the consideration that the wise man ought to have the last word.

It is more appropriate to say that the bearing of Xenophon's praise of tyranny is sufficiently limited, not only by the conversational setting, but above all by the fact that his wise man who praises tyranny makes sufficiently clear the essential shortcomings of tyranny. He describes tyranny at its best, but he lets it be understood that tyranny even at its best suffers from serious defects. This implied criticism of tyranny is much more convincing than Hiero's passionate indictment which serves a selfish purpose and which would be literally true only of the very worst kind of tyranny. To see the broad outline of Simonides' criticism of tyranny at its best, one has only to consider the result of his suggested correction of tyranny in the light of Xenophon's, or Socrates', definition of tyranny. Tyranny is defined in contradistinction to kingship: kingship is such rule as is exercised over willing subjects and is in accordance with the laws of the cities; tyranny is such rule as is exercised over unwilling subjects and accords, not with laws, but with the will of the ruler.[5] This definition covers the common form of tyranny, but not tyranny at its best. Tyranny at its best, tyranny as corrected according to Simonides' suggestions, is no longer rule over unwilling subjects. It is most certainly rule over willing subjects.[6] But it remains rule "not according to laws," i.e., it is absolute government. Simonides, who extols tyranny at its best, refrains from using the very term "law."[7] Tyranny is essentially rule without laws, or, more precisely, monarchic rule without laws.

Before considering the shortcomings of tyranny thus understood, we may dwell for a moment on its positive qualities. As regards the tyrant himself, Simonides asserts without hesitation that he may be perfectly happy. Furthermore, he leaves no doubt that the tyrant may be virtuous, and in fact of outstanding virtue. The correction of tyranny consists in nothing else than the transformation of the unjust or vicious tyrant who is more or less unhappy into a virtuous tyrant who is happy.[8] As for the tyrant's subjects, or his city, Simonides makes it clear that it may be very happy. The tyrant and his subjects may be united by the bonds of mutual kindness. The subjects of the virtuous tyrant are treated, not like little children, but like comrades or companions.[9] They are not deprived by him of honors.[10] They are not disarmed; their military spirit is encouraged.[11] Nor are the mercenaries, without whom tyranny is impossible, undesirable from the point of view of the city: they enable the city to wage war vigorously.[12] When Simonides recommends that the tyrant should make a most ample use of prizes and that he should promote agriculture and commerce, if agriculture to a higher degree than commerce, he simply seems to approve of policies which Xenophon considered to befit a well-ordered commonwealth. He thus creates the impression that according to Xenophon tyrannical government can live up to the highest political standards.[13]

Simonides' praise of beneficent tyranny, which at first sight seems to be boundless and rhetorically vague, proves on closer examination to be most carefully worded and to remain within very precise limits. Just as Simonides avoids in it the term "law," he avoids in it the term "freedom." The practical consequence of the absence of laws, he gives us to understand, is the absence of freedom: no laws, no liberty. All specific suggestions made by Simonides flow from this implied axiom, or reveal their political meaning in its light. For instance, when recommending to the tyrant that he consider the citizens as companions or comrades, he does not mean that the tyrant should treat the citizens as his equals, or even as freemen. For slaves may be companions as well as freemen. Furthermore, Simonides advises the tyrant that he consider the citizens as companions, and his friends as his own children:[14] if his very friends are then in every respect his subordinates, the citizens will be his subordinates in a still more far-reaching sense. The advice just referred to shows in addition that Simonides does not go so far in his praise of beneficent tyranny as to call it "paternal" rule.[15] It is true, the subjects of the beneficent tyrant are not disarmed; but in time of peace at least they do not protect themselves against the slaves and evildoers as the citizens of free commonwealths do; they are protected by the tyrant's bodyguard.[16] They are literally at the mercy of the tyrant and his mercenaries, and they can only wish or pray that the tyrant will become, or remain, beneficent. The true character of tyranny even at its best is clearly indicated by Simonides' "Machiavellian" suggestion that the tyrant should do the gratifying things (such as the awarding of prizes) himself, while entrusting to others the punitive actions.[17] It is hardly necessary to say that the tyrant's refraining from openly taking responsibility for punitive action does not bespeak a particular mildness of this rule: Nontyrannical rulers take that responsibility without any concealment[18] because their authority, deriving from law, is secure. Similarly, the extraordinarily ample use of prizes, especially for the promotion of agriculture, seems to serve the "tyrannical" purpose of keeping the subjects busy with their private concerns rather than with public affairs.[19] At the same time it compensates for the lack of the natural incentives to increase one's wealth, a lack due to the precarious character of property rights under a tyrant. The best tyrant would consider his fatherland his estate. This may be preferable to his impoverishing his fatherland in order to increase his private estate; yet it certainly implies that the best tyrant would consider his fatherland his private property which he would naturally administer according to his own discretion. Thus no subject of a tyrant could have any property rights against the tyrant. The subjects would pay as much as he deems necessary in the form of gifts or voluntary contributions.[20] Nor can the tyrant be said to honor the citizens because he awards prizes or distinctions to some of them; he may be able and willing to enrich his subjects: he cannot accord to them the "equality of honor" which is irreconcilable with tyrannical rule and from the lack of which they may be presumed always to suffer.[21]

These shortcomings of tyranny at its best are not, however, necessarily decisive. How Simonides, and Xenophon, judged of the value of tyranny at its best depends on what they thought of the importance of freedom. As for Simonides, he seems to esteem nothing as highly as honor or praise; and of praise he says that it will be the more pleasant the freer are those who bestow it.[22] This leads to the consequence that the demands of honor or praise cannot be satisfied by tyranny however perfect. The tyrant will not enjoy honor of the highest kind because his subjects lack freedom, and on the other hand the tyrant's subjects will not enjoy full honor for the reason mentioned

before. As for Xenophon himself, we have to start from the facts that
freedom was considered the aim of democracy, as particularly distinguished from aristocracy, the aim of which was said to be virtue;[23]
and that Xenophon was not a democrat. Xenophon's view is reflected
in Hiero's implicit assertion that the wise are not concerned with
freedom.[24] To establish Xenophon's attitude toward tyranny at its best
as characterized by Simonides, we have to consider the relation of
tyranny at its best, not to freedom, but to virtue. Only if virtue were
impossible without freedom, would the demand for freedom be absolutely justified from Xenophon's point of view.

The term "virtue" occurs five times in the *Hiero*. In only two out
of the five cases is it applied to human beings.[25] Only once is it applied
to the tyrant. Never is it applied to the tyrant's subjects. Simonides
advises the tyrant to be proud of "the happiness of his city" rather
than of "the virtue of his chariot horses": he does not mention the
virtue of the city as a possible goal of tyrannical rule. It is safe to say
that a city ruled by a tyrant is not supposed by him to "practice
gentlemanliness as a matter of public concern."[26] But, as has been
proved by Socrates' life, there are virtuous men in cities which do not
"practice gentlemanliness as a matter of public concern." It is therefore an open question whether and how far virtue is possible under a
tyrant. The beneficent tyrant would award prizes for "prowess in war"
and for "justice in contractual relations":[27] he would not be concerned
with fostering prowess simply and justice simply. This confirms
Hiero's assertion that the brave and the just are not desirable as
subjects of a tyrant.[28] Only a qualified, or reduced, form of courage
and justice befits the subjects of a tyrant. For prowess simply is closely
akin to freedom, or love of freedom,[29] and justice simply is obedience
to laws. The justice befitting the subjects of a tyrant is the least political
form of justice, or that form of justice which is most remote from
public-spiritedness: the justice to be observed in contractual, private
relations.[30]

But how can a virtuous man—and Simonides' beneficent tyrant
would seem to be a virtuous man—rest satisfied with the necessity of
preventing his subjects from reaching the summit of virtue? Let us then
reconsider the facts mentioned in the preceding paragraph. As regards
the fact that Simonides ascribes to the tyrant's subjects a qualified form
of prowess only, and fails to ascribe courage to them, we have to
remember that in Xenophon's two lists of the virtues of Socrates,
courage does not occur.[31] As regards Simonides' failure to ascribe to the
tyrant's subjects justice simply, we have to remember that justice can

be understood as a part of moderation and that, according to an explicit statement of Simonides, the tyrant's subjects may very well possess moderation.[32] As regards Simonides' failure to ascribe to the tyrant's subjects virtue as such, we have to remember that virtue is not necessarily a generic term, but may indicate a specific virtue distinguished from justice in particular.[33] However this may be, the question of what Simonides thought about the possibility of virtue under tyrannical rule seems to be definitely settled by an explicit statement of his according to which "gentlemen" may live, and live happily, under a beneficent tyrant.[34] In order not to misinterpret Simonides' ascribing to the tyrant's subjects only qualified forms of courage and justice, we have to compare it with Xenophon's failure, in his *Lacedaemoniorum respublica,* to ascribe justice in any sense to the Spartans themselves. The utmost one is entitled to say is that the virtue possible under a tyrant will have a specific color, a color different from that of republican virtue. It may tentatively be suggested that the place occupied within republican virtue by courage is occupied within the virtue befitting the subjects of the excellent tyrant by moderation which is produced by fear.[35] But one has no right to assume that the virtue befitting the subjects of a good tyrant is meant to be inferior in dignity to republican virtue. How little Xenophon believed that virtue is impossible without freedom is shown most strikingly by his admiration for the younger Cyrus whom he does not hesitate to describe as a "slave."[36]

If gentlemen can live happily under a beneficent tyrant, tyranny as corrected according to Simonides' suggestions might seem to live up to Xenophon's highest political standard. To see at once that this is the case, one merely has to measure Simonides' excellent tyrant by the criterion set forth in Xenophon's, or Socrates', definition of the good ruler. The virtue of the good ruler consists in making happy those he rules. The aim of the good ruler can be achieved by means of laws—this was done, according to Xenophon, in the most remarkable manner in Lycrugus' city—or by rule without laws, i.e., by tyranny: the beneficent tyrant as described by Simonides makes his city happy.[37] It is certainly most significant that, as regards the happiness achieved by means of laws, Xenophon can adduce an actual example (Sparta), whereas as regards the happiness achieved by tyranny, he offers no other evidence than the promise of a poet. In other words, it is of very great importance that, according to Xenophon, the aim of the good ruler is much more likely to be achieved by means of laws than by means of absolute rule. This does not do away, however, with the admission that, as a matter of principle, rule of laws is not essential for good government.

Xenophon does not make this admission in so many words. He presents Simonides as describing tyranny at its best and as declaring that the tyrant can make his city happy. Considering the situation in which Simonides expounds his views of tyranny, the objection is justified that what he says serves the purpose of comforting a somewhat disturbed tyrant or at any rate is said *ad hominem* and ought not to be taken as expressing directly Xenophon's own views. We have therefore to consider whether the thesis that tyranny can live up to the highest political standard is defensible on the basis of Xenophon's, or Socrates', political philosophy.

To begin with, it must appear most paradoxical that Xenophon should have had any liking whatsoever for tyranny however good. Tyranny at its best is still rule without laws and, according to Socrates' definition, justice is identical with legality or obedience to laws.[38] Thus tyranny in any form seems to be irreconcilable with the requirement of justice. On the other hand, tyranny would become morally possible if the identification of "just" and "legal" were not absolutely correct, or if "everything according to law were (only) *somehow* ($\pi\omega\varsigma$) just."[39] The laws which determine what is legal are the rules of conduct upon which the citizens have agreed.[40] "The citizens" may be "the multitude" or "the few"; "the few" may be the rich or the virtuous. That is to say, the laws, and hence what is legal, depend on the political order of the community for which they are given. Could Xenophon or his Socrates have believed that the difference between laws depending on a faulty political order and laws depending on a good political order is wholly irrelevant as far as justice is concerned? Could they have believed that rules prescribed by a monarch, i.e., not by "the citizens," cannot be laws?[41] Besides, is it wholly irrelevant for justice whether what the laws prescribe is reasonable or unreasonable, good or bad? Finally, is it wholly irrelevant for justice whether the laws enacted by the legislator (the many, the few, the monarch) are forcibly imposed on, or voluntarily agreed to by, the other members of the community? Questions such as these are not raised by Xenophon, or his Socrates, but only by Xenophon's young and rash Alcibiades who, however, was a pupil of Socrates at the time when he raised those questions; only Alcibiades, and not Socrates, is presented by Xenophon as raising the Socratic question, "What is law?"[42] Socrates' doubt of the unqualified identification of justice and legality is intimated, however, by the facts that, on the one hand, he considers an enactment of the "legislator" Critias and his fellows a "law" which, he says, he is prepared to obey; and that, on the other hand, he actually disobeys it because it is "against the laws."[43] But apart from the consideration that the identification of "just" and "legal" would make impossible the evidently necessary distinction between just and unjust laws, there are elements of justice which necessarily transcend the dimension of the legal. Ingratitude, e.g., while not being illegal, is unjust.[44] The justice in business dealings—Aristotle's commutative justice proper—which is possible under a tyrant, is for this very reason not essentially dependent on law. Xenophon is thus led to suggest another definition, a more adequate definition, of justice. According to it, the just man is a man who does not hurt anyone, but helps everyone who has dealings with him. To be just, in other words, simply means to be beneficent.[45] If justice is then essentially translegal, rule without laws may very well be just: beneficent absolute rule is just. Absolute rule of a man who knows how to rule, who is a born ruler, is actually superior to the rule of laws, in so far as the good ruler is "a seeing law,"[46] and laws do not "see," or legal justice is blind. Whereas a good ruler is necessarily beneficent, laws are not necessarily beneficent. To say nothing of laws which are actually bad and harmful, even good laws suffer from the fact that they cannot "see." Now, tyranny is absolute monarchic rule. Hence the rule of an excellent tyrant is superior to, or more just than, rule of laws. Xenophon's realization of the problem of law, his understanding of the essence of law, his having raised and answered the Socratic question, "What is law?" enables and compels him to grant that tyranny may live up to the highest political standard. His giving, in the *Hiero,* a greater weight to the praise of tyranny than to the indictment of tyranny is then more than an accidental consequence of his decision to present the teaching concerning tyranny in the form of a dialogue.

Yet Simonides goes much beyond praising beneficent tyranny: he praises in the strongest terms the hoped-for beneficent rule of a tyrant who previously had committed a considerable number of crimes. By impliction he admits that the praiseworthy character of tyranny at its best is not impaired by the unjust manner in which the tyrant originally acquired his power or in which he ruled prior to his conversion. Xenophon would have been prevented from fully agreeing with his Simonides regarding tyranny if he had been a legitimist or constitutionalist. Xenophon's Socrates makes it clear that there is only one sufficient title to rule: only knowledge, and not force and fraud or election, or, we may add, inheritance makes a man a king or ruler. If this is the case, "constitutional" rule, rule derived from elections in particular, is not essentially more legitimate than tyrannical rule, rule derived from force or fraud. Tyrannical rule as well as "constitutional" rule will be legitimate to the extent to which the tyrant or the "constitutional" rulers will listen to the counsels of him who "speaks well" because he "thinks well." At any rate, the rule of a tyrant who, after having come to power by means of force and fraud, or after having committed any number of crimes, listens to the suggestions of reasonable men, is essentially more legitimate than the rule of elected magistrates who refuse to listen to such suggestions, i.e., than the rule of elected magistrates as such. Xenophon's Socrates is so little committed to the cause of "constitutionalism" that he can describe the sensible men who advise the tyrant as the tyrant's "allies." That is to say, he conceives of the relation of the wise to the tyrant in almost exactly the same way as does Simonides.[47]

While Xenophon seems to have believed that beneficent tyranny or the rule of a tyrant who listens to the counsels of the wise is, as a matter of principle, preferable to the rule of laws or to the rule of elected magistrates as such, he seems to have thought that tyranny at its best could hardly, if ever, be realized. This is shown most clearly by the absence of any reference to beneficent and happy tyrants who actually existed, not only from the *Hiero,* but from the *Corpus Xenophonteum* as a whole. It is true, in the *Education of Cyrus* he occasionally refers to a tyrant who was apparently happy;[48] he does not say, however, that he was beneficent or virtuous. Above all, the monarch in question was not a Greek: the chances of tyranny at its best seem to be particularly small among Greeks.[49] The reason why Xenophon was so skeptical regarding the prospects of tyranny at its best is indicated by a feature common to the two thematic treatments of tyranny at its best which occur in his works. In the *Hiero* as well as in the *Memorabilia,* the tyrant is presented as a ruler who needs guidance by another man in order to become a good ruler: even the best tyrant is, as such, an imperfect, an inefficient ruler.[50] Being a tyrant, being called a tyrant and not a king, means having been unable to transform tyranny into kingship, or to transform a title which is generally considered defective into a title which is generally considered valid.[51] The ensuing lack of unquestioned authority leads to the consequence that tyrannical government is essentially more oppressive and hence less stable than nontyrannical government. Thus no tyrant can dispense with a bodyguard which is more loyal to him than to the city and which enables him to maintain his power against the wishes of the city.[52] Reasons such as these explain why Xenophon, or his Socrates, preferred, for all practical purposes, at least as far as Greeks were concerned, the rules of laws to tyranny, and why they identified, for all practical purposes, the just with the legal.

The "tyrannical" teaching—the teaching which expounds the view that a case can be made for beneficent tyranny, and even for a beneficent tyranny which was originally established by force or fraud—has then a purely theoretical meaning. It is not more than a most forceful expression of the problem of law and legitimacy. When Socrates was charged with teaching his pupils to be "tyrannical," this doubtless was due to the popular misunderstanding of a theoretical thesis as a practical proposal. Yet the theoretical thesis by itself necessarily prevented its holders from being unqualifiedly loyal to Athenian democracy, e.g., for it prevented them from believing that democracy is simply the best political order. It prevented them from being "good citizens" (in the precise sense of the term)[53] under a democracy. Xenophon does not even attempt to defend Socrates against the charge that he led the young to look down with contempt on the political order established in Athens.[54] It goes without saying that the theoretical thesis in question might have become embarrassing for its holder in any city not ruled by a tyrant, i.e., in almost every city. Socrates' and Xenophon's acceptance of the "tyrannical" teaching would then explain why they became suspect to their fellow citizens, and, therefore, to a considerable extent, why Socrates was condemned to death and Xenophon was condemned to exile.

It is one thing to accept the theoretical thesis concerning tyranny; it is another thing to expound it publicly. Every written exposition is to a smaller or larger degree a public exposition. The *Hiero* does not expound the "tyrannical" teaching. But it enables, and even compels, its reader to disentangle that teaching from the writings in which Xenophon speaks in his own name or presents the views of Socrates. Only if read in the light of the question posed by the *Hiero* do the relevant passages of Xenophon's other writings reveal their full meaning. The *Hiero* reveals, however, if only indirectly, the conditions under which the "tyrannical" teaching may be expounded. If the city is essentially the community kept together and ruled by law, the "tyrannical" teaching cannot exist for the citizen as citizen. The ultimate reason why the very tyrant Hiero strongly indicts tyranny is precisely that he is at bottom a citizen.[55] Accordingly, Xenophon entrusted the only explicit praise of tyranny which he ever wrote to a "stranger," a man who does not have citizen responsibilities and who, in addition, voices the praise of tyranny not publicly but in a strictly private conversation with a tyrant, and for a purpose which supplies him with an almost perfect excuse. Socrates did not consider it good that the wise man should be simply a stranger;[56] Socrates was a citizen-philosopher. He could not, therefore, with propriety be presented as praising tyranny under any circumstances. There is no fundamental difference in this respect between Xenophon and Plato. Plato entrusted his discussion of the problematic character of the ''rule of laws'' to a stranger: Plato's Socrates is as silent about this grave, not to say awe-inspiring, subject as is Xenophon's Socrates.[57] Simonides fulfills in the *Corpus Xenophonteum* a function comparable to that fulfilled in the *Corpus Platonicum* by the stranger from Elea.

V

The Two Ways of Life

The primary subject of the conversation described in the *Hiero* is not the improvement of tyrannical government, but the difference between tyrannical and private life with regard to human enjoyments and pains. The question concerning that difference is identical, in the context, with the question as to whether tyrannical life is more choiceworthy than private life or *vice versa*. Insofar as "tyrant" is eventually replaced by "ruler," and the life of the ruler is the political life in the strict sense,[1] the question discussed in the *Hiero* concerns the relative desirability of the life of the ruler, or of political life, on the one hand, and of private life on the other. But however the question discussed in the dialogue may be formulated, it is in any case only a special form of the fundamental Socratic question of how man ought to live, or of what way of life is the most choiceworthy.[2]

In the *Hiero,* the difference between the tyrannical and the private life is discussed in a conversation between a tyrant and a private man. This means that the same subject is presented in two different manners. It is presented most obviously by the explicit and thematic statements of the two characters. Yet none of the two characters can be presumed to have stated exactly what Xenophon thought about the subject. In addition, the two characters cannot be presumed to have stated exactly what they themselves thought about it: Hiero is afraid of Simonides, and Simonides is guided by a pedagogic intention. Xenophon presents his view more directly, although less obviously, by the action of the dialogue, by what the characters silently do and unintentionally or occasionally reveal, or by the actual contrast as conceived by him between the tyrant Hiero and the private man Simonides. Insofar as Hiero reveals himself as a citizen in the most

78

radical sense and Simonides proves to be a stranger in the most radical sense, the dialogue presents the contrast between the citizen and the stranger. At any rate, Simonides is not a "private man" simply,[3] and he is not an ordinary representative of private life. However silent he may be about his own way of life, he reveals himself by his being or by deed as a wise man. If one considers the conversational setting, the dialogue reveals itself as an attempt to contrast the tyrannical life, or the life of the ruler, not simply with private life but with the life of the wise man.[4] Or, more specifically, it is an attempt to contrast an educated tyrant, a tyrant who admires, or wishes to admire, the wise, with a wise man who stoops to converse with tyrants.[5] Ultimately, the dialogue serves the purpose of contrasting the two ways of life: the political life and the life devoted to wisdom.[6]

One might object that according to Xenophon there is no contrast between the wise man and the ruler: the ruler in the strict sense is he who knows how to rule, who possesses the most noble kind of knowledge, who is able to teach what is best; and such knowledge is identical with wisdom.[7] Even if this objection were not exposed to any doubts, there would still remain the difference between the wise man or ruler who wishes to rule or does actually rule, and the wise man or ruler (e.g., Socrates and the poet Simonides) who does not wish to rule and does not engage in politics, but leads a life of privacy and leisure.[8]

The ambiguity that characterizes the *Hiero* is illustrated by nothing more strikingly than by the fact that the primary question discussed in the work does not receive a final and explicit answer. To discover the final answer that is implicitly given, we have to start from the explicit, if provisional, answers. In discussing both the explicit or provisional and the implicit or final answers, we have to distinguish between the answers of the two characters; for we have no right to assume that Hiero and Simonides are in agreement.

Hiero's explicit answer is to the effect that private life is absolutely preferable to tyrannical life.[9] But he cannot deny Simonides' contention that tyrants have greater power than private men to do things by means of which men gain love, and he spontaneously praises being loved more highly than anything else. It is true, he retorts that tyrants are also more likely to incur hatred than private men; but Simonides succeeds in silencing this objection by implicitly distinguishing between the good or prudent and the bad or foolish tyrant. In his last utterance, Hiero grants that a ruler or tyrant may gain the affection of his subjects.[10] If one accepts Hiero's premise that love, i.e., being loved, is the most choiceworthy thing, one is led by Simonides' argument to the conclusion that the life of a beneficent tyrant is preferable in the most important respect to private life. As the conclusion follows from Hiero's premise and is eventually not contested by him, we may regard it as his final answer.

Since Hiero is less wise, or competent, than Simonides, his answer is much less important than the poet's. Simonides asserts first that tyrannical life is superior to private life in every respect. He is soon compelled, or able, to admit that tyrannical life is not superior to private life in every respect. But he seems to maintain that tyrannical life is superior to private life in the most important respect: he praises nothing so highly as honor, and he asserts that tyrants are honored above other men.[11] With a view to his subsequent distinction between the good and the bad tyrant, we may state his final thesis as follows: the life of the beneficent tyrant is superior to private life in the most important respect. Simonides and Hiero seem to reach the same conclusion by starting from different premises.

On closer examination, it appears, however, that Simonides' praise of the tyrannical life is ambiguous. In order to lay hold of his view, we have to distinguish in the first place between what he explicitly says and what Hiero believes him to say.[12] Secondly, we have to distinguish between what Simonides says in the first part of the *Hiero* in which he hides his wisdom, and what he says in the second part to which he contributes so much more than to the first part, and in which he speaks no longer as a somewhat diffident pupil but with the confidence of a teacher. We have to attach particular weight to the fact that Simonides' most emphatic statement regarding the superiority of tyrannical life occurs in the first section in which he hides his wisdom to a higher degree than in any subsequent section.[13]

Simonides states to begin with that tyrants experience many more pleasures of all kinds and many fewer pains of all kinds than private men. He grants soon afterward that in a number of minor respects, if not in all minor respects, private life is preferable to tyrannical life. The question arises whether he thus simply retracts or merely qualifies the general statement made at the beginning: Does he believe that tyrannical life is superior to private life in the most important respect? He never answers this question explicitly. When comparing tyrannical and private life with regard to things more important than bodily pleasures, he uses much more reserved language than he did in his initial and general assertion. In particular when speaking about honor, he says, after having enumerated the various ways in which people honor tyrants: "for these are of course the kinds of things that subjects do for the tyrants and to *anyone else* whom they happen to honor at the moment." By this he seems to say that the most outstanding honor is not a preserve of tyrants. On the other hand, he says almost immediately thereafter that "you (*sc.* the tyrants) are honored above (all) other men." What he says in the first part of the dialogue might well appear to be ambiguous or inconclusive to the detached reader of the *Hiero* as distinguished from the rather disturbed interlocutor Hiero.[14] In the second part he nowhere explicitly says that tyrannical life is superior to private life in regard to the greatest pleasure. He does assert that the life of tyrants is superior to private life in regard to love. But he never says anywhere in the dialogue that love, or friendship, is the most pleasant thing.[15]

To arrive at a more exact formulation of the difficulty, we start again from the crucial fact that Simonides praises nothing as highly as honor. His contribution to the first part culminates in the assertion that the characteristic difference between the species "real man" ('ανήρ) and the other kinds of living beings, ordinary human beings of course included, consists in the desire for honor which is characteristic of the former, and in the suggestion that the most outstanding honors are reserved for rulers, if not for tyrants in particular. It is true, he declares in the same context that no human pleasure seems to be superior to the pleasure deriving from honor, and he thus seems to grant that other human pleasures might equal it.[16] On the other hand, he nowhere explicitly excludes the possibility that pleasure is not the sole or ultimate criterion. We have already observed that in the second part of the dialogue the emphasis tacitly shifts from the pleasant to the good and the noble.[17] This change reaches its climax in Simonides' final statement (11.7–15). At its beginning he indicates clearly that the noblest and grandest contest among human beings, and hence the victory in it, is reserved for rulers: victory in that contest consists in rendering very happy the city of which one is the chief. He thus leads one to expect that no human being other than a ruler can reach the summit of happiness: can anything rival victory in the noblest and grandest contest? This question is answered in the concluding sentence, according to which Hiero, by becoming the benefactor of his city, would be possessed of the most noble and the most blessed possession to be met with among human beings: he would be happy without being envied. Simonides does not say that the most noble and most blessed possession accessible to human beings is victory in the most noble and most grand contest among them. He does not even say that one cannot become happy without being envied but by making the city which one rules most happy. In the circumstances he had the strongest reasons for praising the beneficent ruler as emphatically, as explicitly as possible. By refraining from explicitly identifying "making one's city most happy" with "the most noble and most blessed possession," he seems to suggest that there are possibilities of bliss outside of, or beyond, the political life. The very phrasing of the last sentence seems to suggest it. The farmers and artisans who do their work well, are content with their lot and enjoy the simple pleasures of life, are at least as likely to be happy without being envied as rich and powerful rulers however beneficent.[18] What is true of the common people is equally true of other types of men, and in particular of that type which seems to be most important in the conversational situation: those who come to display before the tyrant the wise or beautiful or good things which they possess, who share in the amenities of court life and are rewarded with royal munificence.[19] The highest goal which the greatest ruler could reach only after having made the most extraordinary exertions, seems to be within easy reach of every private man.

This interpretation is open to a very strong objection. We shall not insist on the facts that "being happy" in Simonides' final sentence ("while being happy, you will not be envied") might very well mean "being powerful and wealthy"[20] and that tyrants are superior to private men in regard to power and wealth as not even Hiero can deny. For Simonides might have understood by happiness continuous joy or contentment.[21] Suffice it to say that precisely on account of the essential ambiguity of "being happy" the purport of Simonides' final sentence depends decisively on its second part, viz., the expression "you will not be envied." What this expression means for the decision of the crucial issue becomes clear if we remind ourselves of the following facts: that the purpose of the *Hiero* is to contrast the ruler, not simply with private men in general, but with the wise; that *the* representative of wisdom is Socrates; and that Socrates was exposed, and fell victim, to the envy of his fellow citizens. If the beneficent ruler can be "happy" without being envied, whereas even Socrates' "happiness" was accompanied by envy,[22] the political life, the life of the ruler or of the tyrant, would seem to be unambiguously superior to the life of the wise man. It would seem then that Simonides' praise of tyranny, in spite of his ironical overstatements and his pedagogic intention, is at bottom serious. True happiness—this seems to be Xenophon's thought—is possible only on the basis of excellence or superiority, and there are ultimately only two kinds of excellence—the excellence of the ruler and that of the wise man. All superior men are exposed to envy on account of their excellence. But the ruler, as distinguished from the wise man, is able to do penance for his superiority by becoming the servant of all his subjects: the hardworking and beneficent ruler, and not the retiring wise man, can put envy at rest.[23]

This must be taken with a grain of salt. It goes without saying that the prospect by means of which Simonides attempts to educate Hiero is incapable of fulfillment: Xenophon knew too well that if there are any forms of superiority which do not expose their possessors to envy, political power, however beneficent, would not be one of them. Or, to put it somewhat differently, if it is true that he who wants to receive kindness must first show kindness, it is not certain that his kindness will not be requited with ingratitude.[24] The thought that a superior man who does not successfully hide his superiority would not be exposed to envy is clearly a delusion. It forms the fitting climax of the illusory image of the tyrant who is happy because he is virtuous. Its aptness consists precisely in this: that it makes intelligible the whole illusory image as the momentary illusion of a wise man, i.e., as something more than a noble lie invented for the benefit of an unwise pupil. Being wise, he is most happy and exposed to envy. His bliss would seem to be complete if he could escape envy. If it were true that only experience could fully reveal the character of tyrannical life—it is this assumption on which the explicit argument of the *Hiero* is largely based—the wise man could not be absolutely certain whether the beneficent tyrant would not be beyond the reach of envy. He could indulge the hope that by becoming a beneficent tyrant, i.e., by actually exercising that tyrannical or royal art which flows from wisdom (if it is not identical with wisdom), he would escape envy while retaining his superiority. Simonides' climactic assertion that by acting on his advice Hiero would become happy without being envied intimates the only reason why a wise man could be imagined for a moment to wish to be a ruler or to envy the man who rules well. It thus reveals the truth underlying Hiero's fear of the wise: that fear proves to be based on a misunderstanding of a momentary velleity of the wise. It reveals at the same time the constant preoccupation of Hiero himself: his misunderstanding is the natural outcome of the fact that he himself is greatly tormented by other people's envy of his happiness. It reveals finally the reason why Simonides could not possibly be envious of Hiero. For the irony of Simonides' last sentence consists, above all, in this: that, if *per impossibile* the perfect ruler would escape from envy, his very escape from envy would expose him to envy; by ceasing to be envied by the multitude, he would begin to be envied by the wise. He would be envied for not being envied. Simonides could become dangerous to Hiero only if Hiero followed his advice. Hiero's final silence is a fitting answer to all the implications of Simonides' final statement.

At any rate, the wise are not envious, and the fact that they are envied does not impair their happiness or bliss.[25] Even if they would grant that the life of the ruler is in a certain respect superior to the life of the wise man, they would wonder whether the price which has to be paid for that superiority is worthwhile. The ruler cannot escape envy but by leading a life of perpetual business, care and trouble.[26] The ruler whose specific function is "doing" or "well-doing" has to serve all his subjects. Socrates, on the other hand, whose specific function is "speaking" or discussing, does not engage in discussion except with those with whom he likes to converse. The wise man alone is free.[27]

To sum up, Simonides' final statement does not imply the view that political life is preferable to private life. This conclusion is confirmed by the carefully chosen expression which he uses for describing the character of happiness unmarred by envy. He calls it "the most noble and most blessed possession to be met with among human beings." He does not call it the greatest good. The most noble and most blessed possession for human beings is choiceworthy, but there are other things which are equally or more choiceworthy. It may even be doubted whether it is simply the most choiceworthy "possession." Euthydemus, answering a question of Socrates, says that freedom is a most noble and most magnificent possession for real men and for cities. The older Cyrus says in a speech addressed to the Persian nobility that the most noble and most "political" possession consists in deriving the greatest pleasure from praise. Xenophon himself says to Seuthes that for a real man and in particular a ruler, no possession is more noble or more splendid than virtue and justice and gentility. Antisthenes calls leisure the most delicate or luxurious possession.[28] Socrates, on the other hand, says that a good friend is the best, or the most all-productive, possession and that no possession is more pleasant for a free human being than agriculture.[29] Xenophon's Simonides agrees with Xenophon's Socrates and in fact with Xenophon himself by failing to describe "happiness unmarred by envy" as the most pleasant possession for human beings or as the most noble possession for real men or simply as the best possession.[30] We need not discuss here how Xenophon conceived of the exact relation between "possession" and "good." It is safe to assume that he used "possession" mostly in its less strict sense according to which a possession is a good only conditionally, i.e., only if the possessor knows how to use it or to use it well.[31] If this is the case, even the possession which is simply best would not be identical with the greatest good. While people in general are apt to identify the best possession with the greatest good, Socrates makes a clear distinction between the two things. According to him, the greatest good is wisdom, whereas education is the greatest good for human beings,[32] and the best possession is a good friend. Education cannot be the greatest good simply, because gods do not need education. Education, i.e., the most excellent education, which is education to wisdom, is the greatest good for human beings, i.e., for human beings as such, for men in so far as they do not transcend humanity by approaching divinity: God alone is simply wise.[33] The wise man or the philosopher who partakes of the highest good will be blessed although he does not possess "the most noble and most blessed possession to be met with among human beings."

The *Hiero* is silent about the status of wisdom. Although most explicit about various kinds of pleasure, it is silent about the specific pleasures of the wise, such as, for example, friendly discussion.[34] It is silent about the way of life of the wise. This silence cannot be explained by the fact that the thematic subject of the dialogue is the comparison of the life of the ruler, not with the life of the wise man, but with private life in general. For the thematic subject of the parallel dialogue, the *Oeconomicus,* is the economist, or the management of the household, and yet its central chapter contains a most striking confrontation of the life of the economist (who is a ruler) with the Socratic way of life. The *Hiero* is reserved about the nature of wisdom because the purpose of the dialogue, or of Simonides, requires that "wisdom" be kept in its ordinary ambiguity. If we consider, however, how profoundly Socrates or Xenophon agree with Simonides regarding tyranny, we may be inclined to impute to Xenophon's Simonides the Socratic view that is nowhere contradicted by Xenophon, according to which wisdom is the highest good. Certainly, what Simonides says in his final statement in praise of the life of the ruler accords perfectly with the Socratic view.

In the *Hiero,* Xenophon indicates his view of wisdom by incidental remarks entrusted to Simonides and by the action of the dialogue. Simonides mentions two ways of "taking care" of things which lead to gratification: teaching the things that are best (or teaching what things are best), on the one hand; and praising and honoring him who executes what is best in the finest manner, on the other. When applying this general remark to rulers in particular, he does not mention teaching at all; he silently limits the ruler's ways of taking care which leads to gratification, to praising and honoring, or more specifically to the offering and distributing of prizes. The specific function of the ruler appears to be strictly subordinate to that of the wise man. In the best case imaginable, the ruler would be the one who, by means of honoring, to say nothing of punishing, would put into practice the teaching or the prescriptions of the wise man.[35] The wise man is the ruler of rulers. Similarly, the ruler is supposed merely to encourage the discovery of, or the looking out for, "something good"; he is not supposed to engage in these intellectual activities himself.[36] It deserves mention that the passage in which Simonides adumbrates his view of the relation of wisdom and rule is one of the two chapters in which the very term tyrant is avoided: Simonides describes by the remarks in question not merely the tyrant, but the ruler in general.[37]

The superiority of the wise man to the ruler is brought to light by the action of the dialogue. The tyrannical life, or the life of the ruler, is chosen by Hiero not only prior to the conversation, but again within the conversation itself: he rejects Simonides' veiled suggestion to return to private life. And Hiero proves to be less wise than Simonides, who rejects the political life in favor of the wise man's private life.[38] At the beginning of the conversation, Simonides suggests that not he, but Hiero, has a better knowledge of the two ways of life or their difference. This suggestion does not lack a certain plausibility as long as one understands by the two ways of life the tyrannical life and private life in general; it proves to be simply ironical if it is considered in the light of the setting, i.e., if it is applied to the difference between the life of the ruler and the life of the wise man. For Hiero proves to be ignorant of the life of the wise man and its goal, whereas Simonides knows, not only his own way of life, but the political life as well, as is shown by his ability to teach the art of ruling well. Only Simonides, and not Hiero, is competent to make a choice between the two ways of life.[39] At the beginning, Simonides bows to Hiero's leadership; he even permits Hiero to defeat him. But in the moment of his victory Hiero becomes aware of the fact that far from really defeating Simonides, he has merely prepared his own downfall. The wise man sits leisurely upon the very goal toward which the ruler is blindly and furiously working his way and which he will never reach. At the end, Simonides' leadership is firmly established: the wise man defeats the ruler. This most obvious aspect of the action is a peculiarity of the *Hiero*. In most of Xenophon's dialogues, no change of leadership takes place: Socrates is the leader from the beginning to the end. In Xenophon's Socratic dialogue *par excellence,* the *Oeconomicus,* a change of leadership does occur; but it is a change from the leadership of the wise man (Socrates) to the leadership of the ruler (the economist Ischomachus). Whereas in the *Oeconomicus* the wise man surrenders to the ruler, in the *Hiero* the ruler surrenders to the wise man. The *Hiero,* and not the *Oeconomicus,* reveals by its action the true relation of rule and wisdom. In addition, the *Hiero* is that work of Xenophon which draws our attention most forcefully to the problem of that relation. It can be said to do this for several reasons. In the first place, because its primary subject is the difference between private life and the life of a certain type of ruler. In the second place, because it does contrast a wise man and a ruler more explicitly than any other Xenophontic writing. And finally, the *Hiero*'s most obvious practical aim (the improvement of tyranny) is hardly capable of fulfillment, which precludes the possibility that the obvious practical aim of the work coincides with its final purpose. Here again we may note a profound agreement between Xenophon and Plato. The precise relation between the philosopher and the political man (i.e., their fundamental difference) is the thematic premise, not of the *Republic* and the *Gorgias* in which Socrates as citizen-philosopher is the leading character, but of the *Politicus* in which a stranger occupies the central position.

From what has been said it may be inferred that Simonides' emphatic praise of honor cannot possibly mean that he preferred honor as such to all other things. After all, his statement on honor belongs to that part of the dialogue in which he hides his wisdom almost completely. Besides, its bearing is sufficiently qualified by the sentences with which it opens and ends.[40] One might even think to begin with that his praise of honor can be explained completely by his pedagogic intention. His intention is to show Hiero, who reveals a remarkable indifference to virtue, a way to virtuous rule by appealing, not to virtue or the noble, but to the pleasant; and the pleasure deriving from honor seems to be the natural substitute for the pleasure deriving from virtue. Yet Simonides appeals in his teaching primarily not to Hiero's desire for honor, but to his desire for love. It could not be otherwise since Hiero had bestowed spontaneously the highest praise not on honor, but on love. We may take it then that by extolling honor Simonides reveals his own preferences rather than those of his pupil[41]: Simonides, and not Hiero, prefers the pleasure deriving from honor to the other pleasures explicitly mentioned by him. We may even say that of all desires which are natural, i.e., which "grow" in human beings independently of any education or teaching,[42] he considered the desire for honor the highest because it is the foundation of the desire for any excellence, be it the excellence of the ruler or that of the wise man.[43]

Whereas Simonides is concerned with honor, he is not concerned with love. Hiero has to demonstrate to him not only that as regards love tyrants are worse off than private men, but even that love is a great good and that private men are particularly loved by their children, parents, brothers, wives, and companions. In discussing love, Hiero feels utterly unable to appeal to the poet's experience or previous knowledge as he did when discussing the pleasures of the table and even of sex. He urges him to acquire the rudiments of knowledge regarding love immediately or in the future without being in any way certain Simonides would wish to acquire them.[44]

Just as desire for honor is characteristic of Simonides, desire for love is characteristic of Hiero.[45] In so far as Hiero represents the ruler and Simonides represents the wise man, the difference between love and honor as interpreted in the *Hiero* will throw some light on Xenophon's view of the difference between the ruler and the wise man. What Xenophon has primarily in mind is not simply the difference between love and honor in general: Hiero desires to be loved by "human beings," i.e., not merely by real men, but by everyone regardless of his qualities, and Simonides is concerned with admiration or praise, not by everybody, but by "those who are free in the highest degree."[46] The desire which Xenophon or his Simonides ascribes to Hiero, or the ruler, is fundamentally the same as the erotic desire for the common people which Plato's Socrates ascribes to Callicles.[47] Only because the ruler has the desire to be loved by "human beings" as such is he able to become the willing servant and benefactor of all his subjects and hence to become a good ruler. The wise man, on the other hand, has no such desire; he is satisfied with the admiration, the praise, the approval of a small minority.[48] It would seem, then, that the characteristic difference between the ruler and the wise man manifests itself in the objects of their passionate interest and not in the character of their passion itself.[49] Yet it is no accident that Simonides is primarily concerned with being praised by the competent minority, and not with being loved by them, whereas Hiero is primarily concerned with being loved by human beings in the mass, and not with being admired by them. The characteristic difference between the ruler and the wise man may therefore be presumed to manifest itself somehow in the difference between love and admiration.

The meaning of this difference is indicated by Simonides in his praise of the beneficent ruler. The beneficent ruler will be loved by his subjects, he will be passionately desired by human beings, he will have earned the affectionate regard of many cities, whereas he will be praised by all human beings and will be admirable in the eyes of all. Everyone present, but not everyone absent, will be his ally, just as not everyone will be afraid that something might happen to him and not everyone will desire to serve him. Precisely by making his city happy, he will antagonize and hurt her enemies who cannot be expected to love him and to extol his victory. But even the enemies will have to admit that he is a great man: they will admire him and praise his virtue.[50] The beneficent ruler will be praised and admired by all men, whereas he will not be loved by all men: the range of love is more limited than that of admiration or praise. Each man loves what is somehow his own, his private possession; admiration or praise is concerned with the excellent regardless of whether it is one's own or not. Love as distinguished from admiration requires proximity. The range of love is limited not only in regard to space, but likewise—although Xenophon's Simonides in his delicacy refrains from even alluding to it—in regard to time. A man may be admired many generations after his death whereas he will cease to be loved once those who knew him well are dead.[51] Desire for "inextinguishable fame,"[52] as distinguished from desire for love, enables a man to liberate himself from the shackles of the Here and Now. The beneficent ruler is praised and admired by all men, whereas he is loved mainly by his subjects: the limits of love coincide normally with the borders of the political community, whereas admiration of human excellence knows no boundaries.[53] The beneficent ruler is loved by those whom he benefits or serves on account of his benefits or services,[54] whereas he is admired even by those to whom he has done the greatest harm and certainly by many whom he did not serve or benefit at all: admiration seems to be less mercenary than love. Those who admire the beneficent ruler while loving him do not necessarily make a distinction between their benefactor and the man of excellence; but those who admire him without loving him—e.g., the enemy cities— rise above the vulgar error of mistaking one's benefactor for the man of excellence.[55] Admiration is as much superior to love as the man of excellence is to one's benefactor as such. To express this somewhat differently, love has no criterion of its relevance outside itself, but admiration has. If admiration does not presuppose services rendered by the admired to the admirer, one is led to wonder whether it presupposes any services, or any prospect of services, by the admired at all. This question is answered explicitly in the affirmative by Hiero, and tacitly in the negative by Simonides.[56] Hiero is right as regards the ruler: the ruler does not gain the admiration of all men but by rendering services to his subjects. Simonides is right as regards the wise man:

the wise man is admired, not on account of any services which he renders to others, but simply because he is what he is. The wise man need not be a benefactor at all in order to be admired as a man of excellence.[57] More precisely: the specific function of the ruler is to be beneficent; he is essentially a benefactor; the specific function of the wise man is to understand; he is a benefactor only accidentally. The wise man is as self-sufficient as is humanly possible; the admiration which he gains is essentially a tribute to his perfection, and not a reward for any services.[58] The desire for praise and admiration as distinguished and divorced from the desire for love is the natural foundation for the predominance of the desire for one's own perfection.[59] This is what Xenophon subtly indicates by presenting Simonides as chiefly interested in the pleasures of eating, whereas Hiero appears to be chiefly interested in the pleasures of sex: for the enjoyment of food, as distinguished from sexual enjoyments, one does not need other human beings.[60]

The specific function of the wise man is not bound up with an individual political community: the wise man may live as a stranger. The specific function of the ruler on the other hand consists in rendering happy the individual political community of which he is the chief. The city is essentially the potential enemy of other cities. Hence one cannot define the function of the ruler without thinking of war, enemies, and allies: the city and her ruler need allies, whereas the wise man does not.[61] To the specific functions correspond specific natural inclinations. The born ruler, as distinguished from him who is born to become wise, must have strong warlike inclinations. Hiero mentions the opinion according to which peace is a great good and war a great evil. He does not simply adopt it, however, for he feels too keenly that war affords great pleasures. When enumerating the very great pleasures which private citizens enjoy in war, he assigns the central place to the pleasure which they derive from killing their enemies. He notes with regret that the tyrant cannot have this great pleasure or at least cannot openly show it and boast of the deed. Simonides does not reveal any delight in war or killing. The most he says in favor of war is that Hiero had greatly exaggerated the detrimental effect on appetite and sleep of that fear which fills men's minds before a battle.[62] Not victory in war as such, but the happiness of one's city, is described by him as the goal of the noblest and grandest contest.[63] Hiero's statement about peace and war[64] doubtless serves the purpose of drawing our attention to the particularly close connection between tyranny and war.[65] But a comparison of this passage with what Xenophon tells us about the inclinations of the king Cyrus makes it clear that he considered a streak of cruelty an essential element of the great ruler in general.[66] The difference between the tyrant and the nontyrannical ruler is ultimately not a simple opposition, but rather that in the case of the tyrant certain elements of the character of the ruler are more strongly developed or less easily hidden than in the case of the nontyrannical ruler. Nor is it necessarily true that the pleasure which the ruler takes in hurting enemies is surpassed by his desire to be loved by friends. To say nothing of the fact that what Hiero enjoys most in his sexual relations are the quarrels with the beloved one, he apparently prefers "taking from enemies against their will" to all other pleasures.[67] According to him, the tyrant is compelled to free the slaves, but desirous to enslave the free:[68] if he could afford to indulge his desires everyone would be his slave. Simonides had limited himself to stating that tyrants are most capable of hurting their enemies and helping their friends. When reproducing this statement, Hiero puts a considerably greater weight on "hurting the enemies" than on "helping the friends"; and when discussing it, he implies that Simonides has an interest of his own in helping his friends but none in hurting his enemies: he can easily see Simonides helping his friends; he cannot see him as well hurting his enemies.[69] Since the wise man does not need human beings in the way in which, and to the extent to which, the ruler does, his attitude toward them is free, not passionate, and hence not susceptible of turning into malevolence or hatred. In other words, the wise man alone is capable of justice in the highest sense. When Hiero distinguishes between the wise and the just man, he implies that the just man is the good ruler. Accordingly, he must be presumed to understand by justice political justice, the justice which manifests itself in helping friends and hurting enemies. When Socrates assumes that the wise man is just, he understands by justice transpolitical justice, the justice which is irreconcilable with hurting anyone. The highest form of justice is the preserve of those who have the greatest self-sufficiency which is humanly possible.[70]

VI

Pleasure and Virtue

The *Hiero* almost leads up to the suggestion that tyranny may be perfectly just. It starts from the opinion that tyranny is radically unjust. The tyrant is supposed to reject the just and noble, or virtue, in favor of the pleasant; or, since virtue is human goodness, he is supposed to reject the good in favor of the pleasant. This opinion is based on the general premise that the good and the pleasant are fundamentally different from each other in such a way that the right choice has to be guided by considerations of the good, and not by considerations of the pleasant.[1]

The thesis that tyranny is radically unjust forms the climax of Hiero's indictment of tyranny. That indictment is exaggerated; Hiero simply reproduces without full conviction the gentleman's image of the tyrant.[2] But the very fact that he is capable of using that image for a selfish purpose proves that his thesis is not altogether wrong. Xenophon has taken some pains to make it clear that while Hiero is not as unjust as he declares the tyrant to be, he is remarkably indifferent to virtue. He does not think of mentioning virtue among the greatest goods or the most choice-worthy possessions. At best, he considers virtuous men, i.e., the virtue of others, to be useful. But even the virtue of others is not regarded by him as an object of delight: he does not seek, and never sought, his companions among the virtuous men. Not he, but Simonides, points out the insignificance of bodily pleasures.[3] Only after having been driven into a corner by Simonides does he praise the virtue of the benefactor of human beings with a view to the fact that such virtue is productive of the highest honor and of unimpaired happiness.[4]

In attempting to educate a man of this kind, Simonides has no choice but to appeal to his desire for pleasure. In order to advise Hiero to rule as a virtuous tyrant, he has to show him that the tyrant cannot obtain pleasure, and in particular that kind of pleasure with which Hiero is chiefly concerned, viz., the pleasure deriving from being loved, but by being as virtuous as possible. What he shows Hiero is a way not so much to virtue as to pleasure. Strictly speaking, he does not advise him to become virtuous. He advises him to do the gratifying things himself while entrusting to others the things for which men incur hatred; to encourage certain virtues and pursuits among his subjects by offering prizes; to keep his bodyguard, yet to use it for the benefit of his subjects; and, generally speaking, to be as beneficent to his fellow citizens as possible. Now, the benefactor of his fellow citizens is not necessarily a man of excellence or a virtuous man. Simonides does not advise Hiero to practise any of the things which distinguish the virtuous man from the mere benefactor.

A comparison of the *Hiero* with Isocrates' work on the tyrannical art (*To Nicocles*) makes perfectly clear how amazingly little of moral admonition proper there is in the *Hiero*. Simonides speaks only once of the virtue of the tyrant, and he never mentions any of the special virtues (moderation, courage, justice, wisdom, and so on) when speaking of the tyrant. Isocrates, on the other hand, does not tire of admonishing Nicocles to cultivate his mind, to practise virtue, wisdom, piety, truthfulness, meekness, self-control, moderation, urbanity, and dignity; he advises him to love peace and to prefer a noble death to a base life, as well as to take care of just legislation and adjudication; he calls a good counsellor the most useful and most "tyrannical" possession.[5]

If Simonides can be said to recommend virtue at all, he recommends it, not as an end, but as a means. He recommends just and noble actions to the tyrant as means to pleasure. In order to do this, Simonides, or Xenophon, had to have at his disposal a hedonistic justification of virtue. Moreoever, Simonides prepares his teaching by starting a discussion of whether tyrannical life is superior to private life from the point of view of pleasure. In discussing this subject, Hiero, and Simonides are compelled to examine a number of valuable things from the point of view of pleasure. The *Hiero* could only have been written by a man who had at his disposal a comprehensive hedonistic interpretation of human life.

Expression of essential parts of that hedonistic interpretation has been entrusted to Simonides who in one of his poems had said: "For what life of mortals, or what tyranny, is desirable without pleasure. Without her not even the lasting life of gods is to be envied."[6] It is difficult to say how Simonides conceived of the relation between pleasure and virtue except that he cannot have considered desirable a virtuous life which is devoid of pleasure. From the verses which he addressed to Scopas, it appears that he considered virtue essentially dependent on a man's fate: no one is protected against coming into situations in which he is compelled to do base things.[7] He gave the advice to be playful throughout, and not to be entirely serious about anything. Play is pleasant, and virtue, or gentlemanliness, is the serious thing *par excellence*.[8] If a sophist is a man who uses his wisdom for the sake of gain and who employs arts of deception, Simonides was a sophist.[9] The way in which he is presented in the *Hiero* does not contradict what we are told about the historical Simonides. Xenophon's Simonides is an "economist"; he rejects the gentleman's view of what is most desirable in favor of the view of the "real man"; he would be capable of going to any length in "contriving something"; and he is free from the responsibility of the citizen.[10] While he speaks of the noblest and grandest contest and of the noblest and most blessed possession, he does not speak of the noblest and grandest, or most splendid possession ("virtue and justice and gentility"): he reserves his highest praise, not for virtue, but for happiness unmarred by envy, and, above all, for honor.[11] The amazingly amoral nature of the tyrannical teaching embodied in the second part of the *Hiero* as well as the hedonistic consideration of human things that is given in the first part accord perfectly with Simonides' character.

Xenophon's Simonides not only has a definite leaning toward hedonism; he even has at his disposal a philosophic justification for his views about the importance of pleasure. What he says in his initial statement about the various kinds of pleasure and pain reveals a definite theoretical interest in the subject. He divides all pleasures into three classes: pleasures of the body, pleasures of the soul, and pleasures common to body and soul. He subdivides the pleasures of the body into those related to a special organ (eyes, ears, nose, sexual organs) and those related to the whole body. His failure to subdivide the pleasures of the soul may not be due merely to his wish to stress the pleasures of the body in order to present himself as a lover of those pleasures; it may have to be traced also to the theoretical reasons that there are no parts of the soul in the sense in which there are parts of the body and that the pleasures common to men and brutes are more fundamental and therefore, from a certain theoretical point of view, more important than those characteristic of human beings.[12] He makes it clear that all pleasures and pains presuppose some kind of knowledge, an act of distinction or judgment, a perception of the senses or of thought.[13] He distinguishes the knowledge presupposed by every pleasure and pain from the knowledge or perception of our pleasure or pain. He does not consider it unimportant to indicate that whereas we feel our own pleasures and pains, we merely observe those of others. He possibly alludes to a distinction between the δι' οὖ and the ᾧ with regard to pleasures and perceptions.[14] When mentioning the pleasure deriving from sleep, he does not limit himself to pointing out that sleep is unambiguously pleasant; he raises in addition the theoretical question of how and by what and when we enjoy sleep; since he feels that he cannot answer this question, he explains why it is so particularly difficult to answer it.

If we understand by hedonism the thesis that the pleasant is identical with the good, Xenophon's Simonides is not a hedonist. Before he ever mentions the pleasant, he mentions the good: he mentions at the very outset "better" knowledge, by which, of course, he does not mean "more pleasant" knowledge.[15] In his enumeration of the various kinds of pleasure he makes it clear that he considers the pleasant and the good fundamentally different from each other: the good and the bad things are sometimes pleasant and sometimes painful. He does not explicitly say how he conceives of the precise relation between the pleasant and the good.[16] To establish his view on the subject, we have to pay proper attention to the nonhedonistic principle of preference which he recognizes when he speaks with emphasis of "(ordinary) human beings" and of "(real) men." First, regarding "human beings," he seems to make a distinction between such pleasures as are in accordance with human nature and such pleasures as are against human nature:[17] the preferable or good pleasures are those which agree with human nature. Simonides' nonhedonistic principle of preference would then be "what agrees with human nature." Now, ordinary human beings may enjoy as much pleasure as real men; yet real men are to be esteemed more highly than ordinary human beings.[18] Hence, we may define Simonides' nonhedonistic principle of preference more precisely by identifying it with "what agrees with the nature of real men." Seeing that he praises nothing as highly as honor, and honor is most pleasant to real men as distinguished from ordinary human beings, we may say that the ultimate and complete principle of preference to which Simonides refers in the *Hiero* is the pleasure which agrees with the nature of real men. What he praises most highly is pleasant indeed, but pleasure alone does not define it sufficiently; it is pleasant on a certain level, and that level is determined, not by pleasure, but by the hierarchy of beings.[19] He is then a hedonist only in so far as he rejects the view that considerations of pleasure are irrelevant for right choice: the right goal towards which one has to aim, or with reference to which one has to judge, must be something which is intrinsically pleasant. This view seems to have been held by the historical Simonides as is shown by his verses on pleasure quoted above. We may ascribe the same view to Xenophon's Hiero, who admits the distinction between the good and the pleasant and who characterizes friendship, than which he praises nothing more highly, as both very good and very pleasant.[20]

This qualified hedonism guides Simonides and Hiero in their examination of a number of valuable things. That examination leads to the conclusion suggested by Hiero that friendship has a higher value than city or fatherland or patriotism.[21] Friendship, i.e., being loved and cared for by the small number of human beings whom one knows intimately (one's nearest relatives and companions) is not only "a very great good"; it is also "very pleasant." It is a very great good because it is intrinsically pleasant. Trust, i.e., one's trusting others, is "a great good." It is not a very great good, because it is not so much intrinsically pleasant as the *conditio sine qua non* of intrinsically pleasant relations. A man whom one trusts is not yet a friend: a servant or a bodyguard must be trustworthy, but there is no reason why they ought to be one's friends. While trust is not intrinsically pleasant, it stands in a fairly close relation to pleasure: when discussing trust, Hiero mentions pleasure three times. On the other hand, in the passage immediately following in which he discusses "fatherlands," he does not mention pleasure at all.[22] Not only are "fatherlands" not intrinsically pleasant; they do not even stand in a close relation to pleasure. "Fatherlands are worth very much" because the citizens afford each other protection without pay against violent death and thus enable each citizen to live in safety. That for which the fatherland is "worth very much" is life in safety; safety, or freedom from fear, the spoiler of all pleasures, is the *conditio sine qua non* of every pleasure however insignificant; but to live in safety and to live pleasantly are clearly two different things. More precisely, the fatherland is not, as is trust, the specific condition of the great pleasures deriving from friendship: "strangers," men like Simonides, may enjoy friendship.[23] Friendship and trust are good for human beings as such, but the cities are good primarily, not to say exclusively, for the citizens and the rulers; they are certainly less good for strangers, and still less good for slaves.[24] The fatherland, or the city, is good for the citizens because it liberates them from fear. This does not mean that it abolishes fear; it rather replaces one kind of fear (the fear of enemies, evil-doers, and slaves) by another (the fear of the laws or of the law-enforcing authorities).[25] The city, as distinguished from friendship and trust, is not possible without compulsion; and compulsion, constraint, or necessity (ἀνάγκη) is essentially unpleasant.[26] Friendship, i.e., being loved, is pleasant, while being patriotic is necessary.[26] While friendship, as praised by Hiero, is not only pleasant but also good, its goodness is not moral goodness or nobility: Hiero praises him who has friends regardless of whether the friends are morally good or not.[28] In so far as friendship is being loved, preferring friendship to fatherland is tantamount to preferring oneself to others: when speaking about friendship, Hiero is silent about the mutuality to which he explicitly refers when discussing trust and fatherland. It is tantamount to preferring one's pleasure to one's duties to others.

The thesis that friendship is a greater good than the fatherland is suggested by Hiero who has a strong motive for asserting that private life is superior to the life of the ruler which is the political life *par excellence*. But that thesis is more than a weapon convenient for Hiero's purpose. Simonides, who could have been induced by his pedagogic intention rather to prefer fatherland to friendship, tacitly adopts Hiero's thesis by advising the tyrant to consider his fatherland as his estate, his fellow citizens as his comrades, his friends as his children, and his sons as the same thing as his life or soul.[29] He is even less capable than Hiero of assigning to the fatherland the most exalted place among the objects of human attachment. He adopts Hiero's thesis not only "by speech," but "by deed" as well: he lives as a stranger; he chooses to live as a stranger. Contrary to Hiero, he never praises the fatherland or the city. When he urges Hiero to think of the common good, and of the happiness of the city, he emphasizes the fact that this advice is addressed to a tyrant or ruler. Not Simonides, but Hiero, is concerned with being loved by "human beings" in the mass and therefore has to be a lover of the city in order to reach his goal. Simonides desires nothing as much as praise by the small number of competent judges: he can be satisfied with a small group of friends.[30] It is hardly necessary to repeat that his spontaneous praise of honor is concerned exclusively with the benefit of him who is honored or praised and is silent about the benefits to be rendered to others or the duties to others.

The view that a nonpolitical good such as friendship is more valuable than the city was not the view of the citizen as such.[31] It remains to be considered whether it was acceptable to citizen philosophers. Socrates agrees with Hiero as regards the fact that "the father-lands are worth very much" because they afford safety, or protection against injury, to the citizens.[32] Xenophon seems to indicate by the plan of the *Memorabilia* that Socrates attached a greater importance to the self than to the city.[33] This is in accordance with Xenophon's distinction between the man of excellence and the benefactor of his fellow citizens. Xenophon himself was induced to accompany Cyrus, an old enemy of Athens, on his expedition against his brother by the promise of Proxenus, an old guest-friend of his, that he would make him a friend of Cyrus if he would come. Proxenus, a pupil of Gorgias, of a man who had no fixed domicile in any city,[34] explicitly stated that he himself considered Cyrus worth more to him than his fatherland. Xenophon does not say in so many words that he might conceivably come to consider Cyrus' friendship preferable to his fatherland; but he certainly was not shocked by Proxenus' statement and he certainly acted as if he were capable of sharing Proxenus' sentiment. Socrates had some misgivings regarding Xenophon's becoming a friend of Cyrus and he advised him therefore to consult Apollo about the journey; but Xenophon was so anxious to join Cyrus or to leave his fatherland that he decided at once to accept Proxenus' invitation. Even after every-thing had gone wrong with Cyrus' expedition, Xenophon was not anxious to return to his fatherland, although he was not yet exiled. If his comrades had not passionately protested, he would have founded a city "in some barbarian place"; not Xenophon, but his opponents, felt that one ought not to esteem anything more highly than Greece.[35] Later on, he did not hesitate to accompany Agesilaus on his cam-paign against Athens and her allies which culminated in the battle of Coronea.[36]

Lest we be carried away by blind indignation,[37] we shall try to understand what we might call Xenophon's theoretical and practical depreciation of the fatherland or the city[38] in the light of his political teaching in general and of the teaching of the *Hiero* in particular. If wisdom or virtue is the highest good, the fatherland or the city cannot be the highest good. If virtue is the highest good, not the fatherland as such, but only the virtuous community or the best political order can command a good man's undivided loyalty. If he has to choose between a fatherland which is corrupt and a foreign city which is well ordered, he may be justified in preferring that foreign city to his fatherland. Precisely because he is a good man, he will not be a good citizen in a bad polity.[39] Just as in choosing horses one looks for the best, and not for those which are born in the country, the wise general will fill the ranks of his army not merely with his fellow citizens but with every available man who can be expected to be virtuous.[40] In the spirit of this maxim Xenophon himself devoted his most extensive work to an idealizing description of the achievements of the "barbarian" Cyrus.

The reason why the city as such cannot lay claim to man's ultimate attachment is implied in Xenophon's "tyrannical" teaching. We have stated that according to that teaching beneficent tyranny is theoretically superior and practically inferior to rule of laws and legitimate government. In doing so, we might seem to have imputed to Xenophon the misologist view that a political teaching may be "morally and politically false . . . in proportion as (it is) metaphysically true." But a pupil of Socrates must be presumed to have believed rather that nothing which is practically false can be theoretically true.[41] If Xenophon did then not seriously hold the view that beneficent tyranny is superior to rule of laws and legitimate government, why did he suggest it at all? The "tyrannical" teaching, we shall answer, serves the purpose, not of solving the problem of the best political order, but of bringing to light the nature of political things. The "theoretical" thesis which favors beneficent tyranny is indispensable in order to make clear a crucial implication of the practically and hence theoretically true thesis which favors rule of law and legitimate government. The "theoretical" thesis is a most striking expression of the problem, or of the problematic character, of law and legitimacy: legal justice is a justice which is imperfect and more or less blind, and legitimate government is not necessarily "good government" and almost certainly will not be government by the wise. Law and legitimacy are problematic from the highest point of view, namely, from that of wisdom. In so far as the city is the community kept together, nay, constituted, by law, the city cannot so much as aspire to that highest moral and intellectual level attainable by certain individuals. Hence the best city is morally and intellectually on a lower plane than the best individual.[42] The city as such exists on a lower plane than the individual as such. "Individualism" thus understood is at the bottom of Xenophon's "cosmopolitanism."

The emphasis on pleasure which characterizes the argument of the *Hiero* leads to a certain depreciation of virtue. For there is nothing in the dialogue to suggest that Simonides considered virtue intrinsically pleasant. The beneficence or virtue of the good tyrant procures for him the most noble and most blessed possession: it is not itself that possession. Simonides replaces the praise of virtue by a praise of honor. As appears from the context, this does not mean that only virtue can lead to honor. But even if it is meant this much, his praise of honor would imply that not virtue, but the reward or result of virtue, is intrinsically pleasant.[43]

Xenophon might seem to have revealed his, or his Socrates', attitude toward hedonism, however understood, in a conversation between Socrates and Aristippus which he has recorded or invented. That conversation is chiefly concerned with the unequivocal connection between love of pleasure and the rejection of the life of a ruler: the pleasure-loving Aristippus goes so far as to prefer explicitly the life of a stranger to political life in any sense. Socrates concludes the conversation by reciting a summary of Prodicus' writing on Hercules in which the pursuit of pleasure is almost identified with vice.[44] This is appropriate only if Aristippus' view is taken to imply a remarkable depreciation of virtue. It is not impossible that the historical Aristippus has served to some extent as a model for Xenophon's Simonides. To say nothing of his hedonistic teaching, he was the first of the Socratics to take pay for his teaching and he could adjust himself to places, times, and men so well that he was particularly popular with the Syracusan tyrant Dionysius.[45]

Be this as it may, the conversation referred to between Socrates and Aristippus tells us very little about Xenophon's attitude toward hedonism. After all, Socrates and Aristippus discuss almost exclusively the pleasures of the body; they barely mention the pleasures deriving from honor or praise. Besides, it would be rash to exclude the possibility that Xenophon's account of that conversation is to a certain extent ironical. That possibility is suggested by the disproportionately ample use which Socrates explicitly makes of an epideictic writing of the sophist Prodicus as an instrument of moral education.[46] Let us not forget the fact that in the only conversation between Socrates and Xenophon which is recorded in the latter's Socratic writings, Xenophon presents himself as a lover of certain sensual pleasures and as being rebuked by Socrates in much more severe terms than Aristippus ever was. This is not surprising, of course, since Xenophon is more explicit than Aristippus in praising the pursuit of sensual pleasure.[47] To point, therefore, to facts which are perhaps less ambiguous, Xenophon no more than his Simonides contends that virtue is the most blessed possession; he indicates that virtue is dependent on external goods and, far from being an end in itself, ought to be in the service of the acquisition of pleasure, wealth, and honors.[48]

At first glance, it is not altogether wrong to ascribe the same view even to Socrates. A distinguished historian did ascribe it, not only to

Xenophon's Socrates, but to Plato's as well. "D'une part, son bon sens et sa grande sagesse pratique lui font sentir qu'il doit y avoir un principe d'action supérieur à l'agréable ou au plaisir immédiat; d'autre part, quand il s'efforce de déterminer ce principe lui-même, il ne parvient pas à le distinguer de l'utile, et l'utile lui-même ne diffère pas essentiellement de l'agréable." Yet one cannot leave it at that; one has to acknowledge that Socrates' teaching is characterized by a fundamental contradiction: "Socreate recommande de pratiquer les diverses vertus à cause des avantages matériels qu'elles sont susceptibles de nous procurer; mais ces avantages il n'en jouit jamais."[49] Could Socrates, who insisted so strongly on the indispensable harmony between deed and speech completely have failed to account "by speech" for what he was revealing "by deed"? To solve the contradiction in question, one merely has to remind oneself of the distinction which Xenophon's Socrates makes silently and Plato's Socrates makes explicitly between two kinds of virtue or gentlemanliness: between common or political virtue, whose ends are wealth and honor, and true virtue which is identical with self-sufficient wisdom.[50] The fact that Socrates sometimes creates the impression that he was oblivious of true virtue, or that he mistook common virtue for true virtue, is explained by his habit of leading his discussions, as far as possible, "through the opinions accepted by human beings."[51] Thus the question of Socrates' attitude toward hedonism is reduced to the question as to whether wisdom, the highest good, is intrinsically pleasant. If we may trust Xenophon, Socrates has disclosed his answer in his last conversation: not so much wisdom, or true virtue itself, as one's consciousness of one's progress in wisdom or virtue, affords the highest pleasure.[52] Thus Socrates ultimately leaves no doubt as to the fundamental difference between the good and the pleasant. No man can be simply wise; therefore, not wisdom, but progress toward wisdom is the highest good for man. Wisdom cannot be separated from self-knowledge; therefore, progress toward wisdom will be accompanied by awareness of that progress. And that awareness is necessarily pleasant. This whole—the progress and the awareness of it—is both the best and the most pleasant thing for man. It is in this sense that the highest good is intrinsically pleasant. Concerning the thesis that the most choiceworthy thing must be intrinsically pleasant, there is then no difference between the historical Simonides, Xenophon's Simonides, and Xenophon's Socrates, and, indeed, Plato's Socrates.[53] Nor is this all. There is even an important agreement between Xenophon's Simonides and his Socrates as regards the object of the highest pleasure. For what else is the pleasant consciousness of one's progress in wisdom or virtue but one's reasonable and deserved satisfaction with, and even admiration of,[54] oneself? The difference between Socrates and Simonides seems then to be that Socrates is not at all concerned with being admired or praised by others, whereas Simonides is concerned exclusively with it. To reduce this difference to its proper proportions, it is well to remember that Simonides' statement on praise or honor is meant to serve a pedagogical function. The *Hiero* does not supply us then with the most adequate formulation of Xenophon's view regarding the relation of pleasure and virtue. But it is the only writing of Xenophon which has the merit, and even the function, of posing the problem of that relation in its most radical form: in the form of the question as to whether the demands of virtue cannot be completely replaced by, or reduced to, the desire for pleasure, if for the highest pleasure.

VII

Piety and Law

After advising the democratic rulers of Athens how they could overcome the necessity under which they found themselves of acting unjustly, Xenophon reminds them of the limitations of his advice, and, indeed, of all human advice, by giving them the additional advice to inquire of the gods in Dodona and in Delphi whether the reforms suggested by him would be salutary to the city both now and in the future. Yet even divine approval of his suggestions would not suffice. He gives the Athenians the crowning advice, in case the gods should approve of his suggestions, that they further ask the gods to which of the gods they ought to sacrifice in order to be successful. Divine approval and divine assistance seem to be indispensable for salutary political action. These remarks must be of special interest to the interpreter of the *Hiero* on account of the place where they occur in the *Corpus Xenophonteum*, for they occur at the end of the *Ways and Means*.[1] Still, their content cannot be surprising to any reader of our author: pious sentiments are expressed, more or less forcefully, in all those of his writings in which he speaks in his own or in Socrates' name.

One of the most surprising features of the *Hiero*, i.e., of the only work of Xenophon in which he never speaks in the first person, is its complete silence about piety. Simonides never mentions piety. He does not say a word about the advisability of asking any gods whether his suggestions regarding the improvement of tyrannical rule would be salutary. Nor does he remind Hiero of the need of divine assistance. He does not admonish him in any way to worship the gods.[2] Hiero, too, is silent about piety. In particular, when enumerating the various virtues, he was almost compelled to mention piety: he fails to do so.

103

It might seem that this silence is sufficiently explained by the subject matter of the work. The tyrant, and indeed any absolute ruler, may be said to usurp honors rightfully belonging to the gods alone.[3] Yet the *Hiero* deals, not so much with how tyrants usually live, as with how tyranny can best be preserved or rather improved. If we may believe Aristotle, piety is rather more necessary for preserving and improving tyrannical government than it is for the preservation and improvement of any other political order. We might be inclined to credit Xenophon with the same view, since he indicates that the regime of Cyrus became the more pious in proportion as it became more absolute.[4] But Cyrus is not a tyrant strictly speaking. According to Xenophon, tyranny is in any case rule without laws, and according to his Socrates, piety is knowledge of the laws concerning the gods:[5] where there are no laws, there cannot be piety. However, the identification of piety with knowledge of the laws concerning the gods is not Xenophon's last word on the subject. In his final characterization of Socrates he says that Socrates was so pious that he would do nothing without the consent of the gods. When he describes how Socrates made his companions pious, he shows how he led them to a recognition of divine providence by making them consider the purposeful character of the universe and its parts.[6] It seems, then, that just as he admits a translegal justice, although his Socrates identifies justice with legality, so he admits a piety which emerges out of the contemplation of nature and which has no necessary relation to law; a piety, that is, whose possibility is virtually denied by the definition suggested by his Socrates. We shall conclude that the silence of the *Hiero* about piety cannot be fully explained by the subject matter of the work. For a full explanation one would have to consider the conversational situation, the fact that the *Hiero* is a dialogue between an educated tyrant and a wise man who is not a citizen-philosopher.

While the *Hiero* is silent about piety, it is not silent about the gods. But the silence about piety is reflected in what it says, or does not say, about the gods. In the sentence with which he concludes his statement about friendship, Hiero uses an expression which is reminiscent of an expression used in a similar context by Ischomachus in the *Oeconomicus*. Hiero speaks of those who are born by nature, and at the same time compelled by law, to love. Whereas Hiero speaks of a cooperation of nature and law, Ischomachus speaks of a cooperation of the god (or the gods) and law.[7] Hiero replaces "the god" or "the gods" by "nature." Xenophon's Simonides never corrects him. He seems to be the same Simonides who is said repeatedly to have postponed and finally abandoned the attempt to answer the question which Hiero had posed him, What is God?[8] It is true, both Hiero and Simonides mention "the gods," but there is no apparent connection between what they say about "nature" and what they say about "the gods."[9] It is possible that what they mean by "the gods" is chance rather than "nature" or the origin of the natural order.[10]

The practical bearing of the difference between Ischomachus' and Hiero's statements appears from the different ways in which they describe the cooperation of gods or nature and law in the parallel passages cited. Ischomachus says that a certain order which has been established by the gods is at the same time praised by the law. Hiero says that men are prompted by nature to a certain action or feeling, to which they are at the same time compelled by the law. Ischomachus, who traces the natural order to the gods, describes the specific work of the law as praising; Hiero who does not take that step, describes it as compelling. One's manner of understanding and evaluating the man-made law depends then on one's manner of understanding the order which is not man-made and which is only confirmed by the law. If the natural order is traced to the gods, the compulsory character of the law recedes into the background. Conversely, the law as such is less likely to appear as an immediate source of pleasure if one does not go beyond the natural order itself. The law assumes a higher dignity if the universe is of divine origin. The notion linking "praise" and "gods" is gentlemanliness. Praise as distinguished from compulsion suffices for the guidance of gentlemen, and the gods delight at gentlemanliness.[11] As we have seen, Hiero's and Simonides' gentlemanliness is not altogether beyond doubt. Ischomachus, on the other hand, who traces the natural order to the gods and who describes in the cited passage the work of the law as praising, is the gentleman *par excellence*. What the attitude of the citizen-philosopher Socrates was can be ascertained only by a comprehensive and detailed analysis of Xenophon's Socratic writings.

Notes to
On Tyranny

Introduction

1. Compare *Social Research*, v. 13, 1946, pp. 123–124.—Hobbes, *Leviathan*, "A Review and Conclusion" (ed. by A. R. Waller, p. 523): " . . . the name of Tyranny, signifieth nothing more, nor lesse, than the name of Sovereignty, be it in one, or many men, saving that they that use the former word, are understood to be angry with them they call Tyrants. . . ."—Montesquieu, *De l'Esprit des Lois*, XI 9: "L'embarras d'Aristote paraît visiblement quand il traite de la monarchie. Il en établit cinq espèces: il ne les distingue pas par la forme de la constitution, mais par des choses d'accident, comme les vertus ou les vices des princes. . . ."

2. *Principe*, ch. 15, beginning; *Discorsi* I, beginning.

3. The most important reference to the *Cyropaedia* occurs in the *Principe*. It occurs a few lines before the passage in which Machiavelli expresses his intention to break with the whole tradition (ch. 14, toward the end). The *Cyropaedia* is clearly referred to in the *Discorsi* at least four times. If I am not mistaken, Machiavelli mentions Xenophon in the *Principe* and in the *Discorsi* more frequently than he does Plato, Aristotle, and Cicero taken together.

4. *Discorsi* II 2.

5. Classical political science took its bearings by man's perfection or by how men ought to live, and it culminated in the description of the best political order. Such an order was meant to be one whose realization was possible without a miraculous or nonmiraculous change in human nature, but its realization was not considered probable, because it was thought to depend on chance. Machiavelli attacks this view both by demanding that one should take one's bearings, not by how men ought to live but by how they actually live, and by suggesting that chance could or should be controlled. It is this attack which laid the foundation for all specifically modern political thought. The concern with a guarantee for the realization of the "ideal" led to both a lowering of the standards of political life and to the emergence of "philosophy of history": even the modern opponents of Machiavelli could not restore the sober view of the classics regarding the relation of "ideal" and "reality."

I. The Problem

1. *Hiero* 1.8–10; 2.3–6; 3.3–6; 8.1–7; 11.7–15.

2. *Memorabilia* II 1.21; *Cyropaedia* VIII 2.12. Compare Aristotle, *Politics* 1325a 34 ff. and Euripides, *Phoenissae* 524–5.

106

3. *Memorabilia* I 2.56.

4. *Hiero* 1.1; 2.5.

5. *Hiero* 8.1. Compare *Memorabilia* IV 2.23–24 with *ibid.* 16–17.

6. *Hiero* 1.14–15; 7.2. Compare Plato, *Seventh Letter* 332d6–7 and Isocrates, *To Nicocles* 3–4.

II. The Title and the Form

1. How necessary it is to consider carefully the titles of Xenophon's writings is shown most clearly by the difficulties presented by the titles of the *Anabasis*, of the *Cyropaedia* and, though less obviously, of the *Memorabilia*. Regarding the title of the *Hiero*, see also IV note 50, below.

2. There is only one more writing of Xenophon which would seem to serve the purpose of teaching a skill, the π. ἱππικῆς; we cannot discuss here the question why it is not entitled Ἱππικός. The purpose of the *Cyropaedia* is theoretical rather than practical, as appears from the first chapter of the work.

3. Compare *Cyropaedia* I 3.18 with Plato, *Theages* 124e11–125e7 and *Amatores* 138b15 ff.

4. *De vectigalibus* 1.1. Compare *Memorabilia* IV 4.11–12 and *Symposium* 4. 1–2.

5. *Hiero* 4.9–11; 7.10, 12; 8.10; 10.8; 11.1.

6. *Memorabilia* I 2.9–11; III 9.10; IV 6.12 (compare IV 4). *Oeconomicus* 21.12. *Resp. Lac.* 10.7; 15.7–8. *Agesilaus* 7.2. *Hellenica* VI 4.33–35; VII 1.46 (compare V 4.1; VII 3.7–8). The opening sentence of the *Cyropaedia* implies that tyranny is the least stable regime. (See Aristotle, *Politics* 1315b10 ff.).

7. *Hiero* 4.5. *Hellenica* V 4.9, 13; VI 4.32. Compare *Hiero* 7.10 with *Hellenica* VII 3.7. See also Isocrates, *Nicocles* 24.

8. Plato, *Republic* 393C11.

9. *Memorabilia* III 4.7–12; 6.14; IV 2.11.

10. *Oeconomicus* 1.23; 4.2–19; 5.13–16; 6.5–10; 8.4–8; 9.13–15; 13.4–5; 14.3–10, 20.6–9; 21.2–12. The derogatory remark on tyrants at the end of the work is a fitting conclusion for a writing devoted to the royal art as such. Since Plato shares the "Socratic" view according to which the political art is not essentially different from the economic art, one may also say that it can only be due to secondary considerations that his *Politicus* is not entitled *Oeconomicus*.

11. *Memorabilia* IV 6.12.

12. *Apologia Socratis* 34.

13. *Memorabilia* I 2.31 ff.; III 7.5–6.

14. Plato, *Hipparchus* 228b–c (cf. 229b). Aristotle, *Resp. Athen.* 18.1.

15. Plato, *Second Letter* 310e5 ff.

16. *Memorabilia* I 5.6.

17. Aristophanes, *Pax* 698–9. Aristotle, *Rhetoric* 1391a8–11; 1405b24–28. See also Plato, *Hipparchus* 228c. Lessing called Simonides the Greek Voltaire.

18. *Oeconomicus* 6.4; 2.2, 12 ff. Compare *Memorabilia* IV 7.1 with *ibid.* III 1.1 ff. Compare *Anabasis* VI 1.23 with *ibid.* I 10.12.

19. *Hiero* 9.7–11; 11.4, 13–14, Compare *Oeconomicus* 1.15.

20. *Hiero* 1.2, 10; 2.6.

21. Note the almost complete absence of proper names from the *Hiero*. The only proper name that occurs in the work (apart, of course, from the names of Hiero, Simonides, Zeus, and the Greeks) is that of Daïlochus, Hiero's favorite. George

Grote, *Plato and the other companions of Socrates* (London, 1888, v. I, 222), makes the following just remark: "When we read the recommendations addressed by Simonides, teaching Hiero how he might render himself popular, we perceive at once that they are alike well intentioned and ineffectual. Xenophon could neither find any real Grecian despot correspondingly to this portion . . . nor coud he invent one with any show of plausibility." Grote continues, however, as follows: "He was forced to resort to other countries and other habits different from those of Greece. To this necessity probably we owe the Cyropaedia." For the moment, it suffices to remark that, according to Xenophon, Cyrus is not a tyrant but a king. Grote's error is due to the identification of "tyrant" with "despot."

22. Simonides barely alludes to the mortality of Hiero or of tyrants in general (*Hiero* 10.4): Hiero, being a tyrant, must be supposed to live in perpetual fear of assassination. Compare especially *Hiero* 11.7, end, with *Agesilaus* 9.7 end. Compare also *Hiero* 7.2 and 7.7 ff. as well as 8.3 ff. (the ways of honoring people) with *Hellenica* VI 1.6 (honoring by solemnity of burial). Cf. *Hiero* 11.7, 15 with Plato, *Republic* 465d2–e2.

III. The Setting

A. THE CHARACTERS AND THEIR INTENTIONS

1. *Hiero* 1.12; 2.8. Compare Plato, *Republic* 579b3–c3.
2. Aristotle, *Rhetoric* 1391a8–11.
3. *Hiero* 1.13; 6.13; 11.10.
4. *Memorabilia* I 2.33. *Oeconomicus* 7.2. *Cyropaedia* I 4.13; III 1.14; VIII 4.9.
5. *Hiero* 1.1–2.
6. Aristotle, *Politics* 1311a4–5. Compare the thesis of Callicles in Plato's *Gorgias*.
7. Observe the repeated εἰκός in *Hiero* 1.1–2. The meaning of this indication is revealed by what happens during the conversation. In order to know better than Simonides how the two ways of life differ in regard to pleasures and pains, Hiero would have to possess actual knowledge of both ways of life; i.e., Hiero must not have forgotten the pleasures and pains characteristic of private life; yet Hiero suggests that he does not remember them sufficiently (1.3). Furthermore, knowledge of the difference in question is acquired by means of calculation or reasoning (1.11, 3), and the calculation required presupposes knowledge of the different value, or of the different degree of importance, of the various kinds of pleasure and pain; yet Hiero has to learn from Simonides that some kinds of pleasure are of minor importance as compared with others (2.1; 7.3–4). Besides, in order to know better than Simonides the difference in question, Hiero would have to possess at least as great a power of calculating or reasoning as Simonides; yet Simonides shows that Hiero's alleged knowledge of the difference (a knowledge which he had not acquired but with the assistance of Simonides) is based on the fatal disregard of a most relevant factor (8.1–7). The thesis that a man who has experienced both ways of life knows the manner of their difference better than he who has experienced only one of them is then true only if important qualifications are added; in itself, it is the result of an enthymeme and merely plausible.

8. *Hiero* 1.8, 14, 16. Simonides says that tyrants are universally admired or envied (1.9), and he implies that the same is of course not true of private men as such. His somewhat more reserved statements in 2.1–2 and 7.1–4 about specific kinds of pleasure must be understood, to begin with, in the light of his general statement about

all kinds of pleasure in 1.8. The statement that Simonides makes in 2.1–2 is understood by Hiero in the light of Simonides' general statement, as appears from 2.3–5; 4.6; and 6.12. (Compare also 8.7 with 3.3.) For the interpretation of Simonides' initial question, consider Isocrates, *To Nicocles* 4–5.

9. *Hiero* 2.3–5. One should also not forget the fact that the author of the *Hiero* never was a tyrant. Compare Plato, *Republic* 577a-b and *Gorgias* 470d5–e11.

10. *Memorabilia* I 3.2; IV 8.6; 5.9–10. Compare *Anabasis* VI 1.17–21.

11. *Memorabilia* IV 6.1, 7; III 3.11; I 2.14.

12. *Hiero* 1.21, 31.

13. Compare *Hiero* 11.5–6 and *Agesilaus* 9.6–7 with Pindar, *Ol.* I and *Pyth*. I–III.

14. *Hiero* 1.14. The same rule of conduct was observed by Socrates. Compare the manner in which he behaved when talking to the "legislators" Critias and Charicles, with his open blame of the Thirty which he pronounced "somewhere," i.e., not in the presence of the tyrants, and which had to be "reported" to Critias and Charicles (*Memorabilia* I 2.32–38; observe the repetition of ἀπαγγελθέντος). In Plato's *Protagoras* (345e–346b8) Socrates excuses Simonides for having praised tyrants under compulsion.

15. *Hiero* 1.9–10, 16–17; 2.3–5.

16. *Hiero* 1.10; 8.1.

17. *Hiero* 2.3–5.

18. While all men consider tyrants enviable, while the multitude is deceived by the outward splendor of tyrants, the multitude does not wish to be ruled by tyrants but rather by the just. Compare *Hiero* 2.3–5 with *ibid*. 5.1 and 4.5. Compare Plato, *Republic* 344b5–c1.

19. Compare the end of the *Oeconomicus* with *ibid*. 6.12 ff. See also *Memorabilia* II 6.22 ff.

20. *Hiero* 5.1; 1.1.

21. *Hiero* 6.5. Aristotle, *Politics* 1314a10–13.

22. *Hiero* 4.2. See note 14 above.

23. *Hiero* 5.1–2.

24. Hiero mentions "contriving something bad and base" in 4.10, i.e., almost immediately before the crucial passage. Compare also 1.22–23.

25. *Memorabilia* I 2.31; IV 2.33; *Symposium* 6.6. *Apologia Socratis* 20–21. *Cyropaedia* III 1.39. Compare Plato, *Apol. Socr.* 23d4–7 and 28a6–b1, as well as *Seventh Letter* 344c1–3.

26. *Memorabilia* I 6.12–13.

27. Compare *Oeconomicus* 6.12 ff. and 11.1 ff with *Memorabilia* I 1.16 and IV 6.7. Compare Plato, *Republic* 489e3–490a3. The distinction between the two meanings of "gentleman" corresponds to the Platonic distinction between common or political virtue and genuine virtue.

28. *Cyropaedia* I 1.1. *Memorabilia* I 2.56; 6.11–12. Compare *Memorabilia* IV 2.33 with *Sympoisum* 3.4. See Plato, *Seventh Letter* 333b3 ff. and 334a1–3 as well as *Gorgias* 468e6–9 and 469c3 (cf. 492d2–3); also *Republic* 493a6 ff.

29. *Memorabilia* I 2.31 ff.; IV 4.3. *Symposium* 4.13. Compare Plato, *Apol. Socr.* 20e8–21a3 and 32c4–d8 as well as *Gorgias* 480e6 ff.; also *Protagoras* 329e2–330a2. Cf. note 14 above.

30. *Hellenica* IV 4.6. Compare *Symposium* 3.4.

31. Whereas Hiero asserts that the tyrant is unjust, he does not say that he is foolish. Whereas he asserts that the entourage of the tyrant consists of the unjust, the

intemperate, and the servile, he does not say that it consists of fools. Consider the lack of correspondence between the virtues mentioned in *Hiero* 5.1. and the vices mentioned in 5.2. Moreover, by proving that he is wiser than the wise Simonides, Hiero proves that the tyrant may be wise indeed.

32. According to Xenophon's Socrates, he who possesses the specific knowledge required for ruling well is *eo ipso* a ruler (*Memorabilia* III 9.10; 1.4). Hence he who possesses the tyrannical art is *eo ipso* a tyrant. From Xenophon's point of view, Hiero's distrust of Simonides is an ironic reflection of the Socratic truth. It is ironic for the following reason: From Xenophon's point of view, the wise teacher of the royal art, or of the tyrannical art, is not a potential ruler in the ordinary sense of the term, because he who knows how to rule does not necessarily wish to rule. Even Hiero grants by implication that the just do not wish to rule, or that they wish merely to mind their own business (*cf. Hiero* 5.1 with *Memorabilia* I 2.48 and II 9.1). If the wise man is necessarily just, the wise teacher of the tyrannical art will not wish to be a tyrant. But it is precisely the necessary connection between wisdom and justice which is questioned by Hiero's distinction between the wise and the just.

33. *Hiero* 2.3–5 (compare the wording with that used *ibid.* 1.9 and in *Cyropaedia* IV 2.28). It should be emphasized that in this important passage Hiero does not speak explicitly of wisdom. (His only explicit remark on wisdom occurs in the central passage, in 5.1). Furthermore, Hiero silently qualifies what he says about happiness in 2.3–5 in a later passage (7.9–10) where he admits that bliss requires outward or visible signs.

34. *Hiero* 2.6; 1.10.

35. Hiero states at the beginning that Simonides is a wise *man* (ἀνήρ); but as Simonides explains in 7.3–4, [real] men (ἄνδρες) as distinguished from [ordinary] human beings (ἄνθρωποι) are swayed by ambition and hence apt to aspire to tyrannical power. (The ἀνδρὸς at the end of 1.1 corresponds to the ἀνθρώποις at the end of 1.2. Cf. also 7.9 beginning.) Shortly after the beginning, Hiero remarks that Simonides is "at present still a private man" (1.3), thus implying that he might well become a tyrant. Accordingly, Hiero speaks only once of "you [private men]," whereas Simonides speaks fairly frequently of "you [tyrants]": Hiero hesitates to consider Simonides as merely a private man (6.10. The "you" in 2.5 refers to the reputedly wise men as distinguished from the multitude. Simonides speaks of "you tyrants" in the following passages: 1.14, 16, 24, 26; 2.2; 7.2, 4; 8.7). For the distinction between "real men" and "ordinary human beings," compare also *Anabasis* I 7.4; *Cyropaedia* IV 2.25; V 5.33; Plato, *Republic* 550a1; *Protagoras* 316c5–317b5.

36. *Hiero* 1.9; 6.12. ζηλόω, the term used by Simonides and later on by Hiero, designates jealousy, the noble counterpart of envy rather than envy proper (cf. Aristotle, *Rhetoric* II 11). That the tyrant is exposed to envy in the strict sense of the term appears from Hiero's remark in 7.10 and from Simonides' emphatic promise at the end of the dialogue: the tyrant who has become the benefactor of his subjects will be happy without being envied. Cf. also 11.6, where it is implied that a tyrant like Hiero is envied (cf. note 13 above). In *Hiero* 1.9, Simonides avoids speaking of "envy" because the term might suggest that all men bear ill-will to the tyrant, and this implication would spoil completely the effect of his statement. Hiero's statement in 6.12, which refers not only to 1.9 but to 2.2 as well, amounts to a correction of what Simonides had said in the former passage; Hiero suggests that not all men, but only men like Simonides, are jealous of the tyrant's wealth and power. As for Simonides' distinction (in 1.9) between "all men" who are jealous of tyrants and the "many" who desire to be tyrants, it has to be understood as follows: many who consider a thing an enviable

possession do not seriously desire it, because they are convinced of their inability to acquire it. Compare Aristotle, *Politics* 1311a29–31 and 1313a17–23.

37. By using the tyrant's fear as a means for his betterment, Simonides acts in accordance with a pedagogic principle of Xenophon; see *Hipparchicus* 1.8; *Memorabilia* III 5.5–6; *Cyropaedia* III 1.23–24.

38. Compare *Hiero* 1.14 with 1.16. Note the emphatic character of Simonides' assent to Hiero's reply. (1.16, beginning). Compare also 2.2 with 11.2–5.

39. Compare *Hiero* 4.5 with *Hellenica* VI 4.32 and VII 3.4–6.

40. Compare *Hiero* 6.14 with *Hellenica* VII 3.12.

41. Compare *Hiero* 6.1–3 with *Cyropaedia* I 3.10, 18.

42. Compare *Hiero* 8.6 with *ibid.* 2.1. The statement is not contradicted by Hiero; it is prepared, and thus to a certain extent confirmed, by what Hiero says in 1.27 (Νῦν δή) and 1.29. In 7.5, Hiero indicates that agreement had been reached between him and Simonides on the subject of sex.

43. *Hiero* 2.12–18.

44. By showing this, Hiero elaborates what we may call the gentleman's image of the tyrant. Xenophon pays a great compliment to Hiero's education by entrusting to him the only elaborate presentation of the gentleman's view of tyranny which he ever wrote. Compare p. 31 above on the relation between the *Hiero* and the *Agesilaus*. The relation of Hiero's indictment of tyranny to the true account of tyranny can be compared to the relation of the Athenian story about the family of Pisistratus to Thucydides' "exact" account. One may also compare it to the relation of the *Agesilaus* to the corresponding sections of the *Hellenica*.

45. *Memorabilia* IV 4.10. *Agesilaus* 1.6. As for the purpose of the *Hellenica*, compare IV 8.1 and V 1.4 with II 3.56 as well as with *Symposium* 1.1 and *Cyropaedia* VIII 7.24.

46. *Memorabilia* I 2.58–61. While Xenophon denies the charge that Socrates had interpreted the verses in question in a particularly obnoxious manner, he does not deny the fact that Socrates frequently quoted the verses. Why Socrates liked them, or how he interpreted them, is indicated *ibid.* IV 6.13–15: Socrates used two types of dialectics, one which leads to the truth and another which, by never leaving the dimension of generally accepted opinions, leads to (political) agreement. For the interpretation of the passage, compare *Symposium* 4.59–60 with *ibid.* 4.56–58.

47. *Symposium* 3.6. Compare Plato, *Republic* 378d6–8 and a1–6.

48. To summarize our argument, we shall say that if Hiero is supposed to state the truth or even merely to be completely frank, the whole *Hiero* becomes unintelligible. If one accepts either supposition, one will be compelled to agree with the following criticism by Ernst Richter ("Xenophon-Studien," *Fleckeisen's Jahrbücher für classische Philologie*, 19. Supplementband, 1893, 149): "Einem solchen Manne, der sich so freimüthig über sich selbst äussert, und diese lobenswerten Gesinnungen hegt, möchte man kaum die Schreckensthaten zutrauen, die er als von der Tyrannen-herrschaft unzertrennlich hinstellt. Hat er aber wirklich soviel Menschen getötet und übt er täglich noch soviel Übelthaten aus, ist für ihn wirklich das Beste der Strick—und er musste es ja wissen—, so kommen die Ermahnungen des Simonides in zweiten Teil ganz gewiss zu spät. . . . Simonides gibt Ratschläge, wie sie nur bei einem Fürsten vom Schlage des Kyros oder Agesilaos angebracht sind, nie aber bei einem Tyrannen, wie ihn Hieron beschreibt, der schon gar nicht mehr weiss, wie er sich vor seinen Todfeinden schützen kann." Not to repeat what we have said in the text, the quick transition from Hiero's indictment of the tyrant's injustice (7.7–13) to his remark that

the tyrants punish the unjust (8.9) is unintelligible but for the fact that his account is exaggerated. If one supposes then that Hiero exaggerates, one has to wonder why he exaggerates. Now, Hiero himself makes the following assertions: that the tyrants trust no one; that they fear the wise; that Simonides is a real man; and |that Simonides admires, or is jealous of, the tyrants' power. These assertions of Hiero supply us with the only authentic clue to the riddle of the dialogue. Some of the assertions referred to are without doubt as much suspect of being exaggerated as almost all other assertions of Hiero. But this very fact implies that they contain an element of truth, or that they are true if taken with a grain of salt.

B. THE ACTION OF THE DIALOGUE

1. *Hiero* 1.3. As for the duration of Hiero's reign, see Aristotle, *Politics* 1315b35 ff. and Diodorus Siculus XI 38. Hiero shows later on (*Hiero* 6.1–2) that he recalls very well certain pleasures of private men of which he had not been reminded by Simonides.

2. *Hiero* 1.4–5. The "we" in "we all know" in 1.4 refers of course to private men and tyrants alike. Compare 1.29 and 10.4.

3. *Hiero* 1.4–6. To begin with, i.e., before Simonides has aroused his opposition, Hiero does not find any difference between tyrants and private men in regard to sleep (1.7). Later on, in an entirely different conversational situation, Hiero takes up "the pleasures of private men of which the tyrant is deprived"; in that context, while elaborating the gentleman's image of the tyrant (with which Simonides must be presumed to have been familiar from the outset), Hiero speaks in the strongest terms of the difference between tyrants and private men in regard to the enjoyment of sleep (6.3, 7–10).

4. Twelve out of fifteen classes of pleasant or painful things are unambiguously of a bodily nature. The three remaining classes are (1) the good things, (2) the bad things, and (3) sleep. As for the good and the bad things, Simonides says that they please or pain us sometimes through the working of the soul alone and sometimes through that of the soul and the body together. As regards sleep, he leaves open the question by means of what kind of organ or faculty we enjoy it.

5. Compare *Hiero* 2.1 and 7.3 with *Memorabilia* II 1.

6. *Hiero* 1.19. Compare Isocrates, *To Nicocles* 4.

7. Compare *Hiero* 4.8–9 with *Memorabilia* IV 2.37–38.

8. *Hiero* 1.7–10. Hiero's oath in 1.10 is the first oath occurring in the dialogue. Hiero uses the emphatic form μὰ τὸν Δία.

9. See in *Hiero* 1.10 the explicit reference to the order of Simonides' enumeration.

10. The proof is based on λογισμός, i.e., on a comparison of data that are supplied by experience or observation. Compare *Hiero* 1.11 (λογιζόμενος εὑρίσκω) with the reference to ἐμπειρία in 1.10. Compare *Memorabilia* IV 3.11 and *Hellenica* VII 4.2.

11. The passage consists of five parts: (1) "sights" (Hiero contributes 163 words, Simonides is silent); (2) "sounds" (Hiero 36 words, Simonides 68 words); (3) "food" (Hiero 230 words, Simonides 76 words); (4) "odors" (Hiero is silent, Simonides 32 words); (5) "sex" (Hiero 411 words, Simonides 42 words). Hiero is most vocal concerning "sex"; Simonides is most vocal concerning "food."

12. Compare III A, note 42, and III B, notes 11 and 19. As for the connection between sexual love and tyranny, cf. Plato, *Republic* 573e6-7, 574e2 and 575a1–2.

13. *Hiero* 1.31–33.

14. Compare *Hiero* 1.16 with the parallels in 1.14, 24, 26.

15. Simonides' first oath (μὰ τὸν Δία) occurs in the passage dealing with sounds, i.e., with praise (1.16).

16. Rudolf Hirzel, *Der Dialog*, I. Leipzig, 1895, 171, notes "die geringe Lebendigkeit des Gesprächs, die vorherrschende Neigung zu längeren Vorträgen": all the more striking is the character of the discussion of "food."

17. Simonides grants this by implication in *Hiero* 1.26.

18. Mr. Marchant (Xenophon, *Scripta Minora*, *Loeb's Classical Library*, XV-XVI) says: "There is no attempt at characterization in the persons of the dialogue. . . . The remark of the poet at c.1.22 is singularly inappropriate to a man who had a liking for good living." In the passage referred to, Simonides declares that "acid, pungent, astringent and kindred things" are "very unnatural for human beings": he says nothing at all against "sweet and kindred things." The view that bitter, acid, etc., things are "against nature," was shared by Plato (*Timaeus* 65c–66c), by Aristotle (*Eth. Nic.* 1153a5–6; cf. *De anima* 422b 10–14) and, it seems, by Alcmæon (cf. Aristotle, *Metaphysics* 986a22–34). Moreover, Simonides says that acid, pungent, etc., things are unnatural for "human beings"; but "human beings" may have to be understood in contradistinction to "real men" (cf. III A, note 35 above). At any rate, the fare censured by Simonides is recommended as a fare for soldiers by Cyrus in a speech addressed to "real men" (*Cyropaedia* VI 2.31). (Compare also *Symposium* 4.9). Above all, Marchant who describes the *Hiero* as "a naive little work, not unattractive," somewhat naively overlooks the fact that Simonides' utterances serve primarily the purpose, not of characterizing Simonides, but of influencing Hiero; they characterize the poet in a more subtle way than the one which alone is considered by Marchant: the fact that Simonides indicates, or fails to indicate, his likes or dislikes according to the requirements of his pedagogic intentions, characterizes him as wise.

19. *Hiero* 1.26. "Sex" is the only motive of which Simonides ever explicitly says that it could be the only motive for desiring tyrannical power. Compare note 12 above.

20. *Hiero* 7.5–6.

21. *Hiero* 8.6.

22. Note the increased emphasis on "(real) men" in *Hiero* 2.1. In the parallel passage of the first section (1.9), Simonides had spoken of "most able (real) men." Compare the corresponding change of emphasis in Hiero's replies (see the following note).

23. Compare *Hiero* 1.16–17 with 2.1, where Simonides declares that the bodily pleasures appear to him to be very minor things and that, as he observes, many of those who are reputed to be real men do not attach any great value to those pleasures. Hiero's general statement in 2.3–5, which is so much stronger than his corresponding statement in the first section (1.10), amounts to a tacit rejection of Simonides' claim: Hiero states that the view expressed by Simonides in 2.1–2, far from being nonvulgar, is *the* vulgar view.

24. *Hiero* 2.1–2. Simonides does not explicitly speak of "wealth and power." "Wealth and power" had been mentioned by Hiero in 1.27. (Compare Aristotle, *Politics* 1311a8–12.) On the basis of Simonides' initial enumeration (1.4–6), one would expect that the second section (ch. 2–6) would deal with the three kinds of pleasure that had not been discussed in the first section, *viz.* the objects perceived by the whole body, the good and bad things, and sleep. Only good and bad things and, to a lesser degree, sleep are clearly discernible as subjects of the second section. As for good and bad things, see the following passages: 2.6–7, 3.1, 3, 5; 4.1; 5.2, 4. (Compare also 2.2 with *Anabasis* III 1.19–20.) As for sleep, see 6.3–9. As for objects

perceived by the whole body, compare 1.5 and 2.2 with *Memorabilia* III 8.8–9 and 10.13. Sleep (the last item of the initial enumeration) is not yet mentioned in the retrospective summary at the beginning of the second section, whereas it is mentioned in the parallel at the beginning of the third section (cf. 2.1 with 7.3); in this manner Xenophon indicates that the discussion of the subjects mentioned in the initial enumeration is completed at the end of the second section: the third section deals with an entirely new subject.

25. Simonides merely intimates it, for he does not say in so many words that "they aspire to greater things, to power and wealth." Taken by itself, the statement with which Simonides opens the second section is much less far-reaching than the statements with which he had opened the discussion of the first section (1.8–9, 16). But one has to understand the later statement in the light of the earlier ones, if one wants to understand the conversational situation. Compare III A, note 8 above.

26. Simonides fails to mention above all the field or farm which occupies the central position among the objects desired by private men (*Hiero* 4.7) and whose cultivation is praised by Socrates as a particularly pleasant possession (*Oeconomicus* 5.11). Compare also *Hiero* 11.1–4 with *ibid*. 4.7 and *Memorabilia* III 11.4. Simonides pushes into the background the pleasures of private men who limit themselves to minding their own business instead of being swayed by political ambition (see *Memorabilia* I. 2.48 and II 9.1). Farming is a skill of peace (*Oeconomicus* 4.12 and 1.17). Simonides also fails to mention dogs (compare *Hiero* 2.2 with *Agesilaus* 9.6). Compare *De vectigalibus* 4.8.

27. Whereas we find in the first section an explicit reference to the order of Simonides' enumeration (1.10), no such reference occurs in the second section. In the second section Hiero refers only once explicitly to the statement with which Simonides had opened the section, i.e., to 2.1–2; he does this, however, only after (and in fact almost immediately after) Simonides has made his only contribution to the discussion of the second section (6.12–13). An obvious, although implicit, reference to 2.2 occurs in 4.6–7. (Cf. especially the θᾶττον . . . . . . κατεργάζεσθαι in 4.7 with the ταχυ κατεργάζεσθε in 2.2). The αυτίκα in 2.7 (peace-war) refers to the last item mentioned in 2.2 (enemies-friends). These references merely underline the deviation of Hiero's speech from Simonides' enumeration. Simonides' silence is emphasized by Xenophon's repeated mention of the fact that Simonides has been listening to Hiero's speeches, i.e., that Simonides had not spoken (see 6.9; 7.1, 11). There is no mention of Hiero's listening to Simonides' statements.

28. See note 25 above.

29. As for Simonides, see p. 33 above. Hiero's concern with wealth is indicated by the fact that, deviating from Simonides, he explicitly mentions the receiving of gifts among the signs of honor (compare 7.7–9 with 7.2). To comply with Hiero's desire, Simonides promises him later on (11.12) gifts among other things. Compare Aristotle, *Politics* 1311a8 ff. and note 74 below. Consider also the emphatic use of "possession" in Simonides' final promise. Simonides' silence about love of gain as distinguished from love of honor (compare *Hiero* 7.1–4 with *Oeconomicus* 14.9–10) is remarkable. It appears from *Hiero* 9.11 and 11.12–13 that the same measures which would render the tyrant honored, would render him rich as well.

30. Friendship as discussed by Hiero in ch. 3 is something different from "helping friends" which is mentioned by Simonides in 2.2. The latter topic is discussed by Hiero in 6.12–13.

31. Compare 2.8 with 1.11–12; 3.7–9 with 1.38; 3.8 and 4.1–2 with 1.27–29; 4.2 with 1.17–25. In the cited passages of ch. 1, as distinguished from the parallels in ch. 2 ff., no mention of "killing of tyrants" occurs. Compare also the insistence on the moral depravity of the tyrant, or on his injustice, in the second section (5.1–2 and 4.11) with the only mention of "injustice" in the first section (1.12): in the first section only the "injustice" *suffered* by tyrants is mentioned. As regards, 1.36, see note 41 below.

32. Marchant (*loc. cit*, XVI) remarks that Xenophon "makes no attempt anywhere to represent the courtier poet; had he done so he must have made Simonides bring in the subject of verse panegyrics on princes at c. I.14." It is hard to judge this suggested improvement on the *Hiero* since Marchant does not tell us how far the remark on verse panegyrics on princes would have been more conducive than what Xenophon's Simonides actually says toward the achievement of Simonides' aim. Besides, compare *Hiero* 9.4 with 9.2. We read in Macauley's essay on Frederick the Great: "Nothing can be conceived more whimsical than the conferences which took place between the first literary man and the first practical man of the age, whom a strange weakness had induced to exchange their parts. The great poet would talk of nothing but treaties and guarantees, and the great king of nothing but metaphors and rhymes."

33. *Hiero* 3.6; 4.6; 5.1.

34. Note the frequent use of the second person singular in ch. 13, and the ascent from the καταθέασαι in 3.1 to the εἰ βούλει εἰδέναι, ἐπίσκεψαι in 3.6 and finally to the εἰ τοίνυν εθέλεις κατανοεῖν in 3.8.

35. *Hiero* 6.1–6.

36. Compare *Hiero* 6.7 with *ibid*. 6.3

37. *Hiero* 6.7–9. The importance of Simonides' remark is underlined by the following three features of Hiero's reply: First, that reply opens with the only oath that occurs in the second section. Second, that reply, being one of the three passages of the *Hiero* in which laws are mentioned (3.9; 4.4; 6.10), is the only passage in the dialogue in which it is clearly intimated that tyrannical government is government without laws, i.e., it is the only passage in Xenophon's only work on tyranny in which the essential character of tyranny comes, more or less, to light. Third, Hiero's reply is the only passage of the *Hiero* in which Hiero speaks of "you (private men)" (see III A, note 35 above). Compare also III B, note 27 above.

38. The character of Simonides' only contribution to the discussion of the second section can also be described as follows: While he was silent when friendship was being discussed, he talks in a context in which war is mentioned; he is more vocal regarding war than regarding friendship. See note 26 above.

39. The situation is illustrated by the following figures: In the first section (1.10–38) Simonides contributes about 218 words out of about 1058; in the second section (2.3–6.16) he contributes 28 words out of about 2,000; in the third section (ch. 7) he contributes 220 words out of 522; in the fourth section (ch. 8–11) he contributes about 1,475 words out of about 1,600.—K. Lincke, "Xenophons Hiero und Demetrios von Phaleron," *Philologus*, v. 58, 1899, 226, correctly describes the "Sinnesänderung" of Hiero as "die Peripetie des Dialogs."

40. Compare note 24 above. The initial enumeration had dealt explicitly with the pleasures of "human beings" (see III a, note 35 above), but honor, the subject of the third section, is the aim, not of "human beings," but of "real men." One has no right

to assume that the subject of the third section is the pleasures or pains of the soul, and the subject of the second section is the pleasures or pains common to body and soul. In the first place, the pleasures or pains of the soul precede in the initial enumeration the pleasures or pains common to body and soul; besides ἐπινοεῖν, which is mentioned in the enumeration that opens the second section (2.2), is certainly an activity of the soul alone; finally, the relation of honor to praise as well as the examples adduced by Simonides show clearly that the pleasure connected with honor is not meant to be a pleasure of the soul alone (compare 7.2–3 with 1.14). When Simonides says that no human pleasure comes nearer to the divine than the pleasure concerning honors, he does not imply that that pleasure is a pleasure of the soul alone, for, apart from other considerations, it is an open question whether Simonides, or Xenophon, considered the deity an incorporeal being. As for Xenophon's view on this subject, compare *Memorabilia* I 4.17 and context (for the interpretation consider Cicero, *De natura deorum* I 12.30–31 and III 10.26–27) as well as *ibid*. IV 3.13–14. Compare *Cynegeticus* 12.19 ff.

41. Compare *Hiero* 7.1–4 with *ibid*. 2.1–2. See III A, note 8, and III B, note 22 above. The "many" (in the expression "for many of those who are reputed to be real men") is emphasized by the insertion of "he said" after "for many" (2.1), and the purpose of this emphasis is to draw our attention to the still limited character of the thesis that opens the second section. This is not the only case in which Xenophon employs this simple device for directing the reader's attention. The "he said" after "we seem" in 1.5 draws our attention to the fact that Simonides uses here for the first time the first person when speaking of private men. The two redundant "he said" 's in 1.7–8 emphasize the "he answered" which precedes the first of these two "he said" 's, thus making it clear that Simonides' preceding enumeration of pleasures has the character of a question addressed to Hiero, or that Simonides is testing Hiero. The second "he said" in 1.31 draws our attention to the preceding σύ, i.e., to the fact that Hiero's assertion concerning tyrants in general is now applied by Simonides to Hiero in particular. The "he said" in 1.36 draws our attention to the fact that the tyrant Hiero hates to behave like a brigand. The redundant "he said" in 7.1 draws our attention to the fact that the following praise of honor is based on εἰκότα. The "he said" in 7.13 emphasizes the preceding ἴσθι, i.e., the fact that Hiero does not use in this context the normally used εὖ ἴσθι, for he is now describing in the strongest possible terms how bad tyranny is.

42. *Hiero* 7.5–10.

43. Compare *Hiero* 7.3 with *ibid*. 1.14–15.

44. In the third section, Simonides completely abandons the vulgar opinion in favor not of the gentleman's opinion but of the opinion of the real man. The aim of the real man is distinguished from that of the gentleman by the fact that honor as striven for by the former does not essentially presuppose a just life. Compare *Hiero* 7.3 with *Oeconomicus* 14.9.

45. *Hiero* 7.11–13. I have put in parentheses the thoughts which Hiero does not express. As for Simonides' question, compare *Anabasis* VII 7.28.

46. *Hiero* 1.12. As for the tyrant's fear of punishment, see *ibid*. 5.2.

47. Regarding strangers, see *Hiero* 1.28; 5.3; 6.5.

48. Compare *Hiero* 8.9 with *ibid*. 7.7 and 5.2.

49. Simonides continues asserting that tyrannical life is superior to private life; compare *Hiero* 8.1–7 with *ibid*. 1.8 ff.; 2.1–2; 7.1 ff.

50. *Hiero* 7.12–13.

51. When comparing *Hiero* 7.13 with *Apologia Socratis* 7 and 32, one is led to wonder why Hiero is contemplating such an unpleasant form of death as hanging: does he belong to those who never gave thought to the question of the easiest way of dying? Or does he thus reveal that he never seriously considered committing suicide? Compare also *Anabasis* II 6.29.

52. *Memorabilia* I 2.10–11, 14.

53. "You are out of heart with tyranny because you believe. . . ." (*Hiero* 8.1).

54. Compare also the transition from "tyranny" to the more general "rule" in *Hiero* 8.1 ff. Regarding the relation of "tyranny" and "rule," see *Memorabilia* IV 6.12; Plato, *Republic* 338d7–11; Aristotle, *Politics* 1276a2–4.

55. *Hiero* 7.5–6, 9; compare *ibid*. 1.37–38 and 3.8–9.

56. *Hiero* 8.1.

57. *Hiero* 8.1–7. Compare note 54 above.

58. Compare *Hiero* 1.36–38.

59. In this context (8.3), there occur allusions to the topics discussed in 1.10 ff: ἰδών (sights), ἐπαινεσάντων (sounds), θύσας (food). The purpose of this is to indicate the fact that Simonides is now discussing the subject matter of the first part from the opposite point of view.

60. *Memorabilia* II 1.27–28; 3.10–14; 6.10–16. Compare *Anabasis* I 9.20 ff.

61. If Simonides had acted differently, he would have appeared as a just man, and Hiero would fear him. Whereas Hiero's fear of the just is definite, his fear of the wise is indeterminate (see pp. 41–45 above); it may prove to be unfounded in a given case. This is what actually happens in the *Hiero*: Simonides convinces Hiero that the wise can be friends of tyrants. One cannot help being struck by the contrast between Simonides' "censure" of the tyrant Hiero and the prophet Nathan's accusation of the Lord's anointed King David (II Samuel 12).

62. *Hiero* 8.8. The equally unique πάλιν (εἶπεν)a in 9.1 draws our attention to the εὐθύς in 8.8.

63. *Hiero* 8.8–10. Compare *ibid*. 6.12–13.

64. *Hiero* 9.1. Observe the negative formulation of Simonides' assent to a statement dealing with unpleasant aspects of tyrannical rule.

65. Simonides' speech consists of two parts. In the fairly short first part (9.1–4), he states the general principle. In the more extensive second part (9.5–11), he makes specific proposals regarding its application by the tyrant. In the second part punishment and the like are no longer mentioned. The unpleasant aspects of tyranny, or of government in general, are also barely alluded to in the subsequent chapters. Probably the most charming expression of the poet's dignified silence about these disturbing things occurs in 10.8. There, Simonides refrains from mentioning the possibility that the tyrant's mercenaries, these angels of mercy, might actually punish the evildoers: he merely mentions how they should behave toward the innocent, toward those who intend to do evil and toward the injured. Compare the preceding note. Compare also the statement of the Athenian stranger in Plato's *Laws* 711b4–c2 with the subsequent statement of Clinias.

66. As for bewitching tricks to be used by absolute rulers, see *Cyropaedia* VIII 1.40–42; 2.26; 3.1. These less reserved remarks are those of a historian or a spectator rather than of an adviser. Compare Aristotle, *Politics* 1314a40: the tyrant ought to *play* the king.

67. Ch. 9 and ch. 10 are the only parts of the *Hiero* in which "tyrant" and derivatives are avoided.

68. Compare especially *Hiero* 9.10 with *ibid*. 11.10.

69. *Hiero* 9.7, 11.

70. *Hiero* 9.6. Compare Aristotle, *Politics* 1315a31–40.

71. *Hiero* 8.10.

72. *Hiero* 10.1.

73. *Hiero* 10.2. Compare Aristotle, *Politics* 1314a33 ff.

74. Compare *Hiero* 4.9, 11 with 4.3 ("without pay") and 10.8.

75. Compare *Hiero* 11.1 with 9.7–11 and 10.8.

76. *Hiero* 11.1–6. Compare p. 38 above. One is tempted to suggest that the *Hiero* represents Xenophon's interpretation of the contest between Simonides and Pindar.

77. *Hiero* 11.7–15. Compare Plato, *Republic* 465d2–e2.

78. K. Lincke (*loc. cit*, 244), however, feels "dass Hiero eines Besseren belehrt worden wäre, muss der Leser sich hinzudenken, obgleich es . . . besser wäre, wenn man die Zustimmung ausgesprochen sähe." The Platonic parallel to Hiero's silence at the end of the *Hiero* is Callicles' silence at the end of the *Gorgias* and Thrasymachus' silence in books II-X of the *Republic*.

C. THE USE OF CHARACTERISTIC TERMS

1. Marchant, *loc. cit*, XVI.

2. For instance, Nabis is called "principe" in *Principe* IX and "tiranno" in *Discorsi* I 40, and Pandolfo Petruzzi is called "principe" in *Principe* XX and XXII, and "tiranno" in *Discorsi* III 6. Compare also the transition from "tyrant" to "ruler" in the second part of the *Hiero*.

3. Compare *Hellenica* VI 3.8, end.

4. *Hiero* 9.6.

5. *Hiero* 11.6; 1.31. Compare *Apologia Socratis* 28, a remark which Socrates made "laughingly."

6. Compare the absence of courage (or manliness) from the lists of Socrates' virtues: *Memorabilia* IV 8.11 (cf. IV 4.1 ff.) and *Apologia Socratis* 14, 16. Compare *Symposium* 9.1 with *Hiero* 7.3. But consider also II, note 22 above.

7. Compare *Hiero* 9.8 on the one hand with 1.8, 19 and 5.1–2 on the other.

8. *Hiero* 10.1.

IV. The Teaching Concerning Tyranny

1. Aristotle, *Politics* 1313a33–38.

2. This explanation does not contradict the one suggested on pp. 32–33 above, for the difference between a wise man who does not care to discover, or to teach, the tyrannical art and a wise man who does remains important and requires an explanation.

3. *Hiero* 1.9–10; 2.3, 5.

4. Compare *Hiero* 5.2 with the situations in *Cyropaedia* VII 2.10 on the one hand, and *ibid*. VII 5.47 on the other.

5. *Memorabilia* IV 6.12. Compare *Cyropaedia* I 3.18 and 1.1; *Hellenica* VII 1.46; *Agesilaus* 1.4; *De vectigalibus* 3.11; Aristotle, *Politics* 1295a15–18.

6. *Hiero* 11.12. Compare *Hellenica* V 1.3–4.

7. Compare pp. 64–65 and III B, note 37 above. In *Hiero* 7.2 Simonides says that *all* subjects of tyrants execute *every* command of the tyrant. Compare his additional

remark that all rise from their seats in honor of the tyrant with *Resp. Lac.* 15.6: no ephors limit the tyrant's power. According to Rousseau (*Contrat social* III 10), the *Hiero* confirms his thesis that the Greeks understood by a tyrant not, as Aristotle in particular did, a bad monarch but a usurper of royal authority regardless of the quality of his rule. According to the *Hiero*, the tyrant is necessarily "lawless" not merely because of the manner in which he acquired his position, but above all because of the manner in which he rules: he follows his own will, which may be good or bad, and not any law. Xenophon's "tyrant" is identical with Rousseau's "despot" (*Contrat social* III 10 end). Compare Montesquieu, *De l'esprit des lois* XI 9 and XIV 13 note.

8. *Hiero* 11.8, 15. Compare *ibid.* 8.9 with 7.10–12, 7 and 11.1. Compare also 1.11–14 with the parallel in the *Memorabilia* (II 1.31). Regarding the fact that the tyrant may be just, compare *Plato, Phaedrus* 248e3–5.

9. *Hiero* 11.5, 7, 14–15.

10. *Hiero* 8.3 and 9.2–10.

11. *Hiero* 9.6 and 11.3, 12. Compare *Hellenica* II 3.41; also Aristotle, *Politics* 1315a32–40 and Machiavelli, *Principe* XX.

12. *Hiero* 10.6. Compare *Hellenica* IV 4.14.

13. As regards prizes, compare especially *Hiero* 9.11 with *Hipparchicus* 1.26. Ernst Richter (*loc. cit*, 107) goes so far as to say that "die Forderungen des zweiten (Teils des *Hiero*) genau die des Sokrates (sind)."

14. *Hiero* 11.14; compare *ibid.* 6.3 and 3.8.

15. Compare *Cyropaedia* VIII 1.1 and 8.1.

16. Compare *Hiero* 10.4 with *ibid.* 4.3.

17. *Hiero* 9.1 ff. Compare Machiavelli, *Principe* XIX and XXI, toward the end as well as Aristotle, *Politics* 1315a4–8. See also Montesquieu, *De l'esprit des lois* XII 23–24. As for the reference to the division of the city into sections in Hiero 9.5–6 (cf. Machiavelli, *Principe* XXI, toward the end), one might compare Aristotle, *Politics* 1305a30–34 and Hume's "Idea of a perfect commonwealth" (toward the end).

18. *Memorabilia* III 4.8, *Oeconomicus* 4.7–8; 9.14–15; 12.19. *Resp. Lac.* 4.6 and 8.4. *Cyropaedia* V 1.13, *Anabasis* V 8.18 and II 6.19–20. Compare, however, *Cyropaedia* VIII 1.18.

19. Compare *Hiero* 9.7–8 with *Resp. Lac.* 7.1–2. Compare Aristotle, *Politics* 1305a18–22 and 1313b18–28 as well as Montesquieu, *De l'esprit des lois* XIV 9.

20. *Hiero* 11.12–14. Compare *Cyropaedia* VIII 2.15, 19; 1.17 ff.

21. Compare *Hiero* 8.10 and 11.13 with *Oeconomicus* 14.9.

22. *Hiero* 1.16.

23. Plato, *Republic* 562b9–c3; *Euthydemus* 292b4–c1. Aristotle, *Eth. Nic.* 1131a26–29 and 1161a6–9; *Politics* 1294a10–13; *Rhetoric* 1365b29 ff.

24. Compare p. 43 above.

25. *Hiero* 7.9 and 11.8. Compare *ibid.* 2.2 (horses), 6.15 (horses) and 11.5 (chariots). The horse is the example used for the indirect characterization of political virtue in the *Oeconomicus* (11.3–6): a horse can possess virtue without possessing wealth; whether a human being can possess virtue without possessing wealth, remains there an open question. The political answer to the question is given in the *Cyropaedia* (I 2.15) where it is shown that aristocracy is the rule of well-bred men of independent means. Compare page 70 above about the insecurity of property rights under a tyrant.

26. *Resp. Lac.* 10.4 (cf. Aristotle, *Eth. Nic.* 1180a24 ff.). *Cyropaedia* I 2.2 ff.

27. *Hiero* 9.6.

28. *Hiero* 5.1–2.

29. Compare *Hiero* 9.6 with *ibid.* 5.3–4, *Anabasis* IV 3.4 and *Hellenica* VI 1.12. Compare *Hiero* 9.6 with the parallel in the *Cyropaedia* (I 2.12). A reduced form of prowess might seem to be characteristic of eunuchs; see *Cyropaedia* VII 5.61 ff.

30. This is the kind of justice that might exist in a nonpolitical society like Plato's first city or city of pigs (*Republic* 371e12–372a4). Compare *Oeconomicus* 14.3–4 with Aristotle, *Eth. Nic.* 1130b6, 30 ff.

31. *Memorabilia* IV 8.11. *Apol Socr.* 14, 16.

32. Compare *Hiero* 9.8 with *Memorabilia* IV 3.1 and *Hellenica* VII 3.6. Compare Plato, *Gorgias* 507a7–c3.

33. *Anabasis* VII 7.41.

34. *Hiero* 10.3. Compare Montesquieu, *De l'esprit des lois* III 9: "Comme il faut de la vertu dans une république, et dans une monarchie de l'honneur, il faut de la crainte dans un gouvernement despotique: pour la vertu, elle n'y est pas *nécessaire*, et l'honneur y serait *dangereux*." Virtue is then not dangerous to "despotism." (The italics are mine.)

35. Compare *Hiero* 10.3 with *Cyropaedia* III 1.16 ff. and VIII 4.14 as well as with *Anabasis* VII 7.30.

36. *Anabasis* I 9.29.

37. Compare *Hiero* 11.5, 8 with *Memorabilia* III 2 and *Resp. Lac.* 1.2.

38. *Memorabilia* IV 4.12 ff. Compare *ibid.* IV 6.5–6 and *Cyropaedia* I 3.17.

39. Aristotle, *Eth. Nic.* 1129b12.

40. *Memorabilia* IV 4.13.

41. *Oeconomicus* 14.6–7.

42. *Memorabilia* I 2.39–47 and I 1.16.

43. *Memorabilia* I 2.31 ff.; IV 4.3.

44. *Agesilaus* 4.2. Compare *Cyropaedia* I 2.7.

45. Compare *Memorabilia* IV 8.11 with *ibid.* I 2.7 and *Apol Socr.* 26. See also *Agesilaus* 11.8. Compare Plato, *Crito* 49b10 ff. (cf. Burnet ad loc.); *Republic* 335d11–13 and 486b10–12; *Clitopho* 410a7–b3; Aristotle, *Politics* 1255a17–18 and *Rhetoric* 1367b5–6.

46. *Cyropaedia* VIII 1.22. In *Hiero* 9.9–10 Simonides recommends honors for those who discover something useful for the city. There is a connection between this suggestion, which entails the acceptance of many and frequent changes, and the nature of tyrannical government as government not limited by laws. When Aristotle discusses the same suggestion which had been made by Hippodamus, he rejects it as dangerous to political stability and he is quite naturally led to state the principle that the "rule of law" requires as infrequent changes of laws as possible (*Politics* 1268a6–8, b 22 ff.). The rule of laws as the classics understood it can exist only in a "conservative" society. On the other hand, the speedy introduction of improvements of all kinds is obviously compatible with beneficent tyranny.

47. *Hiero* 11.10–11. *Memorabilia* III 9.10–13. Compare Aristotle, *Politics* 1313a9–10. It may be useful to compare the thesis of Xenophon with the thesis of such a convinced constitutionalist as Burke. Burke says (in his "Speech on a motion for leave to bring in a bill to repeal and alter certain acts respecting religious opinions"): " . . . it is not perhaps so much by the assumption of unlawful powers, as by the unwise or unwarrantable use of those which are most legal, that governments oppose their true end and object, for there is such a thing as tyranny as well as usurpation."

48. *Cyropaedia* I. 3.18.

49. Compare *Anabasis* III 2.13. Incidentally, the fact mentioned in the text accounts for the way in which tyranny is treated in Xenophon's emphatically Greek work, the *Hellenica*.

50. *Memorabilia* III 9.12–13. Compare Plato, *Laws* 710c5–d1. We are now in a position to state more clearly than we could at the beginning (pp. 31–32 above) the conclusion to be drawn from the title of the *Hiero*. The title expresses the view that Hiero is a man of eminence (cf. III A, note 44 above), but of questionable eminence; that the questionable character of his eminence is revealed by the fact that he is in need of a teacher of the tyrannical art; and that this is due, not only to his particular shortcomings, but to the nature of tyranny as such. The tyrant needs essentially a teacher, whereas the king (Agesilaus and Cyrus, e.g.) does not. We need not insist on the reverse side of this fact, *viz.*, that the tyrant rather than the king has any use for the wise man or the philosopher (consider the relation between Cyrus and the Armenian counterpart of Socrates in the *Cyropaedia*). If the social fabric is in order, if the regime is legitimate according to the generally accepted standards of legitimacy, the need for, and perhaps even the legitimacy of, philosophy is less evident than in the opposite case. Compare note 46 above and V, note 60 below.

51. For an example of such transformations, compare *Cyropaedia* I 3.18 with *ibid.* I 2.1.

52. *Hiero* 10.1–8. Compare Aristotle, *Politics* 1311a7–8 and 1314a34 ff.

53. Aristotle, *Politics* 1276b29–36; 1278b1–5; 1293b3–7.

54. *Memorabilia* I 2.9–11.

55. Compare pp. 56–57 above.

56. *Memorabilia* II 1.13–15.

57. Compare also the qualified praise of the good tyrant by the Athenian stranger in Plato's *Laws* (709d10 ff. and 735d). In 709d10 ff. the Athenian stranger declines responsibility for the recommendation of the use of a tyrant by emphatically ascribing that recommendation to "the legislator."

V. The Two Ways of Life

1. *Memorabilia* I 1.8; IV 6.14.

2. Compare *Hiero* 1.2, 7 with *Cyropaedia* II 3.11 and VIII 3.35–48; *Memorabilia* II 1 and I 2.15–16; also Plato, *Gorgias* 500c–d.

3. Consider the twofold meaning of ἰδιώτης in *Hiero* 4.6. Compare Aristotle, *Politics* 1266a31–32. Whereas Hiero often uses "the tyrants" and "we" promiscuously, and Simonides often uses "the tyrants" and "you" promiscuously, Hiero makes only once a promiscuous use of "private men" and "you." Simonides speaks unambiguously of "we (private men)" in *Hiero* 1.5, 6 and 6.9. For other uses of the first person plural by Simonides see the following passages: 1.4, 6, 16; 8.2, 5; 9.4; 10.4; 11.2. Compare III a, note 35 and III b. notes 2 and 41 above.

4. Rudolf Hirzel, *loc cit.*, 170 n. 3: "Am Ende klingt aus allen diesen (im Umlauf befindlichen) Erzählungen (über Gespräche zwischen Weisen und Herrschern) . . . dasselbe Thema wieder von dem *Gegensatz*, der zwischen den Mächtigen der Erde und den Weisen besteht und in deren gesamter Lebensauffassung und Anschauungsweise zu Tage tritt." (Italics mine.)

5. *Hiero* 5.1. See p. 34 and III A, note 44 above.

6. Plato, *Gorgias* 500c–d. Aristotle, *Politics* 1324a24 ff.

7. Compare *Hiero* 9.2 with *Memorabilia* III 9.5, 10–11. Compare III A, note 32 above.

8. *Memorabilia* I 2.16, 39, 47–48; 6.15; II 9.1; III 11.16.

9. *Hiero* 7.13.

10. Compare *Hiero* 8.1–10.1 with *ibid.* 3.3–5 and 11.8–12.

11. *Hiero* 7.4. Compare *ibid.* 1.8–9 with 1.14, 16, 21–22, 24, 26 and 2.1–2.

12. The difference between Simonides' explicit statements and Hiero's interpretation of them appears most clearly from a comparison of *Hiero* 2.1–2 with the following passages: 2.3–5; 4.6; 6.12.

13. See pp. 39f and 51f and III B, notes 39 and 44 above. In the second part (i.e., the fourth section) to which he contributes about three times as much as to the first part, Simonides uses expressions like "it seems to me" or "I believe" much less frequently than in the first part, while he uses in the second part three times ἐγὼ φημί which he never uses in the first part.

14. *Hiero* 7.2,4. The ambiguity of διαφερόντως in 7.4 ("above other men" or "differently from other men") is not accidental. Compare with διαφερόντως in 7.4 the πολὺ διαφέρετε in 2.2, the πολὺ διαφερόντως in 1.29 and the πολλαπλάσια in 1.8. Compare III A, note 8 and III B, notes 25 and 40 above.

15. *Hiero* 8.1–7. Compare III B, note 38 above.

16. *Hiero* 7.3–4.

17. See pp. 62 and 65 above. Regarding the connection between "honor" and "noble," see *Cyropaedia* VII 1.13; *Memorabilia* III 1.1; 3.13; 5.28; *Oeconomicus* 21.6; *Resp. Lac.* 4.3–4; *Hipparchicus* 2.2.

18. *Memorabilia* II 7.7–14 and III 9.14–15. *Cyropaedia* VIII 3.40 ff.

19. *Hiero* 11.10; 1.13; 6.13. Compare *Cyropaedia* VII 2.26–29.

20. In *Hiero* 11.15, the only passage in which Simonides applies "happy" and "blessed" to individuals, he does not explain the meaning of these terms. In the two passages in which he speaks of the happiness of the city, he understands by happiness power, wealth, and renown (11.5, 7. *Cf. Resp. Lac.* 1.1–2). Accordingly, one could expect that he understands by the most noble and most blessed possession that possession of power, wealth, and renown which is not marred by envy. This expectation is, to say the least, not disproved by 11.13–15. Compare also *Cyropaedia* VIII 7.6–7; *Memorabilia* IV 2.34–35; *Oeconomicus* 4.23–5.1; *Hellenica* IV 1.36.

21. It is Hiero who on a certain occasion alludes to this meaning of "happiness" (2.3–5). Compare III A, note 33 above.

22. *Memorabilia* IV 8.11; I 6.14. Compare p. 42 and III A, note 25 above.

23. As for the danger of envy, see *Hiero* 11.6 and 7.10. As for the work and toil of the ruler, see 11.15 (ταῦτα πάντα) and 7.1–2. Compare *Memorabilia* II 1.10.

24. *De vectigalibus* 4.5; *Resp. Lac.* 15.8; *Symposium* 3.9 and 4.2–3; *Anabasis* V 7.10. Compare also *Cyropaedia* I 6.24 and p. 62 above.

25. *Memorabilia* III 9.8; *Cynegeticus* 1.17. Compare Socrates' statements in the *Memorabilia* (IV 2.33) and the *Apol. Socr.* (26) with Xenophon's own statement in the *Cynegeticus* (1.11).

26. Compare note 23 above. Compare *Memorabilia* III 11.16; *Oeconomicus* 7.1 and 11.9; *Symposium* 4.44.

27. *Memorabilia* I. 2.6; 5.6; 6.5; II 6.28–29; IV 1.2. *Symposium* 8.41. Compare *Memorabilia* IV 2.2 and *Cyropaedia* I 6.46. Consider the fact that the second part of the *Hiero* is characterized by the fairly frequent occurrence, not only of χάρις but of ἀνάγκη as well (see p. 65 above).

28. *Memorabilia* IV 5.2; *Cyropaedia* I 5.12; *Anabasis* VII 7.41–42; *Symposium* 4.44.

29. *Memorabilia* II 4.5, 7; *Oeconomicus* 5.11. Compare III B, note 26 above.

30. As for the agreement between Simonides' final statement and the views expressed by Socrates and Xenophon, compare *Hiero* 11.5 with *Memorabilia* III 9.14, and *Hiero* 11.7 with *Agesilaus* 9.7.

31. Compare *Oeconomicus* 1.7 ff. with *Cyropaedia* I 3.17. Compare Isocrates, *To Demonicus* 28.

32. *Memorabilia* IV 5.6 and *Apol. Socr.* 21. Compare *Memorabilia* II 2.3; 4.2; I 2.7. As regards the depreciating remark on wisdom in *Memorabilia* IV 2.33, one has to consider the specific purpose of the whole chapter as indicated at its beginning. Ruling over willing subjects is called an almost divine good, not by Socrates but by Ischomachus (*Oeconomicus* 21.11–12).

33. *Memorabilia* I 4 and 6.10; IV 2.1 and 6.7. Regarding the distinction between education and wisdom, see also Plato, *Laws* 653a5–c4 and 659c9 ff., and Aristotle, *Politics* 1282a3–8. Compare also *Memorabilia* II 1.27, where the παιδεία of Heracles is presented as preceding his deliberate choice betwen virtue and vice.

34. Compare *Hiero* 3.2 (and 6.1–3) with the parallel in the *Symposium* (8.18).

35. *Hiero* 9.1–11. Simonides does not explain what the best things are. From 9.4 it appears that according to Xenophon's Simonides the things which are taught by the teachers of choruses do not belong to the best things: the instruction given by the teachers of choruses is not gratifying to the pupils, and instruction in the best things is gratifying to the pupils. Following Simonides, we shall leave it open whether the subjects mentioned in 9.6 (military discipline, horsemanship, justice in business dealings, etc.) meet the minimum requirements demanded of the best things, *viz.*, that instruction in them is gratifying to the pupils. The fact that he who executes these things well is honored by prizes, does not prove that they belong to the best things (cf. 9.4 and *Cyropaedia* III 3.53). Whether the things Simonides teaches are the best things will depend on whether the instruction that he gives to the tyrant is gratifying to the latter. The answer to this question remains as ambiguous as Hiero's silence at the end of the dialogue. Xenophon uses in the *Hiero* the terms εὖ εἰδέναι and εὖ ποιεῖν fairly frequently (note especially the "meeting" of the two terms in 6.13 and 11.15). He thus draws our attention to the question of the relation of knowing and doing. He indicates his answer by the synonymous use of βέλτιον εἰδέναι and μᾶλλον εἰδέναι in the opening passage (1.1–2; observe the density of εἰδέναι). Knowledge is intrinsically good, whereas action is not (cf. Plato, *Gorgias* 467e ff.): to know to a greater degree is to know better, wheras to do to a greater degree is not necessarily to "do" better. Κακῶς ποιεῖν is as much ποιεῖν as is εὖ ποιεῖν whereas κακῶς εἰδέναι is practically identical with not knowing at all. (See *Cyropaedia* III 3.9 and II 3.13).

36. *Hiero* 9.9–10. The opposite view is stated by Isocrates in his *To Nicocles* 17.

37. The distinction suggested by Simonides between the wise and the rulers reminds one of Socrates' distinction between his own pursuit which consists in making people capable of political action on the one hand, and political activity proper on the other (*Memorabilia* I 6.15). According to Socrates, the specific understanding required of the ruler is not identical with wisdom, strictly speaking. (Compare the explicit definition of wisdom in *Memorabilia* IV 6.7—see also *ibid.* 6.1 and I 1.16—with the explicit definition of rule in III 9.10–13 where the term "wisdom" is studiously avoided.) In accordance with this, Xenophon hesitates to speak of the wisdom of either of the two Cyruses, and when calling Agesilaus "wise," he evidently uses the term in a loose sense, not to say in the vulgar sense (*Agesilaus* 6.4–8 and 11.9). In the *Cyropaedia*,

he adumbrates the relation between the ruler and the wise man by the conversations between Cyrus on the one hand, his father (whose manner of speaking is reminiscent of that of Socrates) and Tigranes (the pupil of a sophist whose fate is reminiscent of the fate of Socrates) on the other. Compare pp. 34 and 65 above. Compare IV, note 50 above.

38. See pp. 40–41 above. Compare Plato, *Republic* 620c3–d2.

39. See pp. 22–23 above. Compare Plato, *Republic* 581e6–582e9.

40. "Honor *seems* to be something great" and "no human pleasure *seems* to come nearer to divinity than the enjoyment connected with honors." (*Hiero* 7.1, 4). See also the ὡς ἔοικε in 7.2 and the εἰκότως δοκεῖτε in 7.4. Compare III B, note 41 above.

41. Since the preferences of a wise man are wise, we may say that Simonides reveals his wisdom in his statement on honor to a much higher degree than in his preceding utterances. The effect of that statement on Hiero would therefore ultimately be due to the fact that through it he faces Simonides' wisdom for the first time in the conversation. Without doubt, he interprets Simonides' wisdom, at least to begin with, in accordance with his own view—the vulgar view—of wisdom. Compare note 12 above.

42. ἐμφύεται . . . ἐμφύῃ (Hiero 7.3). Compare *Cyropaedia* I 2.1–2 and *Oeconomicus* 13.9.

43. In *Hiero* 8.5–6 (as distinguished from *ibid*. 7.1–4) Simonides does not suggest that rulers are honored more than private men. He does not say that only rulers, and not private men, are honored by the gods (cf. *Apol. Socr.* 14–18). He says that a given individual is honored more highly when being a ruler than when living as a private man; he does not exclude the possibility that that individual is in all circumstances less honored than another man who never rules. In the last part of 8.5 he replaces "ruler" by the more general "those honored above others" (cf. *Apol. Socr.* 21). The bearing of 8.6 is still more limited as appears from a comparison of the passage with 2.1 and 7.3. Love of honor may seem to be characteristic of those wise men who converse with tyrants. Plato's Socrates says of Simonides that he was desirous of honor in regard to wisdom (*Protagoras* 343b7–c3).

44. *Hiero* 3.1, 6, 8. Compare *ibid*. 1.19, 21–23, 29 and 4.8. See III B, note 34 above.

45. Compare *Hiero* 3.1–9 with *ibid*. 8.1 and 11.8 (the emphatic "you"). See also Hieros' last utterance in 10.1. Hiero's praise of honor in 7.9–10 is clearly not spontaneous but solicited by Simonides' praise of honor in 7.1–4. Hiero's praise of honor differs from Simonides' in this, that only according to the former is love a necessary element of honor. Furthermore, it should be noted that Hiero makes a distinction between pleasure and the satisfaction of ambition (1.27). Xenophon's characterization of Hiero does not contradict the obvious fact that the tyrant is desirous of honors (cf. 4.6 as well as the emphasis on Hiero's concern with being loved with Aristotle's analysis in *Eth. Nic.* 1159a12 ff.). But Xenophon asserts by implication that the tyrant's, or the ruler's, desire for honor is inseparable from the desire for being loved by human beings. The most obvious explanation of the fact that Hiero stresses "love" and Simonides stresses "honor" would of course be this: Hiero stresses the things which the tyrant lacks, whereas Simonides stresses the things which the tyrant enjoys. Now, tyrants are commonly hated (cf. Aristotle, *Politics* 1312b19–20) but they are honored. This explanation is correct but insufficient because it does not account for Simonides' genuine concern with honor or praise and for his genuine indifference to being loved by human beings.

46. Compare *Hiero* 7.1–4 with *ibid.* 1.16 and the passages cited in the preceding note. The forms of honor other than praise and admiration partake of the characteristic features of love rather than of those of praise and admiration. The fact that Simonides speaks in the crucial passage (*Hiero* 7.1–4) of honor in general, is due to his adaptation to Hiero's concern with love. Consider also the emphasis on honor rather than on praise in ch. 9.

47. Plato, *Gorgias* 481d4–5 and 513c7–8. Compare also the characterization of the tyrant in the *Republic* (see III B, note 12 above). As regards the disagreement between Hiero and Simonides concerning the status of "human beings," compare the disagreement between the politician and the philosopher on the same subject in Plato's *Laws* (804b5–c1).

48. This explains also the different attitude of the two types to envy. See p. 84 above.

49. Compare Plato, *Gorgias* 481d4–5.

50. *Hiero* 11.8–15. Compare *Agesilaus* 6.5 and 11.15.

51. *Hiero* 7.9. Compare Plato, *Republic* 330c3–6 and *Laws* 873c2–4; Aristotle, *Politics* 1262b22–24. Compare also p. 34 and II, note 22 above. Cf. 1 Peter 1.8 and Cardinal Newman's comment: "St. Peter makes it almost a description of the Christian, that he loves whom he has not seen."

52. Simonides fr. 99 Bergk.

53. Cf. the use of φίλοι in the sense of fellow-citizens as opposed to strangers or enemies in *Hiero* 11.15, *Memorabilia* I 3.3, and *Cyropaedia* II 2.15.

54. *Hiero* 8.1–7. That this is not the last word of Xenophon on love, appears most clearly from *Oeconomicus* 20.29.

55. Compare *Hiero* 7.9 and 11.14–15 with *Hellenica* VII 3.12 (*Cyropaedia* III 3.4) and *Memorabilia* IV 8.7. The popular view is apparently adopted in Aristotle's *Politics* 1286b11–12 (cf. 1310b33 ff.). Compare Plato, *Gorgias* 513e5 ff. and 520e7–11.

56. Compare *Hiero* 7.9 with *ibid.* 7.1–4.

57. Men of excellence in an emphatic sense are Hesiod, Epicharmus, and Prodicus (*Memorabilia* II 1.20–21). Compare also *Memorabilia* I 4.2–3 and 6.14.

58. *Memorabilia* I 2.3 and 6.10. Simonides' statement that no human pleasure seems to come nearer to the divine than the enjoyment connected with honors (*Hiero* 7.4) is ambiguous. In particular, it may refer to the belief that the very gods derive pleasure from being honored (whereas they presumably do not enjoy the other pleasures discussed in the dialogue) or it may refer to the connection between the highest ambition and godlike self-sufficiency. Compare VI note 6 below.

59. As for the connection between this kind of selfishness and wisdom, compare Plato, *Gorgias* 458a2–7 and the definition of justice in the *Republic*. Considerations which were in one respect similar to those indicated in our text seem to have induced Hegel to abandon his youthful "dialectics of love" in favor of the "dialectics of the desire for recognition." See A. Kojève, *Introduction à l'étude de Hegel*, Paris (Gallimard), 1947, 187 and 510–12, and the same author's "Hegel, Marx et le Christianisme," *Critique*, 1946, 350–52.

60. Compare Simonides' disparaging remark on a kind of pleasure which is enjoyed by others rather than by oneself in *Hiero* 1.24 (cf. III B, note 11 above). Consider also the ambiguity of "food" (*Memorabilia* III 5.10; Plato, *Protagoras* 313c5–7). As regards the connection between friendship ("love") and sex, cf. *Hiero* 1.33, 36–38 and 7.6. The explanation suggested in the text can easily be reconciled with the fact that Hiero's

concern with the pleasures of sex, if taken literally, would seem to characterize him, not as a ruler in general, but as an imperfect ruler. Xenophon's most perfect ruler, the older Cyrus, is characterizd by the almost complete absence of concern with such pleasures. What is true of the perfect ruler, is still more true of the wise: whereas Cyrus does not dare to look at the beautiful Panthea, Socrates visits the beautiful Theodote without any hesitation (cf *Cyropaedia* V 1.7 ff. with *Memorabilia* III 11.1; *Memorabilia* I 2.1 and 3.8–15; *Oeconomicus* 12.13–14; *Agesilaus* 5.4–5). To use the Aristotelian terms, whereas Cyrus is continent, Socrates is temperate or moderate. In other words, Cyrus' temperance is combined with inability or unwillingness to look at the beautiful or to admire it (cf. *Cyropaedia* V 1.8 and VIII 1.42), whereas Socrates' temperance is the foundation for his ability and willingness to look at the beautiful and to admire it. To return to Hiero, he reveals a strong interest in the pleasures of sight (*Hiero* 1.11–13; cf. 11.10). He is concerned not so much with the pleasures of sex in general as with those of homosexuality. This connects him somehow with Socrates: love of men seems to bespeak a higher aspiration than love of women. (*Symposium* 8.2, 29; *Cyropaedia* II 2.28; Plato, *Symposium* 208d ff. Cf. Montesquieu, *De l'esprit des lois* VII 9 note: "Quant au vrai amour, dit Plutarque, les femmes n'y ont aucune part. Il parlait comme son siècle. Voyez Xénophon, au dialogue intitulé *Hiéron*.") Hiero is presented as a ruler who is capable of conversing with the wise and of appreciating them (cf. III A, note 44 above). Does Hiero's education explain why he is not a perfect ruler? Only the full understanding of the education of Cyrus would enable one to answer this question. Compare IV, note 50 above.

61. *Hiero* 11.7, 11–15. *Memorabilia* I 2.11.

62. *Hiero* 6.9. How little Simonides impresses Hiero, a good judge in this matter, as being warlike, is indicated by the latter's "*if* you too have experience of war" (6.7) as compared with his "I know well that you too have experience" regarding the pleasures of the table (1.19). Cf. also *ibid.* 1.29, 23. Consider Simonides' silence about "manliness" (p. 64 above), and compare III B, notes 18 and 38, and III C, note 6 above.

63. *Hiero* 11.7. In the parallel in the *Agesilaus* (9.7) the qualifying words "among human beings" are omitted.

64. *Hiero* 2.7–18. (Consider the conditional clauses in 2.7.) The emphasis in this passage is certainly on war. The passage consists of two parts: In the first part (2.7–11) in which Hiero shows that if peace is good and war bad, tyrants are worse off than private citizens, "peace" occurs three times and "war" (and derivations) seven times, in the second part (2.12–18) in which he shows that as regards the pleasures of war—or more specifically as regards the pleasures of wars waged against forcibly subjected people, i.e., against rebellious subjects—tyrants are worse off than private citizens, "peace" does not occur at all but "war" (and derivatives) occurs seven times.

65. Plato, *Republic* 566e6–567a9. Aristotle, *Politics* 1313b28–30 and 1305a18–22.

66. *Cyropaedia* I 4.24; VII 1.13. *Memorabilia* III 1.6. Compare Plato, *Republic* 375c1–2 and 537a6–7 with Aristotle, *Politics* 1327b38–1328a11.

67. *Hiero* 1.34–35. As regards the relation between Eros and Ares, compare Simonides fr. 43 Bergk and Aristotle, *Politics* 1269b24–32.

68. *Hiero* 6.5; compare *ibid.* 6.14.

69. *Hiero* 2.2; 6.12–14. Compare the use of the second person singular in 6.13 on the one hand, and in 6.14 on the other.

70. *Hiero* 5.1. *Apol. Socr.* 16. *Memorabilia* I 6.10. Socrates does not teach strategy whereas he does teach economics (compare *Memorabilia* III 1 and IV 7.1 with the

Oeconomicus). Compare Plato, *Republic* 366c7–d1 and the passages indicated in IV, note 45 above.

VI. Pleasure and Virtue

1. Compare *Memorabilia* IV 8.11.
2. See pp. 45–48 and III a, note 44 above.
3. Compare *Hiero* 8.6 with *ibid.* 2.1 and 7.3. Compare *Hiero* 5.1–2 with *ibid.* 3.1–9 and 6.1–3 on the one hand, and with *Memorabilia* II 4 and I 6.14 on the other. Compare *Hiero* 1.11–14 with *Memorabilia* II 1.31: Hiero does not mention one's own virtuous actions as the most pleasant sight. Compare *Hiero* 3.2 with *Symposium* 8.18: he does not mention the common enjoyment of friends about their noble actions among the pleasures of friendship. He replaces Simonides' ἐπινοεῖν by ἐπιθυμεῖν (*Hiero* 2.2 and 4.7).
4. *Hiero* 7.9–10.
5. Aristotle's suggestions for the improvement of tyrannical government (in the fifth book of the *Politics*) are more akin in spirit to Xenophon's suggestions than to Isocrates'; they are, however, somewhat more moralistic than those made in the *Hiero*.
6. Fr. 71 Bergk. When Xenophon's Simonides says that no human pleasure seems to come nearer to the divine than the enjoyment connected with honors, he may imply that "the divine" is pure pleasure. Compare V, note 58 above.
7. Compare *Hiero* 4.10 with frs. 5, 38, 39 and 42 Bergk. Compare Plato, *Protagoras* 346b5–8. Compare also Simonides' definition of nobility as old wealth with Aristotle's view according to which it is not so much wealth as virtue that is of the essence of nobility (*Politics* 1255a32 ff., 1283a33–38, 1301b3–4).
8. *Lyra Graeca*, ed. by J. M. Edmonds, vol. 2, revised and augmented edition, 258. Compare p. 64 above. See *Hellenica* II 3.19 and *Apol. Socr.* 30.
9. *Lyra Graeca, ed. cit.*, 250, 256 and 260. Compare Plato, *Protagoras* 316d3–7, 338e6 ff. and 340e9 ff.; also *Republic* 331e1–4 and context (Simonides did not say that to say the truth is of the essence of justice).
10. Compare pp. 34, 40, 51f., 53, 55f., 76f.
11. Compare pp. 87 ff. above.
12. This would also explain why Simonides emphasizes somewhat later the pleasures connected with food: food is the fundamental need of all animals (*Memorabilia* II 1.1). In *Hiero* 7.3, where he hides his wisdom to a lesser degree than in the preceding sections, he does not call, as he did in 2.1, the pleasures of the body "small things."
13. Compare *Memorabilia* I 4.5 and IV 3.11.
14. Compare Plato, *Theatetus* 184c5–7 and 185e6–7.
15. *Hiero* 1.1. Compare the κάλλιον θεᾶσθαι in 2.5 with the ἥδιον θεᾶσθαι in 8.6.
16. *Hiero* 1.5. A remark which Simonides makes later on (9.10) might induce one to believe that he identified the good with the useful, and this might be thought to imply that the end for which the good things are useful, is pleasure. This interpretation would not take account of the facts which we discuss in the text. Simonides must therefore be presumed to have distinguished between the good which is good because it is useful for something else, and the good which is intrinsically good and not identical with the pleasant.
17. *Hiero* 1.22.
18. *Hiero* 1.9; 2.1; 7.3.

19. See the reference to the divine in *Hiero* 7.4.

20. *Hiero* 1.27; 3.3; 6.16.

21. The importance of the problem "fatherland-friendship" for the understanding of the *Hiero* is shown by the fact that that problem determines the plan of the bulk of the second section (ch. 3–6). This is the plan of ch. 3–6: I (a) friendship (3.1–9); (b) trust (4.1–2); (c) fatherland (4.3–5). II (a) possessions (4.6–11); (b) good men or the virtues (5.1–2); (c) fatherland (5.3–4). III (a) pleasures of private men (6.1–3); (b) fear, protection, laws (6.4–11); (c) helping friends and hurting enemies (6.12–15). The difference between "fatherland" and "trust" is not as clear-cut as that between either of them and "friendship": both fatherland and trust are good with regard to protection, or freedom from fear, whereas friendship is intrinsically pleasant. "Friendship" can be replaced by "possessions" for the reason given in *Hiero* 3.6, *Memorabilia* II 4.3–7 and *Oeconomicus* 1.14; "friendship" can be replaced by "pleasures of private men" for the reason given in *Hiero* 6.1–3. "Trust" can be replaced by "virtue" (cf. Plato, *Laws* 630b2–c6) as well as by "protection" (trustworthiness is the specific virtue of guards: *Hiero* 6.11). "Fatherland" can be replaced by "helping the friends and hurting the enemies" with a view to the fact that helping the friends, i.e., the fellow citizens, and hurting the enemies, i.e., the enemies of the city, is the essence of patriotism (cf. *Symposium* 8.38). The same distinction which governs the plan of ch. 3–6, governs the plan of ch. 8–11 as well: (a) friendship (ch. 8–9; see 10.1); (b) protection (guards) (ch. 10); (c) fatherland or city (ch. 11; see 11.1).

22. Compare *Hiero* 3.3 with 4.1 on the one hand, and with 4.3–5 on the other. Compare 4.2 and 6.11.

23. *Hiero* 4.3–4. Compare 6.6, 10. In what may best be called the repetition of the statement on the fatherland (5.3–4), Hiero says it is necessary to be patriotic because one cannot be preserved or be happy without the city. Compare the οὐκ ἄνευ in 5.3 with the (οὐκ) ἄνευ in 4.1. From 5.3–4 it appears that the power and renown of the fatherland is normally pleasant. When speaking of friendship, Hiero had not spoken of the power and renown of friends; he had not implied that only powerful and renowned friends are pleasant (compare *Agesilaus* 11.3). Not the fatherland, but power and renown are pleasant, and the power and renown of one's city are pleasant because they contribute to one's own power and renown. Compare *Hiero* 11.13. When speaking of the pleasures which he enjoyed while being a private man, Hiero mentions friendship; he does not mention the city or the fatherland (6.1–3).

24. *Hiero* 4.3–4 and 5.3.

25. Compare *Hiero* 4.3 and 10.4 with 6.10.

26. *Hiero* 9.2–4 (cf. 1.37; 5.2–3; 8.9). Compare also Hiero's emphasis (in his statement on friendship: 3.7–9) on the relations within the family, with the opposite emphasis in Xenophon's account of Socrates' character (*Memorabilia* II 2–10): the blood relations are "necessary" (*Memorabilia* II 1.14). *Cyropaedia* IV 2.11. *Anabasis* VII 7.29. *Memorabilia* II 1.18. Compare Aristotle, *Rhetoric* 1370a8–17 and Empedocles fr. 116 (Diels, *Vorsokratiker*, first ed.). See V, note 27 above.

27. Compare *Hiero* 5.3 and 4.9 with 3.1–9.

28. Observe that friendship and virtue occur in different columns of the plan of ch. 3–6 (see note 21 above). Compare Hiero's praise of the friend with Socrates' praise of the good friend (*Memorabilia* II 4 and 6).

29. *Hiero* 11.14.

30. *Hiero* 11.1,5–6. Compare pp. 87 ff. above.

31. Compare *Hellenica* I 7.21.

32. Compare *Hiero* 4.3 with *Memorabilia* II 3.2 and 1.13–15.

33. Only the fairly short first part of the *Memorabilia* (I 1–2) deals with "Socrates and the city," whereas the bulk of the work deals with "Socrates' character"; see the two perorations: I 2.62–64 and IV 8.11. As regards the plan of the *Memorabilia*, see Emma Edelstein, *Xenophontisches und Platonisches Bild des Sokrates*, Berlin, 1935, 78–137.

34. Isocrates, *Antidosis* 155–56.

35. *Anabasis* III 1.4–9; V 6.15–37. Compare *ibid*. V 3.7 and VII 7.57. The sentiment of Proxenus is akin to that expressed by Hermes in Aristophanes' *Plutus* 1151 (*Ubi bene ibi patria*). (Compare *Hiero* 5.1 and 6.4 with *Plutus* 1 and 89.). Compare Cicero, *Tusc. disput.* V 37.106 ff.

36. *Anabasis* V 3.6 and *Hellenica* IV 3.15 (cf. IV 2.17).

37. B. G. Niebuhr, "Ueber Xenophons Hellenika," *Kleine historische und philosophische Schriften*, I, Bonn, 1828, 467: "Wahrlich einen ausgearteteren Sohn hat kein Staat jemals ausgestossen als diesen Xenophon. Plato war auch kein guter Bürger, Athens wert war er nicht, unbegreifliche Schritte hat er getan, er steht wie ein Sünder gegen die Heiligen, Thukydides und Demosthenes, aber doch wie ganz anders als dieser alte Tor!"

38. *Hiero* 4.3–5 and 5.3.

39. See pp. 75f. above.

40. *Cyropaedia* II 2.24–26. Dakyns comments on the passage as follows: "Xenophon's breadth of view: virtue is not confined to citizens, but we have the pick of the whole world. Cosmopolitan Hellenism." Consider the conditional clauses in *Agesilaus* 7.4, 7. Compare *Hipparchicus* 9.6 and *De vectigalibus* 2.1–5.

41. Compare Burke, *Reflections on the Revolution in France*, Everyman's Library ed., p. 59, on the one hand, and Pascal, *Provinciales* XIII as well as Kant, "Über den Gemeinspruch: Das mag in der Theorie richtig sein, taugt aber nicht für die Praxis," on the other.

42. Socrates' statement that cities and nations are "the wisest of human things" (*Memorabilia* I 4.16) does not mean then that the collective wisdom of political societies is superior to the wisdom of wise individuals. The positive meaning of the statement cannot be established but by detailed interpretation of the conversation during which the statement is made.

43. The only special virtues of which Simonides speaks with some emphasis, are moderation and justice. Moderation may be produced by fear, the spoiler of all pleasures (*Hiero* 10.2–3 and 6.6; cf. IV, note 35 above), and it goes along with lack of leisure (9.8). As for justice, Simonides speaks once of a special kind of justice, the justice in business relations, and twice of "doing injustice" (9.6 and 10.8). Now, the term "justice" designates in Xenophon's works a variety of kindred phenomena which range from the most narrow legalism to the confines of pure and universal beneficence. Justice may be identical with moderation, it may be a subdivision of moderation, and it may be a virtue apart from moderation. It is certain that Simonides does not understand by justice legality, and there is no reason to suppose that he identified justice with beneficence. He apparently holds a considerably more narrow view of justice than does Hiero. (For Hiero's view of justice, see especially 5.1–2 and 4.11.) He replaces Hiero's "unjust men" by "those who commit unjust actions" (for the interpretation consider Aristotle, *Eth. Nic.* 1134a17 ff.). Whereas Hiero identifies justice and moder-

ation by using ἀδικεῖν and ὑβρίζειν synonymously, Simonides distinguishes the two virtues from each other: he identifies ἀδικεῖν and κακουργεῖν and he distinguishes between κακουργεῖν and ὑβρίζειν (see 8.9; 9.8; 10.8, 2–4; cf. Aristotle, *Rhetoric* 1389b7–8 and 1390a17–18; Plato, *Protagoras* 326a4–5). It seems that Simonides understands by justice the abstaining from harming others (cf. *Agesilaus* 11.8 and *Memorabilia* IV 4.11–12; consider *Symposium* 4.15) and that he thus makes allowance for the problem inherent in benefiting "human beings" (as distinguished from "real men" or "men of excellence"). It is easy to see that justice thus understood, as distinguished from its motives and results, is not intrinsically pleasant.

44. *Memorabilia* II 1.23, 26, 29.

45. Diogenes Laertius II 65–66.

46. Compare *Memorabilia* II 1.34 with *ibid* I 6.13, *Symposium* 1.5 and 4.62 and *Cynegeticus* 13.

47. *Memorabilia* I 3.8–13.

48. Compare *Hiero* 11.15 with *Anabasis* VII 7.41. See *Anabasis* II 1.12 (cf. Simonides fr. 5 Bergk) and *Cyropaedia* I 5.8–10; also Agesilaus 10.3.

49. V. Brochard, *Études de philosophie ancienne et de philosophie moderne*, Paris (Vrin), 1926, 43.

50. Compare III A, note 27 and IV, note 25 above.

51. *Memorabilia* IV 6. 15.

52. *Memorabilia* IV 8.6–8 (cf. I 6.9 and IV 5.9–10). *Apol. Socr.* 5–6 and 32.

53. Compare Plato, *Republic* 357b4–358a3.

54. *Apol. Socr.* 5. Compare *Memorabilia* II 1.19. Regarding *sibi ipsi placere* see especially Spinoza, *Ethics* III, aff. deff. 25. As for the difference between Socrates and Simonides, compare also p. 94 above.

VII. Piety and Law

1. *De vectigalibus* 6.2–3. Compare pp. 31f. above.

2. When Simonides suggests to Hiero that he should spend money for the adornment of his city with temples *inter alia* (*Hiero* 11.1–2), he does not admonish him to practice piety; he merely adivses him to spend his money in a way proper to a ruler. Aristotle's ethics which is silent about piety, mentions expenses for the worship of the gods under the heading "munificence." (*Eth. Nic.* 1122b19–23. Compare *Politics* 1321a35 ff. Cf. also J. F. Gronovius' note to Grotius' *De jure belli ac pacis*, Prolegg. §45: "Aristoteli ignoscendum, si inter virtutes morales non posuit religionem. . . . Nam illi ut veteribus omnibus extra Ecclesiam cultus deorum sub magnificentia ponitur.")

3. *Agesilaus* 1.34 and *Anabasis* III 2.13. Compare Plato, *Republic* 573c3–6.

4. *Politics* 1314b39 ff. No remark of this kind occurs in Aristotle's discussion of the preservation of the other regimes in the fifth book of the *Politics*. *Cyropaedia* VIII 1.23. Compare Isocrates, *To Nicocles* 20 and Machiavelli, *Principle* XVIII.

5. *Memorabilia* IV 6.2–4.

6. *Memorabilia* IV 8.11; I 4; IV 3.

7. *Hiero* 3.9. Compare *Oeconomicus* 7.16, 29–30 (cf. 7.22–28).

8. Cicero, *De natura deorum* I 22.60.

9. Φύσις and φύειν (or derivatives) occur in *Hiero* 1.22, 31, 33; 3.9; 7.3; 9.8 θεοὶ occurs in 3.5; 4.2; 8.5. Τὸ θεῖον occurs in 7.4. Compare the remarks on ἱερά in 4.5, 11 with *Hellenica* VI 4.30.

10. Compare *Anabasis* V 2.24–25 and Plato, *Laws* 709b7–8. Considering the relation between "nature" and "truth" (*Oeconomicus* 10.2 and *Memorabilia* II 1.22), the distinction between nature and law may imply the view that the law necessarily contains fictitious elements. In *Hiero* 3.3 Hiero says: "It has not even escaped the cities that friendship is a very great good and most pleasant to human beings. At any rate, many cities have a law (νομίζουσι) that only adulterers may be killed with impunity, evidently for this reason, because they believe (νομίζουσι) that they (the adulterers) are the destroyers of the wives' friendship with their husbands." The law that adulterers may be killed with impunity is based on the belief that the adulterers as distinguished from the wives are responsible for the wives' faithlessness. The question arises whether this belief is always sound. Xenophon alludes to this difficulty by making Hiero take up the question of the possible guilt of the wife in the subsequent sentence: "Since when the wife has been raped, husbands do not honor their wives any less on that account, provided the wives' love remains inviolate." It seems that the men's belief in the modesty of women is considered conducive to that modesty. Compare Montesquieu, *De l'esprit des lois* VI 17: "Parce que les hommes sont méchants, la loi est obligée de les supposer meilleurs qu'ils ne sont. Ainsi . . . on juge . . . que tout enfant conçu pendant le mariage est légitime; la loi a confiance en la mère comme si elle était la pudicité même." Cf. also Rousseau, *Emile* V (ed. Garnier, vol. 2, 147–48) Similarly, by considering (νομίζων) one's sons as the same thing as one's life or soul (*Hiero* 11.14), whereas in truth one's sons are not one's life or soul, one will be induced to act more beneficently than one otherwise would.

11. *Anabasis* II 6.19–20 (cf. Aristotle, *Eth. Nic.* 1179b4 ff.). *Symposium* 4.19.

II

The Strauss-Kojève
Debate

Alexandre Kojève

Tyranny and Wisdom*

In my opinion it is not only Xenophon who is impor-
tant in the book Strauss has devoted to him. Perhaps in spite of what
its author may think about it, this book of Strauss's is truly important
not because it purports to reveal to us the authentic and misunderstood thought of a contemporary and compatriot of Plato's, but
because of the problem which it raises and discusses.

Xenophon's dialogue, as interpreted by Strauss, sets a disillu-
sioned tyrant who claims to be discontented with his condition as a
tyrant, against a wise man who has come from afar to advise him on
how to govern his State in a way that will provide him with satisfaction
from the exercise of tyranny. Xenophon makes these two characters
speak, and he tells us between the lines what to think about what they
say. Strauss fully spells out Xenophon's thought, and tells us between
the lines what to think about it. More precisely, by presenting himself
in his book not as a wise man in possession of knowledge but as a

*Kojève's essay first appeared under the title "L'action politique des philosophes," in *Critique*
(1950, 6: 46–55, 138–155). The expanded version subsequently published under the title
"Tyranny and Wisdom" omits the opening paragraphs of the original article.

In a brilliant and impassioned book, but in the guise of a calmly objective work of
scholarship, Leo Strauss interprets Xenophon's dialogue in which a tyrant and a wise man
discuss the advantages and disadvantages of exercising tyranny. He shows us wherein the
interpretation of a work differs from a mere commentary or an analysis. Through his
interpretation Xenophon appears to us as no longer the somewhat dull and flat author we
know, but as a brilliant and subtle writer, an original and profound thinker. What is more,

philosopher in quest of it, Strauss tells us not *what* to think about all this, but only what to think *about* when speaking of the relations between tyranny or government in general on the one hand, and Wisdom or philosophy on the other. In other words, he leaves it at raising problems; but he raises them with a view to solving them.

It is about some of these problems explicitly or implicitly raised by Strauss in the preceding pages that I should like to speak in what follows.

Let us first take up the question of tyranny.

Let us note that it is not Hiero who asks Simonides for advice on how to exercise tyranny. Simonides gives him that advice spontaneously. Still, the fact remains that Hiero listens to it (in a moment of leisure, it is true). And having heard it, he says nothing. That silence shows us that he has nothing to say in response. We may therefore conclude that he judges, as we ourselves do, following Xenophon and Strauss, that Simonides's advice is full of wisdom. But since he does not say so, and since he does not say that he will follow it, we assume that he will do nothing of the kind. And that was probably Simonides's own opinion, for according to Xenophon he does not even ask whether Hiero intends to implement the advice he has just given him.

Faced with this situation, we are naturally inclined to be shocked. We do, to be sure, understand why Hiero was willing to listen attentively to Simonides's advice since, by his own admission, he was unable to exercise his tyranny on his own in a way that was satisfying, if only to himself. But we, if we had been "in his place," would spontaneously have asked for advice just as soon as we became aware of our inability. We would even have done so "long ago;" and not in a moment of leisure, but "dropping everything." Above all, as soon as

---

in interpreting this forgotten dialogue, Strauss lays bare great moral and political problems that are still ours.

He has searched through the maze of the dialogue for the true meaning of Xenophon's teaching. Xenophon presumably took care to hide it from the view of the vulgar. Strauss therefore had to resort to the method of the detective who, by a subtle interpretation of the apparent facts, finally finds the criminal . . .

Truth to tell, the temptation is great in the end to deny the discovery. Indeed, the book cannot end as detective novels do, with the unmasked "criminal's" confession. Let the reader judge . . .

However, it matters only incidentally to know whether the interpretation is irrefutable, for the importance of Strauss's book goes well beyond Xenophon's authentic and perhaps unknown thought. It owes its importance to the importance of the problem which it raises and discusses.

we had realized how excellent the advice was which we had received, we would have loudly proclaimed it, and done everything in our power to implement it. And, once again, we would have done so "dropping everything."

But before yielding to this natural impulse, I believe that we ought to reflect. Let us first ask ourselves whether it is really true that "in Hiero's place" we could have carried out our noble intentions by "dropping everything." Hiero himself does not think so, since he says to Simonides (end of ch. 7): "In this too is tyranny most miserable: it is not possible to be rid of it." And he may be right. For the tyrant always has some "current business" which it is impossible to drop without first completing it. And it may well be that the nature of this business is such that to attend to it proves incompatible with the measures that would have to be taken in order to implement the wise man's advice, or more exactly, in order to institute the ideal state of things which he recommends. It may also be that it takes more years to conclude "current business" than there are years in the tyrant's own life. And what if some of it required centuries of effort to conclude fully?

Hiero draws Simonides's attention to the fact that in order to *come* to power, the tyrant necessarily has to take, let us say, "unpopular" measures (in fact, Hiero considers them "criminal"). Simonides does not deny it, but he asserts that the tyrant could *maintain* himself in power without recourse to violence, by taking appropriate measures to achieve "popularity." But Simonides does not say how to go about abrogating the "unpopular" measures without immediately imperiling the tyrant's life or power (and hence also imperiling the very reforms which he was ready to introduce as a result of the wise man's intervention), or even the State's existence as such. Nor does he explain how the nonviolent "popular" regime could have been established without abrogating the measures in question.

Yet that is obviously what Simonides should have explained to Hiero if he had really wanted him to follow his advice. By not doing so, Simonides seems to have behaved not so much like a wise man as like a typical "Intellectual" who criticizes the real world in which he lives from the standpoint of an "ideal" constructed in the universe of discourse, an "ideal" to which one attributes an "eternal" value, primarily because it does not now exist and never has existed in the past. In fact, Simonides presents his "ideal" in the form of a "utopia." For the ideal presented in the form of a "utopia" differs from the same ideal presented as an "active" (revolutionary) idea precisely in this, that the utopia does not show us how, here and now, to begin to transform the given concrete reality with a view to bringing it into conformity with the proposed ideal in the future.

Strauss may therefore be right in telling us that Simonides, who believes he is a wise man, is really only a poet. Confronted by a poetical vision, a dream, a utopia, Hiero reacts not like a "tyrant," but simply like a statesman, and a "liberal" statesman at that. In order not to encourage his critics, he does not want to proclaim openly that he recognizes the "theoretical" value of the ideal Simonides depicts to him. He does not want to do so not only because he knows that he could not *actualize* this ideal (in the present state of things), but also, and above all, because he is not told what first step he would have to take in order to move toward it. Hence, like a good liberal, he leaves it at remaining *silent*: he *does* nothing, *decides* nothing, and allows Simonides to *speak* and to *depart* in peace.

According to Strauss, Xenophon was perfectly well aware of the necessarily utopian character of the sort of advice Simonides offers. He presumably thought that the "enlightened" and "popular" tyranny he has Simonides depict is an unrealizable ideal, and that the aim of his Dialogue is to convince us that it would therefore be better to renounce tyranny in any form before even having tried to establish it. Strauss and Xenophon thus appear to reject the very idea of "tyrannical" government. But that is another question entirely and, what is more, it is an extremely difficult question. Advice against tyranny would no longer have anything to do with the advice a wise man might give a tyrant with a view to an "ideal" *tyranny*.

In order to gauge the meaning and true import of this new advice, one would have to know whether, in certain specific cases, renouncing "tyranny" would not be tantamount to renouncing government altogether, and whether that would not entail either the ruin of the State, or abandoning any real prospect of progress in a particular State or for the whole of mankind (at least at a given historical moment). But before we take up that question, we have to see whether Hiero, Simonides, Xenophon, and Strauss are really right in asserting that the "ideal" tyranny sketched by Simonides is only a utopia.

Now, when one reads the last three chapters of the Dialogue, in which Simonides describes the "ideal" tyranny, one finds that what might have appeared utopian to Xenophon has nowadays become an almost commonplace reality. Indeed, here is what is said in those chapters. First of all, the tyrant should distribute all kinds of "prizes," especially honorific ones, in order to establish "Stakhanovite" emulation in his State in the fields of agriculture, industry, and commerce (ch. 9). Next, instead of maintaining a mercenary corps of bodyguards, the tyrant should organize a State police (which will "always be needed"), and a permanent armed force which would serve as the nucleus of the army mobilized in case of war (ch. 10). Besides, the tyrant should not disarm his subjects, but introduce compulsory military service, and resort to general mobilization if necessary. Finally, he should spend a part of his "personal" fortune for the common good and construct public buildings rather than palaces. Generally speaking, the tyrant would gain his subjects' "affection" by making them happier and by considering "the fatherland his estate, the citizens his comrades" (ch. 11).

It is understandable that Xenophon should have considered all this utopian. Indeed, he knew only tyrannies exercised for the benefit of an already established social class, or for the sake of personal or family ambitions, or with the vague idea of doing better than anyone else, though wanting the same thing they did. He had not seen "tyrannies" exercised in the service of truly revolutionary political, social, or economic ideas (that is to say, in the service of objectives differing radically from anything already in existence) with a national, racial, imperial, or humanitarian basis. But it is surprising to find our contemporary, Strauss, apparently sharing this way of looking at things. Personally, I do not accept Strauss's position in this matter, because in my opinion the Simonides-Xenophon utopia has been *actualized* by modern "tyrannies" (by Salazar, for example). It may even be that what was utopian in Xenophon's time could be actualized at a later time precisely because the time needed to conclude the "current business" I spoke about has elapsed, and that that "current business" had to be concluded before the measures needed to actualize the ideal advocated by Simonides could be taken. But does it follow that these modern "tyrannies" are (philosophically) justified by Xenophon's Dialogue? Are we to conclude that the modern "tyrant" could actualize the "philosophic" ideal of tyranny without recourse to the advice of the Wise or of the philosophers, or must we grant that he could do so only because a Simonides once advised a Hiero?

I will try to answer the second question below. As for the first, in order to answer it we will have to go to the heart of the matter.

At the culminating point of the Dialogue (ch. 7), Simonides explains to Hiero that his grievances against tyranny are worthless because men's supreme goal and ultimate motive is honor and, as regards honor, the tyrant is better off than anyone else.

Let us briefly pause at this argument. Simonides adopts, in full self-awareness, the "pagan" or even "aristocratic" existential attitude which Hegel will later call that of the "Master" (as opposed to the attitude of the "Slave," which is that of "Judeo-Christian" or even "bourgeois" man). And Simonides states this view in an extremely radical manner. Indeed, when he says that "honor is something great, and human beings undergo all toil and endure all danger striving for it," his point is not simply that man struggles and labors exclusively for the sake of glory. He goes very much further, asserting that "a real man differs from the other animals in this striving for honor." But like any consistent "pagan," "aristocrat," or "Master," Simonides does not believe that the quest for glory is the distinctive feature of *all* creatures with a human form. The quest for glory is specifically and necessarily characteristic only of *born* Masters, and it is *irremediably* missing in "servile" natures which, by that very fact, are not truly human (and deserve to be treated accordingly). "Those in whom love of honor and praise arises by *nature* are the ones who already far surpass the brutes, and who are also believed to be no longer human beings merely [in appearance only], but real men." And these "real" men who live for glory are to a certain extent "divine" beings. For, "no human pleasure comes closer to what is divine than the joy concerning honors."

This "aristocratic" and "pagan" profession of faith would no doubt have shocked the "bourgeois" who did (or do) live in the Judeo-Christian world. In that world neither philosophers nor even tyrants *said* such things, and insofar as they wanted to *justify* tyranny, they used other arguments. It would be vain to enumerate them all because, in my opinion, only one of them is really valid. But that one deserves our full attention. I think it would be false to say, with Simonides, that *only* the "desire to be honored" and the "joy which comes from honor" makes one "endure *any* labor and brave *any* danger." The *joy* that comes from labor itself, and the desire to *succeed* in an undertaking, can, by themselves alone, prompt a man to undertake painful and dangerous labors (as is already shown in the ancient myth of Hercules). A man can work hard risking his life for no other reason than to experience the joy he always derives from *carrying out* his project or, what is the same thing, from transforming his "idea" or even "ideal" into a *reality* shaped by his own *efforts*. A child, alone on a beach, makes sand-patties which he will perhaps never show anyone; and a painter may cover the cliffs of some desert island with drawings, knowing all the while that he will never leave it. Thus, although that is an extreme case, a man can aspire to tyranny in the same way that a "conscientious" and "enthusiastic" workman can aspire to adequate conditions for his labor. Indeed, a "legitimate" monarch who attains and retains power without effort and who is not susceptible to glory could, nevertheless, avoid sinking into a life of pleasure, and devote himself actively to the government of the State. But that monarch, and in general the "bourgeois" statesman who renounces glory on principle, will exercise his hard political "trade" only if he has a "laborer's" mentality. And he will want to justify his tyranny as nothing but a necessary condition for the success of his "labor."

In my opinion, this "bourgeois" way of looking at things and of justifying tyranny (a way that, to some extent and for some time, made it possible to live in the "Judeo-Christian" political world in which men were in theory asked to renounce glory) must complement the "aristrocratic" theory of which Simonides makes himself the spokesman, and which only accounts for the attitude of the *idle* "aristocrat" devoting the best of his powers to (possibly bloody) struggles with other men for the sake of the *honor* victory will bring him.

But we should not isolate the "bourgeois" point of view by forgetting or denying the "aristrocratic" theory. We should not forget that, to return to our examples, the "desire to be honored" and the joy that arises from "honors" come into play and become decisive as soon as the child makes his sand-patties in the presence of adults or of his friends, and as soon as the painter returns home and exhibits the reproduction of his cliff-drawings, as soon, generally speaking, as that *emulation* among men appears which, in fact, is never absent, and which, according to Simonides (ch. 9), is necessary even for agriculture, industry, and commerce truly to prosper. But for this proposition to apply to the statesman, there has to be a *struggle* for power and *emulation* in the exercise of power, in the strict sense of "struggle" and "emulation." To be sure, in theory the statesman could have done away with his rivals without thinking of glory, just as a laborer, absorbed in his labor and indifferent to what surrounds him, almost unconsciously does away with the objects that disturb him in his labor. But in fact, and this is particularly true of those who aspire to "tyranny," one does away with one's rivals because one does not want the goal attained, the job done, by *another*, even if this other could do it equally well. In cases involving "emulation" or "competition" one does in fact act for the sake of glory, and it is only in order to justify oneself from a "Christian" or "bourgeois" point of view, that one believes or claims that one is doing so exclusively because one is or imagines that one is more "capable" or "better equipped" than the others.

Be that as it may. Hiero, in his role as an authentic "pagan aristrocrat," accepts Simonides's point of view without reservation. However, he rejects Simonides's argument as a *justification* of tyranny: while he grants that man's highest goal is honor, he holds that the tyrant never attains that goal.

Hiero explains to Simonides (ch. 7, second paragraph) that the tyrant rules by terror, and that therefore the honors paid him by his subjects are dictated only by the fear he inspires in them. Now, "services of those under fear are not honors. . . . [such acts] would probably be regarded as acts of slavery." And the acts of a Slave give no satisfaction to that aristrocratic Master, the ancient tyrant.

In describing his situation, Hiero describes the tragedy of the Master analyzed by Hegel in the *Phenomenology of Mind* (ch. iv, section A). The Master enters into a struggle to the death in order to make his adversary recognize his exclusive human dignity. But if his adversary is himself a Master, he will be animated by the same desire for "recognition," and will fight to the death: his own or the other's. And if the adversary submits (through fear of death), he shows himself to be a Slave. His "recognition" is therefore worthless to the victorious Master in whose eyes the Slave is not a truly human being. The victor in this bloody struggle for pure prestige will therefore not be "satisfied" by his victory. His situation is thus essentially tragic, since there is no possible way out of it.

Truth to tell, Xenophon's text is less precise than Hegel's. Hiero confuses spontaneously granted "sexual love" with the "affection" of subjects who "recognize" him. Simonides corrects him by making him see that the tyrant as such is interested not in his "lovers" but in his subjects taken as citizens. But Simonides does retain the idea of "affection" (ch. 11). Moreover, Hiero would like to be happy by virtue of his tyranny and of "honors" in general, and Simonides, too, says that he will be "happy" (last sentence of the Dialogue) if he follows his advice, and thus gains his fellow citizens' "affection." Now, it is perfectly obvious that tyranny or political action in general cannot, as such, engender "love" or "affection" or "happiness," for these three phenomena involve elements that have nothing to do with politics: a mediocre politician can be the object of his fellow citizens' intense and authentic "affection," just as a great statesman may be universally admired without arousing love of any kind, and the most complete political success is perfectly compatible with a profoundly unhappy private life. It is therefore preferable to stay with Hegel's precise formulation, which refers not to "affection" or "happiness," but to "recognition" and to the "satisfaction" that comes from "recognition." For the desire to be "recognized" in one's eminent human reality and dignity (by those whom one "recognizes" in return) effectively is, I believe, the ultimate motive of all *emulation* among men, and hence of all political *struggle*, including the struggle that leads to tyranny. And the man who has satisfied this desire by his own action is, by that very fact, effectively "satisfied," regardless of whether or not he is happy or beloved.

We may, then, grant that tyrants (and Hiero himself) will seek Hegelian "recognition" above all else. We may also grant that Hiero, not having obtained this recognition, is not effectively "satisfied" in the strong sense of the term. We therefore understand why he listens to the advice of the wise man who promises him "satisfaction" by pointing out to him the means of obtaining "recognition."

In any case, both Hiero and Simonides know perfectly well what is at issue. Hiero would like his subjects "*willingly* to give way in the streets" (ch. 7, second paragraph) and Simonides promises him that if he follows his advice his subjects will be "*willing* men obeying." (ch. 11, twelfth paragraph). That is to say that both of them are concerned with *authority*.[1] For to get oneself "recognized" by someone without inspiring fear (in the final analysis, fear of violent death) or love in him, is to enjoy *authority* in his eyes. To acquire authority in someone's eyes, is to get him to *recognize* that authority. Now a man's authority (that is to say, in the final analysis, his eminently human value, though not necessarily his *superiority*), is *recognized* by another when that other follows or carries out his advice or his orders not because he cannot do otherwise (physically, or because of fear or of any other "passion"), but because he spontaneously considers them

---

[1]Hiero (*ibid.*), it is true, would like his subjects to "crown him for his public *virtue*" and he believes that at the present time they condemn him "for his *injustice*." But "injustice" disturbs him only to the extent that it prevents his being "recognized," and it is only in order to obtain "recognition" that he would practice "virtue." In other words, "virtue" and "justice" are for him only means by which to impose his *authority* on his subjects, and not ends in themselves. The sequel shows that Simonides's attitude is exactly the same: the tyrant must be "virtuous" and "just" in order to win his subjects' "affection"; in order, that is, to do the thing that will make his subjects obey "without being constrained," and—ultimately—in order to be "happy without being envied." This attitude is surely not "Socratic." We may grant, with Strauss, that Simonides, as an advisor to a tyrant, adopts Hiero's point of view for pedagogical reasons only, and without himself sharing it (in his capacity as a wise man).

worthy of being followed or carried out, and he does so not because he himself recognizes their intrinsic value, but only because *this particular person* gives this advice or these orders (as an oracle might), that is to say, precisely because he recognizes the "authority" of the person who gives them to him. We may therefore grant that Hiero, like any political man, actively sought tyranny because (consciously or not) he wanted to impose his exclusive *authority* on his fellow citizens.

We may therefore believe Hiero when he says that he is not "satisfied." He has indeed failed in his enterprise, since he admits that he has to have recourse to *force*, that is to say that he has to exploit his subjects' fear (of death). But Hiero surely exaggerates (and, according to Strauss, he does so deliberately, in order to discourage potential rivals, and Simonides in particular, from tyranny) when he says that tyranny does not provide him *any* "satisfaction" because he enjoys *no* authority and governs *solely* through terror. For, contrary to a rather common prejudice, such a situation is absolutely impossible. Pure terror presupposes force alone, which, in the final analysis, is to say physical force. Now, by physical force alone a man can dominate children, old men, and some women, at the outside two or three adults, but he cannot in this way impose himself for long on a group of able-bodied men, however small it may be. That is to say that "despotism" properly so called is possible only within isolated families, and that the head of any State whatsoever always has recourse to something besides force. In fact, a political chief always has recourse to his *authority*, and it is to it that he owes his power. The whole question is to know by *whom* this authority is recognized, *who* "obeys him without constraint"? Indeed, the authority of a head of State may be recognized either by a more or less extensive majority of the citizens, or by a more or less restricted minority. Until very recently it was not thought possible that one could speak of "tyranny" in the pejorative sense of the term, except where a minority (guided by an authority it alone recognizes) rules the majority of the citizens by force or "terror" (that is to say, by exploiting their fear of death). Of course, only citizens recognized as such by the State were taken into account. For even nowadays, no one criticizes the governing of children or criminals or madmen by force, and in the past governing women, slaves, or aliens for example, by force, was not criticized. But this way of seeing things, while logically possible, does not in fact correspond to people's natural reactions. It was finally realized that it does not correspond to them, and recent political experiences, as well as the current polemics between "Western" and "Eastern" democrats, have enabled us to provide a more adequate definition of tyranny.

In fact, there is tyranny (in the morally neutral sense of the term) when a fraction of the citizens (it matters little whether it be a majority or a minority) imposes on all the other citizens its own ideas and actions, ideas and actions that are guided by an authority which this fraction recognizes spontaneously, but which it has not succeeded in getting the others to recognize; and where this fraction imposes it on those others without "coming to terms" with them, without trying to reach some "compromise" with them, and without taking account of their ideas and desires (determined by another authority, which those others recognize spontaneously). Clearly this fraction can do so only by "force" or "terror," ultimately by manipulating the others' fear of the violent death it can inflict on them. In this situation the others may therefore be said to be "enslaved," since they in fact behave like slaves ready to do anything to save their lives. And it is this situation that some of our contemporaries label *tyranny* in the pejorative sense of the term.

Be that as it may. It is clear that Hiero is not fully "satisfied," not because he has *no* authority and governs *solely* by force, but because his authority, recognized by some, is not recognized by *all* of those whom he himself considers to be citizens, that is to say men worthy of recognizing it, and hence supposed to do so. By behaving in this manner, Hiero, who symbolizes the ancient tyrant for us, is in full agreement with Hegel's analysis of "satisfaction" (achieved by emulation or action that is "political" in the broad sense of the term).

Hegel says that the political man acts in terms of the desire for "recognition," and that he can be fully "satisfied" only if he has completely satisfied *this* desire. Now this desire is by definition limitless: man wants to be effectively "recognized" by *all* of those whom he considers capable and hence worthy of "recognizing" him. To the extent that the citizens of a foreign State, animated by a "spirit of independence," successfully resist the head of some given State, he must necessarily recognize their human worth. He will therefore want to extend his authority over them. And if they do not resist him, it is because they already recognize his authority, if only the way the Slave recognizes his Master's authority. So that in the final analysis, the head of State will be *fully* "satisfied" only when his State encompasses the whole of mankind. But he will also want to extend his *authority* as far as possible within the State itself, by reducing to a minimum the number of those capable of only a servile obedience. In order to make it possible for him to be "satisfied" by their authentic "recognition," he will tend to "enfranchise" the slaves, "emancipate" the women, and reduce the authority of families over children by granting them their "majority" as soon as possible, to reduce the number of criminals and of the "unbalanced" of every variety, and to raise the "cultural" level (which clearly depends on the economic level) of all social classes to the highest degree possible.

At all events, he will want to be "recognized" by all those who resist him out of "disinterested" motives, that is to say out of "ideological" or "political" motives properly so called, because their very resistance is the measure of their human worth. He will want to be recognized by them as soon as such a resistance manifests itself, and he will give up wanting to be recognized by them (and give it up regretfully) only when, for one reason or another, he finds himself forced to *kill* the "resistants." In fact, the political man, acting consciously in terms of the desire for "recognition" (or for "glory") will be *fully* "satisfied" only when he is at the head of a State that is not only *universal* but also politically and socially *homogeneous* (with allowances for irreducible physiological differences), that is to say of a State that is the goal and the outcome of the collective labor of all and of each. If one grants that this State is the actualization of the supreme political ideal of mankind, then the "satisfaction" of the head of this State may be said to constitute a sufficient "justification" (not only subjective, but also objective) of his activity. Now, from this point of view, the modern tyrant, while in fact implementing Simonides's advice and thus achieving more "satisfying" results than those of which Hiero complained, is not *fully* "satisfied" either. He is not fully satisfied because the State he rules is in fact neither universal nor homogeneous, so that his authority, like Hiero's, is not recognized by *all* those who, according to him, could and should have recognized it.

Since he is not fully satisfied by his State or by his own political actions, the modern tyrant thus has the same reasons as Hiero for lending an ear to the advice of the Wise. But in order to avoid the tyrant's having the same reasons for not following that advice, or for reacting to it with a "silence" that might be infinitely less "liberal" than Hiero's, the new Simonides would have to avoid his "poetic" predecessor's error. He would have to avoid *utopia*.

The description, even the eloquent description, of an idyllic state of things lacking any real connections with the present state of things, will touch a tyrant or a statesman in general as little as would "utopian" advice that lacked any direct relation to current concerns and business. Such "advice" will interest the modern tyrant all the less as he, having perhaps been instructed by some wise man other than Simonides, might very well already know the ideal which the "advisor" is ready to reveal to him, and he might already be consciously working toward its actualization. It would be just as vain to try to oppose this "ideal" to the concrete measures this tyrant is taking with a view to actualizing it, as it would be to try and carry out a concrete policy (tyrannical or other) which explicitly or tacitly rejects the "ideal" on which it is based.

On the other hand, if the wise man, granting that the tyrant seeks "glory" and hence could only be fully "satisfied" by the recognition of his authority in a universal and homogeneous State, were prepared to give "realistic" and "concrete" advice by explaining to the tyrant who consciously accepts the ideal of "universal recognition" how, starting at the *present* state of things, one might attain that ideal, and attain it better and faster than one could by this tyrant's own measures, then the tyrant could perfectly well have accepted and followed this advice openly. In any event, the tyrant's refusal would then be absolutely "unreasonable" or "unjustified," and it would not raise any questions of principle.

The question of principle that remains to be resolved is whether or not the wise man, in his capacity as a wise man, *can* do anything but talk about a political "ideal," and whether he *wants* to leave the realm of "utopia" and "general" or even "abstract ideas," and to confront concrete reality by giving the tyrant "realistic" advice.

In order to answer this twofold question, we must carefully distinguish between the wise man properly so called, and the philosopher, for the situation is far from being the same in the two cases. In order to simplify things, I will speak only about the latter. Anyway, neither Xenophon nor Strauss seem to admit the existence of the wise man properly so called.

By definition, the philosopher does not possess Wisdom (that is to say full self-consciousness, or—in fact—omniscience); but (a Hegelian would have to specify: in a given epoch) he is more advanced on the road that leads to Wisdom than any non-philosopher or "uninitiate," including the tyrant. Also by definition, the philosopher is supposed to "dedicate his life" to the quest for Wisdom.

Taking this twofold definition as our point of departure, we must ask ourselves: "*can* the philosopher govern men or participate in their governance, and does he *want* to do so; in particular, *can* and does he *want* to do so by giving the tyrant concrete political advice?"

Let us first ask ourselves whether he *can* do so, or, more precisely, whether, as a philosopher, he enjoys any *advantage* over the "uninitiate" (and the tyrant is an uninitiate) when it comes to questions of government.

I believe that the negative answer that is usually given rests on a misunderstanding, on a total misconception of what philosophy is and of what the philosopher is.

For the purposes at hand, I need only recall three traits that are distinctive of the philosopher in contrast to the "uninitiate." In the first place, the philosopher is more expert in the art of *dialectic* or *discussion* in general: he sees better than his "uninitiate" interlocutor the inadequacies of the latter's argument, and he knows better how to make the most of his own arguments and how to refute the objections of others. In the second place, the art of dialectic enables the philosopher to free himself of *prejudices* to a greater extent than the "uninitiate": he is thus more open to reality as it is, and he is less dependent on the way in which men, at a given historical moment, imagine it to be. Finally, in the third place, since he is more open to the real, he comes closer to the *concrete* than does the "uninitiate," who confines himself to abstractions, without, however, being aware of their abstract, even unreal, character.[2]

Now these three distinctive traits of the philosopher are so many advantages he in principle enjoys over the "uninitiate" when it comes to governing.

Strauss points out that Hiero, realizing Simonides's dialectical superiority, mistrusts him, seeing in him a potential and formidable rival. And I think that Hiero is right. Indeed, governmental action within an already constituted State is purely *discursive* in origin, and whoever is a master of discourse or "dialectic" can equally well become master of the government. If Simonides was able to defeat Hiero

---

[2]This assertion appears paradoxical only if one fails to think about the specific meaning of the words "concrete" and "abstract." One reaches the "abstract" when one "neglects" or *abstracts* some features implied in the "concrete," that is to say the real. Thus, for example, when in speaking of a tree one abstracts everything that is not it (the earth, the air, the planet Earth, the solar system, etc.), one is speaking of an abstraction that does not exist in reality (for the tree can exist only if there is the earth, the air, the rays of the sun, etc.). Hence all the particular sciences deal, in varying degrees, with abstractions. Similarly, an exclusively "national" politics is necessarily abstract (as is a "pure" politics that would, for example, abstract from religion or art). The isolated "particular" is by definition *abstract*. It is precisely in seeking the *concrete* that the philosopher rises to the "general ideas" which the "uninitiate" claims to scorn.

in their oratorical joust, if he was able to "maneuver" him as he pleased, there is no reason at all why he could not defeat and out-maneuver him in the realm of politics, and in particular, why he could not replace him at the head of the government—if he should ever desire to do so.

If the philosopher were to take power by means of his "dialec-tics," he would exercise it better, other things being equal, than any "uninitiate." And he would do so not only because of his greater dialectical skill. His government would be better because of a relative absence of *prejudices* and of the relatively more *concrete* character of his thought.

Of course, when it is simply a matter of maintaining an estab-lished state of things, without proceeding to "structural reforms" or to a "revolution," there is no particular disadvantage to *unconsciously* relying on generally accepted prejudices. That is to say that in such situations one can, without much harm, forego having philosophers in or near power. But where "structural reforms" or "revolutionary action" are objectively possible and hence necessary, the philosopher is particularly suited to set them in motion or to recommend them, since he, in contrast to the "uninitiate" ruler, knows that what has to be reformed or opposed is nothing but "prejudices," that is to say something unreal and hence relatively unresistant.

Finally, in "revolutionary" as well as in "conservative" periods, it is always preferable for the rulers not to lose sight of *concrete* reality. To be sure, that reality is extremely difficult and dense. That is why, in order to understand it with a view to dominating it, the man of action is compelled (since he thinks and acts *in time*) to simplify it by means of *abstractions*: he makes cuts and isolates certain parts or aspects by "abstracting" them from the rest and treating them "in themselves." But there is no reason to suppose that the philosopher could not do so as well. He would deserve the reproach commonly leveled at philoso-phers, that they have a predilection for "general ideas," only if these general ideas prevented him from seeing the particular *abstractions* which the "uninitiate" wrongly calls "*concrete* cases." But such a reproach, if it were justified, could only pertain to someone's con-tingent defects, not to the specific character of the philosopher. As a philosopher he handles abstractions as well as the "uninitiate," if not better. But since he is aware of the fact that he has performed an *abstraction*, he will be able to handle the "particular case" better than the "uninitiate" who believes that what is involved is a *concrete* reality which really is isolated from the rest, and can be treated as such. The philosopher will thus see the implications of the particular problem which escape the "uninitiate": he will see *farther* in space and in time.

For all these reasons, to which many more could have been added, I believe, with Hiero, Xenophon, and Strauss, and contrary to a widely held opinion, that the philosopher is perfectly capable of assuming power, and of governing or participating in government, for example by giving political advice to the tyrant.

The whole question then is whether or not he *wants* to do so. Now, one need only to raise this question (keeping in mind the *definition* of the philosopher) in order to see that it is exceedingly complex, and even insoluble.

The complexity and the difficulty of the question are due to the banal fact that man *needs time* to think and to act, and that the time at his disposal is in fact very limited.

It is this twofold fact, namely, man's essential temporality and finitude, that forces him to *choose* among his various existential possibilities (and that accounts for the being of *liberty* by, incidentally, also making for its ontological possibility). In particular, it is on account of his own temporality and finitude that the philosopher is compelled to *choose* between the quest for Wisdom and, for example, political activity, even if only the political activity of advising the tyrant. Now, at first sight, and according to the very definition of the philosopher, the philosopher will devote "all of his time" to the quest for Wisdom, that being his supreme value and goal. He will therefore renounce not only "vulgar pleasures," but also all *action* properly so-called, including that of governing, either directly or indirectly. Such was, at all events, the attitude taken by the "*Epicurean*" *philosophers*. And it is this "Epicurean" attitude that has inspired the popular image of the philosophical life. According to this image, the philosopher lives "outside the world": he retires into himself, isolates himself from other men, and has no interest in public life; he devotes all his time to the quest for "truth," which is pure "theory" or "contemplation" with no necessary connections with "action" of any kind. To be sure, a tyrant can disturb this philosopher. But such a philosopher would not disturb the tyrant, for he has not the slightest desire to meddle in his affairs, even if only by giving him advice. All this philosopher asks of the tyrant, his only "advice" to him, is not to pay any atttention to the philosopher's life, which is entirely devoted to the quest for a purely *theoretical* "truth" or an "ideal" of a strictly *isolated* life.

Two principal variants of this "Epicurean" attitude can be observed in the course of history. The pagan or aristocratic Epicurean, who is more or less wealthy or in any case does not work for a living (and as a rule finds a Maecenas to support him), isolates himself in a "garden," which he would like the government to treat as an inviolable castle, and from which he can be expected not to make any "sorties." The Christian or bourgeois Epicurean, the more or less poor intellectual who has to do something (write, teach, etc.) to secure his subsistence, cannot afford the luxury of the aristocratic Epicurean's "splendid isolation." He therefore replaces the private "garden" by what Pierre Bayle so aptly describes under the heading "the Republic of Letters." Here the atmosphere is less serene than it is in the "garden"; for here "the struggle for existence" and "economic competition" reign supreme. But the enterprise remains essentially "peaceful" in the sense that the "bourgeois republican," just like the "aristocratic castellan," is ready to renounce all *active* interference in public affairs in return for being "tolerated" by the government or the tyrant: the government or the tyrant would "leave him in peace" and permit him to exercise his trade of thinker, orator, or writer unimpeded, it being understood that his thoughts, speeches (lectures), and writings will remain purely "theoretical"; and that he will do nothing that could lead, directly or indirectly, to an *action* properly so called, and in particular to a *political* action of any kind.

Of course, it is practically impossible for the philosopher to keep this (generally sincere) promise of noninterference in the affairs of the State, and that is why rulers, and above all "tyrants," have always looked upon these Epicurean "republics" or "gardens" with suspicion. But that is of no interest to us at the present. What concerns us is the philosopher's attitude, and at first sight the Epicurean attitude appears to us irrefutable, and indeed even implied by the very definition of philosophy.

But at first sight only. For in fact the Epicurean attitude follows from the definition of philosophy as the quest for Wisdom or truth only if one assumes, regarding that quest, something that is not at all self-evident and that, from the perspective of the Hegelian conception, is even fundamentally mistaken. Indeed, in order to justify the philosopher's absolute *isolation,* one has to grant that Being is essentially immutable in itself and eternally identical with itself, and that it is completely revealed for all eternity in and by an intelligence that is perfect from the first; and this adequate revelation of the timeless totality of Being is, then, the Truth. Man (the philosopher) can *at any moment* participate in this Truth, either as the result of an action issuing from the Truth itself ("divine revelation"), or by his own *individual* effort to understand (the Platonic "intellectual intuition"), the only condition for such an effort being the innate "talent" of the one making this effort, independently of where he may happen to be situated in space (in the State) or in time (in history). If such is indeed the case, then the philosopher can and must isolate himself from the changing and tumultuous world (which is nothing but pure "appearance"), and live in a quiet "garden" or, if necessary, in a "Republic of Letters" where intellectual quarrels are at least less "unsettling" than are the political struggles on the outside. The quietude of this isolation, this total lack of interest in one's fellows and in any "society" whatever, offer the best prospects of attaining the Truth to the pursuit of which one has decided to devote one's entire life as an absolutely *egoistical* philosopher.[3]

But if one does not accept this *theistic* conception of Truth (and of Being), if one accepts the radical Hegelian atheism according to which Being itself is essentially temporal (Being=Becoming) and creates itself insofar as it is discursively revealed in the course of history (or as history: revealed Being=Truth=Man=History), and if one does not want to sink into the skeptical relativism which ruins the very idea of Truth and thus the quest for it or philosophy, then one has to flee the absolute solitude and isolation of the "garden" as well as the narrow society (the relative solitude and isolation) of the "Republic of Letters" and, like Socrates, frequent not the "trees and cicadas" but the "citizens of the City" (cf. *Phaedrus*). If Being creates itself ("becomes") in the course of History, then it is not by isolating oneself from History that one can reveal Being (transform it by *Discourse* into the *Truth* man "possesses" in the form of *Wisdom*). In order to reveal Being, the philosopher must, on the contrary, "participate" in history, and it is not clear why he should then not participate in it *actively*, for example by advising the tyrant, since, as a philosopher, he is better able to govern than any "uninitiate." The only thing that could keep him from it is *lack of time*. And so we come to the fundamental problem of the philosophical life, which the Epicureans wrongly believed they had disposed of.

I shall return later to this Hegelian problem of the philosophical life. For the moment we must take a somewhat closer look at the Epicurean attitude, for it is open to criticism, even allowing the *theistic*

---

[3]Strauss, in agreement with Xenophon, seems to grant this radical egoism of the philosophical life. Indeed he says that "the wise man is as self-sufficient as is humanly possible." The wise man is thus absolutely "uninterested" in other men.

conception of Being and Truth. Indeed, it involves and presupposes a most questionable conception of *Truth* (although it is generally accepted by pre-Hegelian philosophy), according to which "subjective certainty" (*Gewissheit*) everywhere and always coincides with "objective truth" (*Wahrheit*): one is presumed to be effectively in possession of the Truth (or of *a* truth) as soon as one is subjectively "sure and certain" of having it (for example, by having a "clear and distinct idea").

In other words, the isolated philosopher necessarily has to grant that the necessary and sufficient criterion of truth consists in the feeling of "evidence" that is presumably prompted by the "intellectual intuition" of the real and of Being, or that accompanies "clear and distinct ideas" or even "axioms," or that immediately attaches to divine revelations. This criterion of "evidence" was accepted by all "rationalist" philosophers from Plato to Husserl, passing by way of Descartes. Unfortunately, the criterion itself is not at all "evident," and I think that it is invalidated by the sole fact that there have always been *illuminati* and "false prophets" on earth, who never had the least doubt concerning the truth of their "intuitions" or of the authenticity of the "revelations" they received in one form or another. In short, an "isolated" thinker's subjective "evidence" is invalidated as a *criterion* of truth by the simple fact that there is madness which, insofar as it is a correct deduction from subjectively "evident" premises, can be "systematic" or "logical."

Strauss seems to follow Xenophon (and the ancient tradition in general) in justifying (explaining) the *isolated* philosopher's indifference ("egoism") and pride by the fact that he knows something more—and something different—than does the "uninitiate" whom he despises. But the madman who believes that he is made of glass, or who identifies with God the Father or with Napoleon, also believes that he knows something the others do not know. And we can call his knowledge madness only because he is *entirely alone* in taking this knowledge (which, incidentally, is subjectively "evident") for a truth, and because even the other madmen refuse to believe it. So too, it is only by seeing our ideas shared by others (or at least by *an* other) or accepted by them as *worth discussing* (even if only because they are regarded as wrong) that we can be sure of not finding ourselves in the realm of madness (without being sure that we are in the realm of truth). Hence the Epicurean philosopher, living strictly isolated in his "garden," could never know whether he has attained Wisdom or sunk into madness, and as a philosopher he would therefore have to flee the "garden" and its isolation. In fact, the Epicurean, recalling his Socratic origins, does not live in absolute isolation, and he receives philosophical *friends* in his "garden" with whom he engages in discussion. From this point of view there is, then, no essential difference between the aristocratic "garden" and the bourgeois intellectual's "Republic of Letters": the difference consists only in the number of the "elect." Both the "garden" and the "Republic" where one "discusses" from morning till night, provide a sufficient guarantee against the danger of madness. Although by taste, and by virtue of their very profession, the "lettered citizens" never agree among themselves, they will always be unanimous when it rightly comes to sending one of their number to an asylum. One may therefore be confident that, perhaps in spite of appearances, one will meet in the "garden" or in the "Republic" only persons who, although they may occasionally be odd, are essentially of sound mind (and sometimes mimic madness only in order to appear "original").

But the fact that one is never alone in the "garden" is not the only feature it has in common with the "Republic." There is also the fact that the "many" are excluded from it. To be sure, a "Republic of Letters" is generally more populated than an Epicurean "garden." But both are populated by a relatively small "elite" with a marked tendency to withdraw into itself and to exclude the "uninitiated."

Here again Strauss seems to follow Xenophon (who conforms to the ancient tradition) and to justify this kind of behavior. The wise man, he says, "is satisfied with the approval of a small minority." He seeks only the approval of those who are "worthy," and this can only be a very small number. The philosopher will therefore have recourse to *esoteric* (preferably oral) instruction which permits him, among other things, to select the "best" and to eliminate those "of limited capacity" who are incapable of understanding hidden allusions and tacit implications.

I must say that here again I differ from Strauss and the ancient tradition he would like to follow, which, in my opinion, rests on an aristocratic *prejudice* (perhaps characteristic of a *conquering* people). For I believe that the idea and the practice of the "intellectual elite" involves a very serious danger which the philosopher as such should want to avoid at any cost.

The danger to which the inhabitants of various "gardens," "academies," "lyceums," and "Republics of Letters" are exposed stems from what is called the "cloistered mind." To be sure, the "cloister," which is a society, does exclude *madness*, which is essentially asocial. But far from excluding *prejudices,* it tends, on the contrary, to foster them by perpetuating them: it can easily happen that only those are admitted in its midst, who accept the prejudices on which the "cloister" believes it can pride itself. Now, Philosophy is, by definition, something other than Wisdom: it necessarily involves "subjective certainties" that are not *the* Truth, in other words "prejudices." The philosopher's duty is to turn away from these prejudices as quickly and as completely as possible. Now, any closed society that adopts a doctrine, any "elite" selected in terms of a doctrinal teaching, tends to consolidate the prejudices entailed by that doctrine. The philosopher who shuns prejudices therefore has to try to live in the wide world (in the "market place" or "in the street," like Socrates) rather than in a "cloister" of any kind, "republican" or "aristocratic."[4]

The "cloistered" life, while dangerous on any hypothesis, is strictly unacceptable for the philosopher who with Hegel, acknowledges that reality (at least *human* reality), is not given once and for all, but creates itself in the course of time (at least in the course of *historical* time). For if that is the case, then the members of the "cloister," isolated from the rest of the world and not really taking part in public life in its historical evolution, will, sooner or later, be "left behind by events." Indeed, even what at one time was "true," can later become "false," change into a "prejudice," and only the "cloister" will fail to notice what has happened.

But the question of the philosophical "elite" can be dealt with fully only in the context of the general problem of "recognition," as that problem bears on the philosopher. Indeed, that is the perspective in which Strauss himself raises the question. And it is about this aspect of the question that I should now like to speak.

According to Strauss, the essential difference between Hiero, the tyrant, and Simonides, the philosopher, consists in this: Hiero would like "to be *loved* by *human beings* as such," while Simonides "is satisfied by the admiration, the praise, the approval of a *small minority.*" It is to win his subjects' *love* that Hiero must become their *benefactor*; Simonides lets himself be admired without *doing* anything to gain this admiration. In other words, Simonides is admired solely for his own *perfection,* while Hiero would like to be loved for his benefac-

---

[4]As Queneau has reminded us in *les Temps Modernes,* the philosopher is essentially a "voyou." <i.e. a hooligan: "Philosophes et voyous," *Temps Modernes,* 1951, No. 63, pp. 1193–1205; Kojève's reference involves a pun: the root of *voyou* is *voie,* street or road; so that "the philosopher who lives 'in the street' " would be a *voyou.* >

tions, even without being himself perfect. That is why the desire for admiration, independently of the desire for love, is "the natural foundation for the predominance of the desire for one's own perfection," whereas the need for love does not impel one to self-perfection and hence is not a "philosophical" desire.

This conception of the difference between the philosopher and the tyrant (which is, indeed, neither Strauss's nor, according to him, Xenophon's) does not seem to me to be satisfactory.

If one accepts (with Goethe and Hegel) that man is *loved* solely because he *is,* and independently of what he *does* (a mother loves her son in spite of his faults), while "admiration" or "recognition" are a function of the *actions* of the person one "admires" or "recognizes," it is clear that the tyrant, and the statesman in general, seeks *recognition* and not *love*: *love* thrives in the family, and the young man leaves his family and devotes himself to public life in search not of love, but of *recognition* by the State's citizens. Simonides rather < than Hiero > would have to be said to seek love, if he truly wanted to have a positive (even absolute) value attributed, not to his *actions,* but to his (perfect) *being.* But, in fact, it is simply not the case that he does. Simonides wants to be admired for his *perfection* and not for his *being* pure and simple, whatever that may be. Now love is specifically characterized by the fact that it attributes a positive value to the beloved or to the *being* of the beloved *without reason.* So that what Simonides seeks is, indeed, the recognition of his perfection and not the love of his being: he would like to be recognized for his perfection and therefore *desires* his perfection. Now, *desire* is actualized by *action* (negating action, since the aim is to negate existing imperfection, perfection being only desired and not yet attained). Hence it is by virtue of his *actions* (of self-perfection) that Simonides in fact is and wants to be recognized, just as Hiero is and wants to be recognized by virtue of his actions.

It is not true that the tyrant and the statesman in general are *by definition* content with a "gratuitous" admiration or recognition: just like the philosopher, they wish to "deserve" this admiration and recognition by truly being or becoming such as they appear to others to be. Hence the tyrant seeking recognition will also make an effort at self-perfection, if only for safety's sake, since an impostor or hypocrite always runs the risk of being "unmasked" sooner or later.

From this perspective there is therefore *in principle* no difference whatsoever between the statesman and the philosopher: both seek *recognition,* and both *act* with a view to deserving it (imposture can, in fact, be met with in both cases).

There remains the question of knowing whether it is true that the statesman seeks recognition by the "many," while the philosopher seeks to be recognized only by the "elect" few.

First of all, it does not seem that this is necessarily so with respect to the statesman as such. It is, indeed, for the most part so with respect to "democratic" leaders, who are dependent on the opinion of the majority. But "tyrants" have not always sought "popularity" (Tiberius, for example), and they have often had to be satisfied with the approval of a small circle of "political friends." Besides, there is no reason why the acclaim of the "many" should be incompatible with the approval of competent judges, and there is no reason why the statesman should prefer that acclaim to this approval. Conversely, it is not at all evident why the philosopher should systematically eschew the praise of the "many" (which undoubtedly gives him pleasure). What matters is that the philosopher not sacrifice the approval of the "elect" to "popular" acclaim, and that he not adapt his conduct to the demands of the "worst." But if a statesman (tyrant or not) were to behave differently in this matter than the philosopher, he would immediately be called a "demagogue"; and nothing says that statesmen are, by definition, "demagogues."

In fact, a man is fully satisfied only by the recognition of those he himself recognizes as worthy of recognizing him. And that is as true of the statesman as it is of the philosopher.

Now, to the extent that a man seeks recognition, he should do everything in his power to make the number of those "worthy" of recognizing him as large as possible. Consciously or not, statesmen have often assumed this task of political pedagogy (the "enlightened despot," the "pedagogical" tyrant). And philosophers have generally done the same, by devoting a portion of their time to philosophical pedagogy. Now, it is not clear why the number of the philosopher's initiates or disciples necessarily has to be limited or, for that matter, smaller than the number of the political man's *competent* admirers. If a philosopher artificially limited this number by proclaiming that he does not, under any circumstances *want* many initiates, he would only prove that he is less conscious of himself than the "uninitiated" political man who consciously strives for an unlimited extension of his recognition by competent judges. And if he maintained *a priori* and without empirical evidence that the number of people to whom philosophy is accessible is smaller than the number of people who can knowledgeably judge a political doctrine or a political action, he would be speaking on the basis of an undemonstrated "opinion" and thus be prey to a "prejudice" that is at best valid under certain social conditions and at a particular historical moment. In either case he would, therefore, not truly be a philosopher.

Besides, the prejudice in favor of an "elite" is all the more serious as it can bring about a total reversal of the situation. In principle the philosopher should only seek the admiration or approval of those he deems *worthy* of "recognizing" him. But if he never leaves the intentionally narrow circle of a deliberately recruited "elite" or of carefully chosen "friends," he runs the risk of considering "worthy" those and only those who approve of him or admire him. And it has to be acknowledged that this particularly disagreeable form of limited reciprocal recognition has always prevailed in Epicurean "gardens" and intellectual "cloisters."

Be that as it may. If, with Simonides, one grants that the philosopher seeks recognition (or admiration), and if, with Hegel, one recognizes that the statesman does so as well, then one has to conclude that, from this perspective, there is no essential difference between the tyrant and the philosopher. That is probably why Xenophon (according to Strauss), and Strauss himself, do not side with Simonides. According to Strauss, Xenophon contrasts Simonides with Socrates, who is not in the least interested in "the admiration or the praise of others," whereas Simonides is interested in nothing else. And one has the impression that Strauss agrees with this "Socratic" attitude: to the extent that the philosopher seeks recognition and admiration, he should exclusively give thought to his own recognition of his own worth and to his admiration for himself.

As for myself, I confess that I do not understand this very well, and I do not see how it could enable us to find an *essential* difference between the philosopher (or the wise man) and the tyrant (or the statesman in general).

If one takes the attitude of the Xenophon-Strauss Socrates literally, one is brought back to the case of the *isolated* philosopher who is utterly uninterested in other people's opinion of him. That is not a self-contradictory ("absurd") attitude, if the philosopher is prepared to grant that he may attain the Truth by some direct personal vision of Being or by an individual revelation proceeding from a transcendent God. But if he does grant this, then he will have no philosophically valid reason to *communicate* his knowledge (orally or in writing) to others (unless it be with a view to gaining their "recognition" or admiration, which is excluded by definition), and he will therefore not do so if he is truly a philosopher (who does not act "without reason").

We will therefore not know anything about him; we will not even know whether he exists, and hence whether he is a philosopher or simply a madman. What is more, in my opinion he will not even know it himself since he will be deprived of every social control, which is the only way to weed out "pathological" cases. In any event, his "solipsist" attitude, excluding as it does all "discussion," would be fundamentally anti-Socratic.

Let us therefore grant that "Socrates," who does engage in "discussion" with others, is in the highest degree interested in the opinion they have or will have about what he says and does, at least to the extent to which they are, in his view, "competent." If "Socrates" is a true philosopher, he makes progress in Wisdom (which implies knowledge and "virtue"), and he is conscious of his progress. If he is not perverted by the prejudice of Christian humility to the point of being hypocritical with himself, he will be more or less *satisfied* with his progress, that is to say with himself: let us say, without being afraid of the word, that he will have more or less self-*admiration* (above all if he considers himself more "advanced" than the *others*). If those who express opinions about him are "competent," they will appreciate him in the same way he appreciates himself (on the assumption that he is not deluding himself), that is to say that, if they are not blinded by envy, they will admire him to the same extent that he admires himself. And if "Socrates" is not a "Christian," he will acknowledge (to himself and to others) that being admired by others brings (a certain) "satisfaction" and (a certain) "pleasure." Admittedly, that does not mean that the mere fact of (consciously) making progress on the road to Wisdom gives "Socrates" no other "pleasure" and "satisfaction" than he gets from being able to admire himself and being admired by others: everyone knows the "pure joy" one derives from the acquisition of knowledge, and the "disinterested satisfaction" that comes with the feeling of "having done one's duty." Nor does it follow that it is *in principle* impossible to seek knowledge and do one's duty without being motivated by the *resulting* "pleasure." Indeed, is it not possible to engage in sports just for the "love" of it, and without particularly seeking the "pleasure" of the "victor's crown" in a *competition?*

On the contrary, it is evident that, in fact, all these things are absolutely inseparable. It is certainly possible to draw subtle distinctions "in theory," but "in practice" it is impossible to eliminate one of the elements while retaining the others. That is to say that there can be no verifying *experiment* in this realm, and that therefore nothing regarding this question can be *known* in the "scientific" sense of the term.

It is known that there are pleasures that have nothing to do with knowledge or virtue. It is also known that men have at times renounced these pleasures in order to devote themselves fully to the quest for truth or to the exercise of virtue. But since this quest and this exercise are in fact inseparably linked with *sui generis* "pleasures," there is absolutely no way of knowing whether what makes men act that way is in fact a choice between different "pleasures," or a choice between "pleasure" and "duty" or "knowledge." Now these *sui generis* "pleasures" are in turn *inseparably* linked with the specific "pleasure" that comes from self-satisfaction or self-admiration: regardless of what Christians may say, one cannot be wise and virtuous (that is to say, in fact wiser and more virtuous than all, or at least than some others) without deriving a certain "satisfaction" and a sort of "pleasure" from it.[5] There is therefore no knowing whether, in fact, the "primary motive" of conduct is the "pure" joy that comes from Wisdom (knowledge + virtue), or whether it is the sometimes condemned "pleasure" that comes from the wise man's self-admiration (regardless of whether it is influenced by other people's admiration of him or not).

The same ambiguity is apparent when one considers "Socrates" in his relations with others. We have granted that he is interested in the opinion others have of him to the extent that it enables him to test whether or not the opinion he has of himself is well founded. But everything else is ambiguous. One can maintain, as Xenophon-Strauss seem to do, that Socrates is interested only in other people's "theoretical" judgments of him, and that he is completely uninterested in their *admiration* of him: he derives his "pleasure" solely from *self*-admiration (which either determines his philosophical activity, or merely accompanies it). But one can just as well say that the self-admiration of a man who is not mad, necessarily implies and presupposes admiration by others; that a "normal" person cannot be truly "satisfied" with himself without being not only judged, but also "recognized" by all or

---

[5]As a matter of fact, Christians only succeeded in "spoiling this pleasure" by playing on the disagreeable sentiment that manifests itself in the form of "jealousy" or "envy," among others: one is dissatisfied with oneself (sometimes one even despises oneself) when one is "worse than someone else." Now a Christian always has at his disposal an other who is better than himself, this Other being God himself, who made himself man in order to facilitate the comparison. To the extent that this man to whom he compares himself and whom he tries in vain to imitate is for him a God, the Christian experiences neither "envy" nor "jealousy" toward him, but only an "inferiority complex" pure and simple, which does, however, suffice to keep him from recognizing his own wisdom or virtue and from "enjoying" that recognition.

at least some others. One might even go further, and say that the pleasure involved in self-admiration is relatively worthless when compared with the pleasure one gets from being admired by someone else. These are some *possible* psychological analyses of the phenomenon of "recognition," but since it is impossible to perform experiments that separate its various aspects, it is impossible to settle the issue conclusively in favor of any one of these analyses.

It would certainly be wrong to suppose that "Socrates" seeks knowledge and practices virtue *solely* for the sake of "recognition" by others. For experience shows that one can pursue science for the pure love of it on a desert island without hope of return, and be "virtuous" without witnesses (human or even divine), simply out of fear of falling short in one's own eyes. But nothing prevents our asserting that, when "Socrates" *communicates* with others and practices his virtue *in public,* he does so not only in order to test himself, but also (and perhaps even above all) with a view to external "recognition." By what right can we maintain that he does not seek this "recognition," since he *necessarily* finds it in fact?

Truth to tell, all these distinctions make sense only if one accepts the existence of a God who sees clearly into men's hearts and judges them according to their intentions (which may, of course, be unconscious). If one is truly an atheist, none of this any longer makes sense. For it is evident that in that case only introspection could provide the elements of an answer. Now, as long as a man is alone in knowing something, he can never be sure that he truly *knows* it. If, as a consistent atheist, one replaces God (understood as consciousness and will surpassing individual human consciousness and will) by Society (the State) and History, one has to say that whatever is, in fact, beyond the range of social and historical verification, is forever relegated to the realm of *opinion (doxa).*

That is why I do not agree with Strauss when he says that Xenophon posed the problem of the relationship between pleasure and virtue in a radical way. I do not agree for the simple reason that I do not think that (from the atheistic point of view) there is a problem there which could be resolved by some form of *knowledge (epistēmē).* More exactly, the problem admits of several possible solutions, none of which is truly *certain.* For it is impossible to know whether the philosopher (the wise man) seeks knowledge and practices virtue "for their own sakes" (or "out of duty"), or whether he seeks it for the sake of the "pleasure" (joy) he experiences in doing so, or, finally, whether he acts this way in order to experience self-admiration (influenced or not by other people's admiration). This question obviously cannot be settled "from outside," and there is therefore no way to assess the "subjective certainty" achieved by introspection, nor to decide among these "certainties" if they should disagree.[6]

What is worth retaining from what has gone so far, is that some philosophers' "Epicurean" conception is not in any way justified by a comprehensive and consistent system of thought. That conception becomes questionable as soon as one takes the problem of "recognition" into account, as I have just done, and it is problematic even when one restricts oneself to the problem of the criterion of truth, as I did at first.

To the extent that the philosopher looks upon "discussion" (dialogue, dialectic) as a method of investigation and a criterion of truth, he necessarily has to "educate" his interlocutors. And we have seen that he has no reason to place an *a priori* limit on the number of his possible interlocutors. That is to say that the philosopher has to be a pedagogue and has to try to extend his (direct or indirect) pedagogical activity indefinitely. But in so doing, he will always sooner or later encroach on the field of action of the statesman or of the tyrant, who themselves also are (more or less consciously) "educators."

As a rule, the interference of the philosopher's pedagogical activity with the tyrant's takes the form of a more or less acute conflict. Thus "corrupting the young" was the principal charge brought against Socrates. The philosopher-pedagogue will therefore be naturally inclined to try to influence the tyrant (or the government in general) with a view to getting him to create conditions that permit the exercise of philosophical pedagogy. But in fact the State is itself a pedagogical institution. The pedagogy practiced and controlled by the government is an integral part of governmental activity in general, and it is a

---

[6]Observation of "conduct" cannot *settle* the question. But the fact remains that in observing philosophers (for want of wise men) one really does not get the impression that they are insensitive to praise, or even to flattery. One can even say that, like all intellectuals, they are on the whole more vain than men of action. Indeed, it is readily understandable why they would be. Men do the specific things they do in order to *succeed* or "to achieve success" (and not to fail). Now, the "success" of an undertaking involving action can be measured by its objective "outcome" (a bridge that does not collapse, a business that makes money, a war won, a state that is strong and prosperous, etc.), independently of other people's opinion of it, while the "success" of a book or of an intellectual discourse is nothing but other people's recognition of its value. So that the intellectual depends very much more than does the man of action (including the tyrant) on other people's admiration, and he is more sensitive than the man of action to the absence of such admiration. Without it, he has absolutely no valid reason to admire himself, while the man of action can admire himself on account of his objective (even solitary) "successes." And that is why, as a general rule, the intellectual who does nothing but talk and write is more "vain" than the man who acts, in the strong sense of the term.

function of the very structure of the State. Hence to want to influence the government with a view to introducing or to administering a philosophical pedagogy is to want to influence the government in general, it is to want to determine or to co-determine its policy as such. Now, the philosopher cannot give up pedagogy. Indeed, the "success" of his philosophical pedagogy is the sole "objective" criterion of the truth of the philosopher's "doctrine": the fact of his having disciples (either in a narrow or in a broad sense) is his guarantee against the danger of madness, and his disciples' "success" in private and public life is the "objective" proof of the (relative) "truth" of his doctrine, at least in the sense of its adequacy to the given historical reality.

So that if one does not want to leave it at the merely subjective criteria of "evidence" or of "revelation" (which do not exclude the danger of madness), one cannot be a philosopher without at the same time wanting to be a philosophical *pedagogue*. And if the philosopher does not want artificially or unduly to restrict the scope of his pedagogical activity (and thereby risk being subject to the prejudices of the "cloister"), he will necessarily be strongly inclined to participate, in one way or another, in government as a whole, so that the State might be organized and governed in a way that makes his philosophical pedagogy both possible and effective.

It is probably for this (more or less consciously acknowledged) reason that most philosophers, including the greatest, gave up their "Epicurean" isolation and engaged in political activity, either by personal interventions or through their writings. Plato's voyages to Syracuse, and the collaboration between Spinoza and De Witt, are familiar examples of direct intervention. And it is well known that nearly all philosophers have published works dealing with the State and with government.[7]

But here the conflict that stems from man's temporality and finitude, and about which I spoke earlier, comes into play. On the one hand, the philosopher's supreme goal is the quest for Wisdom or Truth, and this quest, which a philosopher by definition never completes, is supposed to take *all of his time*. On the other hand, it also takes time, and even a great deal of time, to govern a State, however small it may be. Truth to tell, governing a State also takes *all of a man's time*.

Since they cannot devote *all of their time* both to philosophy and to government, philosophers have generally looked for a compromise solution. While they wanted to be involved in politics, they did not

---

[7]The case of Descartes is too complicated to discuss here.

give up their strictly philosophical involvement, but only agreed to limit somewhat the time they devoted to it. They therefore gave up the idea of taking over the governance of the State, and left it at devoting the little time they set aside from philosophy to giving the rulers of the day (oral or written) *advice*.

Unfortunately, this compromise has proven unworkable. To be sure, Philosophy has not particularly suffered from the philosophers' political "distractions." But the direct and immediate effect of their political advice has been strictly nil.

Truth to tell, the philosophers who left it at giving written, indeed "bookish" advice, did not look upon their failure as a tragedy. For the most part they had enough good sense not to expect the powers that be to read their writings, and to expect even less that they would be guided by them in their daily work. In resigning themselves to being active exclusively through writing, they resigned themselves to being politically ineffectual in the short run. However, those who did deign to go to some personal trouble in order to give political advice may have taken the lack of readiness to follow that advice rather ill, and they may have had the impression of really having "wasted their time."

Of course, we do not know Plato's reactions after his Sicilian failure. The fact that he renewed his abortive attempt suggests that, in his view, both sides were to blame for it, and that if he had acted differently, he could have done better and accomplished more. But in general, the common opinion of more or less philosophical intellectuals heaps opprobrium and contempt on reluctant rulers. I nevertheless persist in believing that it is entirely wrong to do so.

First of all, there is a tendency to blame the "tyrannical" character of a government unresponsive to philosophical advice. Yet it seems to me that the philosopher is in a particularly poor position to criticize tyranny as such. On the one hand the philosopher-advisor is, by definition, in a great hurry: he is entirely prepared to contribute to the reform of the State, but he would like to lose as little time as possible in the process. Now, if he wants to succeed *quickly*, he has to address himself to the tyrant rather than to the democratic leader. Indeed, philosophers who wanted to *act* in the political present have, at all times, been drawn to tyranny. Whenever there has been a powerful and effective tyrant contemporary with the philosopher, it is precisely on him that the philosopher lavished his advice, even if the tyrant lived in a foreign country. On the other hand, it is difficult to imagine a philosopher himself (*per impossibile*) becoming a statesman, except as some sort of "tyrant." In a hurry "to have done" with politics and to return to more noble occupations, he will scarcely be endowed with exceptional political patience. Despising the "great mass," indifferent to its praise, he will not want patiently to play the role of a "democratic" ruler, solicitous of the opinions and desires of the "masses" and the "militants." Besides, how could he implement his reform programs, which are necessarily radical and opposed to the commonly received ideas, *rapidly*, without resorting to political procedures that have always been taxed with being "tyrannical"? In fact, as soon as a philosopher who was not himself involved in affairs of State steered one of his disciples in that direction, the disciple—for example Alcibiades—did immediately resort to typically "tyrannical" methods. Inversely, whenever a statesman openly acted in the name of a philosophy, he did so as a "tyrant," just as "tyrants" of a certain grandeur have generally had more or less direct and more or less conscious and acknowledged philosophical origins.

In short, of all possible statesmen, the tyrant is unquestionably the most likely to receive and to implement the philosopher's advice. If, having received it, he does not implement it, he must have very good reasons for not doing so. What is more, in my opinion these reasons would be even more cogent in the case of a non-"tyrannical" ruler.

I have already indicated what these reasons are. A statesman, regardless of whether he is or not a tyrant, simply cannot follow "utopian" advice: since he can *act* only in the *present,* he cannot take into account ideas that have no *direct* connection with the concrete given situation. So that in order to obtain a hearing, the philosopher would have had to give advice about "current business." But in order to give such advice, one has to keep up with current business on a daily basis, and hence to devote *all of one's time* to it. Yet that is precisely what the philosopher does not *want* to do. In his capacity as a philosopher he even *cannot* do so. For to do so would mean to abandon the very quest for truth that makes him a philosopher and that, in his eyes, is his only authentic claim to being the tyrant's *philosophical* advisor, that is to say to being an advisor entitled to something more than and different from an "uninitiated" advisor, regardless of how intelligent and capable that uninitiated advisor might otherwise be. To devote *all of one's time* to government is to cease to be a philosopher and hence to lose any advantage one might have over the tyrant and his "uninitiated" advisors.

As a matter of fact, that is not the only reason why the philosopher's every attempt at directly influencing the tyrant is necessarily ineffectual. For example, let us suppose that Plato had remained in Syracuse to the end of his days, that he had climbed (rapidly, of course) the various rungs leading to a position whose holder may make decisions and hence influence the general political direction. It is practically certain that, *in that case,* Plato would have had the tyrant's ear, and could in effect have guided his policy. But what would happen in that case? On the one hand, Dionysus, eager to carry out the "radical" reforms suggested by Plato, would surely have had to intensify the "tyrannical" character of his government more and more. His philosophical advisor would then soon have found himself faced with "cases of conscience" as his quest for an "objective truth" embodied in the "ideal" State came into conflict with his conception of a "virtue" at odds with "violence," which he would nevertheless like to continue to practice. On the other hand, Plato, conscious (in contrast to Dionysus) of the limits of his own knowledge, would soon have become aware of having reached these limits: whereupon he would grow hesitant in his advice, and hence unable to give it *in time.* Now, these theoretical uncertainties and moral conflicts, against the background of the "guilty conscience" aroused by the fact that he no longer has the time to devote himself to philosophy, will soon have disgusted the philosopher with all direct and concrete political action. And since, in the meantime, he will have understood that it is either ridiculous or hypocritical to offer the tyrant "general ideas" or "utopian" advice, the philosopher, upon submitting his resignation, would leave the tyrant "in peace," and spare him any advice *as well as any criticism*: most particularly if he knew that the tyrant is pursuing the same goal he himself had been pursuing during his—voluntarily aborted—career as advisor.

Which is as much as to say that the conflict of the philosopher confronted with the tyrant is nothing else than the conflict of the intellectual faced with action, or, more precisely, faced with the inclination, or even the necessity, to act. According to Hegel, that conflict is the only authentic *tragedy* that takes place in the Christian or bourgeois world: the tragedy of Hamlet and of Faust. It is a *tragic* conflict because it is a conflict with no way out, a problem with no possible resolution.

Faced with the impossibility of *acting* politically without giving up philosophy, the philosopher gives up political action. But has he any *reasons* for giving it up?

The preceding considerations can in no way be invoked to "justify" such a choice. And by definition the philosopher should not reach a decision without "sufficient reason," nor assume a position that "can not be justified" within the framework of a coherent system of thought. It therefore remains for us to see how, in his own judgment, the philosopher could "justify" giving up political *action* in the precise sense of the term.

The first "justification" one might be tempted to offer is easy. The fact that he has not solved a problem need not disturb the philosopher. Since he is not a wise man, he, by definition, lives in a world of questions which, for him, remain open. All that is required for him to be a philosopher, is that he be aware of the existence of these questions, and that he . . . *seek* to solve them. The best method to use in that search (at least according to the Platonists), is "dialectics," that is to say "meditation" tested and stimulated by "dialogue." In other words, the best method is "discussion." So that, in our case, instead of giving the tyrant of the day political advice or, alternatively, abstaining from all criticism of the government in power, the philosopher could leave it at "discussing" the question of whether he himself should govern, or whether he should only advise the tyrant, or whether he should not rather abstain from all political action and even from all concrete criticism of the government by devoting all his time to theoretical pursuits of a more "elevated" and less "mundane" kind. Now, discussing this question is what philosophers have been doing forever. In particular, that is what Xenophon did in his dialogue, what Strauss does in his book, and what I myself am doing in the present critical essay. Thus everything seems to be in order. Yet one cannot help being somewhat disappointed by the fact that this "discussion" of the problem at hand, after having gone on for more than two thousand years, has not resulted in some kind of *solution*.

Perhaps one might try to *resolve* the question by going beyond *discussion* with philosophers and using the "objective" method Hegel used in order to reach "indisputable" solutions.

That is the method of *historical verification*.

For Hegel, the outcome of the classical "dialectic" of the "dialogue," that is, the victory won in a purely *verbal* "discussion," is not a sufficient criterion of the truth. In other words, discursive "dialectic" as such cannot, according to him, lead to the *definitive* solution of a problem (that is to say, a solution that remains unchanging for *all* time to *come*), for the simple reason that, if one leaves it at *talking*, one will never succeed in definitively "eliminating" the contradictor or, consequently, the contradiction itself; for to *refute* someone is not necessarily to *convince* him. "Contradiction" or "controversy" (between Man and Nature on the one hand or, on the other hand, between man and man, or even between a man and his social and historical milieu) can be "dialectically done away with" (that is to say, *done away with* insofar as they are "false," but *preserved* insofar as they are "true," and *raised* to a higher level of "discussion") only to the extent that they are played out on the *historical* plane of *active social* life where one argues by *acts* of Work (against Nature) and of Struggle (against men). Admittedly, Truth emerges from this active "dialogue," this historical dialectic, only once it is completed, that is to say once history reaches its final stage <*terme final*> in and through the universal and homogeneous State which, since it implies the citizens' "satisfaction," excludes any possibility of negating *action,* hence of all *negation* in general, and, hence, of any new "discussion" of what has already been established. But, even without wishing to assume, with the author of the *Phenomenology of Mind,* that history is already virtually "completed" in our time, one can assert that if the "solution" to a problem has, in fact, been historically or socially "valid" throughout the entire period that has elapsed since, then, short of (historical) *proof* to the contrary, one has the *right* to regard it as philosophically "valid," in spite of the philosophers' ongoing "discussion" of the problem. In so regarding it, one may assume that, at the opportune moment, History itself will take care to put an end to the endlessly ongoing "philosophical discussion" of a problem it has virtually "resolved."

Let us therefore see whether understanding our historical past enables us to resolve the problem of the relation between Wisdom and Tyranny, and thus to decide what should be the Philosopher's "reasonable," that is to say "philosophical," conduct with respect to government.

A priori it seems plausible that history could resolve the question or conflict which the philosophers' *individual* meditations (including mine) have so far been unable to settle. Indeed, we have seen that the conflict itself, as well as its "tragic" character, are due to the *finitude,* that is to say to the *finite temporality* of man in general and of the philosopher in particular. If he were *eternal,* in the sense of not needing *time* to act and to think, or if he had unlimited time to act and to think, the question would not even arise (as it does not arise for God). Now, history *transcends* the finite duration of man's individual existence. To be sure, it is not "eternal" in the classical sense of the term, since it is only the integration with respect to time of *temporal* acts and thoughts. But if, with Hegel, one grants (and anyone who would like to be able to grant, as Hegel does, that there is a *meaning* to history and historical *progress,* should have agreed with him on this point), that history can *reach completion* in and by itself, and that the "Absolute Knowledge" (=discursive Wisdom or Truth) that results from "understanding" or "explaining" integral history (or history integrated in and by this very Knowledge) by a "coherent discourse" (*Logos*) that is "circular" or "uni-total" in the sense of exhausting all the possibilities (assumed to be *finite*) of "rational" (that is to say of inherently non-contradictory) thought, if one grants all this, I say, then one can equate History (completed and integrated in and by this "absolute" discursive Knowledge) with *eternity* understood as the *totality of time* (historical, that is to say of human time, that is to say of time capable of containing any "discussion" whatsoever, in deed or in speech), *beyond* which no one single man could go, anymore than could Man as such. In short, if an individual properly so-called has not yet been able to solve the problem that interests us because it is *insoluble* on the individual level, there is no *a priori* reason why the "great individual" of whom Pascal speaks (who will not *always* learn, but who does *learn* some things in the strict sense of the term), might not have solved it long ago and "definitively" (even if not a single *individual* has as yet noticed it).

Let us then see what history teaches us about the relations between tyrants and philosophers (on the premise that so far there has not been a wise man on earth).

At first sight history confirms common opinion. Not only has no philosopher ever yet in fact governed a State, but all political men, and "tyrants" foremost among them, have always despised the philosophers' "general ideas," and dismissed their political "advice." The political action of philosophers thus appears to have been nil, and the lesson they might draw from history would seem to encourage them to devote themselves to "contemplation" or "pure theory," without concern for what "men of action," and in particular "rulers" of every kind might be doing in the meantime.

But upon closer examination, the lesson to be drawn from history appears to be an entirely different one. Within the geographic realm of Western philosophy, perhaps the greatest Statesman, and certainly the one whom the great tyrants of our world have imitated for centuries (and who was only recently again imitated by an imitator of Napoleon who imitated Caesar, who was himself an imitator) was Alexander the

Great. Now Alexander had perhaps read the dialogues of Xenophon. He had certainly been a student of Aristotle, who had been a student of Plato, a student of Socrates. So that Alexander, without a doubt, indirectly received the same teaching as Alcibiades. Either because he was politically more gifted than Alcibiades, or simply because he came "at the right time," Alexander succeeded where Alcibiades failed. But both wanted the same thing, and both tried to go beyond the rigid and narrow confines of the ancient City. Nothing prevents our assuming that these two political attempts, only one of which met with failure, can be traced back to the philosophical teaching of Socrates.

Admittedly this is no more than a simple historical hypothesis. But an analysis of the facts about Alexander renders this hypothesis plausible.

What characterizes the political action of Alexander in contrast to the political action of all of his Greek predecessors and contemporaries, is that it was guided by the idea of *empire,* that is to say of a *universal* State, at least in the sense that this State had no *a priori given* limits (geographic, ethnic, or otherwise), no *pre-established* "capital," nor even a geographically and ethnically *fixed* center destined to exercise political dominion over its periphery. To be sure, there have at all times been conquerors ready to extend the realm of their conquests indefinitely. But as a rule they sought to establish the same type of relation between conquerors and conquered as that between Master and Slave. Alexander, by contrast, was clearly ready to dissolve the whole of Macedonia and of Greece in the new political unit created by his conquest, and to govern this unit from a geographical point he would have *freely* (rationally) chosen in terms of the new *whole.* Moreover, by requiring Macedonians and Greeks to enter into mixed marriages with "Barbarians," he was surely intending to create a new ruling stratum that would be independent of all rigid and *given* ethnic support.

Now, what might account for the fact that it should have been the head of a *national* State (and not of a "city" or a *polis*) with a sufficiently broad ethnic and geographic base to allow him to exercise over Greece and the Orient a one-sided political dominion of the traditional type, who conceived of the idea of a truly *universal* State or of an *Empire* in the strict sense of the term, in which conqueror and conquered are merged? It was an utterly new political idea that only began to be *actualized* with the Edict of Caracalla, that is still not anywhere actualized in all its purity, having in the meantime (and only lately) suffered some spectacular eclipses, and that is still a subject of "discussion." What might account for the fact that it was a hereditary monarch who consented to expatriate himself and who wanted to merge the victorious nobility of his native land with the newly vanquished? Instead of establishing the domination of his *race* and imposing the rule of his *fatherland* over the rest of the world, he chose to dissolve the race and to eliminate the fatherland itself for all political intents and purposes.

One is tempted to ascribe all this to Aristotle's education and to the general influence of "Socratic-Platonic" *philosophy* (which is also the foundation of the Sophists' properly political teaching to which Alexander was exposed). A student of Aristotle's might have thought it necessary to create a *biological* foundation for the unity of the Empire (by means of mixed marriages). But only the disciple of Socrates-Plato could have conceived of this unity by taking as his point of departure the "idea" or the "general notion" of Man that had been elaborated by Greek philosophy. All men can become citizens of one and the same State (=Empire) because they *have* (or acquire as a result of *biological* unions) one and the same "essence." And in the last analysis this single "essence" common to all men is "*Logos*" (language-science), that is to say what nowadays we call (Greek) "civilization" or "culture." The Empire which Alexander had projected is not the political expression of a *people* or a *caste*. It is the political expression of a *civilization,* the material actualization of a "logical" entity, universal and one, just as the *Logos* itself is universal and one.

Long before Alexander, the Pharaoh Ikhnaton also probably conceived the idea of Empire in the sense of a trans-ethnic (trans-national) political unit. Indeed, an Amarnian bas-relief depicts the traditional Asiatic, Nubian, and Libyan not as shackled by the Egyptian, but as worshiping with him, *as equals,* one and the same god: Aton. Only here the unity of the Empire had a *religious* (theistic), not a philosophical (anthropological), origin: its basis was a common *god* and not the "essential" unity of men in their capacity as humans (=rational). It was not the unity of their reason and of their culture (*Logos*), but the unity of their god and the community of their worship that united the citizens.

Since Ikhnaton, who failed woefully, the idea of an Empire with a *transcendent* (religious) unifying basis has frequently been taken up again. Through the intermediary of the Hebrew prophets it was adopted by St. Paul and the Christians, on the one hand, and by Islam on the other (to speak only of the most spectacular political attempts). But what has stood the test of history by lasting up to the present is not Muslim *theocracy,* nor the Germanic *Holy Empire,* nor even the Pope's secular power, but the universal *Church,* which is something altogether different from a *State* properly so called. One may therefore conclude that, in the final analysis, it is exclusively the *philosophical* idea going all the way back to Socrates that acts *politically* on earth, and that continues in our time to guide the political actions and entities striving to actualize the *universal* State or Empire.

But the political goal humanity is pursuing (or fighting) at present is not only that of the politically *universal* State; it is just as much that of the socially *homogeneous* State or of the "classless Society."

Here again the *remote* origins of the political idea are found in the *religious* universalist conception that is already present in Ikhnaton and that culminates in St. Paul. It is the idea of the *fundamental equality* of all who believe in the same God. This transcendent conception of social equality differs radically from the Socratic-Platonic conception of the identity of all the beings that have the same *immanent* "essence." For Alexander, the disciple of the Greek philosophers, Greek and Barbarian have the same claim to political citizenship in the Empire in so far as they HAVE the same human (i.e. rational, logical, discursive) "nature" (=essence, idea, form, etc.), or that they *identify* "essentially" with one another as a result of a direct (="immediate") "mixture" of their innate qualities (achieved by biological union). For St. Paul there is no "essential" (irreducible) difference between Greek and Jew because both can BECOME Christians, and they would do so not by "mixing" Greek and Jewish "qualities" but by *negating* and "synthesizing" them in and by this very negation into a homogeneous unity that is not innate or given but (freely) *created* by "conversion." Because of the *negating* character of this Christian "synthesis," no incompatible or even "contradictory" (=mutually exclusive) "qualities" remain. For Alexander, the Greek philosopher, no "mixture" of Masters and Slaves was possible, because they were "contraries." Thus his *universal* State, which did away with *races,* could not be *homogeneous* in the sense of also doing away with "classes." For St. Paul, on the other hand, the negation (which is *active* inasmuch as "faith" is an *act* and is "dead" without "acts") of the opposition between pagan Mastery and Slavery could engender an "essentially" *new* Christian unity (which, moreover, is also active or acting, and even "affective," rather than purely rational or discursive, that is to say "logical") capable of providing the basis not only of the State's political *universality* but also of its social *homogeneity.*

But in fact, universality and homogeneity on a transcendent, theistic, religious basis did not and could not engender a *State* properly so called. They only served as the basis of the universal and homogeneous *Church*'s "mystical body" and are supposed to be fully actualized only in the *beyond* (the "Kingdom of Heaven," provided one abstracts from the *permanent* existence of hell). In fact, the *universal* State is the one goal which *politics*, entirely under the twin influence of ancient pagan *philosophy* and Christian *religion*, has pursued, although it has so far never attained it.

But in our day the universal and *homogeneous* State has become a *political* goal as well. Now here again, politics is derivative from *philosophy*. To be sure, this philosophy (being the *negation* of religious Christianity) is in turn derivative from St. Paul (whom it presupposes since it "negates" him). But the religious Christian idea of human homogeneity could achieve real *political* import only once modern philosophy succeeded in *secularizing* it (=rationalizing it, transforming it into coherent discourse).

As regards social homogeneity, the filiation between philosophy and politics is less direct than it is as regards political universality, but, in return, it is absolutely certain. In the case of universality, we only know that the Statesman who took the first effective step toward actualizing it was educated by a disciple twice removed from its theoretical initiator, and we can only assume the filiation of ideas. By contrast, in the case of homogeneity we know that there was a filiation of ideas, although we have no direct oral tradition to confirm it. The tyrant who here initiates the *real* political movement toward homogeneity consciously followed the teaching of the intellectual who deliberately transformed the idea of the philosopher so that it might cease to be a "utopian" ideal (which, incidentally, was erroneously thought to describe an already existing political reality: the Empire of Napoleon) and become, instead, a political theory in terms of which one might give tyrants concrete advice, advice which they could follow. Thus, while recognizing that the tyrant has "falsified" (*verkehrt*) the philosophical idea, we know that he has done so only in order to "transpose it (*verkehren*) from the realm of abstraction into that of reality."

I leave it at citing these two historical examples, although it would be easy to multiply their number. But these two examples for all intents and purposes exhaust the great political themes of History. And if one grants that, in these two cases, all that the "tyrannical" king and the tyrant properly so-called did was to put into political practice the philosophers' teaching (meanwhile suitably prepared by intellectuals), then one can conclude that the philosophers' political advice has essentially been followed.

To be sure, the philosophers' teaching, even when it has a political cast, could never be implemented *directly* or "immediately." One might therefore view it as by definition *inapplicable* because it lacked *direct* or "immediate" connections with the concrete political reality prevailing at the time it appears. But "intellectual mediators" have always taken hold of it and confronted it with contemporary reality by trying to discover or to construct a bridge between the two. This purely intellectual labor of bringing the philosophical idea and the political reality more closely together could go on for a more or less long time. But sooner or later some tyrant always sought guidance in his day-to-day actions from the *usable* (oral or written) advice issuing from these "mediators." When history is viewed in this light, it appears as a continuous succession of political actions guided more or less directly by the evolution of *philosophy.*

From the Hegelian perspective, based on the understanding of history, the relations between Tyranny and Wisdom may therefore be described as follows.

As long as man has not become fully conscious of a given political situation at a given historical moment by discursive *philosophical* reflection, he has no "distance" with respect to it. He cannot "take a stand," he cannot consciously and freely decide for or against it. He is simply "passive" with respect to the political world, just as the animal is passive with respect to the natural world in which it lives. But once he has achieved full philosophical consciousness, man can distinguish between the *given* political reality and his idea of it "in his head," an idea that can then serve as an "ideal." However, if man leaves it at philosophically *understanding* (=explaining or justifying) the given political reality, he will never be able to *go beyond* this reality or the philosophical idea that corresponds to it. For a "going beyond" or for philosophical *progress* toward Wisdom (=Truth) to occur, the political given (which *can* be negated) must actually be *negated* by Action (Struggle and Work), so that a new historical or political (that is to say human) reality be, first of all, *created* in and by this active negation of the already existing and philosophically understood real, and, then, *understood* within the framework of a new philosophy. This new philosophy will preserve only that part of the old which has survived the test of the creative political negation of the historical reality that corresponded to it, and it will transform or "sublimate" this preserved part by synthesizing it (in and by a coherent discourse) with its own revelation of the new historical reality. Only by proceeding in this fashion will philosophy make its way toward absolute Knowledge or Wisdom, which it will be in a position to attain only once all possible active (political) negations have been accomplished.

In short, if philosophers gave Statesmen no political "advice" at all, in the sense that no political teaching whatsoever could (directly or indirectly) be drawn from their ideas, there would be no historical *progress,* and hence no History properly so called. But if the Statesmen did not eventually *actualize* the philosophically based "advice" by their day-to-day political action, there would be no philosophical *progress* (toward Wisdom or Truth) and hence no Philosophy in the strict sense of the term. So-called "philosophical" *books* would of course get written indefinitely, but we would never have *the* book ("Bible") of Wisdom that could *definitively* replace the book by that title which we have had for nearly two thousand years. Now, wherever it has been a matter of actively negating a given political reality in its very "essence," we have always, in the course of history, seen political *tyrants* arise. One may therefore conclude that while the emergence of a reforming tyrant is not conceivable without the prior existence of the philosopher, the coming of the wise man must necessarily be preceded by the revolutionary political action of the tyrant (who will realize the universal and homogeneous State).

Be that as it may. When I compare the reflections prompted by Xenophon's Dialogue and by Strauss's interpretation with the lessons that emerge from history, I have the impression that the relations between the philosopher and the tyrant have always been "reasonable" in the course of historical evolution: on the one hand the philosophers' "reasonable" advice has always been actualized by tyrants *sooner or later*; on the other hand, philosophers and tyrants have always behaved toward each other "in accordance with reason."

The tyrant is perfectly right not to try to implement a *utopian* philosophical theory, that is to say a philosophical theory without direct connections with the political reality with which he has to deal: for he has no time to fill the *theoretical* gap between utopia and reality. As for the philosopher, he too is right when he refrains from elaborating his theories to the point where they speak directly to the questions raised by current political affairs: if he did, he would have no time left for philosophy, he would cease to be a philosopher and hence would cease to have any claim to giving the tyrant *politico-philosophical* advice. The philosopher is right to leave the responsibility for bringing about a convergence on the theoretical plane between his philosophical ideas and political reality to a constellation of intellectuals of all shades (more or less spread out in time and space); the intellectuals are right to dedicate themselves to this task and, if the occasion arises, to give the tyrant direct advice when, in their theories, they have reached the level of the concrete problems raised by current political affairs; the tyrant is right not to follow (and not to listen) to such advice until it has reached this level. In short, they all behave *reasonably* within historical *reality,* and it is by behaving *reasonably* that, in the end, all of them directly or indirectly achieve *real* results.

On the other hand, it would be perfectly *unreasonable* for the Statesman to want to deny the philosophical value of a theory solely because it cannot be implemented "as is" in a given political situation (which, of course, does not mean that the Statesman may not have politically valid reasons for *prohibiting* this theory within the context of that situation). It would be equally *unreasonable* for the philosopher to condemn Tyranny *as such* "on principle," since a "tyranny" can be "condemned" or "justified" only within the context of a concrete political situation. Generally speaking, it would be *unreasonable* if, solely in terms of his philosophy, the philosopher were in any way whatsoever to criticize the concrete political measures taken by the statesman, regardless of whether or not he is a tyrant, especially when he takes them so that the very ideal advocated by the philosopher might be actualized at some future time. In both cases the judgments passed on philosophy or on politics would be *incompetent*. As such, they would be more excusable (but no more justified) in the mouth of an "uninitiated" statesman or tyrant, than in that of the philosopher who is by definition "rational." As for the "mediating" intellectuals, they would be *unreasonable* if they did not recognize the philosopher's right to judge the philosophical value of their theories, or the statesman's right to choose the theories which he regards as capable of being actualized in the given circumstances and to discard the rest, even "tyrannically."

In general terms, it is history itself that attends to "judging" (by "achievement" or "success") the deeds of statesmen or tyrants, which they perform (consciously or not) as a function of the ideas of philosophers, adapted for practical purposes by intellectuals.

Leo Strauss

Restatement on Xenophon's *Hiero*

A social science that cannot speak of tyranny with the same confidence with which medicine speaks, for example, of cancer, cannot understand social phenomena as what they are. It is therefore not scientific. Present-day social science finds itself in this condition. If it is true that present-day social science is the inevitable result of modern social science and of modern philosophy, one is forced to think of the restoration of classical social science. Once we have learned again from the classics what tyranny is, we shall be enabled and compelled to diagnose as tyrannies a number of contemporary regimes which appear in the guise of dictatorships. This diagnosis can only be the first step toward an exact analysis of present-day tyranny, for present-day tyranny is fundamentally different from the tyranny analyzed by the classics.

But is this not tantamount to admitting that the classics were wholly unfamiliar with tyranny in its contemporary form? Must one not therefore conclude that the classical concept of tyranny is too narrow and hence that the classical frame of reference must be radically modified, i.e., abandoned? In other words, is the attempt to restore classical social science not utopian since it implies that the classical

From Leo Strauss, *What Is Political Philosophy?* (New York: The Free Press of Glencoe, 1959).

orientation has not been made obsolete by the triumph of the biblical orientation?

This seems to be the chief objection to which my study of Xenophon's *Hiero* is exposed. At any rate, this is the gist of the only criticisms of my study from which one could learn anything. Those criticisms were written in complete independence of each other and their authors, Professor Eric Voegelin and M. Alexandre Kojève, have, so to speak, nothing in common. Before discussing their arguments, I must restate my contention.

The fact that there is a fundamental difference between classical tyranny and present-day tyranny, or that the classics did not even dream of present-day tyranny, is not a good or sufficient reason for abandoning the classical frame of reference. For that fact is perfectly compatible with the possibility that present-day tyranny finds its place within the classical framework, i.e., that it cannot be understood adequately except within the classical framework. The difference between present-day tyranny and classical tyranny has its root in the difference between the modern notion of philosophy or science and the classical notion of philosophy or science. Present-day tyranny, in contradistinction to classical tyranny, is based on the unlimited progress in the "conquest of nature" which is made possible by modern science, as well as on the popularization or diffusion of philosophic or scientific knowledge. Both possibilities—the possibility of a science that issues in the conquest of nature and the possibility of the popularization of philosophy or science—were known to the classics. (Compare Xenophon, *Memorabilia* I 1.15 with Empedocles, fr. 111; Plato, *Theaetetus* 180c7–d5.) But the classics rejected them as "unnatural," i.e., as destructive of humanity. They did not dream of present-day tyranny because they regarded its basic presuppositions as so preposterous that they turned their imagination in entirely different directions.

Voegelin, one of the leading contemporary historians of political thought, seems to contend (*The Review of Politics*, 1949, pp. 241–44) that the classical concept of tyranny is too narrow because it does not cover the phenomenon known as Caesarism: when calling a given regime tyrannical, we imply that "constitutional" government is a viable alternative to it; but Caesarism emerges only after "the final breakdown of the republican constitutional order"; hence Caesarism or "postconstitutional" rule cannot be understood as a subdivision of tyranny in the classical sense of tyranny. There is no reason to quarrel with the view that genuine Caesarism is not tyranny, but this does not justify the conclusion that Caesarism is incomprehensible on the basis of classical political philosophy: Caesarism is still a subdivision of absolute monarchy as the classics understood it. If in a given situation "the republican constitutional order" has completely broken down, and there is no reasonable prospect of its restoration within all the foreseeable future, the establishment of permanent absolute rule cannot, as such, be justly blamed; therefore it is fundamentally different from the establishment of tyranny. Just blame could attach only to the manner in which that permanent absolute rule that is truly necessary is established and exercised; as Voegelin emphasizes, there are tyrannical as well as royal Caesars. One has only to read Coluccio Salutati's defense of Caesar against the charge that he was a tyrant—a defense which in all essential points is conceived in the spirit of the classics—in order to see that the distinction between Caesarism and tyranny fits perfectly into the classical framework.

But the phenomenon of Caesarism is one thing; the current concept of Caesarism is another. The current concept of Caesarism is certainly incompatible with classical principles. The question thus arises whether the current concept or the classical concept is more nearly adequate. More particularly, the question concerns the validity of the two implications of the current concept which Voegelin seems to regard as indispensable, and which originated in nineteenth-century historicism. In the first place, he seems to believe that the difference between "the constitutional situation" and "the post-constitutional situation" is more fundamental than the difference between the good king or the good Caesar on the one hand and the bad king or the bad Caesar on the other. But is not the difference between good and bad the most fundamental of all practical or political distinctions? Secondly, Voegelin seems to believe that "postconstitutional" rule is not per se inferior to "constitutional" rule. But is not "postconstitutional" rule justified by necessity or, as Voegelin says, by "historical necessity"? And is not the necessary essentially inferior to the noble or to what is choiceworthy for its own sake? Necessity excuses: what is justified by necessity is in need of excuse. The Caesar, as Voegelin conceives of him, is "the avenger of the misdeeds of a corrupt people." Caesarism is then essentially related to a corrupt people, to a low level of political life, to a decline of society. It presupposes the decline, if not the extinction, of civic virtue or of public spirit, and it necessarily perpetuates that condition. Caesarism belongs to a degraded society, and it thrives on its degradation. Caesarism is just, whereas tyranny is unjust. But Caesarism is just in the way in which deserved punishment is just. It is as little choiceworthy for its own sake as is deserved punishment. Cato refused to see what his time demanded because he saw too clearly the degraded and degrading character of what his time demanded. It is much more important to realize the low level of Caesarism (for, to repeat, Caesarism cannot be divorced from the society which deserves Caesarism) than to realize that under certain conditions Caesarism is necessary and hence legitimate.

While the classics were perfectly capable of doing justice to the merits of Caesarism, they were not particularly concerned with elaborating a doctrine of Caesarism. Since they were primarily concerned with the best regime, they paid less attention to "postconstitutional" rule or to late kingship, than to "preconstitutional" rule or to early kingship: rustic simplicity is a better soil for the good life than is sophisticated rottenness. But there was another reason which induced the classics to be almost silent about "postconstitutional" rule. To stress the fact that it is just to replace constitutional rule by absolute rule, if the common good requires that change, means to cast a doubt on the absolute sanctity of the established constitutional order. It means encouraging dangerous men to confuse the issue by bringing about a state of affairs in which the common good requires the establishment of their absolute rule. The true doctrine of the legitimacy of Caesarism is a dangerous doctrine. The true distinction between Caesarism and tyranny is too subtle for ordinary political use. It is better for the people to remain ignorant of that distinction and to regard the potential Caesar as a potential tyrant. No harm can come from this theoretical error which becomes a practical truth if the people have the mettle to act upon it. No harm can come from the political identification of Caesarism and tyranny: Caesars can take care of themselves.

The classics could easily have elaborated a doctrine of Caesarism or of late kingship if they had wanted, but they did not want to do it. Voegelin however contends that they were forced by their historical situation to grope for a doctrine of Caesarism, and that they failed to discover it. He tries to substantiate his contention by referring to Xenophon and to Plato. As for Plato, Voegelin was forced by considerations of space to limit himself to a summary reference to the royal ruler in the *Statesman*. As for Xenophon, he rightly asserts that it is not sufficient to oppose "the *Cyropaedia* as a mirror of the perfect king to the *Hiero* as a mirror of the tyrant," since the perfect king Cyrus and the improved tyrant who is described by Simonides "look much more opposed to each other than they really are." He explains this fact by suggesting that "both works fundamentally face the same historical problem of the new [*sc*. postconstitutional] rulership," and that one cannot solve this problem except by obliterating at the first stage the distinction between king and tyrant. To justify this explanation he contends that "the very motivation of the *Cyropaedia* is the search for a stable rule that will make an end to the dreary overturning of democracies and tyrannies in the Hellenic polis." This contention is not supported by what Xenophon says or indicates in regard to the intention of the *Cyropaedia*. Its explicit intention is to make intelligible Cyrus' astonishing success in solving the problem of ruling human beings. Xenophon conceives of this problem as one that is coeval with man. Like Plato in the *Statesman*, he does not make the slightest reference to the particular "historical" problem of stable rule in "the postconstitutional situation." In particular, he does not refer to "the dreary overturning of democracies and tyrannies in the Hellenic polis": he speaks of the frequent overturning of democracies, monarchies, and oligarchies and of the essential instability of all tyrannies. As for the implicit intention of the *Cyropaedia*, it is partly revealed by the remark, toward the end of the work, that "after Cyrus died, his sons immediately quarrelled, cities and nations immediately revolted, and all things turned to the worse." If Xenophon was not a fool, he did not intend to present Cyrus' regime as a model. He knew too well that the good order of society requires stability and continuity. (Compare the opening of the *Cyropaedia* with the parallel in the *Agesilaus*, 1. 4.) He rather used Cyrus' meteoric success and the way in which it was brought about as an example for making intelligible the nature of political things. The work, which describes Cyrus' whole life, is entitled *The Education of Cyrus*: the education of Cyrus is the clue to his whole life, to his astonishing success, and hence to Xenophon's intention. A very rough sketch must here suffice. Xenophon's Cyrus was the son of the king of Persia, and until he was about twelve years old he was educated according to the laws of the Persians. The laws and the policy of Xenophon's Persians, however, are an improved version of the laws and polity of the Spartans. The Persia in which Cyrus was raised was an aristocracy superior to Sparta. The political activity of Cyrus—his extraordinary success—consisted in transforming a stable and healthy aristocracy into an unstable "Oriental despotism" whose rottenness showed itself at the latest immediately after his death. The first step in this transformation was a speech which Cyrus addressed to the Persian nobles and in which he convinced them that they ought to deviate from the habit of their ancestors by practicing virtue no longer for its own sake, but for the sake of its rewards. The destruction of aristocracy begins, as one would expect, with the corruption of its principle. (*Cyropaedia* I 5.5–14; compare Aristotle, *Eudemian Ethics* 1248b 38 ff., where the view of virtue which Xenophon's Cyrus instills into the minds of the Persian gentlemen is described as the Spartan view.) The quick success of Cyrus' first action forces the reader to wonder whether the Persian aristocracy was a genuine aristocracy; or more precisely, whether the gentleman in the political or social sense is a true gentleman. This question is identical with the question which Plato answers explicitly in the negative in his story of Er. Socrates says outright that a man who has lived in his former life in a well-ordered regime, participating in virtue by habit and without philosophy, will choose for his next life "the greatest tyranny," for "mostly people make their choice according to the habits of their former life" (*Republic* 619b6–620a3). There is no adequate solution to the problem of virtue or happiness on the political or social plane. Still, while aristocracy is always on the verge of declining into oligarchy or something worse, it is the best possible political solution of the human problem. It must here suffice to note that Cyrus' second step is the democratization of the army, and that the end of the process is a regime that might seem barely distinguishable from the least intolerable form of tyranny. But one must not overlook the essential difference between Cyrus' rule and tyranny, a distinction that is never obliterated. Cyrus is and remains a legitimate ruler. He is born as the legitimate heir to the reigning king, a scion of an old royal house. He becomes the king of other nations through inheritance or marriage and through just conquest, for he enlarges the boundaries of Persia in the Roman manner: by defending the allies of Persia. The difference between Cyrus and a Hiero educated by Simonides is comparable to the difference between William III and Oliver Cromwell. A cursory comparison of the history of England with the history of certain other European nations suffices to show that this difference is not unimportant to the well-being of peoples. Xenophon did not even attempt to obliterate the distinction between the best tyrant and the king because he appreciated too well the charms, nay, the blessings of legitimacy. He expressed this appreciation by subscribing to the maxim (which must be reasonably understood and applied) that the just is identical with the legal.

Voegelin might reply that what is decisive is not Xenophon's conscious intention, stated or implied, but the historical meaning of his work, the historical meaning of a work being determined by the historical situation as distinguished from the conscious intention of the author. Yet opposing the historical meaning of Xenophon's work to his conscious intention implies that we are better judges of the situation in which Xenophon thought than Xenophon himself was. But we cannot be better judges of that situation if we do not have a clearer grasp than he had of the principles in whose light historical situations reveal their meaning. After the experience of our generation, the burden of proof would seem to rest on those who assert rather than on those who deny that we have progressed beyond the classics. And even if it were true that we could understand the classics better than they understood themselves, we would become certain of our superiority only after understanding them exactly as they understood themselves. Otherwise we might mistake our superiority to our notion of the classics for superiority to the classics.

According to Voegelin, it was Machiavelli, as distinguished from the classics, who "achieved the theoretical creation of a concept of rulership in the postconstitutional situation," and this achievement was due to the influence on Machiavelli of the Biblical tradition. He refers especially to Machiavelli's remark about the "armed prophets" (*Prince* VI). The difficulty to which Voegelin's contention is exposed is indicated by these two facts: he speaks on the one hand of "the apocalyptic [hence thoroughly non-classical] aspects of the 'armed prophet' in the *Prince*," whereas on the other hand he says that Machiavelli claimed "for [the] paternity" of the "armed prophet" "besides Romulus, Moses and Theseus, precisely the Xenophontic Cyrus." This amounts to an admission that certainly Machiavelli himself was not aware of any non-classical implication of his notion of "armed prophets." There is nothing unclassical about Romulus, Theseus, and Xenophon's Cyrus. It is true that Machiavelli adds Moses; but, after having made his bow to the Biblical interpretation of Moses, he speaks of Moses in exactly the same manner in which every classical political philosopher would have spoken of him; Moses was one of the greatest legislators or founders (*fondatori: Discorsi* I 9) who ever lived. When reading Voegelin's statement on this subject, one receives the impression that in speaking of armed prophets, Machiavelli put the emphasis on "prophets" as distinguished from nonprophetic rulers like Cyrus, for example. But Machiavelli puts the emphasis not on "prophets," but on "armed." He opposes the armed prophets, among whom he counts Cyrus, Romulus, and Theseus as well as Moses, to unarmed prophets like Savonarola. He states the lesson which he intends to convey with remarkable candor: "All armed prophets succeed and the unarmed ones come to ruin." It is difficult to believe that in writing this sentence Machiavelli should have been completely oblivious of the most famous of all unarmed prophets. One certainly cannot understand Machiavelli's remark on the "unarmed prophets" without taking into consideration what he says about the "unarmed heaven" and "the effeminacy of the world" which, according to him, are due to Christianity. (*Discorsi* II 2 and III 1.) The tradition which Machiavelli continues, while radically modifying it, is not, as Voegelin suggests, that represented by Joachim of Floris, for example, but the one which we still call, with pardonable ignorance, the Averroistic tradition. Machiavelli declares that Savonarola, that unarmed prophet, was right in saying that the ruin of Italy was caused by "our sins," "but our sins were not what he believed they were," namely, religious sins, "but those which I have narrated," namely, political or military sins (*Prince* XII). In the same vein Maimonides declares that the ruin of the Jewish kingdom was caused by the "sins of our fathers," namely, by their idolatry; but idolatry worked its effect in a perfectly natural manner: it led to astrology and thus induced the Jewish people to devote themselves to astrology instead of to the practice of the arts of war and the conquest of countries. But apart from all this, Voegelin does not give any indication of what the armed prophets have to do with "the postconstitutional situation." Certainly Romulus, Theseus, and Moses were "preconstitutional" rulers. Voegelin also refers to "Machiavelli's complete drawing of the savior prince in the *Vita di Castruccio Castracani*" which, he says, "is hardly thinkable without the standardized model of the *Life of Timur*." Apart from the fact that Voegelin has failed to show any connection between the *Castruccio* and the *Life of Timur* and between the *Life of Timur* and the Biblical tradition, the *Castruccio* is perhaps the most impressive document of Machiavelli's longing for classical *virtù* as distinguished from, and opposed to, Biblical righteousness. Castruccio, that idealized condottiere who preferred in so single-minded a manner the life of the soldier to the life of the priest, is compared by Machiavelli himself to Philip of Macedon and to Scipio of Rome.

Machiavelli's longing for classical *virtù* is only the reverse side of his rejection of classical political philosophy. He rejects classical political philosophy because of its orientation by the perfection of the nature of man. The abandonment of the contemplative ideal leads to a radical change in the character of wisdom: Machiavellian wisdom has no necessary connection with moderation. Machiavelli separates wisdom from moderation. The ultimate reason why the *Hiero* comes so close to the *Prince* is that in the *Hiero* Xenophon experiments with a type of wisdom which comes relatively close to a wisdom divorced from moderation: Simonides seems to have an inordinate desire for the pleasures of the table. It is impossible to say how far the epoch-making change that was effected by Machiavelli is due to the indirect influence of the Biblical tradition, before that change has been fully understood in itself.

The peculiar character of the *Hiero* does not disclose itself to cursory reading. It will not disclose itself to the tenth reading, however painstaking, if the reading is not productive of a change of orientation. This change was much easier to achieve for the eighteenth-century reader than for the reader in our century who has been brought up on the brutal and sentimental literature of the last five generations. We are in need of a second education in order to accustom our eyes to the noble reserve and the quiet grandeur of the classics. Xenophon, as it were, limited himself to cultivating exclusively that character of classical writing which is wholly foreign to the modern reader. No wonder that he is today despised or ignored. An unknown ancient critic, who must have been a man of uncommon discernment, called him most bashful. Those modern readers who are so fortunate as to have a natural preference for Jane Austen rather than for Dostoievski, in particular, have an easier access to Xenophon than others might have; to understand Xenophon, they have only to combine the love of philosophy with their natural preference. In the words of Xenophon, "it is both noble and just, and pious and more pleasant to remember the good things rather than the bad ones." In the *Hiero*, Xenophon experimented with the pleasure that comes from remembering bad things, with a pleasure that admittedly is of doubtful morality and piety.

For someone who is trying to form his taste or his mind by studying Xenophon, it is almost shocking to be suddenly confronted by the more than Machiavellian bluntness with which Kojève speaks of such terrible things as atheism and tyranny and takes them for granted. At least on one occasion he goes so far as to call "unpopular" certain measures which the very tyrant Hiero had declared to be criminal. He does not hesitate to proclaim that present-day dictators are tyrants without regarding this in the least as an objection to their rule. As for reverence for legitimacy, he has none. But the nascent shock is absorbed by the realization, or rather the knowledge of long standing, that Kojève belongs to the very few who know how to think and who love to think. He does not belong to the many who today are unabashed atheists and more than Byzantine flatterers of tyrants for the same reason for which they would have been addicted to the grossest superstitions, both religious and legal, had they lived in an earlier age. In a word, Kojève is a philosopher and not an intellectual.

Since he is a philosopher, he knows that the philosopher is, in principle, more capable of ruling than other men and hence will be regarded by a tyrant like Hiero as a most dangerous competitor for tyrannical rule. It would not occur to him for a moment to compare the relationship between Hiero and Simonides with the relationship, say, between Stefan George or Thomas Mann and Hitler. For, to say nothing of considerations too obvious to be mentioned, he could not overlook the obvious fact that the *hypothesis* of the *Hiero* demanded a tyrant of whom it was at least imaginable that he could be taught. In particular, he knows without having to be reminded of the *Seventh Letter* that the difference between a philosopher who is a subject of the tyrant and a philosopher who merely visits the tyrant is immaterial as far as the tyrant's fear of philosophers is concerned. His understanding does not permit him to rest satisfied with the vulgar separation of theory from practice. He knows too well that there never was and there never will be reasonable security for sound practice except after theory has overcome the powerful obstacles to sound practice which originate in theoretical misconceptions of a certain kind. Finally, he brushes aside in sovereign contempt the implicit claim of current, i.e., running or heedless thought to have solved the problems that were raised by the classics—a claim that is only implicit because current thought is unaware of the existence of those problems.

Yet while admitting and even stressing the absolute superiority of classical thought to current thought, Kojève rejects the classical solution of the basic problems. He regards unlimited technological progress and universal enlightenment as essential for the genuine satisfaction of what is human in man. He denies that present-day social science is the inevitable outcome of modern philosophy. According to him, present-day social science is merely the inevitable product of the inevitable decay of that modern philosophy which has refused to learn the decisive lesson from Hegel. He regards Hegel's teaching as the genuine synthesis of Socratic and Machiavellian (or Hobbian) politics, which, as such, is superior to its component elements. In fact, he regards Hegel's teaching, as in principle, the final teaching.

Kojève directs his criticism in the first place against the classical notion of tyranny. Xenophon reveals an important part of that notion by making Hiero answer with silence to Simonides' description of the good tyrant. As Kojève rightly judges, Hiero's silence signifies that he will not attempt to put into practice Simonides' proposals. Kojève suggests, at least provisionally, that this is the fault of Simonides, who did not tell Hiero what the first step is which the tyrant must take in order to transform bad tyranny into good tyranny. But would it not have been up to Hiero if he seriously desired to become a good tyrant, to ask Simonides about the first step? How does Kojève know that Simonides was not waiting in vain for this very question? Or perhaps Simonides has answered it already implicitly. Yet this defense of Simonides is insufficient. The question returns, for, as Kojève again rightly observes, the attempt to realize Simonides' vision of a good tyrant is confronted with an almost insurmountable difficulty. The only question which Hiero raises while Simonides discusses the improvement of tyranny concerns the mercenaries. Hiero's imperfect tyranny rests on the support of his mercenaries. The improvement of tyranny would require a shift of part of the power from the mercenaries to the citizens. By attempting such a shift, the tyrant would antagonize the mercenaries without being at all certain that he could regain by that concession, or by any concession, the confidence of the citizens. He would end by sitting between two chairs. Simonides seems to disregard this state of things and thus to reveal a poor understanding of Hiero's situation or a lack of wisdom. To save Simonides' reputation, one seems compelled to suggest that the poet himself did not believe in the viability of his improved tyranny, that he regarded the good tyranny as a utopia, or that he rejected tyranny as a hopelessly bad regime. But, Kojève continues, does this suggestion not imply that Simonides' attempt to educate Hiero is futile? And a wise man does not attempt futile things.

This criticism may be said to be based on an insufficient appreciation of the value of utopias. The utopia in the strict sense describes the simply good social order. As such it merely makes explicit what is implied in every attempt at social improvement. There is no difficulty in enlarging the strict meaning of utopia in such a manner that one can speak of the utopia of the best tyranny. As Kojève emphasizes, under certain conditions the abolition of tyranny may be out of the question. The best one could hope for is that the tyranny be improved, i.e., that the tyrannical rule be exercised as little inhumanely or irrationally as possible. Every specific reform or improvement of which a sensible man could think, if reduced to its principle, forms part of the complete picture of the maximum improvement that is still compatible with the continued existence of tyranny, it being understood that the maximum improvement is possible only under the most favorable conditions. The maximum improvement of tyranny would require, above all, the shift of part of the power from the mercenaries to the citizens. Such a shift is not absolutely impossible, but its actualization is safe only in circumstances which man cannot create or which no sensible man would create (e.g., an extreme danger threatening equally the mercenaries and the citizens, like the danger of Syracuse being conquered, and all its inhabitants being put to the sword, by barbarians). A sensible man like Simonides would think that he had deserved well of his fellow men if he could induce the tyrant to act humanely or rationally within a small area, or perhaps even in a single instance, where, without his advice, the tyrant would have continued an inhuman or irrational practice. Xenophon indicates an example: Hiero's participating at the Olympian and Pythian games. If Hiero followed Simonides' advice to abandon this practice, he would improve his standing with his subjects and in the world at large, and he would indirectly benefit his subjects. Xenophon leaves it to the intelligence of his reader to replace that particular example by another one which the reader, on the basis of his particular experience, might consider to be more apt. The general lesson is to the effect that the wise man who happens to have a chance to influence a tyrant should use his influence for benefiting his fellow men. One may say that the lesson is trivial. It would be more accurate to say that it was trivial in former ages, for today such little actions like that of Simonides are not taken seriously because we are in the habit of expecting too much. What is not trivial is what we learn from Xenophon about how the wise man has to proceed in his undertaking, which is beset with great difficulties and even with dangers.

Kojève denies our contention that the good tyranny is a utopia. To substantiate his denial, he mentions one example by name: the rule of Salazar. I have never been to Portugal, but from all that I have heard about that country, I am inclined to believe that Kojève is right, except that I am not quite certain whether Salazar's rule should not be called "postconstitutional" rather than tyrannical. Yet one swallow does not make a summer, and we never denied that good tyranny is possible under very favorable circumstances. But Kojève contends that Salazar is not an exception. He thinks that circumstances favorable to good tyranny are easily available today. He contends that all present-day tyrants are good tyrants in Xenophon's sense. He alludes to Stalin. He notes in particular that the tyranny improved according to Simonides' suggestions is characterized by Stakhanovistic emulation. But Stalin's rule would live up to Simonides' standards only if the introduction of Stakhanovistic emulation had been accompanied by a considerable decline in the use of the NKVD or of "labor" camps. Would Kojève go so far as to say that Stalin could travel outside of the Iron Curtain wherever he liked in order to see sights without having anything to fear? (*Hiero* 11.10 and 1.12.). Would Kojève go so far as to say that everyone living behind the Iron Curtain is an ally of Stalin, or that Stalin regards all citizens of Soviet Russia and the other "people's democracies" as his comrades? (*Hiero* 11.11 and 11.14.)

However this may be, Kojève contends that present-day tyranny, and perhaps even classical tyranny, cannot be understood on the basis of Xenophon's principles, and that the classical frame of reference must be modified radically by the introduction of an element of Biblical origin. He argues as follows. Simonides maintains that honor is the supreme or sole goal of the tyrant in particular and of the highest type of human being (the Master) in general. This shows that the poet sees only half of the truth. The other half is supplied by the Biblical morality of Slaves or Workers. The actions of men, and hence also the actions of tyrants, can be, and frequently are, prompted by desire for the pleasure deriving from the successful execution of their work, their projects, or their ideals. There is such a thing as devotion to one's work, or to a cause, "conscientious" work, into which no thought of honor or glory enters. But this fact must not induce us to minimize hypocritically the essential contribution of the desire for honor or prestige to the completion of man. The desire for prestige, recognition, or authority is the primary motive of all political struggles, and in particular of the struggle that leads a man to tyrannical power. It is perfectly unobjectionable for an aspiring statesman or a potential tyrant to try for no other reason than for the sake of his preferment to oust the incumbent ruler or rulers although he knows that he is in no way better equipped for the job than they are. There is no reason to find fault with such a course of action, for the desire for recognition necessarily transforms itself, in all cases which are of any consequence, into devotion to the work to be done or to a cause. The synthesis of the morality of Masters with the morality of Slaves is superior to its component elements.

Simonides is very far from accepting the morality of Masters or from maintaining that honor is the supreme goal of the highest human type. In translating one of the crucial passages (the last sentence of *Hiero* 7.4), Kojève omits the qualifying *dokei* ("no human pleasure *seems* to come closer to what is divine than the joy concerning honors"). Nor does he pay attention to the implication of the fact that Simonides declares the desire for honor to be the dominating passion of *andres* (whom Kojève calls Masters) as distinguished from *anthropoi* (whom he calls Slaves). For, according to Xenophon, and hence according to his Simonides, the *anēr* is by no means the highest human type. The highest human type is the wise man. A Hegelian will have no difficulty in admitting that, since the wise man is distinguished from the Master, he will have something important in common with the Slave. This was certainly Xenophon's view. In the statement of the Master's principle, which he entrusted to Simonides, the poet cannot help admitting implicitly the unity of the human species which his statement explictly denies. And the unity of the human species is thought to be more easily seen by the Slave than by the Master. One does not characterize Socrates adequately by calling him a Master. Xenophon contrasts him with Ischomachus, who is the prototype of the *kalos te kagathos anēr*. Since the work and the knowledge which is best for the type represented by Ischomachus is agriculture and Socrates was not an agriculturist, Socrates was not a *kalos te kagathos anēr*. As Lycon explicitly says, Socrates was a *kalos te kagathos anthropos* (*Symposium* 9.1; *Oeconomicus* 6.8, 12). In this context we may note that in the passage of the *Hiero* which deals with gentlemen living under a tyrant (10.3), Simonides characteristically omits *andres: kaloí te kagathoi andres* could not live happily under a tyrant however good (compare *Hiero* 9.6 and 5.1–2). Xenophon indicates his view most succinctly by failing to mention manliness in his two lists of Socrates' virtues. He sees in Socrates' military activity a sign not of his manliness, but of his justice (*Memorabilia* IV 4.1).

Since Xenophon or his Simonides did not believe that honor is the highest good, or since they did not accept the morality of Masters, there is no apparent need for supplementing their teaching by an element taken from the morality of Slaves or Workers. According to the classics, the highest good is a life devoted to wisdom or to virtue, honor being no more than a very pleasant, but secondary and dispensable, reward. What Kojève calls the pleasure deriving from doing one's work well or from realizing one's projects or one's ideals was called by the classics the pleasure deriving from virtuous or noble activity. The classical interpretation would seem to be truer to the facts. Kojève refers to the pleasure which a solitary child or a solitary painter may derive from executing his projects well. But one can easily imagine a solitary safecracker deriving pleasure from executing his project well, and without a thought of the external rewards (wealth or admiration of his competence) which he reaps. There are artists in all walks of life. It does make a difference what kind of a "job" is the source of disinterested pleasure: whether the job is criminal or innocent, whether it is mere play or serious, and so on. By thinking through this observation one arrives at the view that the highest kind of job, or the only job that is truly human, is noble or virtuous activity, or noble or virtuous work. If one is fond of this manner of looking at things, one may say that noble work is the synthesis effected by the classics between the morality of workless nobility and the morality of ignoble work (cf. Plato, *Meno* 81d3 ff.).

Simonides is therefore justified in saying that the desire for honor is the supreme motive of men who aspire to tyrannical power. Kojève seems to think that a man may aspire to tyrannical power chiefly because he is attracted by "objective" tasks of the highest order, by tasks whose performance requires tyrannical power, and that this motive will radically transform his desire for honor or recognition. The classics denied that this is possible. They were struck by the similarity between Kojève's tyrant and the man who is more attracted to safe-cracking by its exciting problems than by its rewards. One cannot become a tyrant and remain a tyrant without stooping to do base things; hence, a self-respecting man will not aspire to tyrannical power. But, Kojève might object, this still does not prove that the tyrant is motivated chiefly or exclusively by a desire for honor or prestige. He may be motivated, e.g., by a misguided desire to benefit his fellow men. This defense would hold good if error in such matters were difficult to avoid. But it is easy to know that tyranny is base; we all learn as children that one must not give others bad examples and that one must not do base things for the sake of the good that may come out of them. The potential or actual tyrant does not know what every reasonably well-bred child knows, because he is blinded by passion. By what passion? The most charitable answer is that he is blinded by desire for honor or prestige.

Syntheses effect miracles. Kojève's or Hegel's synthesis of classical and Biblical morality effects the miracle of producing an amazingly lax morality out of two moralities both of which made very strict demands on self-restraint. Neither Biblical nor classical morality encourages us to try, solely for the sake of our preferment or our glory, to oust from their positions men who do the required work as well as we could. (Consider Aristotle, *Politics* 1271a10–19.) Neither Biblical nor classical morality encourages all statesmen to try to extend their authority over all men in order to achieve universal recognition. It does not seem to be sound that Kojève encourages others by his speech to a course of action to which he himself would never stoop in deed. If he did not suppress his better knowledge, it would be given him to see that there is no need for having recourse to a miracle in order to understand Hegel's moral and political teaching. Hegel continued, and in a certain respect radicalized, the modern tradition that emancipated the passions and hence "competition." That tradition was originated by Machiavelli and perfected by such men as Hobbes and Adam Smith. It came into being through a conscious break with the strict moral demands made by both the Bible and classical philosophy; those demands were explicitly rejected as too strict. Hegel's moral or political teaching is indeed a synthesis: it is a synthesis of Socratic and Machiavellian or Hobbian politics. Kojève knows as well as anyone living that Hegel's fundamental teaching regarding master and slave is based on Hobbes' doctrine of the state of nature. If Hobbes' doctrine of the state of nature is abandoned *en pleine connaissance de cause* (as indeed it should be abandoned), Hegel's fundamental teaching will lose the evidence which it apparently still possesses for Kojève. Hegel's teaching is much more sophisticated than Hobbes', but it is as much a construction as the latter. Both doctrines construct human society by starting from the untrue assumption that man as man is thinkable as a being that lacks awareness of sacred restraints or as a being that is guided by nothing but a desire for recognition.

But Kojève is likely to become somewhat impatient with what, as I fear, he might call our Victorian or pre-Victorian *niaiseries*. He probably will maintain that the whole previous discussion is irrelevant because it is based on a dogmatic assumption. We assume indeed that the classical concept of tyranny is derived from an adequate analysis of the fundamental social phenomena. The classics understand tyranny as the opposite of the best regime, and they hold that the best regime is the rule of the best or aristocracy. But, Kojève argues, aristocracy is the rule of a minority over the majority of citizens or of adult residents of a given territory, a rule that rests, in the last resort, on force or terror. Would it then not be more proper to admit that aristocracy is a form of tyranny? Yet Kojève apparently thinks that force or terror are indispensable in every regime, while he does not think that all regimes are equally good or bad and hence equally tyrannical. If I understand him correctly, he is satisfied that "the universal and homogeneous state" is the simply best social order. Lest we get entangled in a merely verbal difficulty, I shall state his view as follows: the universal and homogeneous state is the only one which is essentially just; the aristocracy of the classics in particular is essentially unjust.

To see the classical view in the proper light, let us make the assumption that the wise do not desire to rule. The unwise are very unlikely to force the wise to rule over them. For the wise cannot rule as wise if they do not have absolute power or if they are in any way responsible to the unwise. No broil in which the unwise may find themselves could be great enough to induce them to surrender absolute control to the wise, whose first measure would probably be to expel everyone above the age of ten from the city (Plato, *Republic* 540d–541a). Hence, what pretends to be absolute rule of the wise will in fact be absolute rule of unwise men. But if this is the case, the universal state would seem to be impossible. For the universal state requires universal agreement regarding the fundamentals, and such agreement is possible only on the basis of genuine knowledge or of wisdom. Agreement based on opinion can never become universal agreement. Every faith that lays claim to universality, i.e., to be universally accepted, of necessity provokes a counter-faith which raises the same claim. The diffusion among the unwise of genuine knowledge that was acquired by the wise would be of no help, for through its diffusion or dilution, knowledge inevitably transforms itself into opinion, prejudice, or mere belief. The utmost in the direction of universality that one could expect is, then, an absolute rule of unwise men who control about half of the globe, the other half being ruled by other unwise men. It is not obvious that the extinction of all independent states but two will be a blessing. But it is obvious that absolute rule of the unwise is less desirable than their limited rule: the unwise ought to rule under law. In addition, it is more probable that in a situation that is favorable to radical change, the citizen body will for once follow the advice of a wise man or a founding father by adopting a code of laws which he has elaborated, than that they will ever submit to perpetual and absolute rule of a succession of wise men. Yet laws must be applied or are in need of interpretation. The full authority under law should therefore be given to men who, thanks to their good upbringing, are capable of "completing" the laws (*Memorabilia* IV 6.12) or of interpreting them equitably. "Constitutional" authority ought to be given to the equitable men (*epieikeis*), i.e., to gentlemen—preferably an urban patriciate which derives its income from the cultivation of its landed estates. It is true that it is at least partly a matter of accident—of the accident of birth—whether a given individual does or does not belong to the class of gentlemen and has thereby had an opportunity of being brought up in the proper manner. But in the absence of absolute rule of the wise on the one hand, and on the other hand of a degree of abundance which is possible only on the basis of unlimited technological progress with all its terrible hazards, the apparently just alternative to aristocracy open or disguised will be permanent revolution, i.e., permanent chaos in which life will be not only poor and short but brutish as well. It would not be difficult to show that the classical argument cannot be disposed of as easily as is now generally thought, and that liberal or constitutional democracy comes closer to what the classics demanded than any alternative that is viable in our age. In the last analysis, however, the classical argument derives its strength from the assumption that the wise do not desire to rule.

In discussing the fundamental issue which concerns the relation of wisdom to rule or to tyranny, Kojève starts from the observation that at least up to now there have been no wise men but at best men who strove for wisdom, i.e., philosophers. Since the philosopher is the man who devotes his whole life to the quest for wisdom, he has no time for political activity of any kind: the philosopher cannot possibly desire to rule. His only demand on the political men is that they leave him alone. He justifies his demand by honestly declaring that his pursuit is purely theoretical and does not interfere in any way with the business of the political men. This simple solution presents itself at first glance as the strict consequence from the definition of the philosopher. Yet a short reflection shows already that it suffers from a fatal weakness. The philosopher cannot lead an absolutely solitary life because legitimate "subjective certainty" and the "subjective certainty" of the lunatic are indistinguishable. Genuine certainty must be "intersubjective." The classics were fully aware of the essential weakness of the mind of the individual. Hence their teaching about the philosophic life is a teaching about friendship: the philosopher is as philosopher in need of friends. To be of service to the philosopher in his philosophizing, the friends must be competent men: they must themselves be actual or potential philosophers, i.e., members of the natural "elite." Friendship presupposes a measure of conscious agreement. The things regarding which the philosophic friends must agree cannot be known or evident truths. For philosophy is not wisdom but quest for wisdom. The things regarding which the philosophic friends agree will then be opinions or prejudices. But there is necessarily a variety of opinions or prejudices. Hence there will be a variety of groups of philosophic friends: philosophy, as distinguished from wisdom, necessarily appears in the form of philosophic schools or of sects. Friendship as the classics understood it offers then no solution to the problem of "subjective certainty." Friendship is bound to lead to, or to consist in, the cultivation and perpetuation of common prejudices by a closely knit group of kindred spirits. It is therefore incompatible with the idea of philosophy. The philosopher must leave the closed and charmed circle of the "initiated" if he intends to remain a philosopher. He must go out to the market place; the conflict with the political men cannot be avoided. And this conflict by itself, to say nothing of its cause or its effect, is a political action.

The whole history of philosophy testifies that the danger eloquently described by Kojève is inevitable. He is equally right in saying that that danger cannot be avoided by abandoning the sect in favor of what he regards as its modern substitute, the Republic of Letters. The Republic of Letters indeed lacks the narrowness of the sect: it embraces men of all philosophic persuasions. But precisely for this reason, the first article of the constitution of the Republic of Letters stipulates that no philosophic persuasion must be taken too seriously or that every philosophic persuasion must be treated with as much respect as any other. The Republic of Letters is relativistic. Or if it tries to avoid this pitfall, it becomes eclectic. A certain vague middle line, which is perhaps barely tolerable for the most easy-going members of the different persuasions if they are in their drowsiest mood, is set up as The Truth or as Common Sense; the substantive and irrepressible conflicts are dismissed as merely "semantic." Whereas the sect is narrow because it is passionately concerned with the true issues, the Republic of Letters is comprehensive because it is indifferent to the true issues: it prefers agreement to truth or to the quest for truth. If we have to choose between the sect and the Republic of Letters, we must choose the sect. Nor will it do that we abandon the sect in favor of the party or more precisely—since a party which is not a mass party is still something like a sect—of the mass party. For the mass party is nothing but a sect with a disproportionately long tail. The "subjective certainty" of the members of the sect, and especially of the weaker brethren, may be increased if the tenets of the sect are repeated by millions of parrots instead of by a few dozens of human beings, but this obviously has no effect on the claim of the tenets in question to "objective truth." Much as we loathe the snobbish silence or whispering of the sect, we loathe even more the savage noise of the loudspeakers of the mass party. The problem stated by Kojève is not then solved by dropping the distinction between those who are able and willing to think and those who are not. If we must choose between the sect and the party, we must choose the sect.

But must we choose the sect? The decisive premise of Kojève's argument is that philosophy "implies necessarily 'subjective certainties' which are not 'objective truths' or, in other words, which are prejudices." But philosophy in the original meaning of the term is nothing but knowledge of one's ignorance. The "subjective certainty" that one does not know coincides with the "objective truth" of that certainty. But one cannot know that one does not know without knowing what one does not know. What Pascal said with anti-philosophic intent about the impotence of both dogmatism and skepticism, is the only possible justification of philosophy which as such is neither dogmatic nor skeptic, and still less "decisionist," but zetetic (or skeptic in the original sense of the term). Philosophy as such is nothing but genuine awareness of the problems, i.e., of the fundamental and comprehensive problems. It is impossible to think about these problems without becoming inclined toward a solution, toward one or the other of the very few typical solutions. Yet as long as there is no wisdom but only quest for wisdom, the evidence of all solutions is necessarily smaller than the evidence of the problems. Therefore the philosopher ceases to be a philosopher at the moment at which the "subjective certainty" of a solution becomes stronger than his awareness of the problematic character of that solution. At that moment the sectarian is born. The danger of succumbing to the attraction of solutions is essential to philosophy which, without incurring this danger, would degenerate into playing with the problems. But the philosopher does not necessarily succumb to this danger, as is shown by Socrates, who never belonged to a sect and never founded one. And even if the philosophic friends are compelled to be members of a sect or to found one, they are not necessarily members of one and the same sect: *Amicus Plato*.

At this point we seem to get involved in a self contradiction. For, if Socrates is the representative *par excellence* of the philosophic life, the philosopher cannot possibly be satisfied with a group of philosophic friends but has to go out to the market place where, as everyone knows, Socrates spent much or most of his time. However, the same Socrates suggested that there is no essential difference between the city and the family, and the thesis of Friedrich Mentz, *Socrates nec officiosus maritus nec laudandus paterfamilias* (Leipzig 1716), is defensible: Xenophon goes so far as not to count the husband of Xanthippe among the married *men (Symposium, in fine)*.

The difficulty cannot be discussed here except within the context of a limited exegetic problem. Xenophon indicates in the *Hiero* that the motivation of the philosophic life is the desire for being honored or admired by a small minority, and ultimately the desire for "self-admiration," whereas the motivation of the political life is the desire for love, i.e., for being loved by human beings irrespective of their qualities. Kojève rejects this view altogether. He is of the opinion that the philosopher and the ruler or tyrant are equally motivated by the desire for satisfaction, i.e., for recognition (honor) and ultimately for universal recognition, and that neither of the two is motivated by a desire for love. A human being is loved because he is and regardless of what he does. Hence love is at home within the family rather than in the public spheres of politics and of philosophy. Kojève regards it as particularly unfortunate that Xenophon tries to establish a connection between the "tyrannical" desire and sexual desire. He is equally averse to the suggestion that whereas the tyrant is guided by the desire for recognition by others, the philosopher is concerned exclusively with "self-admiration"; the self-satisfied philosopher is as such not distinguishable from the self-satisfied lunatic. The philosopher is then necessarily concerned with approval or admiration by others and he cannot help being pleased with it when he gets it. It is practically impossible to say whether the primary motive of the philosopher is the desire for admiration or the desire for the pleasures deriving from understanding. The very distinction has no practical meaning unless we gratuitously assume that there is an omniscient God who demands from men a pure heart.

What Xenophon indicated in the *Hiero* about the motivations of the two ways of life is admittedly incomplete. How can any man in his senses ever have overlooked the role played by ambition in political life? How can a friend of Socrates ever have overlooked the role played by love in the philosophic life? Simonides' speech on honor alone, to say nothing of Xenophon's other writings, proves abundantly that what Xenophon indicates in the *Hiero* about the motivations of the two ways of life is deliberately incomplete. It is incomplete because it proceeds from a complete disregard of everything but what one may call the most fundamental difference between the philosopher and the ruler. To understand this difference, one must start from the desire which the philosopher and the ruler have in common with each other and indeed with all men. All men desire "satisfaction." But satisfaction cannot be identified with recognition and even universal recognition. The classics identified satisfaction with happiness. The difference between the philosopher and the political man will then be a difference with respect to happiness. The philosopher's dominating passion is the desire for truth, i.e., for knowledge of the eternal order, or the eternal cause or causes of the whole. As he looks up in search for the eternal order, all human things and all human concerns reveal themselves to him in all clarity as paltry and ephemeral, and no one can find solid happiness in what he knows to be paltry and ephemeral. He has then the same experience regarding all human things, nay, regarding man himself, which the man of high ambition has regarding the low and narrow goals, or the cheap happiness, of the general run of men. The philosopher, being the man of the largest views, is the only man who can be properly described as possessing *megaloprepreia* (which is commonly rendered by "magnificence") (Plato, *Republic* 486a). Or, as Xenophon indicates, the philosopher is the only man who is truly ambitious. Chiefly concerned with eternal beings, or the "ideas," and hence also with the "idea" of man, he is as unconcerned as possible with individual and perishable human beings and hence also with his own "individuality," or his body, as well as with the sum total of all individual human beings and their "historical" procession. He knows as little as possible about the way to the market place, to say nothing of the market place itself, and he almost as little knows whether his very neighbor is a human being or some other animal (Plato, *Theaetetus* 173c8–d1, 174b1–6). The political man must reject this way altogether. He cannot tolerate this radical depreciation of man and of all human things (Plato, *Laws* 804b5–c1). He could not devote himself to his work with all his heart or without reservation if he did not attach absolute importance to man and to human things. He must "care" for human beings as such. He is essentially attached to human beings. This attachment is at the bottom of his desire to rule human beings, or of his ambition. But to rule human beings means to serve them. Certainly an attachment to beings which prompts one to serve them may well be called love of them. Attachment to human beings is not peculiar to the ruler; it is characteristic of all men as mere men. The difference between the political man and the private man is that in the case of the former, the attachment enervates all private concerns; the political man is consumed by erotic desire, not for this or that human being, or for a few, but for the large multitude, for the *demos* (Plato, *Gorgias* 481d1–5, 513d7–8; *Republic* 573e6–7, 574e2, 575a1–2), and in principle, for all human beings. But erotic desire craves reciprocity: the political man desires to be loved by all his subjects. The political man is characterized by the concern with being loved by all human beings regardless of their quality.

Kojève will have no difficulty in granting that the family man can be characterized by "love" and the ruler by "honor." But if, as we have seen, the philosopher is related to the ruler in a way comparable to that in which the ruler is related to the family man, there can be no difficulty in characterizing the ruler, in contradistinction to the philosopher, by "love" and the philosopher by "honor." Furthermore, prior to the coming of the universal state, the ruler is concerned with, and cares for, his own subjects as distinguished from the subjects of other rulers, just as the mother is concerned with, and cares for, her own children as distinguished from the children of other mothers; and the concern with, or care for, what is one's own is what is frequently meant by "love." The philosopher on the other hand is concerned with what can never become private or exclusive property. We cannot then accept Kojève's doctrine regarding love. According to him, we love someone "because he *is* and independently of what he *does*." He refers to the mother who loves her son in spite of all his faults. But, to repeat, the mother loves her son, not because he is, but because he is her own, or because he has the quality of being her own. (Compare Plato, *Republic* 330c3–6).

But if the philosopher is radically detached from human beings as human beings, why does he communicate his knowledge, or his questionings, to others? Why was the same Socrates, who said that the philosopher does not even know the way to the market place, almost constantly in the market place? Why was the same Socrates, who said that the philosopher barely knows whether his neighbor is a human being, so well informed about so many trivial details regarding his neighbors? The philosopher's radical detachment from human beings must then be compatible with an attachment to human beings. While trying to transcend humanity (for wisdom is divine) or while trying to make it his sole business to die and to be dead to all human things, the philosopher cannot help living as a human being who as such cannot be dead to human concerns, although his soul will not be in these concerns. The philosopher cannot devote his life to his own work if other people do not take care of the needs of his body. Philosophy is possible only in a society in which there is "division of labor." The philosopher needs the services of other human beings and has to pay for them with services of his own if he does not want to be reproved as a thief or fraud. But man's need for other men's services is founded on the fact that man is by nature a social animal or that the human individual is not self-sufficient. There is therefore a natural attachment of man to man which is prior to any calculation of mutual benefit. This natural attachment to human beings is weakened in the case of the philosopher by his attachment to the eternal beings. On the other hand, the philosopher is immune to the most common and the most powerful dissolvent of man's natural attachment to man, the desire to have more than one has already and in particular to have more than others have; for he has the greatest self-sufficiency which is humanly possible. Hence the philosopher will not hurt anyone. While he cannot help being more attached to his family and his city than to strangers, he is free from the delusions bred by collective egoisms; his benevolence or humanity extends to all human beings with whom he comes into contact. (*Memorabilia* I 2.60–61; 6.10; IV 8.11.) Since he fully realizes the limits set to all human action and all human planning (for what has come into being must perish again), he does not expect salvation or satisfaction from the establishment of the simply best social order. He will therefore not engage in revolutionary or subversive activity. But he will try to help his fellow man by mitigating, as far as in him lies, the evils which are inseparable from the human condition. (Plato, *Theaetetus* 176a5-b1; *Seventh Letter* 331c7–d5; Aristotle, *Politics* 1301a39–b2.) In particular, he will give advice to his city or to other rulers. Since all advice of this kind presupposes comprehensive reflections which as such are the business of the philosopher, he must first have become a political philosopher. After this preparation he will act as Simonides did when he talked to Hiero, or as Socrates did when he talked to Alcibiades, Critias, Charmides, Critobulus, the younger Pericles and others.

The attachment to human beings as human beings is not peculiar to the philosopher. As philosopher, he is attached to a particular type of human being, namely to actual or potential philosophers or to his friends. His attachment to his friends is deeper than his attachment to other human beings, even to his nearest and dearest, as Plato shows with almost shocking clarity in the *Phaedo*. The philosopher's attachment to his friends is based in the first place on the need which arises from the deficiency of "subjective certainty." Yet we see Socrates frequently engaged in conversations from which he cannot have benefited in any way. We shall try to explain what this means in a popular and hence unorthodox manner. The philosopher's attempt to grasp the eternal order is necessarily an ascent from the perishable things which as such reflect the eternal order. Of all perishable things known to us, those which reflect that order most, or which are most akin to that order, are the souls of men. But the souls of men reflect the eternal order in different degrees. A soul that is in good order or healthy reflects it to a higher degree than a soul that is chaotic or diseased. The philosopher who as such has had a glimpse of the eternal order is therefore particularly sensitive to the difference among human souls. In the first place, he alone knows what a healthy or well-ordered soul is. And secondly, precisely because he has had a glimpse of the eternal order, he cannot help being intensely pleased by the aspect of a healthy or well-ordered soul, and he cannot help being intensely pained by the aspect of a diseased or chaotic soul, without regard to his own needs or benefits. Hence he cannot help being attached to men of well-ordered souls: he desires "to be together" with such men all the time. He admires such men not on account of any services which they may render to him but simply because they are what they are. On the other hand, he cannot help being repelled by ill-ordered souls. He avoids men of ill-ordered souls as much as he can, while trying of course not to offend them. Last but not least, he is highly sensitive to the promise of good or ill order, or of happiness or misery, which is held out by the souls of the young. Hence he cannot help desiring, without any regard to his own needs or benefits, that those among the young whose souls are by nature fitted for it, acquire good order of their souls. But the good order of the soul is philosophizing. The philosopher therefore has the urge to educate potential philosophers simply because he cannot help loving well-ordered souls.

But did we not surreptitiously substitute the wise man for the philosopher? Does the philosopher of whom we have spoken not possess knowledge of many most important things? Philosophy, being knowledge of our ignorance regarding the most important things, is impossible without some knowledge regarding the most important things. By realizing that we are ignorant of the most important things, we realize at the same time that the most important thing for us, or the one thing needful, is quest for knowledge of the most important things, or philosophy. In other words, we realize that only by philosophizing can man's soul become well-ordered. We know how ugly or deformed a boaster's soul is; but everyone who thinks that he knows, while in truth he does not, is a boaster. Still, observations of this kind do not prove the assumption, for example, that the well-ordered soul is more akin to the eternal order, or to the eternal cause or causes of the whole, than is the chaotic soul. And one does not have to make that assumption in order to be a philosopher, as is shown by Democritus and other pre-Socratics, to say nothing of the moderns. If one does not make the assumption mentioned, one will be forced, it seems, to explain the philosopher's desire to communicate his thoughts by his need for remedying the deficiency of "subjective certainty" or by his desire for recognition or by his human kindness. We must leave it open whether one can thus explain, without being forced to use *ad hoc* hypotheses, the immediate pleasure which the philosopher experiences when he sees a well-ordered soul or the immediate pleasure which we experience when we observe signs of human nobility.

We may have explained why the philosopher is urged, not in spite of but because of his radical detachment from human beings as such, to educate human beings of a certain kind. But cannot exactly the same be said of the tyrant or ruler? May a ruler not likewise be penetrated by a sense of the ultimate futility of all human causes? It is undeniable that detachment from human beings, or what is popularly known as the philosophic attitude toward all things which are exposed to the power of chance, is not a preserve of the philosopher. But a detachment from human concerns which is not constantly nourished by genuine attachment to eternal things, i.e., by philosophizing, is bound to wither or to degenerate into lifeless narrowness. The ruler too tries to educate human beings and he too is prompted by love of some kind. Xenophon indicates his view of the ruler's love in the *Education of Cyrus*, which is, at any rate at first glance, his description of the greatest ruler. Xenophon's Cyrus is a cold or unerotic nature. That is to say, the ruler is not motivated by true or Socratic *eros* because he does not know what a well-ordered soul is. The ruler knows political virtue, and nothing prevents his being attracted by it; but political virtue, or the virtue of the nonphilosopher, is a mutilated thing; therefore it cannot elicit more than a shadow or an imitation of true love. The ruler is in fact dominated by love based on need in the common meaning of need, or by mercenary love; for "all men by nature believe they love those things by which they believe they are benefited" (*Oeconomicus* 20.29). In the language of Kojève, the ruler is concerned with human beings because he is concerned with being recognized by them. This explains incidentally why the indications of the *Hiero* about love are so strikingly incomplete; the purpose of the work required the disregard of nonmercenary love just as it required that wisdom be kept in its ordinary ambiguity.

We cannot agree then with Kojève's contention that the educative tendency of the ruler has the same character or scope as that of the philosopher. The ruler is essentially the ruler of all his subjects; his educative effort must therefore be directed toward all his subjects. If every educative effort is a kind of conversation, the ruler is forced by his position to converse with every subject. Socrates, however, is not compelled to converse with anyone except those with whom he likes to converse. If the ruler is concerned with universal recognition, he must be concerned with enlarging universally the class of competent judges of his merits. But Kojève does not seem to believe that all men are capable of becoming competent judges in political matters. He limits himself to contending that the number of men of philosophic competence is not smaller than the number of men of political competence. Yet contrary to what he seems to say in the text of his essay as distinguished from his note number five, many more men are capable of judging competently of the greatness of a ruler than of the greatness of a philosopher. This is the case not merely because a much greater intellectual effort is required for competent judgment of a philosophic achievement than for competent judgment of a political achievement. Rather is it true because philosophy requires liberation from the most potent natural charm whose undiminished power in no way obstructs political competence as the ruler understands political competence: from that charm that consists in unqualified attachment to human things as such. If the philosopher addresses himself, therefore, to a small minority, he is not acting on the basis of an a priori judgement. He is following the constant experience of all times and countries and, no doubt, the experience of Kojève himself. For try as one may to expel nature with a hayfork, it will always come back. The philosopher will certainly not be compelled, either by the need to remedy the deficiency of "subjective certainty" or by ambition, to strive for universal recognition. His friends alone suffice to remedy that deficiency, and no shortcomings in his friends can be remedied by having recourse to utterly incompetent people. And as for ambition, as a philosopher, he is free from it.

According to Kojève, one makes a gratuitous assumption in saying that the philosopher as such is free from ambition or from the desire for recognition. Yet the philosopher as such is concerned with nothing but the quest for wisdom and kindling or nourishing the love of wisdom in those who are by nature capable of it. We do not have to pry into the heart of any one in order to know that, insofar as the philosopher, owing to the weakness of the flesh, becomes concerned with being recognized by others, he ceases to be a philosopher. According to the strict view of the classics he turns into a sophist. The concern with being recognized by others is perfectly compatible with, and in fact required by, the concern essential to the ruler who is the ruler of others. But concern with being recognized by others has no necessary connection with the quest for the eternal order. Therefore, concern with recognition necessarily detracts from the singleness of purpose which is characteristic of the philosopher. It blurs his vision. This fact is not at variance with the other fact that high ambition is frequently a sign by which one can recognize the potential philosopher. But to the extent to which high ambition is not transformed into full devotion to the quest for wisdom, and to the pleasures which accompany that quest, he will not become an actual philosopher. One of the pleasures accompanying the quest for truth comes from the awareness of progress in that quest. Xenophon goes so far as to speak of the self-admiration of the philosopher. This self-admiration or self-satisfaction does not have to be confirmed by the admiration of others in order to be reasonable. If the philosopher, trying to remedy the deficiency of "subjective certainty," engages in conversation with others and observes again and again that his interlocutors, as they themselves are forced to admit, involve themselves in self-contradictions or are unable to give any account of their questionable contentions, he will be reasonably confirmed in his estimate of himself without necessarily finding a single soul who admires him. (Consider Plato, *Apology of Socrates* 21d1–3.) The self-admiration of the philosopher is in this respect akin to "the good conscience" which as such does not require confirmation by others.

The quest for wisdom is inseparable from specific pleasures just as the quest for these pleasures is inseparable from the quest for wisdom. Thus it might seem possible to understand the quest for wisdom in terms of the quest for pleasure. That this is in fact possible is asserted by all hedonists. In the *Hiero*, Xenophon (or his Simonides) is forced to argue on the basis of the hedonistic thesis. Hence the argument of the *Hiero* implies the question whether the philosophic life can be understood in hedonistic terms. It implies the answer that it cannot be so understood because the rank of the various kinds of pleasure ultimately depends upon the rank of the activities to which the pleasures are related. Neither the quantity nor the purity of the pleasures determines in the last resort the rank of human activities. The pleasures are essentially secondary; they cannot be understood but with reference to the activities. The question as to whether the activities or the pleasure are in themselves primary has nothing to do with the question as to whether someone who engages in an activity is prompted to do so primarily by the intrinsic value of the activity or by the pleasure which he expects to enjoy as a consequence of the activity. Kojève may be perfectly right in saying that the latter question does not permit a responsible answer and is unimportant from the point of view of philosophy. But the consideration is irrelevant to Xenophon's argument, which is concerned exclusively with the former question.

While I must disagree with a considerable part of Kojève's reasoning, I agree with his conclusion that the philosopher has to go to the market place, or in other words, that the conflict between the philosopher and the city is inevitable. The philosopher must go to the market place in order to fish there for potential philosophers. His attempts to convert young men to the philosophic life will necessarily be regarded by the city as an attempt to corrupt the young. The philosopher is therefore forced to defend the cause of philosophy. He must therefore act upon the city or upon the ruler. Up to this point Kojève is in perfect agreement with the classics. But does the final consequence mean, as he maintains, that the philosopher must desire to determine or codetermine the politics of the city or of the rulers? Must the philosopher desire "to participate, in one way or another, in the total direction of public affairs, so that the State be organized and governed in such a manner that the philosopher's philosophic pedagogy be possible and effectual"? Or must we conceive of philosophic politics, i.e., of the philosopher's action on behalf of philosophy, in entirely different terms?

Contrary to what Kojève apparently implies it seems to us that there is no necessary connection between the philosopher's indispensable philosophic politics and the efforts which he might or might not make to contribute toward the establishment of the best regime. For philosophy and philosophic education are possible in all kinds of more or less imperfect regimes. One may illustrate this by an example taken from the eighth book of Plato's *Republic*. There Plato contends that the Spartan regime is superior to the Athenian, although he knows that the Athenian is more favorable than the Spartan regime to the possibility and the survival of philosophic education (consider 557c6 and d4). It is true that it was in Athens that Socrates was compelled to drink the hemlock. But he was permitted to live and engage in philosophic education until he was seventy: in Sparta he would have been exposed as an infant. Plato could not have decided, however provisionally, in favor of the Spartan regime, if the philosopher's concern with a good political order were absolutely inseparable from the concern guiding his philosophic politics. In what then does philosophic politics consist? In satisfying the city that the philosophers are not atheists, that they do not desecrate everything sacred to the city, that they reverence what the city reverences, that they are not subversives, in short, that they are not irresponsible adventurers but good citizens and even the best of citizens. This is the defense of philosophy which was required always and everywhere, whatever the regime might have been. For, as the philosopher Montesquieu says, "*dans tous les pays du monde, on veut de la morale*" and "*les hommes, fripons en détail, sont en gros de très honnêtes gens; ils aiment la morale.*" This defense of philosophy before the tribunal of the city was achieved by Plato with a resounding success (Plutarch, *Nicias* ch. 23). The effects have lasted down to the present throughout all ages except the darkest ones. What Plato did in the Greek city and for it was done in and for Rome by Cicero, whose political action on behalf of philosophy has nothing in common with his actions against Catiline and for Pompey, for example. It was done in and for the Islamic world by Fārābī and in and for Judaism by Maimonides. Contrary to what Kojève seems to suggest, the political action of the philosophers on behalf of philosophy has achieved full success. One sometimes wonders whether it has not been too successful.

Kojève, I said, fails to distinguish between philosophic politics and that political action which the philosopher might undertake with a view to establishing the best regime or to the improvement of the actual order. He thus arrives at the conclusion that on the one hand the philosopher does not desire to rule, and on the other hand he must desire to rule, and that this contradiction involves a tragic conflict. The classics did not regard the conflict between philosophy and the city as tragic. Xenophon at any rate seems to have viewed that conflict in the light of Socrates' relation to Xanthippe. At least in this point there appears then something like an agreement between Xenophon and Pascal. For the classics, the conflict between philosophy and the city is as little tragic as the death of Socrates.

Kojève's argument continues as follows: Since the philosopher does not desire to rule because he has no time for ruling, but on the other hand is forced to rule, he has been satisfied with a compromise solution; with devoting a little time to giving advice to tyrants or rulers. Reading the chronicles, one receives the impression that this action of the philosophers has been wholly ineffectual—as ineffectual as Simonides' action that consisted in his conversation with Hiero. This conclusion does not entitle one, however, to infer that the philosopher should abstain from mingling in politics, for the strong reason for mingling in politics remains in force. The problem of what the philosopher should do in regard to the city remains, therefore, an open question, the subject of an unfinishable discussion. But the problem which cannot be solved by the dialectics of discussion may well be solved by the higher dialectics of History. The philosophic study of our past shows that philosophy, far from being politically ineffectual, has radically revolutionized the character of political life. One is even entitled to say that philosophic ideas alone have had significant political effect. For what else is the whole political history of the world except a movement toward the universal and homogeneous state? The decisive stages in the movement were actions of tyrants or rulers (Alexander the Great and Napoleon, e.g.). But these tyrants or rulers were and are pupils of philosophers. Classical philosophy created the idea of the universal state. Modern philosophy, which is the secularized form of Christianity, created the idea of the universal and homogeneous state. On the other hand, the progress of philosophy and its eventual trans-mutation into wisdom requires the "active negation" of the previous political states, i.e., requires the action of the tyrant: only when "all possible active [political] negations" have been effected and thus the final stage of the political development has been reached, can and will the quest for wisdom give way to wisdom.

I need not examine Kojève's sketch of the history of the Western world. That sketch would seem to presuppose the truth of the thesis which it is meant to prove. Certainly the value of the conclusion which he draws from his sketch depends entirely on the truth of the assumption that the universal and homogeneous state is the simply best social order. The simply best social order, as he conceives of it, is the state in which every human being finds his full satisfaction. A human being finds his full satisfaction if his human dignity is universally recognized and if he enjoys "equality of opportunity," i.e., the opportunity, corresponding to his capacities, of deserving well of the state or of the whole. Now if it were true that in the universal and homogeneous state, no one has any good reason for being dissatisfied with that state, or for negating it, it would not yet follow that everyone will in fact be satisfied with it and never think of actively negating it, for men do not always act reasonably. Does Kojève not underestimate the power of the passions? Does he not have an unfounded belief in the eventually rational effect of the movements instigated by the passions? In addition, men will have very good reasons for being dissatisfied with the universal and homogeneous state. To show this, I must have recourse to Kojève's more extensive exposition in his *Introduction à la lecture de Hegel*. There are degrees of satisfaction. The satisfaction of the humble citizen, whose human dignity is universally recognized and who enjoys all opportunities that correspond to his humble capacities and achievements, is not comparable to the satisfaction of the Chief of State. Only the Chief of State is "*really* satisfied." He alone is "truly free" (p. 146). Did Hegel not say something to the effect that the state in which one man is free is the Oriental despotic state? Is the universal and homogeneous state then merely a planetary Oriental despotism? However this may be, there is no guarantee that the incumbent Chief of State deserves his position to a higher degree than others. Those others then have very good reason for dissatisfaction: a state which treats equal men unequally is not just. A change from the universal-homogeneous monarchy into a universal-homogeneous aristocracy would seem to be reasonable. But we cannot stop here. The universal and homogeneous state, being the synthesis of the Masters and the Slaves, is the state of the working warrior or of the war-waging worker. In fact, all its members are warrior workers (pp. 114, 146). But if the state is universal and homogeneous, "wars and revolutions are henceforth impossible" (pp. 145, 561). Besides, work in the strict sense, namely the conquest or domestication of nature, is completed, for otherwise the universal and homogeneous state could not be the basis for wisdom (p. 301). Of course, work of a kind will still go on, but the citizens of the final state will work as little as possible, as Kojève notes with explicit reference to Marx (p. 435). To borrow an expression which someone used recently in the House of Lords on a similar occasion, the citizens of the final state are only so-called workers, workers by courtesy. "There is no longer fight nor work. History has come to its end. There is nothing more to *do*" (pp. 385, 114). This end of History would be most exhilarating but for the fact that, according to Kojève, it is the participation in bloody political struggles as well as in real work or, generally expressed, the negating action, which raises man above the brutes (pp. 490–492, 560, 378n.) The state through which man is said to become reasonably satisfied is, then, the state in which the basis of man's humanity withers away, or in which man loses his humanity. It is the state of Nietzsche's "last man." Kojève in fact confirms the classical view that unlimited technological progress and its accompaniment, which are indispensable conditions of the universal and homogeneous state, are destructive of humanity. It is perhaps possible to say that the universal and homogeneous state is fated to come. But it is certainly impossible to say that man can reasonably be satisfied with it. If the universal and homogeneous state is the goal of History, History is absolutely "tragic." Its completion will reveal that the human problem, and hence in particular the problem of the relation of philosophy and politics, is insoluble.

For centuries and centuries men have unconsciously done nothing but work their way through infinite labors and struggles and agonies, yet ever again catching hope, toward the universal and homogeneous state, and as soon as they have arrived at the end of their journey, they realize that through arriving at it they have destroyed their humanity and thus returned, as in a cycle, to the prehuman beginnings of History. *Vanitas vanitatum. Recognitio recognitionum.* Yet there is no reason for despair as long as human nature has not been conquered completely, i.e., as long as sun and man still generate man. There will always be men (*andres*) who will revolt against a state which is destructive of humanity or in which there is no longer a possibility of noble action and of great deeds. They may be forced into a mere negation of the universal and homogeneous state, into a negation not enlightened by any positive goal, into a nihilistic negation. While perhaps doomed to failure, that nihilistic revolution may be the only action on behalf of man's humanity, the only great and noble deed that is possible once the universal and homogeneous state has become inevitable. But no one can know whether it will fail or succeed. We still know too little about the workings of the universal and homogeneous state to say anything about where and when its corruption will start. What we do know is only that it will perish sooner or later (see Friedrich Engels' *Ludwig Feuerbach*, ed. by Hans Hajek, p. 6). Someone may object that the successful revolt against the universal and homogeneous state could have no other effect than that the identical historical process which has led from the primitive horde to the final state will be repeated. But would such a repetition of the process—a new lease of life for man's humanity—not be preferable to the indefinite continuation of the inhuman end? Do we not enjoy every spring although we know the cycle of the seasons, although we know that winter will come again? Kojève does seem to leave an outlet for action in the universal and homogeneous state. In that state the risk of violent death is still involved in the struggle for political leadership (p. 146). But this opportunity for action can exist only for a tiny minority. And besides, is this not a hideous prospect: a state in which the last refuge of man's humanity is political assassination in the particularly sordid form of the palace revolution? Warriors and workers of all countries, unite, while there is still time, to prevent the coming of "the realm of freedom." Defend with might and main, if it needs to be defended, "the realm of necessity."

But perhaps it is not war nor work but thinking that constitutes the humanity of man. Perhaps it is not recognition (which for many men may lose in its power to satisfy what it gains in universality) but wisdom that is the end of man. Perhaps the universal and homogeneous state is legitimated by the fact that its coming is the necessary and sufficient condition for the coming of wisdom: in the final state all human beings will be reasonably satisfied, they will be truly happy, because all will have acquired wisdom or are about to acquire it. "There is no longer fight nor work; History is completed; there is nothing more to *do*": man is at last free from all drudgery and for the highest and most divine activity, for the contemplation of the unchangeable truth (Kojève, *op. cit.*, p. 385). But if the final state is to satisfy the deepest longing of the human soul, every human being must be capable of becoming wise. The most relevant difference among human beings must have practically disappeared. We understand now why Kojève is so anxious to refute the classical view according to which only a minority of men are capable of the quest for wisdom. If the classics are right, only a few men will be truly happy in the universal and homogeneous state and hence only a few men will find their satisfaction in and through it. Kojève himself observes that the ordinary citizens of the final state are only "potentially satisfied" (p. 146). The actual satisfaction of all human beings, which allegedly is the goal of History, is impossible. It is for this reason, I suppose, that the final social order, as Kojève conceives of it, is a State and not a stateless society: the State, or coercive government, cannot wither away because it is impossible that all human beings should ever become actually satisfied.

The classics thought that, owing to the weakness or dependence of human nature, universal happiness is impossible, and therefore they did not dream of a fulfillment of History and hence not of a meaning of History. They saw with their mind's eye a society within which that happiness of which human nature is capable would be possible in the highest degree: that society is the best regime. But because they saw how limited man's power is, they held that the actualization of the best regime depends on chance. Modern man, dissatisfied with utopias and scorning them, has tried to find a guarantee for the actualization of the best social order. In order to succeed, or rather in order to be able to believe that he could succeed, he had to lower the goal of man. One form in which this was done was to replace moral virtue by universal recognition, or to replace happiness by the satisfaction deriving from universal recognition. The classical solution is utopian in the sense that its actualization is improbable. The modern solution is utopian in the sense that its actualization is impossible. The classical solution supplies a stable standard by which to judge of any actual order. The modern solution eventually destroys the very idea of a standard that is independent of actual situations.

It seems reasonable to assume that only a few, if any, citizens of the universal and homogeneous state will be wise. But neither the wise men nor the philosophers will desire to rule. For this reason alone, to say nothing of others, the Chief of the universal and homogeneous state, or the Universal and Final Tyrant will be an unwise man, as Kojève seems to take for granted. To retain his power, he will be forced to suppress every activity which might lead people into doubt of the essential soundness of the universal and homogeneous state: he must suppress philosophy as an attempt to corrupt the young. In particular he must in the interest of the homogeneity of his universal state forbid every teaching, every suggestion, that there are politically relevant natural differences among men which cannot be abolished or neutralized by progressing scientific technology. He must command his biologists to prove that every human being has, or will acquire, the capacity of being a philosopher or a tyrant. The philosophers in their turn will be forced to defend themselves or the cause of philosophy. They will be obliged, therefore, to try to act on the Tyrant. Everything seems to be a re-enactment of the age-old drama. But this time, the cause of philosophy is lost from the start. For the Final Tyrant presents himself as a philosopher, as the highest philosophic authority, as the supreme exegete of the only true philosophy, as the executor and hangman authorized by the only true philosophy. He claims therefore that he persecutes not philosophy but false philosophies. The experience is not altogether new for philosophers. If philosophers were confronted with claims of this kind in former ages, philosophy went underground. It accommodated itself in its explicit or exoteric teaching to the unfounded commands of rulers who believed they knew things which they did not know. Yet its very exoteric teaching undermined the commands or dogmas of the rulers in such a way as to guide the potential philosophers toward the eternal and unsolved problems. And since there was no universal state in existence, the philosophers could escape to other countries if life became unbearable in the tyrant's dominions. From the Universal Tyrant however there is no escape. Thanks to the conquest of nature and to the completely unabashed substitution of suspicion and terror for law, the Universal and Final Tyrant has at his disposal practically unlimited means for ferreting out, and for extinguishing, the most modest efforts in the direction of thought. Kojève would seem to be right although for the wrong reason: the coming of the universal and homogeneous state will be the end of philosophy on earth.

All I can hope to have proven by opposing Kojève's thesis on the relation between tyranny and wisdom is that Xenophon's thesis on this important topic is not only compatible with the idea of philosophy, but is even required by it. That is not a very great deal, for the question immediately arises whether the idea of philosophy itself does not require legitimation. Philosophy, in the strict, classical sense of the term, is the quest for the eternal order, or for the eternal cause or causes of all things. I assume, then, that there is an eternal and immutable order within which history takes place, and which remains entirely unaffected by history. In other words, I assume that any "realm of freedom" is but a province that depends on the "realm of necessity." In Kojève's terms, this presupposes that "Being is essentially immutable in itself and eternally identical with itself." This hypothesis is not self-evident; Kojève rejects it in favor of the idea that "Being creates itself in the course of history," or that the highest Being is society and history, or that eternity is nothing but the totality of historical time, that is to say finite. On the basis of the classical hypothesis, a radical distinction has to be drawn between the conditions of understanding and its sources, between the conditions for the existence and the pursuit of philosophy (specific kinds of societies, etc.) on the one hand, and the sources of philosophical knowledge on the other. On the basis of Kojève's hypothesis, that distinction is deprived of its most important meaning: social change or chance affect Being if, indeed, they are not identical with it, and they thus affect the truth. On the basis of Kojève's hypothesis, absolute attachment to human interests becomes the source of philosophical knowledge: man ought to feel absolutely at home on earth; he must absolutely be a citizen of the earth, if not a citizen of a particular part of the inhabitable earth. On the basis of the classical hypothesis, philosophy requires radical detachment from human interests: man ought not to feel absolutely at home on earth, but ought to be a citizen of the whole. In our discussion the conflict between the two opposing fundamental hypotheses has barely been mentioned. But we have been constantly mindful of it, for both of us appear to turn our attention away from Being and toward tyranny because we saw that those who lacked the courage to face the consequences of tyranny, who, therefore *et humiliter serviebant et superbe dominabantur*,* were at the same time forced to escape the consequences of Being precisely because they did nothing but speak about Being.

---

* <themselves obsequiously subservient while arrogantly lording it over others. Livy XXIV, 25, viii>

III

The Strauss-Kojève
Correspondence

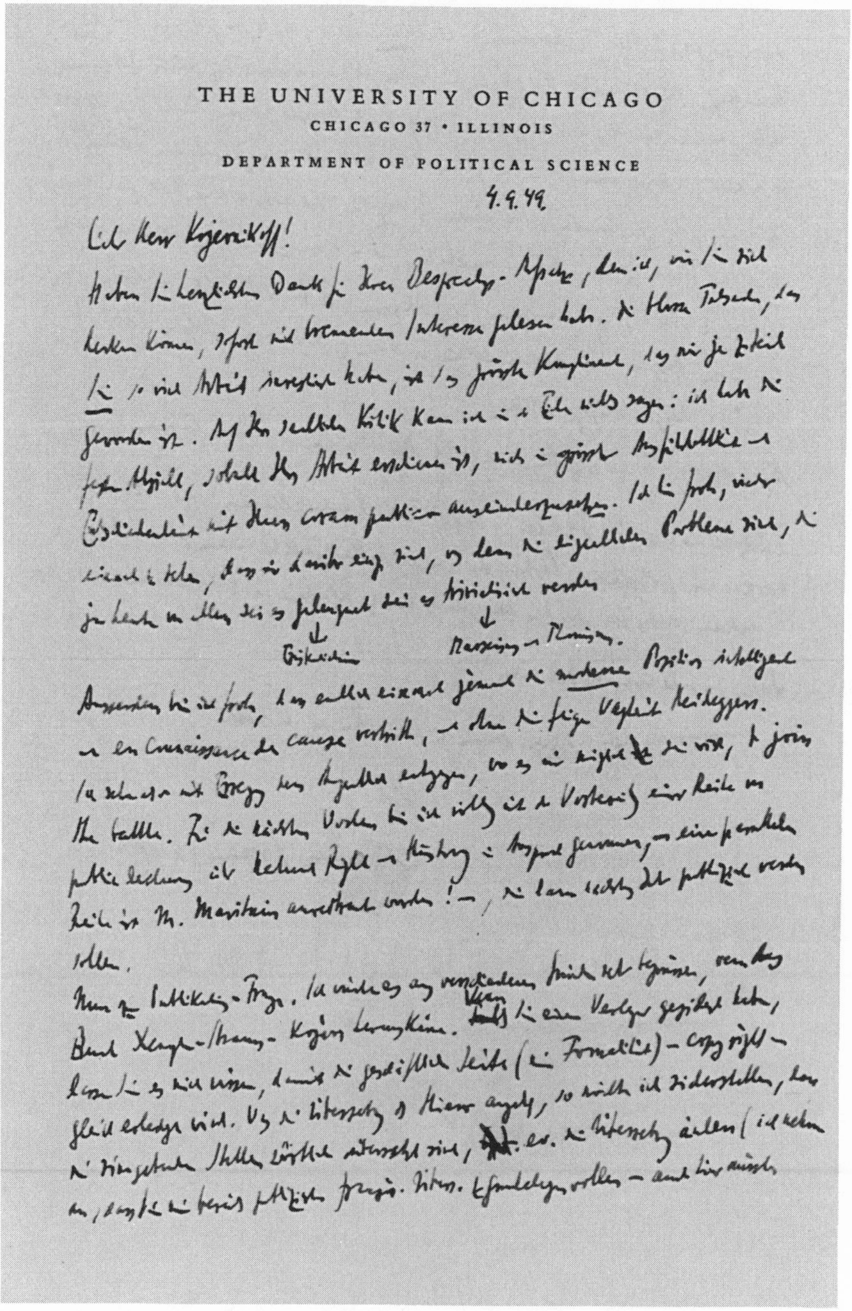
THE UNIVERSITY OF CHICAGO
CHICAGO 37 • ILLINOIS
DEPARTMENT OF POLITICAL SCIENCE

4.9.49

Lieber Herr Kojevnikoff!

Strauss to Kojève (4 September, 1949)

Photograph: James Dee

Kojève to Strauss (1 July, 1957)

Photograph: The University of Chicago Library

Letters

PREFATORY NOTE

We included all of the letters between Strauss and Kojève that we could find. Unfortunately some letters have been lost, and at least one important letter is preserved only in part.

We have corrected occasional minor misspellings of proper names: e.g. Quesneau for Queneau, and obvious slips of the pen: e.g. *Sophist* 361 alongside a passage from *Sophist* 261, whithout calling attention to them. In later years Strauss sometimes dictated his letters, and he did not always catch minor errors by secretaries who were unacquainted with the concepts, texts, or names he was mentioning. We silently corrected these few misspellings. But we never altered references that seemed doubtful without indicating the change. Both Strauss and Kojève often abbreviated titles and names. We consistently spelled them out. But we let stand idiosyncratic spellings of titles or names, e.g. Phaidros, Phailebos . . . ; and we saw no need to italicize titles more consistently than the writers did in their letters.

Strauss's handwriting is notoriously difficult to decipher. His correspondents had to reconstruct his letters as they would assemble a puzzle: copying what they could make out, and leaving blanks to be filled in on subsequent attempts. That is also how we proceeded with most of the letters included here. We wish to record our very special gratitude to the late Professor P. H. v. Blanckenhagen for helping us with some particularly difficult passages at a time when his health was already failing.

Lacunae due either to the fact that one or several words remained illegible even after repeated attempts by various competent readers, or to the fact that the original or the copy from which we were working is defective, are indicated by < . . .> for each missing word or portion of a word.

The writers' frequent, easy shuttling back and forth between languages imparts to this exchange an added liveliness which unfortunately but inevitably gets lost in translation.

The inclusion in this volume of the correspondence between Strauss and Kojève calls for a few brief remarks about them.

They were close contemporaries. Strauss was born in 1899 in Kirchhain, a small town in western Germany; Kojève in 1902 in Moscow. They first met in Berlin in the 1920s. At the time, they both happened to be engaged in studies of religious thought. Strauss's first book is devoted to *Spinoza's Criticism of Religion* (1930), and his second book, *Philosophy and Law* (1935), brings together his early studies of medieval Jewish and Muslim thinkers. Kojève, for his part, wrote his doctoral dissertation under Karl Jaspers in Heidelberg on Vladimir Soloviëv's philosophy of religion.

In 1929 Kojève moved to Paris. Strauss came to Paris on a Rockefeller Fellowship in 1932. They clearly saw a great deal of each other at the time. Their early letters convey something of the difficulties and uncertainties they faced in those troubled years, and the correspondence incidentally traces the main stages in their subsequent careers: Strauss moved to England in 1934, and in 1938 finally obtained a teaching position, his first, at the New School for Social Research in New York. He went on to teach at the University of Chicago from 1949 to 1968. At the time of his death, in 1973, he was the Scott Buchanan Distinguished Scholar in Residence at St. John's College in Annapolis.

In 1933 Kojève took over a seminar on "Hegel's Philosophy of Religion," which Alexandre Koyré had taught at the École pratique des Hautes Études the previous academic year. Koyré had focused on Hegel's early, so-called Jena manuscripts that had only recently been discovered and published. Kojève focused on the *Phenomenology of Mind*. He continued to teach the Hegel seminar every year until 1939, the year the Second World War broke out. In the course of this series of seminars he analyzed and interpreted the text in minute detail, and then went on to discuss a number of key issues in Hegel's teaching. The material for and from these seminars was published in 1947 under the modest title *Introduction à la lecture de Hegel*. As Kojève himself remarks in the letter to Strauss in which he announces the publication of the *Introduction*, it is not a book in the usual sense of the term at all. It combines outlines, notes, exhaustive commentaries, and the transcripts of several series of formal lectures. But this variety, and the fact that sections in which one can almost hear the rhythm of oral delivery alternate with sections that are so clearly *written* that they have to be *seen* in order to be understood, only adds to its impact. It was immediately recognized as a work of uncommon brilliance and penetration. Its pervasive and lasting influence on philosophical thought in France, in the rest of Europe, and in America, cannot be exaggerated.

Kojève did not return to academic life after the War. He entered the French Ministry of Economic Affairs as an Assitant to Robert Marjolin, who had been a participant in the Hegel seminar. He rose very rapidly to a position of eminence in the Ministry, and continued to play an influential role in French international economic policy until his death in 1968. He was the main French architect of the GATT treaty, he actively participated in the establishment of the European Economic Community, and he was widely noted for the special interest he took in what has come to be known as the North-South dialogue.

The correspondence between the two men only confirms what had been perfectly evident from their public exchange on tyranny— that for all of the profound philosophical and political differences that divided them, they had the very highest regard for one another. They valued each other's seriousness and enjoyed each other's intellectual power. Each regarded the other's position as perhaps the only significant philosophical alternative to his own, and each regarded the other as the most intransigent spokesman for that alternative. Superficially they could not have been more different. Strauss was the very embodiment of the scholar and thinker, although he was certainly not as unworldly as he somtimes liked to appear. He was utterly direct and unassuming in manner and bearing. His expression was open, intensely alert, often accompanied by a slightly quizzical, amused twinkle. When he spoke, especially when he rose to speak on formal occasions, he was a commanding presence. He had an uncommon capacity to meet others on their own terms and at their level. The young people who flocked to his courses were at least as much attracted by his ability to listen or to speak directly to their deepest concerns, and by his common sense and sobriety, as they were by his great learning. Yet I believe that even those who knew him well, even those who became his most devoted disciples, only gradually recognized the full range, penetration, and power of his thought. Kojève, by contrast, was worldly and immediately fascinating in the many senses of that term. He, too, was utterly direct. He was a man of wide learning, and his *Introduction* alone gives ample proof of his capacity to combine scrupulous scholarship with bold thinking. But he was not in any way an academic. Strauss may have been right to challenge his remark that the conflict between being a man of action and a philosopher is a tragic conflict. Still, it is not a conflict of which Strauss appears to have had any direct experience, whereas Kojève was living it. He alludes to it in several of his letters, and now and then he spoke of it, though always with irony and detachment. For the most part his conversation simply sparkled with intelligence and a certain playfulness. He could be rather disconcerting and, as he admits in his last letter in this correspondence, occasionally he rather enjoyed being outrageous. At times I experienced in his presence an intellectual power and concentration I have otherwise experienced only in the presence of great works of the mind.

23 rue Racine
to
Mr. Kochevnikoff
15 Bd. du Lycée
Vanves

Dear Mr. Kochevnikoff,   December 6, 1932

In case this card reaches you in time, would you care to come by to our place today (Tuesday), in connection with the main business, but also and above all "in general." And in case this card reaches you too late, then on Wednesday evening. We will be expecting you on Tuesday or Wednesday between 8 and 9 o'clock.

Goodbye.

With best regards
Yours

Leo Strauss

To
M. Alexandre Kochevnikoff
15 Bd. du Lycée
Vanves

December 13, 1932

Dear friend,

As we are in the process of moving, I write just these few lines in order to give you our new address.

Rue de la Glacière runs between the Boulevard Port-Royal and the Boulevard Arago. There is a metro station "Glacière."

We look forward to seeing you on Thursday evening.

Please accept, Monsieur, the expression of my most cordial sentiments.

Leo Strauss

December 17, 1932

Dear Mr. Kochevnikoff,

First, regarding business: enclosed please find the second section of my article; please excuse the stains on the paper and the envelope. I had nothing else handy, and I wanted to get this matter ready for you just as soon as possible.

Then, regarding personal matters: we very much look forward to seeing you and Miss Basjo at our house on Wednesday evening. If you and the records don't mind, could you bring along a few records on Wednesday? As you can imagine, this request comes more from my wife than it does from me. Still, my opposition to music received its first shock last night. Perhaps we can talk about it some day.

So, until Wednesday evening.

Goodbye.

With best regards, also from my wife, to Miss Basjo and yourself,

Yours

Leo Strauss

―――――――――

< undated >

Address: 47 Montague Street, Russell Square, London

Dear friend—I am very thirsty in this moment and I have not the good and cheap French wine. But instead of it we have the wonderful English breakfast—the hams taste too good as to consist of pork, and therefore they are allowed by the M < osaic > law according to atheistic interpretation—, the wonderful E < nglish > puddings and sweets; and, besides it, the English people is < much > politer than the Frenchmen. I cannot realize a greater difference than that between the Préfecture de Police and the Aliens Registration Office. We feel much better here than in Paris—except only that we ha < ve > here no friends: we know only Herr < Hoganer > with his red < . . . >; however we don't see him very often.

How do you do? How is Miss Basjo? Did your beard b<ecome> greater and stronger? Do not forget to send us as often <as> possible photos showing the progresses you made in th<is> regard.

Our boarding house is facing the British Museum. I hope I ob<tain> the card in the beginning of the next week so that I can begin to <use it>. Up to now I only heard two lessons about English phonetics read by two oldish spectacled Misses singing the English wo<rds> in a very funny manner.

I would be very glad if you could write me what is happen<ing> with you since we did not see us.

Yours sincerely,

Leo Strauss

London, January 16th, 1934

Dear friend—

Meanwhile I have acclimatized myself here. I go each day in the British Museum (half a minute's walk) in order to study the English Hobbes-literature and the Hobbes-Mss. The English cooking is much more according to my taste than the French. The most important fact: I saw Downing Street, the seat of the greatest power of the world—much, much smaller than the Wilhelmstrasse. I had a very strong impression.

The address you want is: Dr. Kl.[1] c.o. Dr. Gadamer,[2] [alias Moldauer], Marburg an d. Lahn, Ockershäuser Allee 39, Germany. The quotation you want is: Heidegger, *Die Selbstbehauptung der deutschen Universität*, Breslau 1933, p. 12.[3]

I am sorry—I have not the time to write a real letter. But you want the address and the quotation at once.

I hope, you will write me as soon as possible, and perhaps a little more of "details" of this memorable discussion.

What was the impression you had from Herr Landsberg?[4]

Yours sincerely,

L. Strauss

Did you hear anything from Mr. Koyré?[5]

P.S. It is not necessary to be or become Aristotelian or < . . . > sufficient to become Platonist.

< undated >

Dear Mr. Kochevnikoff,

I am deep in work and worries—in other words in a situation similar to yours. Nothing will come of Palestine: Guttman[1] is going there. So far, prospects are the same as in France. But one must not lose courage.

Be that as it may. Could you please send me Koyré's address right away. I want to write to him very soon.

Saturday I am going to Oxford.

Be well!

With best regards to yourself and Miss Basjo,

Yours

Strauss

My wife sends best regards

New address:
2 Elsworthy Road
St. John's Wood. London

---

2 Elsworthy Road, London NW3

London, April 9, 1934

Dear Mr. Kochevnikoff,

Why do I never hear anything from you? I have not the least idea of how you are, what has happened to your work, your hopes and your worries. Do write me sometime, even if only a card.

Regarding myself, I can only report that I am quite well. I like this country, about which one might say what Diderot said about Hobbes: dry (the pubs close at 10 p.m. sharp here, and the stuff is expensive!), austere and forceful, much more than I do France. And by contrast to the Bibliothèque Nationale, the British Museum is a place to which one enjoys going.

I have become a real Hobbes philologist: Mss., etc. The Hobbes-edition project (do, please, try to be discreet) is not entirely hopeless—the Master of an Oxford College is prepared to sponsor it—and hence also myself. In the most recent Hobbes book, by John Laird, Prof<essor> in Aberdeen, to which Gibson called my attention—the book is better than Lubienski's,[1] but not good, not as good as that by Tönnies[2]—I am described in connection to our joint *Recherches* article, as "a very competent writer,"[3] in which I <mis>use Gibson's introduction. Most important: I may perhaps(!) have found Hobbes's hitherto entirely unknown first writing—a collection of 10 essays, the first five of which deal with vanity and related phenomena. In the worst case, the ms. was written under Hobbes's influence by one of his disciples. The decision will be reached in about a week.

We have a few acquaintances here—but none with whom we enjoy spending time as much as we do with you.

So write again, so that we don't lose track of one another.

My wife and Thomas[4] send "Uncle" Basjo warm greetings, and I greet you no less warmly.

Your

Leo Strauss[5]

May 1, 1934

Dear Mr. Strauss,

Many thanks for your letter.

Please excuse me for not writing all this time. But I have not written to anyone except to my wife and to Miss Basio—not even to Koyré.

That has a romantic reason. This time my July-August moods arose in April. For a change, an "Arian" girl.

During the Easter vacation I did absolutely nothing. I cancelled the first lecture. The second—delivered entirely unprepared (it was by no means the worst). Now my life is becoming more normal, at least I prepare my lectures, and today I write to you and to Koyré.

I am very pleased that you are well, and that you have made your decision. I never had any doubt about the most favorable prospects for your future.

It would give me great pleasure to have more precise details (discretion assured: after all, I do—as a human being—have my eternal nature!).

With me, nothing new, nothing good.

The École has not yet paid anything, and I have become very sceptical on this score.

My application (the equivalence of a *licence* on top of the doctorate, on the basis of my German Ph.D.) was rejected. Hitler is responsible (12 similar applications!). I can therefore not announce my courses, and hence cannot request a research grant.

Naturalization has now (Stavisky[1]) become very difficult. Letters of recommendation are now strictly prohibited. An old debtor has paid me 3000 Francs (such things do happen!). That is what I live off, but it, too, soon comes to an end.

So that I am in a rather somber mood.

As yet I work very little. Almost exclusively at my lectures.

Gordin lectures on medieval philosophy at the École rabbinique.[2] I have never heard anything like it! Heinemann gives lectures at the Sorbonne for Rey,[3] unpaid. Also drivel.

"My" Gurevitsch has become a professor in Bordeaux.[4] I hear nothing interesting from Koyré.

Please write me again soon.

With best regards to yourself and your wife,

Yours

AK

P.S. Enclosed a picture of Hitler which—in my opinion—explains a great deal: the man is really very congenial and "cozy."

Did your wife receive Miss Basio's letter?

––––––––––

Address: 26 Primrose Hill Road, London NW3

London, June 3, 1934

Dear Mr. Kochevnikoff,

Many thanks for your letter. Please excuse me for not having answered it, and be so kind as to regard this writing as a letter.

I write you in a similar mood as you do to me—namely somber. Some influential English professors do, I believe, take an interest in me—but whether and how that interest will manifest itself in terms of bread, cigarettes, and the like, is another matter entirely. And soon it is summer, that is to say a time when it is impossible to undertake anything. I don't want to detail all this for you more fully—after all, you know about it from your own experience.

If I had a modest income, I could be the happiest man in the world. I have already written you about my Hobbes-find. In the meantime I have copied the manuscript, read and studied it, and it is now absolutely certain that it is H < obbes > 's first writing. That is rather nice for all kinds of incidental reasons—but to me it means more: namely the refutation of your own and Koyré's objection, that my Hobbes interpretation is a willful construction. No, now I can prove that I did not construct. Naturally, reality always looks somewhat different than even the most conscientious, complete texts-in-hand reconstruction. That is obvious. But it does help me to render my H < obbes > interpretation concrete in a way I would never have dared to dream possible. I should like briefly to out-line this for you:

In his "youth," i.e. until he was 41, that is to say before he became acquainted with Euclid and thereafter with Galileo etc., H < obbes > had been influenced by four forces: Scholasticism, Puritanism, Humanism, and the aristocratic atmosphere in which he lived. Relatively early—let us say at the age of 22—he broke with Scholasticism. But the break with Scholasticism does not mean he broke with Aristotle. Aristotle, albeit not the scholastic Arist < otle >, still remains the philosopher for him. But the center of gravity has already shifted: from physics and metaphysics to ethics and rhetoric (the teaching about the passions). The place of theory is taken by "heroic virtue" (modified Aristotelian magnanimity), that is to say, virtue (beauty, strength, courage, openness of being, striving after great goals, grand way of life). That is the first point. The second is that, (under Bacon's influence), while he in principle acknowledges ancient, Aristotelian ethics and the inquiry into virtue, < his focus shifts to > the function of virtue and the inquiry into the use and life with others[1] in < . . . > virtue < . . . >. Hence history, which exhibits instances of moral life, assumes greater importance than does philosophical doctrine with its exclusively abstract precepts. This provides a radical explanation of H < obbes >'s < historical > studies in his "youth."
< . . . > in this way H < obbes >'s later break with Aristotle < becomes radically > intelligible. For his later teaching is nothing else than the at-tempt to understand < . . . > on the basis of life with others[1], that is to say on the basis of human "nature" as it now is, that is to say of the ordi-nary, "average" human being < . . . . >

The concrete way in which he did this, the passion with which he did it < . . . . > of this concrete criticism of that modi-fied, distorted Aristot < elian > ethics, that is to say of aristocratic virtue, < . . . > a criticism that was already noticeable in the Essays. The aristo-cratic principle is honor, fame, pride. This criticism, the principle of which is of puritanical origin, by which honor, fame, and vanity are sin-gled out and devalued, requires a revolution in basic moral concepts that results in the antithesis vanity-fear.

The further, most important and most difficult task is then to show how the project of a mechanistic-deterministic account of nature arises from this new moral principle. The essential middle term here is the sig-nificance attached on a priori grounds to the sense of touch, which now becomes the most important sense. That is simply the as-it-were "epistemological'' expression of the < the fact > that the fear of (violent) death becomes the moral principle. (That is my London discovery.)

Please excuse this higher nonsense, which is intended to make up to you for the sober gloom of the beginning of this letter: if you wept then, you may now laugh.

My wife received Miss Basjo's letter, and has written to her in the meantime.

Thomas grows and thrives, he develops morally under my modest moral influence—he often recalls ''Uncle Basjo's'' table-manners with us.

It is a pity that we never meet. Perhaps it will be possible to do so in Autumn. In a fortnight my sister arrives from Egypt for a visit with us. My father would like to meet with his children outside of Germany—perhaps in Paris.

For you, the most sensational news will be that (perhaps!) Klein will join us. He, too, is ''resolved'' to leave Germany.

Be well—delight in the wines of France which we miss more and more—and best regards, also in my wife's name.

from

Your

Leo Strauss

May 9, 1935

Dear Mr. Kochevnikoff,

I was delighted with your letter—in the first place simply because I once again had news of you, and in the second place because precisely this letter gave me great satisfaction. Most immediately that is so with respect to the Parisian ''philosophes'' whom you now—finally!—judge just as I had judged them from the first. I know only one truly intelligent man in Paris, and that is—Kochevnikoff. I do not deny that there are cleverer ''dialecticians'' than you in Paris—but since when has sterile ''sharpness'' (which, incidentally, invariably proves extremely dull on closer inspection) had anything to do with understanding, with insight. Understanding is virtue (virtue = knowledge); whoever has insight into what matters, deals with the issues, is "passionately" interested in the issues and not the busyness—and you are the only person I know in Paris who has an interest in the issues, and <u>therefore</u> you are the brightest of all. (But if you tell this to others, I send your letter with your judgments to Paris!) Of course some are harder-working than you—for example Klein, who has published an absolutely first-rate analysis of Plato's and Aristotle's philosophy of mathematics[1]—indeed—which you have naturally not read—because of your erotic adventures—adventures that of course are more comfortable than the intellectual risks, the experimental shift in perspective to which you too will some day have to resolve yourself if you do not want to sink into a Parisian life of ease. This brings me to the second point, regarding which your letter gratified me and, I should add, my wife: I refer to your remark about Miss Basjo, that your relationship with her is not "resolved," in other words not broken off in the way we were told by some people who are ill-disposed toward Miss Basjo. I need say nothing on this point, since you know my opinion very precisely. If my wife did not have so much work, she would long ago have written Miss Basjo, and invited her to visit us. When you write to her, do please tell her that it would give my wife great pleasure to hear from her, and even greater pleasure if she came to visit her.

Of course we must speak. But since I am no longer a Rockefeller-Fellow, there is only one way in which that is possible, that you come here. We have a small house all to ourselves, and so have enough room even for so distinguished a guest as yourself. So come at Whitsun, for example. The trip cannot be beyond reach.

I am really angry with you for loaning my book[2] to that fool Gordin who is not <u>capable</u> of understanding a single line of it, instead of reading it yourself. Just read the Introduction, and the first essay. The Introduction is very daring and will interest you if only because of that. And then write me your reaction. In my view it is the best thing I have written.

In the meantime my study of "Hobbes's Political Science in its Genesis" is finished. I believe that it is good. Other than the study by Klein which I have already mentioned, it is the first attempt at a radical liberation from the modern prejudice. On several occasions I refer to Hegel, and do not fail to mention your name. The study will appear in the first volume of my posthumous works, since no German publisher or English translator can be found.*

*This morning I got the definitive rejection from the English!

The economic situation is serious. I have a grant until October 1, which does not exceed the minimum for bare existence. It remains an open question whether it will be renewed for another year. After that it is certainly over. Where we turn then, only the gods know. I have no luck, dear Mr. Kochevnikoff.

So: write right away, and come soon.

With best regards, also in my wife's name.

Your

Leo Strauss

Vanves, November 2, 1936

Dear Mr. Strauss:

Many, many thanks for your Hobbes book[1], which I have already read through. To say so right away: it is one of the best history of philosophy books I have read, and it is altogether a <u>very</u> good book. I have learned much from it. Admittedly, I do not know Hobbes. But your interpretation is <u>compelling</u>: it <u>cannot</u> be otherwise, and one has no wish to take issue with you.

I did not answer immediately because I intended to write you a very long letter, both about the Hobbes-Hegel problem, and about the progress of my own reflections. I miss our conversations more than ever. Well—the intention remained and remains unfulfilled: I <u>really</u> have no time for it. In addition to which my arm gives me trouble. I have written too much, and now have a bursitis. In principle I should take two weeks' rest. But that is impossible. I must therefore at least drop all writing that is not absolutely necessary. Hence this brief and inadequate letter—

<u>Hegel</u>—<u>Hobbes</u>:

Everything you write is correct. Hegel undoubtedly takes Hobbes as his point of departure. A comparison is surely worthwhile, and I would have liked to make it—with you.

<u>Major difference</u>: Hegel consciously wants to "return" to the Ancients ("dialectically," that is to say by way of "Hobbes.") There is a summum

bonum, namely full self-understanding through philosophy. But one can only understand (and thus "satisfy") oneself fully in an ideal state (just as according to Plato). That state can only be actualized by means of history and at the end of history. For it is the "reality of the kingdom of heaven." That means, it is this-worldly, like the ancient state; but in this-world, the (Christian) other-world is actualized. That is why the state presupposes not only "knowledge" but also "action" ("volonté!"). Although its final cause is also philosophical knowledge, this knowledge is a knowledge of action, through action (man's "negative," that is to say creative, and not merely uncovering < or revealing > activity). Struggle → the dialectic of master and slave in history → synthesis of the two (master and slave) in the citizen of the ideal state.

Concrete difference: Hobbes fails to see the value of work. The fear of death is not enough to lead man "to reason." The fearing slave attains knowledge (and the idea of freedom → Stoicism → Scepticism → Christianity) only if he also works (in and out of fear), and works for the master, that is to say only if he performs services. This accounts for history as a "class-struggle," that is to say as a master-slave dialectic with a final synthesis.

    Natural science (Galileo-Newton's, that is to say also Hobbes's) is a pseudo sci< ence > of the working slave. The ex-slave liberated by the rev< olution > (1789) gives it up; his science becomes the phil< osophy > (Hegel's) on the basis of which man can understand himself as man (but to that end, the transition through < the stage of > slave labor and its ideology is necessary!). Slave sci< ence > leads 1. to transcendentalism, 2. to subj< ective > idealism, 3. to "phrenology." that is to say to material< ist > anthropology (so, too, in Hobbes). Why? Because the slave who does not want to struggle (Hobbes's bourgeois), necessarily flees into the beyond ("belief"), and seeks his satisfaction there (without ever finding it). The purely theoretical cancellation of the beyond yields subj< ective > idealism (more generally: the intellectuals' ideology of "the thing itself," of "pure" science, etc., that is to say the flight into "absolute" values ["pure insight," that is to say 17th century rationalism]). But in fact these purely intuited values are merely given givens,[2] that is to say nature. The whole process therefore ends up in materialism. The way out: recognition of values-as-duties.[3] Initially that leads to "utopia" ("insanity"). But if man is ready to struggle for them, it leads to revolution. That is the final synthesis (of master and slave): the worker's struggle leads to the struggler's work (univ< ersal > military service as the major consequence of the Fr< ench > revolution, according to Hegel!) That is the "action of each and all" = ideal state, in which <u>everyone</u> is a citizen, that is to say $\left\{\begin{array}{l}\text{soldier---}\\\text{civilian---}\end{array}\right\}$ <u>civil</u> <u>servant</u>, and thus <u>creates</u> and preserves the state by his <u>own</u> actions.

<u>In sum</u>:

Hobbes fails to appreciate the value of work and therefore underestimates the value of struggle ("vanity"). According to Hegel, the <u>working</u> slave realizes 1. the <u>idea</u> of freedom, 2. the <u>actualization</u> of this idea through struggle. Thus: initially "man" is always master <u>or</u> slave; the "full human being"—at the "end" of history—is master <u>and</u> slave (that is to say both and neither). Only this can <u>satisfy</u> his "vanity," in that he is recognized by <u>those he recognizes</u>, and understands himself as such (in [Hegel < 's >] philosophy). Nothing short of this understanding of satisfaction constitutes the summum bonum. But one can understand only <u>satisfaction</u>; and satisfaction presupposes work <u>and</u> struggle. [Fear of death <u>alone</u> can only lead to religion (= unhappiness)]. The master does not kill the slave <u>only</u> so that he might work for him! The gen < uine > master is never afraid.

In the meantime, I have re-read Plato. I continue to believe that you underestimate the *Timaeus*.

1. Plato wants to teach Dion <u>geometry</u> first (and not "virtue" itself).

2. It seems to me that Plato later found "dialectics" inadequate, and went over to the "method of division;" that method implies the primacy of physics (mathem < atical > physics).

3. The "Statesman" <u>presupposes</u> the "Timaeus."

Thus: the "idea" = "ideal" of man cannot be seen in man himself. He has to be grasped as "a place in the cosmos." That <u>place</u> is his "ideal." The organization of the state presupposes the (or some) knowledge of the org < anization > of the cosmos.

What do you think of that?

Now, regarding personal matters.

I have been promised that I would get French citizenship soon. Then I may perhaps receive a fellowship. Until then, much meaningless work in order to earn money. Library (5 hours) + the crazy Frenchman (ghostwriting) (2 hours) + 2 courses. One on Hegel (Chapter VI, B and C); and a second one on Bayle. (I am replacing Koyré, who is in Egypt), I chose

Bayle because I am interested in the problem of tolerance. What for him was Prot < estantism > -Cathol < icism > , is today fasc < ism > -comm < unism > . I believe that in Bayle the motives and the meaning of the middle position are clearer than among modern "democrats."

I regret that we write each other so seldom. It is of course due to slovenliness on my part. But do believe me that it has nothing to do with "intrinsic reasons." "Humanly" and "philosophically" I continue to value and cherish you greatly.

Write me soon, and with best regards also to your wife.

Yours,

AK

Paris, June 22, 1946

Dear Mr. Strauss:

Many thanks for your Farabi essay.[1] I am in no way a specialist in the field. I can therefore not pass an expert judgment on your interpretation. But to a layman it seems most plausible. In any case, the essay is most amusing.

But the problem interests me much more than the historical issues.

I have thought much about wisdom myself, in the course of the past years. My last course was devoted to this problem. I am now bringing out a book. A compendium of my Hegel course by one of those who attended it (Queneau),[2] and transcripts of some lectures. Among others, the full text of the last course about wisdom. The book is very bad. I had no time to work it out. But it contains some interesting things. Above all, about wisdom, fulfillment, and happiness (I follow Hegel in saying: satisfaction.) I would like to know what you think of it. I will send you a copy as soon as it comes out.

I would like to have the opportunity for discussions with you. As well as with Klein. Here I have almost no one. Weil[3] is very intelligent, but he lacks something, I don't quite know what. Koyré is completely dotty. Last year Klein wrote me about the possibility of being invited to

St. John's College.[4] At the time I could not do it. Now I would gladly come. But Klein no longer writes anything about it.

I do not want to ask him directly. Perhaps he does not want to submit my name a second time. But I would be grateful to you, if you raised this question with him.

With best regards to yourself and to your wife

Yours,

Kojève

————————

MINISTÈRE
DE
L'ÉCONOMIE NATIONALE

April 8, 1947

Dear Strauss,

I received your 1943 and 1945 essays[1] almost at the same time. The essay about ancient political philosophies interests me intensely. In any case—many thanks.

I have the impression that basically we do not think as differently as it appears. What a pity that we no longer have the opportunity to talk with one another at length. Because it is not really possible by way of letters. And still less by way of essays and books.

By the way—my book has still not come out. I will send it to you as soon as it does.

Koyré was very affected by your critical attitude toward his Plato book.[2] I mentioned only purely "material" criticism. But he evidently has a "bad conscience" . . .

Surely you can arrange a "research trip" to Europe: after all, there is a lot of money for this sort of thing in the U.S.! For it is scarcely possible for me to come to America for a mere trip.

I have still not written the Löwith review. Nor have I any particular desire to do so.

On May 1 I probably will go to Geneva (Conference), where I may remain 4–6 weeks.

What do you hear from Klein? Will he come to Europe? It would be nice if the two of you could come together.

Weil has finished his big book.[3] Very impressive. Also, very "Hegel-Marxist," and certainly influenced by my course. But it ends à la Schelling: Poetry ~ philosophy, and wisdom as silence. You will finally have to read it. And I regret I did not write the book myself.

Perhaps I will still do it, if I drop administration . . . and find a little money "to do nothing"!

With very best regards to you and yours,

> Your
> A. Kojève.

3202 Oxford Ave., New York 63, N.Y. 22.8.48

Dear Mr. Kojevnikoff:

Finally I get to write to you. Before I turn to the primary object of this letter, I should like to thank you for getting me the Malebranche (how much do I owe you?), and to ask you whether you would be prepared to review my forthcoming small book, *On Tyranny: An Interpretation of Xenophon's Hiero*,[1] in France. I know no one besides yourself and Klein who will understand what I am after (I am one of those who refuse to go through open doors when one can enter just as well through a keyhole), and Klein is endlessly lazy. In any case, I will send you my opusculum.—Now to the issue.

Only now, during the vacation, did I find time to work through your *Introduction*.[2] It is an extraordinary book, by which I also mean this, that it is an uncommonly good and interesting book. With the exception of Heidegger there is probably not a single one of our contemporaries who has written as comprehensive and at the same time as intelligent a book. In other words, no one had made the case for modern thought in our time as brilliantly as you. Quite aside from this general merit, your book has the truly not negligible merit of having made the *Phenomenology of Mind* accessible, not only to myself, I am sure.

The account as a whole leaves the impression that you regard Hegel's philosophy as absolute knowledge, and reject the philosophy of nature together with its implications as a dogmatic and dispensable residue. One is therefore all the more surprised to find you admit that the demonstrative power of the Hegelian argument (the circularity of the system) is absolutely dependent on the philosophy of nature (291 at the bottom; 400, paragraph 3; 64). Indeed, it is evident that the philosophy of nature is indispensable. How else can the uniqueness of the historical process (349 n. 2; 391) be accounted for? It can only be necessarily unique if there can be only one "earth" of finite duration in infinite time. (By the way, are there any explicit statements in Hegel about the earth's beginning and end? In Lasson's edition of the *Encyclopedia* I found nothing on this score, other than the rejection of evolutionary theories. How can that be reconciled with the earth's temporal finiteness?) Besides, why should the one, temporal, finite earth not be subject to cataclysms (every 100,000,000 years), with total or partial repetitions of the historical process? Only a teleological concept of nature can help out here. If nature is not structured or ordered with a view to history, then one is led to a contingency even more radical than Kant's transcendental contingency (which Hegel rejects). (Cp. 397 bottom–398 top, as well as 301 paragraph 2 and 434 middle, with 404 n. 1 and 432 paragraph 2.). But if the philosophy of nature is necessary, it follows that atheism has to be rejected (378).

The deduction of the desire for recognition is convincing if one presupposes that every philosophy consists in grasping the spirit of its time in thought, that is to say if one presupposes everything that is at issue. Otherwise, that deduction is arbitrary. Why should self-consciousness and the striving for recognition not be understood as derivative from the zoon logon echon[3]? Self-consciousness presupposes desire? But is the striving for contemplation not a desire? All desire is directed at what-is-not, but only the desire for desire is directed at non-being as such—but is not recognition (for example of parents by their children, of the stronger by the weaker), always a given?

What makes human beings into human beings is the striving for recognition. Hence human beings are fully satisfied when and only when they are universally recognized. I see an ambiguity here: a) they should be satisfied, dissatisfaction with universal recognition is irrational; b) they are satisfied. Regarding a) human beings are irrational; they manage to destroy the simply rational communal life (implied on p. 400, paragraph 2). Regarding b) human beings are not satisfied; they want to be happy; their happiness is not identical with their being recognized (cp. 334 with 435n).

The recognition for which great men of action strive, is admiration. That recognition is not necessarily satisfied by the End-State. The fact that great deeds are impossible in the End-State, can lead precisely the best to a nihilistic denial of the End-State. There is only one way of avoiding that consequence, namely by the Platonic-Hegelian assumption that "the best" are somehow ruled by the purely rational, the philosophers. Differently stated, only if the striving for recognition is a veiled form of the striving for full self-consciousness or for full rationality, in other words only if a human being, insofar as he is not a philosopher, is not really a human being, if someone who leads a life of action is essentially subordinate to the philosopher—that is to say if one follows Hegel even where (in my view for bad reasons) you diverge from him: cp. 398, paragraph 1, with 398–400, 275–279, 286–291. (Regarding these passages and regarding 293, I should like to remark—and this is only another way of saying what I have just said—that you seem to underestimate the fact that in Hegel's view the Enlightenment refuted the Christian dogma as such. Hegel would rightly reject what you call mysticism as a nonconcept inapplicable to Biblical religion.) Hence it is not recognition but only wisdom that can truly satisfy a human being (which you naturally also say). Hence the end state owes its privilege to wisdom, to the rule of wisdom, to the popularization of wisdom (414a., 385, 387), and not to its universality and homogeneity as such. But if wisdom does not become common property, the mass remains in the thrall of religion, that is to say of an essentially particular and particularizing power (Christianity, Islam, Judaism . . .), which means that the decline and fall of the universal-homogeneous state is unavoidable.

In any case, if not all human beings become wise, then it follows that for almost all human beings the end state is identical with the loss of their humanity (490, 491 and 492), and they can therefore not be rationally satisfied with it. The basic difficulty also shows itself in this, that on the one hand the End-State is referred to as the State of warrior-workers (114, 146, 560 f.), and on the other hand it is said that at this stage there are no more wars, and as little work as possible (indeed, in the strict sense of the term, there is no more work at all (145, 385, 435 n, 560), since nature will have been definitively conquered (301 paragraph 3, et passim). Besides: the masses are only potentially satisfied (145 f.)

If I had more time than I have, I could state more fully, and presumably more clearly, why I am not convinced that the End State as you describe it, can be either the rational or the merely-factual satisfaction of human beings. For the sake of simplicity I refer today to Nietzche's "last men."[4]

When do your travels again bring you this way? In any case, let me hear from you soon. With best regards from

your

Leo Strauss

I have re-read your last two letters—containing among other things, your judgement of Weil. I can only repeat: I have seldom seen such an empty human being. You say: he lacks something—I say: he lacks substance, he is nothing but an idle chatterer.

THE GRADUATE FACULTY OF POLITICAL AND SOCIAL SCIENCE
organized under the New School for Social Research
66 West 12th Street New York 11, Grammercy 7-8464

December 6, 1948

M. Alexandre Kojève
15 Boulevard Stalingrad
Vanves (Seine)
France

Dear Kojève:

I am sending you under separate cover my study on Xenophon. Would it be possible for you to review it in Critique or, for that matter, in any other French periodical. I am very anxious to have a review by you because you are one of the three people who will have a full understanding of what I am driving at.

Sincerely yours,

Leo Strauss

THE UNIVERSITY OF CHICAGO
Chicago 37, Illinois
Department of Political Science

May 13, 1949

Dear Mr. Kojevnikoff:

I was very pleased to see in an earlier issue of *Critique* that you plan
to review my *Xenophon*. Now I see on the back-cover of the April issue
that your name has disappeared, and that instead, M. Weil announces an
article on Machiavelli. Did you abandon your plan? I would regret it very
much—among other things also because I should have liked to take your
account as the occasion for an essay to which I intended to devote the
month of July, and in which I would discuss our differences. Please let me
know where things stand.

A further request: Could you have your friends at *Critique* henceforth send me *Critique* at the above address. You probably know that at
the end of January I went to the University of Chicago as "Professor of
Political Philosophy."

When will you come to these parts again? And how are you and your
Philosophy of Right?[1]

With best regards,
Your

Leo Strauss

Vanves, May 26, 1949

Dear Mr. Strauss,

Thank you so much for your letter of the 13th. I very much apologize for
still not having answered your first, already very old letter.

Really because it poses too many important questions that cannot be
dealt with properly in a short answer. I have thought about the questions,
and have much to say in answer to them, but I never find the time to get it
all down in writing.

Be that as it may—a thousand thanks for the really very friendly judgment about a book which, as regards its form, is beneath all criticism.

I have read your *Xenophon* very attentively, and have learned much from it.

I have <u>not</u> abandoned the idea of reviewing the book (but the cover of *Critique* mentions forthcoming items only <u>once</u>). I have even written 22 (!) pages about it. But that is only about 2/3. Now: in the first place, I do not know <u>when</u> I will write the remaining 10–15 pages; in the second place, the article seems to me too long for *Critique* (although Bataille is ready to print everything I write).

In any event, I will send you a typed copy as soon as I have one. I have another idea. A volume could be brought out (possibly by NRF) that would combine the French translation of the dialogue, a translation of your book (without the notes, or rather the "technical" notes), and my article (which deals with your book). What do you think of that idea?

Naturally you have to see my article in order to be able to decide. But what do you think "in principle?" I believe that it would in any event be better to bring out the translation of your book together with the French text of the dialogue.

Otherwise, I am not especially well: tired, kidneys, heart.

<u>Very</u> much work, much <u>personal</u> success, but really very few results.

I spent a month in Egypt: very impressive.

I am very pleased that the material question is finally solved for you. And how are the students?

With best regards to you and yours,

Your Kojève

P. S. I will speak to Weil regarding your *Critique*.

THE UNIVERSITY OF CHICAGO
Chicago 37, Illinois
Department of Political Science

June 27, 1949

Dear Mr. Kojevnikoff,

Thank you ever so much for your letter. I was so busy, I could not answer. Today, just before the beginning of the summer semester, in terrible heat and humidity, I find a free moment.

I restrict myself to the practical problem. What matters most to me is to get to see your critique in any legible form whatsoever. I very much hope that in the meantime you have written the last third,—the rest of your 22 pages.

As for the publication, I wonder whether both might not be possible: a) your review in *Critique*, and b) the book you suggest (translation of the *Hiero*, my interpretation, and your criticism). I fully agree with the idea for the book, even before having read your criticism. I would be most grateful to you for an early report about where things stand.

I am very sorry to hear that you are physically not well. That $\sigma\omega\mu\alpha$ $\sigma\eta\mu\alpha$[1] makes itself felt more and more unpleasantly every year—to myself as well. What is of course depressing is the fact that the older one grows, the more clearly one sees how little one understands: the darkness gets increasingly dense. It is perhaps a questionable compensation that one sees through the lack of clarity in the ideas of chatterers and cheats more easily and quickly than in earlier years. The $\epsilon\dot{\upsilon}\delta\alpha\iota\mu\nu\acute{\iota}\alpha$ of $\theta\epsilon\omega\rho\epsilon\grave{\iota}\nu$ is really available only $\pi\sigma\tau\epsilon$, ut philosophus dixit.[2]

When will you again come to these parts?

With best regards, also in my wife's name, from

your
Leo Strauss

––––––––––

Vanves, August 15, 1949

Dear Mr. Strauss,

Please excuse that I reply only today to your letter of June 27. But I wanted first to fulfill your request, and give the manuscript a legible form.

That was done only yesterday: I have corrected a typed copy, and sent it to you (c/o the University, with the request to forward). I hope it is not too late, although you wanted to have it at the beginning of August.

Critique is broke: the September issue is the last one.

Perhaps I will publish my review in Sartre's *Temps Modernes*, although I do not much care to do so.

As for the article, I am rather dissatisfied with it. I had to write it in bits and pieces, and the structure is therefore very defective.

Regarding the book (Xenophon—Strauss—Kojève), it will have to wait until the end of the vacation. That way you can let me know whether the idea appeals to you.

With best regards to yourself and to your wife,

Yours,
Kojève

THE UNIVERSITY OF CHICAGO
Chicago 37, Illinois
Department of Political Science

September 4, 1949

Dear Mr. Kojevnikoff,

My warmest thanks for your review essay, which, as you can imagine, I immediately read with the most intense interest. The mere fact that you invested as much work as you did, is the greatest compliment ever paid me. I cannot speak to your substantive criticism in haste: I firmly intend to discuss your position with the utmost thoroughness and decisiveness in a public setting just as soon as your article has appeared. I am glad to see, once again, that we agree about what the genuine problems are, problems which are nowadays on all sides either denied or trivialized.

Existentialism Marxism and Thomism

Besides that I am glad that finally someone represents the <u>modern</u> position intelligently and in full knowledge—and without Heidegger's cowardly vagueness.

I therefore eagerly look forward to the moment when it will be possible to ¹join the battle.¹ In the coming weeks I am totally taken up with the preparation of a series of public lectures on Natural Right and History —Mr. Maritain delivered a series of lectures under the same auspices!— which are then to be published next year.

Now to the question about publication. For a variety of reasons, I would very much welcome it if the Xenophon-Strauss-Kojève book appeared. If you have secured a publisher, let me know, so that the business side (a formality)—copyright—can get settled right away. Regarding the translation of the *Hiero*, I would like to make sure that the crucial passages are translated literally, and if necessary the translation be changed (I assume that you want to proceed on the basis of an already published French translation—hence, too, the copyright problem would have to be resolved). Regarding my contribution, some notes really are essential. If you wish, I can put a list of them together for you.—But all that will require a stretch of time. Therefore I wonder whether it might not be practical to have you go ahead and publish your portion in the Temps Modernes now. I would prefer that. Immediately upon its publication I would then work out my reply (and in this connection include a series of other additions to *On Tyranny*), and publish it. It would then be up to you to decide whether you wish to add a reply and possibly a "final word" to the French edition.

In any event, let me know your intentions and plans soon.

By chance I happened upon Jaspers' *History* (1949):[2] a well-intentioned North-German Protestant Pastor, full of unction and earnestness even in sexual relations, and who for that very reason never achieves clarity or decisiveness.

Let me hear from you again soon.

With warm greetings from my wife and myself,

Your

Leo Strauss

Vanves, October 10, 1949

Dear Mr. Strauss,

Please excuse me for answering your two letters only today. I was on holidays in Spain and came back only the day before yesterday.

To the matter:

I have not yet done anything about my article. But I will try to have it published as soon as possible in some journal. (*Critique* is now definitely dead.)

At the same time I will speak with Gallimard about the "X-St-K" book. I had thought of using some old translation, in order not to have to pay any copyright. Of course some of your notes will have to be translated as well. I really thought that only the strictly technical notes, references, etc., should be omitted. Personally, I would very much welcome it if your reply to my criticism could also be reprinted. But that depends on the publisher (number of pages, etc.)

Your Chicago suggestion interests me very much. I believe that regular contact with you will not only be personally extremely pleasant, but that at least as far as I am concerned it will also be philosophically extremely stimulating.

(Please excuse the blemished first sheet—I had not noticed it.) I will work out my curriculum, discuss it with Koyré, and send it to you. I know no "big shots." But I could have myself recommended by

1. Professor Wilcox (Economics), Chairman of the American Delegation in London, New York, Geneva, Havana, etc.

2. The local ECA ("Marshall Plan") people.

Would that be useful?

Koyré says that he does not want to intervene on his own. But if someone from the University of Chicago asks him about me, he will write favorably.

The Quai d'Orsay is very interested. But Koyré tells me that any official French intervention could only hurt my prospects. Is that so?

A visiting summer appointment lasts about ten weeks? What is the pay for something like that? It is not so much a question of money as of prestige.

In any event—many thanks for the suggestion, and for everything you will undertake on my behalf.

Regarding the articles and the book, I will keep you informed.

With best regards to yourself and your wife,

Your Kojève

THE UNIVERSITY OF CHICAGO
Chicago 37, Illinois
Department of Political Science

October 14, 1949

Dear Mr. Kojevnikoff,

In the utmost haste:

Regarding your article and "X-St-K," I do see that the inclusion of my Reply both increases the cost, and greatly delays it because of my terrible slowness. So: ¹go ahead.¹.

Regarding your vita, etc.—feel free to mention Wilcox and the Paris ECA people. Provided they are not notorious communists—every other foolishness is pardonable.—K<oyré> is perfectly right that an unsolicited initiative on the part of the Quai d'Orsay can only hurt. But a statement about you addressed To Whom It May Concern (or, preferably, the <u>French</u> equivalent), written in <u>French</u> by one of the big shots in the "Affaires Étrangères" would surely be useful: because it would show that you are politically not entirely inexperienced.

Summer course: this <u>should</u> not be a matter of prestige. Everyone, including the prima donnas, prostitues himself <u>this</u> way. I <u>believe</u> you would get the same that Koyré got. (How much that is I do not know.) I cannot undertake anything further until I have your vita.

Best regards from us both,

Your

Leo Strauss

Vanves, December 26, 1949

Merry Christmas, dear Mr. Strauss,

After much reflection (which it would be too tedious to reproduce) I have decided to drop the Chicago project. Among other reasons, because it is a "delicate subject." I hope that you will not hold it against me. In any event, many thanks for the suggestion.

The only thing I really regret is that there is no prospect of a face-to-face discussion with you about the issues that interest us in the foreseeable future. Here I have, for all intents and purposes, no occasion for <u>philosophical</u> discussion.

As regards our book:

Queneau has read your book (+ Xenophon) and is <u>enthusiastic</u>. He also finds my article suitable for publication and interesting. So that he absolutely wants to publish the book, and he expects it to be a great success.

However, he has spoken about the book with such enthusiasm, that Gallimard himself wants to read it, together with my article. But the article has to be corrected, because the only corrected copy is with Merleau-Ponty (for *Temps Modernes*). It will therefore be some time before the official contract is submitted to us.

Queneau is ready to reprint the notes as well, in case you insist. However, it would considerably increase costs (because of the Greek).

And he fears that the notes will scare away some readers, and so restrict the circulation of the book.

On the other hand, he (and I) would very much welcome an "Afterword."

A translator still has to be found for the *Hiero*, as well as one for your book. The translator's honorarium will probably come out of your honorarium. As for the two of us, we will divide the honorarium in proportion to the number of pages. Have you any objections to that suggestion?

I would like to know what you think of my essay. I myself am quite dissatisfied. I wrote it under difficult circumstances, with massive interruptions: as a result it is wide-ranging, and at the same time unclear. But I have neither the time nor the inclination to work on it more. Or do you believe that it is really <u>necessary</u> that I do so?

With best regards to you and yours.

Kojève

THE UNIVERSITY OF CHICAGO
Chicago 37, Illinois
Department of Political Science

January 18, 1950

Dear Mr. Kojevnikoff,

I just received your letter of December 26.

I <u>very</u> <u>much</u> regret that we will not see each other for the time being. I, too, never have the opportunity for discussions περί τῶν μεγίστων τε καί καλλίστων .[1]

I was very pleased by the news about our book. To begin with business-questions: My publisher owns the rights, not I. The situation is different regarding the Afterword, since I am writing it on my own. For reasons that are too tedious, I would propose that you get the honorarium for the Afterword in <u>your</u> name, and after subtracting taxes and so on transferred it to one of my relatives in Paris.

I found your criticism clear and meaningful; stylistic revisions may be desirable, but that is something about which I have no opinion, because I do not know French well enough.

The notes can for the most part be omitted, <u>except</u> some few that are interesting.

As soon as the matter is settled and I have some leisure, I will write the Afterword in <u>English</u>. I assume that the publisher will have no objection to my publishing the Afterword in an American journal: after all, it would also be a bit of pulbicity for the book.

In the meantime I have begun to prepare six public lectures on Natural Right and History. Progress is extremely slow. I am working on the first lecture, a summary criticism of historicism (= existentialism).

Have you ever read Prescott's *Conquest of Mexico* and *Conquest of Peru*? A story more fabulous than any fairy-tale.

With best regards from my wife and myself,

Your

Leo Strauss

––––––––

THE UNIVERSITY OF CHICAGO
Chicago 37, Illinois
Department of Political Science

March 24, 1950

Dear Mr. Kojevnikoff,

My publisher sent me the letter that Gallimard (Mascole) wrote to him. It will be a little while before the formalities are settled (another publisher is just in the process of taking over publication of my book). But this formality should not delay the substantive procedure. I personally attach importance to only two things: (a) I should like to see the translation of my share before it is typeset; (b) translation rights are limited to the translation into French. (That is to say, no translations from the French translation into any other languages are permitted.) It would be desirable not to delay getting the translation out. The financial aspect of this business (a flat fee of $150.00) is o.k.

Have you seen Heidegger's *Holzwege*? Most interesting, much that is outstanding, and on the whole bad: the most extreme historicism.

How are you? Write soon.

Your

Leo Strauss

RÉPUBLIQUE FRANÇAISE

MINISTÈRE DES FINANCES
ET DES
AFFAIRES ÉCONOMIQUES

SECRÉTARIAT D'ÉTAT
AUX FINANCES

(AFFAIRES ÉCONOMIQUES)

41 QUAI BRANLY, PARIS VIIè

Paris, April 9, 1950

Dear Mr. Strauss,

Please excuse me for only now answering your letter of March 24.

I saw Queneau. He says that your two conditions go without saying.

Koyré has a translator in view. I hope work begins soon.

Could you indicate the notes that should be translated and printed?

On the other hand, Merleau-Ponty does <u>not</u> want to publish my article in *Temps Modernes*. The pretext is that *T<emps> M<odernes >* does not publish reviews. In fact he refuses publication for substantive reasons, as is evident from his letter to Weil.

I can understand that. In effect I say in the article that what Merleau-Ponty, among others, does, is politically as well as philosophically senseless.

I have not yet read *Holzwege*. But I will do so.

I assume that the legal issue between your publisher and Gallimard will be settled, and that I do not need to be concerned with it.

With best regards,

Your Kojève

THE UNIVERSITY OF CHICAGO
Chicago 37, Illinois
Department of Political Science

June 26, 1950

Dear Mr. Kojevnikoff,

Please excuse my long silence—but all hell was loose. In the meantime I have signed the contract with Gallimard. I now come to you with the suggestion for a translator. Victor Gourévitch, one of my students, who will be attending the Sorbonne with a University of Chicago Fellowship this fall, and apparently knows French very well, has offered to undertake the translation—independently of how much he gets from the publisher. I would of course regard it as absolutely proper that he receive the usual compensation from the publisher, and I would be most grateful to you if you would arrange for this—in case a translator has not yet been found and begun work. Gourévitch would have the following great advantage: he will be in Chicago for another few weeks, and I could discuss the problems of translation with him in detail. In any event, I earnestly request that you let me know right away whether this arrangement is acceptable. Also for the following reason: in case the translation is completed soon, I would have to start work on my criticism of your criticism quite soon. I have three or four urgent commitments this summer, and therefore have to plan.

How much I would enjoy talking with you περὶ ἀρχῶν (as well as περὶ ἀρχῆς).[1] I have once again been dealing with Historicism, that is to say, with Heidegger, the only radical historicist, and I believe I see some light. On the < . . . >, that is to say, ultimately uninteresting plane, Heidegger's position is the last refuge of nationalism: the state, even "culture'', is done with—all that remains is language—of course with the modifications that became necessary as a consequence of 1933–1945.

Have you seen Lukácz, *The Young Hegel?* Orthodox-Stalinist in thought and writing, but useful as a corrective to Wilhelminian Hegel studies. I have looked into Lenin and Engels—unpalatable and comical.

With best regards,

your

Leo Strauss

THE UNIVERSITY OF CHICAGO
Chicago 37, Illinois
Department of Political Science

July 28, 1950

Dear Mr. Kojevnikoff:

Thank you so much for the information regarding Stephano.

As far as my Conclusion or Afterword is concerned, I intended to write it in August, because during the academic year it is too difficult to concentrate on one subject. However, since I also have to attend to a number of other things, I would like to turn to the Afterword only once it is reasonably certain that the whole thing will be completed and come out in the academic year 1950–1951. Otherwise I would postpone the writing of the Afterword until next Summer (1951). Where do things stand (a) regarding the translation of Xenophon's *Hiero?* Is there not one in the Collection Budé, for example? (b) When does Stephano expect to be done? (c) Is the version of your critique which you sent me, the definitive version? If it is not, I would have to wait until I have the definitive version. In any event, I very much ask you please to answer these three questions by air mail—at my expense, so that I know how to plan my time in August.

It may interest you to learn that Klein has married Husserl's daughter-in-law.

I hope that you are well.

Best regards as ever,

Your

Leo Strauss

THE UNIVERSITY OF CHICAGO
Chicago 37, Illinois
Department of Political Science

August 5, 1950

Dear Mr. Kojevnikoff,

On the reverse side of this sheet, you will find the list of the notes I would like to have included in the translation. I would very much appreciate it if the translator could indicate in his Preface or elsewhere that the English original contains a great many notes that are omitted in the French translation.

I plan to begin work on the Afterword tomorrow.

Best regards.

Your

Leo Strauss

Introduction	note 5
III The Setting	
A. The characters and their iden- tities	notes 14, 31, 32, 44, 46
B. The action	notes 51, 61, 65
C. The use of characteristic terms	note 6 omit the last sentence
IV The Teaching Concerning Tyr- anny	notes 25, 34, 46; 57; 50 change reference "cf. IIIA, note 44 above," and omit reference at the end of note

V The Two Ways of Life	note 47 <u>omit</u> "(see IIIB, note 12 above)"; 59; 70 <u>omit</u> "and the passages indicated in IV, note 45 above.")
VI Pleasure, Virtue	note 49
VII Piety and Law	note 10

THE UNIVERSITY OF CHICAGO
Chicago 37, Illinois
Department of Political Science

September 14, 1950

Dear Mr. Kojevnikoff,

Enclosed, the Afterword. I have called it Restatement, because I regard the problem as entirely open—"Afterword" would create the impression of an apparent finality—and, <u>above all</u>, because I would <u>very much</u> like you to <u>answer</u>. You must clarify the difficulties in which the reader of your *Introduction* gets entangled. If my attack succeeds in getting you to clarify what is unclear, I will be very satisfied.

Unfortunately, I again have a couple of requests. In the first place, I should like Gallimard's assurance that I retain the copyright of the English original of the Restatement, or more precisely, that he requires only the rights to its French translation. In the second place, for various reasons it is necessary that the dedication and the motto (from Macaulay) be retained in the French edition.

I assume that Stephanopoulos will let me see the translation of the Restatement as well.

I would be much obliged to you for an early reply.

How are you?

Best regards,

Your

Leo Strauss

Vanves, September 19, 1950

SECRÉTARIAT D'ÉTAT AUX AFFAIRES ÉCONOMIQUES

Dear Mr. Strauss,

Many thanks for your letter and the Restatement. (I very much like the title; only I don't know how to translate it into French!)

I was in Spain for three weeks, and got your letter on the day of my return to Paris.

I read your reply immediately, and with great interest. Naturally, I would have much to say, but one also has to leave something for the reader: he should go on to think on his own.

I am in full agreement with the conclusion. It might be even clearer to say that the fundamental difference with respect to the question of being pertains not only to the problem of the criterion of truth but also to that of good and evil. You appeal to moral conscience in order to refute my criterion-argument. But the one is as problematic as the other. Did Torquemada or Dzerzhinski have "bad consciences"?![1] The universal and homogeneous state is "good" only because it is the <u>last</u> (because neither war not revolution are conceivable in it:—mere "dissatisfaction" is not enough, it also takes weapons!).

Besides, "not human" can mean "animal" (or, better—automaton) as well as "God." In the final state there naturally are no more "human beings" in our sense of an <u>historical</u> human being. The "healthy" automata are "satisfied" (sports, art, eroticism, etc.), and the "sick" ones get locked up. As for those who are not satisfied with their "purposeless activity" (art, etc.), they are the philosophers (who can attain wisdom if they "contemplate" enough). By doing so they become "gods." The tyrant becomes an administrator, a cog in the "machine" fashioned by automata for automata.

All this seems to me rather "classical." With the one difference that according to Hegel all this <u>is</u> not right from the start, but only <u>becomes</u> right at the end.

Now, in the meantime I have come to understand something new better than before.

Human beings really act only in order to be able to <u>speak</u> about it (or to hear it spoken about) [conversely: one can <u>speak</u> only about action;

about nature one can only be [mathematically, aesthetically, etc.] <u>silent</u>. Historical action necessarily leads to a specific result (hence: deduction), but the ways that lead to this result, are varied (all roads lead to Rome!). The choice between these ways is <u>free</u>, and this choice determines the content of the speeches about the action and the <u>meaning</u> of the result. In other words: materially < i.e., factually > history is unique, but the spoken < i.e., narrated > story can be extremely varied, depending on the free choice of how to act. For example: If the Westerners remain cap-italist (that is to say, also nationalist), they will be defeated by Russia, and <u>that</u> is how the End-State will come about. If, however, they "integrate" their economies and policies (they are on the way to doing so), then <u>they</u> can defeat Russia. And <u>that</u> is how the End-State will be reached (the <u>same</u> universal and homogeneous State). But in the first case it will be spoken about in "Russian" (with Lysenko, etc.), and in the second case—in "European."

As regards myself, I came to Hegel by way of the question of criteria. I see only three possibilities:

(a) Plato's—Husserl's "intuition of essences" (which I do not believe [for one has to <u>believe</u> it]); (b) relativism (in which one cannot <u>live</u>); (c) Hegel and "circularity." If, however, one assumes circularity as the only criterion of truth (including the moral), then everything else follows auto-matically.

For a time I believed in a fourth possibility: nature is "identical," hence the classical criterion can be retained for nature. But now I believe that one can only be <u>silent</u> about nature (mathematics). Hence: either one remains "classically" <u>silent</u> (cp. Plato's *Parmenides* and Seventh Epistle), or one chatters "in the modern manner" (Pierre Bayle), or one is an Hegelian.

But—as I said—all this can be left up to the reader. In itself your Re-statement seems to me very sensible and useful. There is only one pas-sage in your text I would ask you to alter or to strike.

I refer to p. 13: "Kojève denies . . . (*Hiero* II.11 and II.14)."[2]

The passage rests on a misunderstanding, and I am perfectly ready to improve my text in order to[3]

THE UNIVERSITY OF CHICAGO
Chicago 37, Illinois
Department of Political Science

September 28, 1950

Dear Mr. Kojevnikoff,

Many thanks for your letter. Could "restatement" not be translated with something like "reformulation"? Or with a composite expression corresponding to "A Second Statement"? If there is <u>no</u> alternative, I would accept "Réplique" or something like it.

I was aware that some of your arguments are rather exoteric, and I replied to them exoterically. Quite aside from that, the question remains whether I have understood you or you me on all points. Thus, for example, I do not believe that the considerations you adduce in your letter to me were sufficient. But that would lead too far just now (beginning of the academic year).

As regards p. 13 of the Restatement (Hitler), I am perfectly ready to strike the three sentences in the middle of the paragraph: "As is shown by his reference . . . under his rule." But I <u>cannot</u> accept your suggestion to replace "good tyranny" with some other expression. I naturally knew that Stalin was <u>comrade</u>: you see how modern Xenophon is even in this.

Please do not forget to remind Queneau about the copyright of the Restatement.

One of my students—Gourévitch—will try to get in touch with you. He is very impressed by your *Introduction*.

Have you seen the things by Lukácz?

Best regards,
Your

Leo Strauss

THE UNIVERSITY OF CHICAGO
Chicago 37, Illinois
Department of Political Science

January 19, 1951

Dear Mr. Kojevnikoff,

In all haste—What has happened to the translation? And: where do things stand with my right to publish the English original of the Restatement now? I do not doubt I have that right, but would like to have it confirmed by the publisher.

How are things with you? I heard about you and your political outlook from Bertrand de Jouvenel,[1] who is here just now, esteems you greatly, and also esteems your book, but did not know that you, the official, are one and the same as you, the author of the book.

May I ask you for a prompt reply.

Best regards,
Your

Leo Strauss

THE UNIVERSITY OF CHICAGO
Chicago 37, Illinois
Department of Political Science

February 22, 1951

M. Alexandre Kojève
15 Bd. Stalingrad
Vanves (Seine), France

Dear M. Kojève:

Many thanks for your letter of February 5th. It is impossible to open again in a letter the long controversy between us. We must try it again in print.

I am writing to you today in connection with our publication. The NRF confirmed what you wrote in your letter. Thanks very much for that. But another problem has now arisen. I am very much pressed with my time, and I am wondering whether I could not delegate the correction of the translation to Victor Gourévitch. I have full faith in his command of the language as well as in his diligence. This procedure would have the additional value that in case of obvious blunders made by the translator, the thing would be taken care of immediately in a café, and one would not have to bother trans-Atlantic facilities for this problem. Gourévitch could write to me in the very few cases where he himself did not feel quite certain as to the proper translation. (His address is American Wing, Cité Universitaire, University of Paris, Paris, France). If this could be arranged, a great load would be taken off my chest. No problem of a financial nature would bother us in connection with this arrangement. Gourévitch told me that he would enjoy doing this job. I would be very grateful if you would let me know what you think of my idea.

Very sincerely yours,

Leo Strauss

LS/mkm

THE UNIVERSITY OF CHICAGO
Chicago 37, Illinois
Department of Political Science

July 17, 1952

Dear Mr. Kojevnikoff:

Yesterday I sent you an essay and my small book *Persecution and the Art of Writing*. You are acquainted with some of the contents. Would you do me the favor of calling attention to it in *Critique* or somewhere else.[1]

How is *La tyrannie et la sagesse*?

I was very amused by your review of Queneau.[2] I particularly liked your sensible comment about the old women or the adolescents who call themselves philosophers and savor their "tragic" condition instead of making an effort like reasonable people.

Best regards,
Your

Leo Strauss

RÉPUBLIQUE FRANÇAISE

SECRÉTARIAT D'ÉTAT
AUX FINANCES
ET AUX
AFFAIRES ÉCONOMIQUES

Paris, August 11, 1952

Dear Mr. Strauss,

Thank you so much for your letter and the book which arrived the day before yesterday.

I have read the review;[1] the man does not seem to have been a great philosopher; with what you say, I am in complete agreement.

Regarding the *Tyranny* I know nothing. One of your plenipotentiaries should deal with it. The book will surely get published sooner or later. And where "eternal questions" are involved, excessive haste is out of place!

I am in the process of transforming my lecture "The Concept and Time" into a book. I have already written about 150 pages, but that is barely half of it. Up to now it has gone more or less smoothly, because I was dealing with "great unknowns": Parmenides, Plato, Aristotle, Hegel. But now it is Mr. Kojève's turn, and that is a rather delicate matter.

At least I have three weeks of quiet. The rest of the time I can work on it (write) only on Sundays, and make progress by setting down only 12–15 pages every Sunday. It will again be an unreadable book. If only there were something in it!

With best regards,

Your

Kojève

SECRÉTARIAT D'ÉTAT
AUX
AFFAIRES ÉCONOMIQUES

RÉPUBLIQUE FRANÇAISE

Paris, October 29, 1953

Dear Mr. Strauss,

Thank you so much for your *Natural Law*.[1] (I have entrusted the *Critique* matters to Mr. Weil.)

I got the book just a few days ago, and have not yet read it in its entirety. But I already see that it is excellent. One really sees in it what is at stake. I would have liked to review the book in *Critique*. But I am writing a book myself, and have only the weekends at my disposal. Hence. . . .

Regarding the issue, I can only keep repeating the same thing. If there is something like "human nature," then you are surely right in everything. But to deduce from premisses is not the same as to prove these premisses. And to infer premisses from (anyway questionable) consequences is always dangerous.

Your Bible quote about the land of the fathers[2] is already most problematic. From it one can of course deduce a condemnation of collectivization in the USSR and elsewhere. But with it one also justifies permanently preserving a Chinese peasant's animal-like starvation-existence (before Mao-Tse-Tung). Etc., etc.

But all this is hardly philosophy. The task of philosophy is to resolve the <u>fundamental</u> question regarding "human <u>nature</u>." And in that connection the question arises whether there is not a <u>contradiction</u> between speaking about "ethics" and "ought" on the one hand, and about conforming to a "given" or "innate" human <u>nature</u> on the other. For animals, which unquestionably have such a <u>nature</u>, are not morally "good" or "evil," but at most <u>healthy</u> or <u>sick</u>, and <u>wild</u> or <u>trained</u>. One might therefore conclude that it is precisely <u>ancient</u> anthropology that would lead to mass-<u>training</u> and <u>eugenics</u>.[3]

"Modern" anthropology leads to moral anarchy and tasteless "existentialism" only if one assumes, God knows why, that man can give <u>human</u> values. But if, with Hegel, one assumes that at some time he <u>returns</u> to his beginning (by deducing what he <u>says</u> from the mere fact <u>that</u> he <u>speaks</u>), then there indeed is an "ethics" that prescribes that one do everything that leads to <u>this</u> end (= wisdom), and that condemns everything that impedes it—also in the political realm of progress toward the "universal and homogeneous State."

With best greetings,

Your Kojève

———————————

THE UNIVERSITY OF CHICAGO
Chicago 37, Illinois
Department of Political Science

April 28, 1954

M. Alexandre Kojève
15 Blvd. Stalingrad
Vanves (Seine)
France

Dear Kojève:

I received our book.[1] I looked at the translation of my sections and it is sometimes very satisfactory and sometimes less satisfactory. Who is Hélène anyway, and what became of Stephano? I suggest that you ask Queneau to send a review copy to Professor Karl Loewith, Philosophisches Seminar, Heidelberg University. Loewith would have an understanding of the issue controversial between you and me.[2]

I plan to be in Paris during the second half of June. I am anxious to see you. I hope you will be there.

Sincerely yours,

Leo Strauss

THE UNIVERSITY OF CHICAGO
Chicago 37, Illinois
Department of Political Science

June 4, 1956

Dear M. Kojève,

I heard from Tommy that you too are not well. I myself am just recovering slowly from a coronary thrombosis, so our state is similar and so I suppose many similar thoughts are passing through our minds. It is a pity that we have lost contact almost completely. The only link at the moment is Allan Bloom[1] who reminds me on proper occasions of our considerable disagreements as well as our more fundamental agreement. I deplored that I could not talk to you in June 1954, when I was in Paris. But apart from the fact that we had to rush to Switzerland, I was rather disgusted by the company in which I met you, a fellow who is really one of the most unpleasant people I have ever come across. I mean of course Weil not Koyré. At the suggestion of Pines[2] I read his book which restates in a sometimes somewhat more orderly fashion your thesis but with a complete absence of intellectual honesty: the difference between Hegel and your neo-Hegelianism is nowhere mentioned. I would call the book: Prolegomena zu einer jeden künftigen Chuzpa die als absolutes Wissen wird auftreten können.[3] You see that while possibly about to die I'm still trying to keep the flag flying. I wish you a speedy and complete recovery and I hope that it will be given to us to see each other either alone or else in good company. The possible localities of our meeting, if any, are in your opinion, if it has not changed, restricted to a certain part of the surface of the earth. I am more open-minded in this respect. If you see Koyré please give him my regards.

Cordially,

Leo Strauss

———————

Vanves, June 8, 1956

Dear Mr. Strauss,

Your letter brought an unpleasant surprise: I did not know that you were—or still are—ill. Although I have seen Gildin[1] several times (I delivered several longish "lectures" to him), he told me nothing about it. Nor did Koyré, who may not have known anything about it himself.

Anyway, I am very glad the danger is now behind you.

Yes, you are right, we must surely have thought about the same things. And I am sure we fully agree that in this situation, philosophy—if not "consoling"—is nevertheless as reliable and satisfying as ever. In any case, I felt no desire for lectures in dead tongues, with or without musical accompaniment.

Incidentally, my doctor seems to have given up the cancer hypothesis in favor (?!) of a tuberculosis.

Be that as it may, I may no longer go to the Ministry (if only because of the official doctor's refusal to let me work there.) I therefore restrict myself to telephone conversations and a few official visits. That way I again have more leisure and—in conformity with the ancient model—I devote them to philosophy (which I never entirely abandoned anyway). I again work 4–5 hours a day at my book, or rather at its Introduction, or more precisely still, at its Third Introduction, which is intended as a kind of general history of philosophy.

I have talked philosophy only with your two American (?) students. I must say that as regards philosophical "eros" and human "decency," the two young people are OK. They must owe that to you.

As regards Weil, you are right. For a long time now, I have been unable to "discuss" with him; and also have no interest in doing so.

I, too, very much regret that we did not speak with one another. The atmosphere was most disagreeable indeed, and so was I. . . .

As for when and where, it is impossible to say anything for the time being: I am tied to my room for 5–6 months (if all goes "well.") If you think of coming to Paris, it would naturally be very easy to get together.

Bloom may have spoken to you about the Third Part of my book ("Logic," or however else it might be called). In the meantime, I make some progress. Anyway, on my part there is material for "discussion". . . .

With best greetings,

Your

Kojève

———————————

Paris, April 11, 1957

Dear Mr. Strauss,

A few days ago I read a transcript of your St. John's lecture on the *Euthyphro*,[1] which Mr. Hazo had loaned me. Although I had not reread the *Euthyphro* for a long time, I remembered the text quite well. I had the impression that your interpretation is entirely correct. But on one point in your lecture, I noted a possible difference of opinion between us. Specifically, at the point where you mention the famous portrait of the philosopher in the *Thaetetus*. Admittedly you do say, in connection with it, that the text is not altogether univocal. But it seems to me that you do not share my "ironic" interpretation of the entire passage.

As I have already written you [by the way: did you ever get my long Plato letter; I sent it registered by surface mail, probably at the beginning of the year or at the end of '56], it seems to me that Plato sides completely with the "Thracian Maid" (who, by the way, is a pretty girl and laughs so prettily) [the ironic remark about "looking upward" is also found, setting aside the *Republic*, in Alcibiades I]. And that interpretation seems to me to fit very well with your interpretation of the *Euthyphro*. Namely, this way: "Justice without Knowledge" (in the manner of Euthyphro) is just as objectionable or unphilosophical as "Knowledge without Justice" (in the manner of "Thales," that is to say the "learned" or the "theoreticians" in general, people like Thaetetus and Eudoxus, and even Aristotle; people who do not know who their neighbor is and how he lives can naturally not practice justice; but at the end of the Thales passage Socrates says that everything depends on justice); for, philosophy is "knowing justice" or "just knowing." [That is to say: only the philosophy that accounts for the "evident" and "immediate" distinction between right and wrong, can be true; now, neither the Sophists (~ Heraclitus) nor Aristotle do so because of the middle terms in their diairesis[2], to which Plato's diairesis[2] opposes A with a firm non-A and thus excludes the amoral as-well-as or neither-nor].

In the meantime I have reread the *Alcibiades I* (indeed!) The dialogue seems to me not only to be authentic, but also very successful in literary terms. I understand the content as follows [incidentally, it contains a deliciously ironic passage about Sparta and Persia, completely in the style of the *Lacedaemonian Republic*[3] you so brilliantly interpreted: In Sparta two ephors are needed in order to prevent adultery on the part of the queen, and the Persian queen remains faithful only out of fear of others; etc.]: every human being (including Alcibiades) has (even as a child) an "intuition" of right and wrong, which is neither learned nor taught; it is "natural" for human beings to do what is right and avoid what is wrong (passively as well as actively); as long as one simply does not speak, one is a "naturally" decent human being (such as for example Crito or, perhaps also Cephalus in the *Republic*); but when one speaks or hears others speak, one can fail to hear "the voice of conscience": that is the danger of sophists and rhetoricians, and also of "theology"; indeed it looks as if (cp. *Republic* where it is not the father Cephalus, but his "so-phisticated" son who gives impetus to the conversation about justice which the father avoids) philosophy is needed only as a (pedagogical) answer to "sophistry": it is a "dialectical" defence of "natural" justice against the "sophistic" attacks on it. However, Plato evidently does not quite mean it that way. For in the *Phaedo* it is (evidently seriously) said that misology is the worst thing. That would mean that one should speak about justice in spite of the danger of sophistic errors. As regards Alcibiades, responsibility has to be understood in the following way: (Heraclitus--->) Sophists---> Rhetoricians---> Politicians---> the Populace corrupted by the Politicians---> Alcibiades corrupted by the people. If he had spent enough time speaking with Socrates, he would have been cured. But the conversation in *Alcibiades I* was insufficient because Alcibiades did not understand anything: for he believes that he does not know what is right and wrong and that that is what Socrates first has to teach him about, instead of trying (with Socrates's help) to become discursively conscious about what he already knows "intuitively," and to draw important ("logical") conclusions from it. If he had understood this, he would not have been "jealous" of Socrates (as he says at the end of the dialogue). For the rest, Socrates argues ad hominem, from the perspective of Alcibiades's "master-morality," by presenting justice and temperance as courage, and "sensuality" as slavish cowardice. Plato may wish to suggest by this that it is very dangerous to present ("aristocratic") courage as the principal virtue; that the principal virtue is, rather, ("democratic") justice. ["Anamnesis," which is implicit in *Alc<ibiades> I*, is a "mythical" interpretation of the psychological fact of "conscience," that is to say, of the "immediate," "innate" knowledge of good and evil.]

I have also reread the *Phaedrus*, but not yet the *Symposium*. What, in your opinion, is the sequence? *Sym<posium>---> Ph<aedrus>---> Phaedo*, or *Phaedrus---> S<ymposium>---> Ph<aedo>*? Usually it is said: at the end of the *Symposium* the tragicomical character of philosophy is indicated, and then the philosophical comedy (*Phaedrus*) and tragedy (*Phaedo*) are exhibited. But perhaps one could also say: the *Phaedrus* already says that Phil<osophy> = com<edy> + trag<edy>; Socrates's first speech was a comical tragedy, his second speech a tragic comedy (in which case the interpretation of the two speeches at the end <of the dialogue> would be philosophical). The *Symp<osium>* would then be the philosophical comedy in which Socrates is 100% alive (at the end all but Socrates are asleep [= are dead]; in the *Ph<aedo>* all but Socrates are "alive"), while he alone is dying in the *Ph<aedo>*.[4] And

what is "better": to live solitary among the "drunk" (= dead), or to die
(joking!) in the company of such "beastly-earnest" pseudo-philosophers
as Simmias-Cebes? The *Ph < aedo >* ends with the cock to Aesclepius!
And yet Aristoph[anes] falls asleep before Agathon; does that mean the
joke disappears "at the end"??

Some points in "confirmation(?)" of my earlier letter:

1. Parmenides

In his Plato biography, Diogenes Laertius mentions Plato's two
brothers, but appears not to know anything about his presumed "half-
brother." (Antiphon [Antiphon was a Sophist, an enemy of Socrates,
whose disciples he wanted to attract to himself.] = Euclides--- >
Th < eodorus >/Eu < clides > --- > Arist < otle >)

According to tradition, the dialogue bears the subtitle: *P < ar-
menides >* or *About the Ideas.* It is scarcely credible that the dialogue
would have been given that subtitle if it had really contained only the
purely negative-critical passages against the theory of Ideas, and not also
their "refutation."

In *Alc < ibiades >* I, "Pythodorus" is mentioned: "ironically";
in any event not as a genuine philosopher! Even if he is a historical
person, nothing stands in the way of using his name "synthetically" (for
Theo-dorus).

2. Timaeus

In Diogenes Laertius the chapter about Endoxus comes at the end
of the book about the . . . Pythagoreans! Now, Plato also presents
"Timaeus" as an arch-"Pythagorean."

3. Diairesis[2]--- > Ordinal numbers

In a neo-Pythagorean fragment it is said: "He [Pythagoras] said not that
everything arose from number, but that everything was fashioned in conformity to number, since essential order resides in number, and it is only
in participating in that order that the very things that can be numbered
are placed first, second, and so on. "Theano" in Stob < aeus > Ecl. pol. I,
10, 13.

In Philo (for example, *De origine mundi* (ed. Cohen) 91–102), the
ideal numbers are also interpreted as ordinal numbers. He further says (in
conformity with the tradition) that a distinction has to be drawn between
the (ideal) numbers of the same type within and without the decade; for

example, there are "infinitely" many numbers of the type 7 (= seventh) that share the same "qualitative" character ("law of formation"), but are <u>quantitatively</u> differentiated from one another. One might then perhaps say that the first ten ideal numbers (the only ones which, according to Aristotle, Plato "deduced") are "categories" in the modern sense, whereas the "kinds" (to which, according to Aristotle, numbers also correspond, but which surely number more than 10) correspond to the ideal numbers > 10, and are distributed among the 10 "categories." But all this is, as I have said, most problematic.

∙∙

While searching in the (translated) neo-Platonists for indications about Plato's theory of numbers, I made a discovery that will amuse you in case you do not already know the relevant texts. Indeed, I discovered, one right after the other, three authentic and entirely unknown philosophers, namely the emperor Julian (<u>Speeches</u>), "Sallustius" (*On the Gods and the World*, and—[5]last < but > not least[5]—Damascius (*Life of Isidor*). These three "mystical enthusiasts" have revealed themselves as first-class Voltaires. (I vaguely recall that Burkhardt (*Constantin the Great*) had already said that Julian does not believe a single word of what he tells the "people.") Before reading these three, I was <u>prejudiced</u>, and expected to read "mystical" texts. And after a few pages I was pleasantly surprised. So, up to the 6th century there were men who preserved the philosophical tradition in all its purity, and who despised the neo-Platonic nonsense as much as they did Christian "theology." In this they were <u>completely consciously</u> imitating Plato's "Socratic" irony. It is a nice example of "the art of writing" which you discovered! And with that, on the one hand "highly placed" (Julian), and on the other, literarily first class (Julian and Damascius).

<u>Julian</u> was, in ethics, a stoicizing Cynic. In theoretical philosophy, probably a "Democritean." In any case, an atheist. Follows Aristotle in his critique of Plato's doctrine of ideas; but then also follows Xenarchus in his criticism of Aristotelian teleology and theology (against "aether" and any difference between "heavens" and the "sublunar world") (cp. *Hymn to the Mother of the Gods* 162a–165b). He furthermore makes particular fun of Iamblichus. And of "intellectuals" in general (most especially so in *The Epistle to Themistius*).

"<u>Sallustius</u>" about the same: atheistic "materialism" and parody of neo-Platonism. The small book (*On the Gods and the World*) is usually attributed to Julian's friend < Sallustius >, to whom <Julian's> *Mother of the Gods* is dedicated. He was certainly a "partner in thought" of Julian's.

However, I do not believe that this extremely busy official <u>wrote</u>. Sallustius is therefore probably the one mentioned in Damascius's *Life of Isidor*, specifically as one of the (few) "genuine" philosophers. Now, I suspect that this "Sallustius" is nothing but an alias for Damascius himself, who probably is himself the author of the parody *On the Gods and the World*.

<u>Damascius</u>: his *Life* is certainly written (especially against Proclus) in a way that makes Voltaire appear a mere waif by comparison! In other respects, Damascius appears to have been an Aristotelian, but in the manner of Theophantus (whom he praisingly quotes as Asclepiodotos, [where this "Ascl < epiodotos" > may also just be a pseudonym for Dam < ascius >].

In case you have not yet done so, I very much urge you to read all three authors (*The Epistle to Them < istius >*, the two Speeches *Against the Cynics, The Hymn to Helios* and [above all!] the *Hymn to the Mother of the Gods*. In the first place because it is a great intellectual pleasure. In the second place because I would like to know your opinion of them. Because if you agree, I would write an essay about Julian (or Damascius?) for the "Strauss Festschrift"; since I was recently asked to contribute something to it, which I naturally will do with pleasure.

In conclusion I would like to give you some samples of my authors' "art of writing."

<u>Sall < ustius ></u> After having summarized (an incidentally "tempered") neo-Platonism in the first 12 chapters, he begins chapter XIII with the following words: "Regarding the gods, the universe, and human things, what we have said suffices for those who are incapable of delving more deeply into the study of philosophy, and <u>whose</u> <u>souls</u> <u>are</u> <u>not</u> <u>incurable</u>. [So, too, in Julian and Damascius: the neo-Platonic "myths" are worthwhile insofar as they challenge <u>reasonable</u> people to think about them and to oppose something reasonable to this nonsense.] It remains to explain how all things never had a beginning. . . ." That is done in chapter XVII. In between there are 4 chapters (XIII–XVI) in which Sallustius makes fun of sacrifices, etc. Chapter XVII begins as follows: "We have said that the gods do not destroy the universe; it remains to show that it is also by nature incorruptible." There follow 4 pages of "Democritean" theory [where, among other things, one reads: "If what <u>is</u> vanishes into what is not, what is to prevent this from happening even to God?"] And the concluding sentence of the chapter reads: "Having spoken thus for those who require more solid proofs, we pray the world (<u>sic</u>!) itself to be

propitious to us." The concluding chapter (XXI)–(XVIII–XX: ethics)—
reads as follows: "As for the souls that have lived in accordance with virtue, they are in all respects happy, and they will be especially so when,
separated from their irrational principles and purified of all bodily component, they will join the gods and share the government of the entire
universe with them. Even if none of this happened to them, virtue itself
and the honor and happiness they will derive from it, the <u>life</u> free of pains
and of all servitude, would <u>suffice</u> to render happy the life of those who
have chosen to live in accordance with virtue and have proven themselves capable living in accordance with it."—Period—and one has the
impression of hearing the resurrected Socrates having once again told the
"Cebeses" his Phaedo myth, while he himself, like a philosopher, thinks
about <u>dying</u>.

Dam<acius> The entire book is so delightful, I am unable to pick
out some one ironic passage. I therefore cite some (few!) "serious" passages [Das Leben des Philosophen Isodorus, wiederhergestellt von
Asmus, Leipzig, Meiner, 1911][6]

79, 30 ". . . it is not meet for a philosopher to declare divination as
his profession or to practice it, anymore than any other branch of the
hieratic sciences. For the boundaries between the philosophers' and the
priests' realms are as specific as the proverbial boundaries between the
Magerians and the Phrygians." [Strabo cites this proverb in order to emphasize the difficulty (!!) of determining boundaries!].

129, 9 "And [yet] he [an unknown "Diomedes" who was "corrupted" by the neo-Platonist] was a man suited for philosophy; for the
<kind of> philosophy that cannot be injured or corrupted by a <u>foreign</u>
evil, but only, as Socrates says, by <u>its</u> <u>own</u>. That is precisely why philosophy is also injured by this offence [namely neo-Platonism] which arises
from its <u>own</u> midst.

130, 21 "However if, as you [Hegesias] maintain, the activity of the
clergy . . . is more divine, then so do I maintain that it is, but first of all
those who are to become gods have to become human beings. That is
also why Plato said that men can be granted <u>no greater</u> [sic!] happiness
than philosophy. But now philosophy stands on the razor's edge; she has
truly reached the most advanced old age: she has reached this far. . . .
But . . . as for myself I am of the opinion that those who want to be men
and do not want to pant like animals [sic!] after boundless pastures
[namely after the clergy] need only <u>this</u> "divination" [namely genuine
philosophy]. . . ."

It is scarcely possible to express oneself more clearly and incisively. And yet . . . everyone from Zeller etc. to the learned translator (Asmus), see Damascius as nothing but a "mystical enthusiast" who abandons himself to the "most extravagant superstition"!!! Yet Damascius very explicitly says at the end of the *Life* how this < "mystical enthusiasm" > is to be understood. Indeed, he says:

132, 27 "But what even sounds contradictory is that for all his noble and solid dignity he [the ideal < "Dia . . ." >, a symbol of Plato, who never existed] made a cheerful impression on everyone around him, because although he generally spoke seriously to the best of his interlocutors, he also sometimes substituted wit for seriousness, and with innate skill made fun of those who were not there, so that he gave his rebukes a jocular cast."
. . . .
Julian. I urge you read: the *Letter to Themistius*, the two *Speeches against the "Cynics"* (= Christians), *Hymn to Helios*, *Hymn to the Mother of the Gods*. Everything is first-class "Voltaire," and at the same time genuinely philosophical.

It is interesting that in them Julian literally expounds your theory about the "art of writing":

Cynic Heraclios: 207 a/b "Now if an orator [like Jul < ian > himself] fearing the hatred of his audience, hesitates to speak his mind openly, he must hide his exhortations and doctrines in some disguise. That is what manifestly Hesiod also does. After him, Archilochus not infrequently used myths in order as it were to sweeten his poems. . . ."

ib.; 224a: "Furthermore, what is the value of your [presumably the Cynics, in fact, of course, the Christian monks] traveling everywhere, molesting mules and also [?!], I hear, muleteers, who are more afraid of you than they are of soldiers? For I hear that you put your sticks [presumably: Cynics' sticks, but in fact bishops' crooks] to more cruel use than they do their swords. No wonder, then, that you frighten them more."

ib.; 239b: "For one just may not say everything, and even of what may be said, some things must, in my view, be kept from the many."

In other words: all "myths" serve either to camouflage or to "sweeten," including the Platonic myths. Now: what are "myths"?

ib; 205, c ". . . untrue stories in credible form." In other words, in deliberate contrast to Stoicism: ". . . true stories in incredible form." For Julian the Christian as well as the pagan (including the neo-Platonic)

myths are simply nonsense. But the content of the Platonic "myths" is
also false. [The form may be "believable precisely because they are in
fact believed]: in any case, the "soul" is not immortal [according to Plato,
as Jul<ian> understands him]:

ib.; 223, a "However, anyone who composes his stories for the purpose of improving morals, and in the process invokes myths, should address them not to men but to such as are still children in years [?!] or in
understanding, and are still in need of such stories."

It is important that in their "ironic" way of writing, Jul<ian> (as
well as Damascius) consciously imitate the Platonic Socrates. (So that the
good tradition maintained itself well into the 6th century!) The following
passage is therefore particularly important to me (for my *Timaeus* interpretation):

ib.; 237a–c ". . . I would then tell you [presumably the "Cynic
Heraclios," in fact a Bishop (earlier: Heracles = Christ)] things in this connection [about Pythagoras, Plato and Aristotle], that may be unknown to
you, but are for the most part well-known and clear to the others. But
now just listen to what Plato writes [ironically]: "My fear of the gods,
dear Protarchos, is no longer human [?!], but exceeds all measure [?!]. And
although I know Aphrodite as she likes to be known, regarding pleasure, I
know that it has many shapes." This passage occurs in the *Philebus*
[12,c], and another of the same kind[!] in the *Tim<aeus>* [40,d]. What
he requires is that one should simply grant credence to everything [?!] the
poets [?!] say about the gods without requiring any proofs [?!] for it.
<" >But I have referred to this passage here only so [!] that you not in-
voke Socrates's irony as many Platonists do in order to refute Plato's
opinion [double irony!]. For after all, these words are spoken not by Socrates but by Timaeus, who is not in the least given to irony [!!!] Is it not
also entirely reasonable that instead of testing what has been said, we ask
who has said it, and to whom his words are addressed?!" No comment![7]

Julian: Speeches against the "uneducated Cynics" (= Christians) 186,c

<" > . . . it would also not be as noticeable if the wise [here:
Diogenes] made fun in them [namely in his supposed tragedies (which,
according to J<ulian>, he never wrote)], since many philosophers are
known also to have devoted themselves to them. Democritus [!], it is said
used to laugh at his fellows' solemn demeanor. We therefore do not want
to attend to the products of their jesting muse, . . .

. . . Hence, in order to avoid having the same thing happen to us [namely: as to the person who, on approaching a holy city, sees brothels on its out-skirts, and believes that that is the holy place!], by taking seriously every-thing he [Plato] wrote just for fun—and which also contains some not altogether worthless wheat . . . we will therefore take our bearings in what follows by his [i.e. Diogenes qua wise man] deeds, as dogs hunting wild animals begin by sniffing out the spoor."
And that is by far not the only place!

K

THE UNIVERSITY OF CHICAGO
Chicago 37, Illinois
Department of Political Science

April 22, 1957

M. Alexandre Kojève
15 Bd. Stalingrad
Vanves (Seine)
France

Dear M. Kojève:

Many thanks for your second long letter. I received your first long letter, but since I was too busy to study it at the time at which I received it, I sent it on to Klein, who had promised to read it right away and let you know his opinion. Needless to say that I have not heard anything from him since.

My handwriting has become so illegible that I have to dictate my letters, and this means that I have to write to you in English. Now to the subject.

As regards the excursus of the *Theaetetus*, the ironical character of the description of the philosopher is obvious; it flagrantly contradicts Socrates' own familiarity with all Athenian gossip; the philosopher com-bines the understanding of the pure theoretician ("sophist") and of the statesman. I agree: philosophy is just, but I hesitate on the basis of Plato to identify "just" with "moral". As for your remark on Alc < ibiades > I, (of course it is genuine, everything which has come down as genuine is genuine), that "if one does not speak, one is naturally a decent man—e.g., Crito", I do not agree; there is no "conscience" in Plato; anamnesis is not conscience (see *Natural Right and History*, p. 150n. re Polemarchus). Indeed, misology is the worst, as you say; therefore, there is ultimately no superiority of the merely honorable man to the sophist (contrary to Kant) or for that matter to Alc<ibiades> (cf. *N. R. & H*, p. 151). I do not believe in the possibility of a conversation of Socrates with the people (it is not clear to me what you think about this); the relation of the philosopher to the people is mediated by a certain kind of rhetoricians who arouse fear of punishment after death; the philosopher can guide these rhetoricians but can not do their work (this is the meaning of the Gorgias). As for the relation between manliness and justice (to which you refer with regard to *Alc<ibiades> I*), I believe that you underestimate the positive side of manliness; in the Republic everyone is just and moderate, but only the elite is manly (and wise); manliness and wisdom belong together, for philosophy does not wish to be edifying as your hero says.

I am not aware of a "sequence of the *Symposium-Phaedo-Phaedros*"; considering the low position of Phaedros compared with the others there in the *Symp<osium>*, one could say that the *Symp<osium>* is "higher" than the Phaedrus. Your suggestion that at the end of the *Symp<osium>* all are dead except Socrates, and at the end of the *Phaedo* all are alive except Socrates, is very appealing. But this does not yet justify your assertion that the *Symp<osium>* is a comedy and the *Phaedo* a tragedy. All the Dialogues are tragicomedies. (The tragedian is awake while the comedian is sleeping at the end of the *Symp<osium>*.) The dramatic hypothesis of the *Symp<osium>* is that Plato reveals what happened prior to the Sicilian expedition: not Alc<ibiades>, but Socrates divulges the mystery. I am also attracted by the alternative regarding the *Symp<osium>-Phaedo* as stated by you: whether it is better to live among the dead or to die in the society of the dull.

Regarding "ideal numbers" I trust you have read Klein's detailed analysis in his book on logistics and algebra. I was extremely interested and gratified but not altogether surprised to learn of your discoveries regarding Julian &c. Mysticism is one form in which philosophy can appear (cf. beginning of the *Sophist*). Your discovery makes the possibility of Farabi more intelligible. As regards Sallustius, if the division into chapters is authentic, 17 is of course the right place: 17 is the number designating φύσις.[1]

What you say about the volume to be written in my honor was news to me. Needless to say that I shall feel greatly honored by anything you would write.

I expect to send you on one of the next days a copy of an essay of mine on Machiavelli's *Prince*. I hope to have finished my book on Machiavelli by the end of this year. Therefore I must concentrate absolutely on this work and can not even look up the neo-Platonists whom you made so interesting to me. Bloom will do it for me.

Are you well?

As ever yours,

Leo Strauss

LS: mfg

———————

May 28, 1957

M. Alexandre Kojève
15 Bd. Stalingrad
Vanves (Seine)
France

Dear Mr. Kojève:

I have now found the time to read your long letter on Plato. I was unable to look up the texts. I simply tried to follow your argument and to see whether it agrees with what I believe to have been the understanding of Plato. I am sending your letter today to Klein, who promised to read it at the end of the semester, i.e., after June 15th. It is not impossible that you will hear from him then.

The combination "Parmenides . . . Phailebus" makes sense. But so do other combinations, i.e., the combination is arbitrary. One cannot separate as you do Timaeus—Critias from the *Republic* e.g., the Cephalus in the Parmenides alone suffices to establish the connection with the Republic, which also begins with Cephalus.

I disagree with your procedure. The interpretation of Plato always grows out of the thorough interpretation of each individual Dialogue, with as little reliance on extraneous information (even to begin with that supplied by other Platonic Dialogues) as possible. Certainly one cannot treat information supplied by Diogenes Laertius, &c. on the same level as what appears from the Dialogues themselves. This applies also and especially to the Protreptichos—an exoteric writing of which only fragments survive—I would tremble to base any inferences on that.

What you say about Plato's presumed reaction to the Protreptichos in the Parmenides, amounts to this, that Plato maliciously treats Aristotle's criticism of the ideas as old hat with which Socrates was already thoroughly familiar in his earliest youth. While this attracts me as every ingenious malice would, I regard it as perfectly possible that these criticisms of the ideas were Platonic and perhaps even Socratic commonplaces, prior to Aristotle's birth. One can not read the *Republic* without becoming aware of the criticism of the idea of the good as stated in the first book of the Nicomachean Ethics; given the paradoxical character of the doctrine of ideas its criticism is implied in doxa[1] itself (therefore no need for Aristotle's genius).

To understand Aristotle's criticism of Plato, the criticism of which criticism is according to you the thread of your heptalogy, I myself would start from that part of Aristotle's criticism of Plato with which I am most familiar, the critique of the *Republic* in *Politics* II. Aristotle's criticism is absolutely reasonable, he understands perfectly what Plato is doing, but he refuses to treat as ironical what is meant ironically, because he believes that it is possible and necessary to write treatises and not merely Dialogues; therefore, he treats the dialogic thesis of the *Republic* as a treatise thesis; undoubtedly because he believes that wisdom and not merely philosophy is available. This seems to me to be the difference between Plato and Aristotle, a difference which presupposes the acceptance by both of the doctrine of ideas, i.e., of the doctrine that the whole is characterized neither by noetic homogeneity (the exoteric Parmenides, and all "mathematical" philosophy) nor by sensible heterogeneity (four elements, &c.) but by noetic heterogeneity.

Before I turn to this main point, some details. Contrary to what you say, I think that Theatetus is superior to Theodorus. Theodorus is a typical mathematician: nice, unreflective, tactless, lacking instinct, and therefore falls victim to a philosopher (Protagoras) who denies the truth of mathematics itself. (Hence his pupil, Theatetus, does not even think of mathematics when trying to answer the question of what knowledge or science is.) Theatetus is superior: he can converse with Socr<ates>, he is not "stupid and vain," he is indeed not a philosopher; but if the "moderate" Theatetus (he accepts God's making the whole in deference to the Eleatic Stranger) and the "bold" younger Socrates could be combined, they would make a philosopher. (The relation of Theat<etus> and the younger Socrates is the same as that of Adeimantus and Glaucon in the *Republic*.) The boldness of the younger Socr<ates>: he is the addressee of the myth of the Statesman, the most massive meaning of which is denial of Providence—it is the ugly myth. (Generally the *Statesman* is ugly.) Constant dissatisfaction, always something is begun and then dropped unfinished, imitation of Sisyphean human life, of the life of even the philosopher, how it would be without Eros; the Eleatic Stranger advises Socrates to commit suicide, i.e., not to resist the condemnation; the Eleatic Stranger had caught the Sophist (Socrates) and could hand him over to the king, in the *Sophist*, but in the *Statesman* he catches the king, so that the sophist could be freed, (but it is not worthwhile in your age, Socrates.) In a word, the Eleatic Stranger is far from being "a parrot".—As for the depreciation of Astronomy in *Republic* VII, this must be understood in the line of the basic hypothesis of the *Republic* (unreasonable depreciation of "body"); the status of the visible heaven is restored at the end of *Republic* IX.—The Aristotelian "mean" is not "relativistic". Plato's notion of the Metrion, Prepon, and Hikanon[2] is fundamentally the same.—Regarding the irrelevance and stupidity of Antisthenes, I entirely concur (on the basis of Xenophon's *Symposium*).

　　Cephalus at the beginning of Parm<enides> reminds of Cephalus at the beginning of the *Republic*. The latter sacrifices to the gods instead of philosophizing. I assume that the same is true of Cephalus of Clazomeneae—in a way. Claz<omenae> reminds of Anaxagoras' Nous: Anax<agoras>, intelligently understood, would lead to theo-teleology, i.e. perfectly rational account of everything, [3]including the[3] irrational or meaningless or accidental. But this is not philosophy, but rather piety or sacrificing to the gods. Philosophy consists in the escape into Logoi, ideas. In the Parm<enides>, the ideas are represented as separate from the sensible; this thesis has no difficulty for Socr<ates>. As far as opposites are concerned and especially the moral opposites: the latter, as "ideal" ends, necessarily transcend what men achieve. He is doubtful regarding the idea of "man" (cf. the finger, in the *Republ<ic>*,) and especially low things (let me say, worms). But as Par<menides> warns him, this is due to Socrates' youthful contempt for the low and humble, and this contempt means to remain under the spell of popular prejudice. The primary correction, therefore, is this: if philosophy's quest is for the knowledge of the whole, and if the whole must be understood in the light of ideas, there must be ideas of "everything." One must therefore turn to the primary meaning of Idea, or Eidos, as class, as a whole, which is a whole by virtue of a specific character, and this character is in the case of living beings at the same time the end for the individual belonging to the class, and in this sense transcends the individuals (the animal's dominating desire for procreation or for perpetuation of the class.) In the case of man, the end is complex because man is both simply a part of the whole (like the lion or the worm) and that unique part of the whole which is open to the whole. (Only the souls of men have seen the ideas prior to birth.) Therefore, man's form and end is articulated in such a way that justice can come to sight provisionally as simply transcendent, and in no way "the perfection of man."

There is a realm of ideas; hence there must be a hierarchy, an organizing principle: the idea of the good. But as the highest principle it must be the ground not only of the ideas, but of the sensible as well. Hence the idea of the good is "the Good". The problem of diaeresis is the problem of the organization of the realm of ideas, and in particular the problem of the knowability of that organization. If wisdom is not available but only philosophy, the diaeresis as descent from the One to all ideas is not available. We live and think in the derivative and ascend to some extent, but not to the origin of things. The actual diaeresis reflects this in the arbitrariness of its beginning. (The divisions of the Sophist and the Statesman are caricatures; the principle of the caricature is mathematical simplification like division of even numbers by two). The adequate division would presuppose that one could deduce all ideas, especially also the ideas of living; it would presuppose a "rational biology"; this is impossible (see Timaeus); hence what is available is a dualism of a hypothetical mathematical physics and a non-hypothetical understanding of the human soul. The difference between Plato and Aristotle is that Aristotle believes that biology, as a mediation between knowledge of the inanimate and knowledge of man is available, or Aristotle believes in the availability of universal teleology, if not of the simplistic kind sketched in Phaedo 96.

The main point: you have not used your assumption or admission that according to Plato wisdom is not available. If one takes this as seriously as one must, the vision of the One-Good which is mediated by division, and hence the division itself, is not available. As for the choice between Plato and Hegel, I agree with you that Suez and Hungary are more interesting and more real than the Sorbonne; but what has the

Sorbonne to do with Philosophy? The analogon with the Sorbonne is not Suez and Hungary, but the more inept kind of deputies and sous-préfets.

In conclusion, I am sure that the community of ideas is absolutely essential, but I simply do not have the time at the moment to develop this.

Hoping to hear from you soon again,

As ever yours,

Leo Strauss

LS:mfg

Paris, July 1, 1957

Dear Mr. Strauss,

Many thanks for your letter of May 28, 1957. It is, of course, difficult to discuss our theses in writing. But I have no one nearby with whom discussion would be meaningful [as regards Weil, I must, belatedly, admit that you were entirely right: he is <u>not</u> a "philosopher"; and Koyré is a little "dotty": and besides, rather too "sceptical;" anything else is simply not worth even considering!]

To anticipate: Your letter has . . . confirmed me in my conviction (which, naturally, is entirely "natural"). I tell myself: if one of the two Plato experts has no more massive objections than that, then my interpretation is surely <u>possible</u> and perhaps even <u>correct</u>.

Your letter disappointed me greatly in only <u>one</u>, admittedly decisive, point. I refer to the koinonia ton genon.[1] For with regard to it, the "systematic" state of affairs is absolutely unequivocal (although <u>I</u> have known this for only about a year).

If the concept (and hence knowledge) is to be <u>eternal</u>, that is to say "spatial" and not "temporal," then koinonia[2] is sheer nonsense and can therefore only be used as a reductio ad absurdum (either as a mere <u>consequence</u> of empiricism, or as a claim by Eudoxus; which is likely, in view of the well-known passage in the *Metaph<ysics>*). If koinonia[2] is taken seriously, it would follow that the concept is <u>not</u> eternal. One is then faced with choosing between Heraclitean "relativism" (= historicism in

the fashion of Max Weber) according to which: concept = temporal; and
Hegelian "absolutism," according to which: concept = time ("time" =
completed history; knowledge = re-called [completed] history).[3]

Now, to make an Hegelian (let alone an Heraclitean) of Plato; is simply not possible. Be that as it may: if the koinonia[2] is true, then your entire interpretation of Plato is false; that is to say, Plato is then not an
"Ancient." However I believe that your interpretation of the Ancients is
entirely correct, and that that is why koinonia[2] cannot be seriously maintained by an ancient philosopher (Eudoxus was, after all, only a philosopher in the sense that, say, Einstein is one!)

Klein also admits as much—implicitly—in his Algebra Essay (which
is otherwise first rate!).

For he says that the logos (he of course means the ancient, that is to
say, eternal Logos) is transcended by the koinonia. Certainly! But if for
Plato it were a matter of maintaining silence, then the theos-agathon[4]
would be entirely sufficient (cp. the "first hyp<othesis>" of the
Parm<enides>). After all, the entire doctrine of ideas was invented in
order to make discursive knowledge possible. Hence, if the doctrine of
ideas is reduced to silence by koinonia, then that is a reductio ad absurdum of koinonia, at least as Plato understands it. [The Ancients proceed
on the basis of two axioms:

1. Knowledge = eternal, that is to say, infinitely repeatable speech that
   does not change in meaning over time; (this axiom is "evident" and is
   naturally retained by Hegel);
2. Knowledge = a (discursive) sense[5] that "corresponds" to an "essence"
   subsisting outside speech and its sense; [this is naturally "senseless";
   necessarily leads to skepticism; is not recognized by Hegel; according
   to Hegel, the "eternal" in speech is guaranteed by its completeness (its
   circularity shows or "proves" completeness): whoever has said everything can only repeat himself, and no one can contradict him].
3. From the Ancients' axioms it follows that: there can be knowledge
   only of eternal beings; regarding the temporal (always understood as
   in-complete) there can only be opinion which can, however, be right
   if it agrees with its object; but since that object is temporal, "right"
   knowledge of it is also temporal, and that is precisely not genuine
   knowledge but a (by definition changeable) opinion.
4. The eternal, on the other hand, is un-changeable, and hence koinonia
   is there either impossible or it is a mere mixture: the night of the absolute, in which all cows are black.]

Besides, Plato says so himself in the *Soph<ist>* (although "ironically"). The Stranger says that everything can be mixed except motion and rest. Now, everyone knows that there are different speeds and mixing motion and rest is a perfectly obvious thing to do! Much more so than, for example, to mix being and not-being. The fact that the Stranger regards it as "self-evident" that the mixture of motion and rest has to be rejected— strikes one as comical. However what it means is: rest = idea, motion = phenomenon, these two should, then, not be mixed. So that the point is only to establish the chorismos[6] of the ideas (in the name of Eudoxus who in fact denies the separateness of the ideas!). Koinonia, on the other hand, is motion. Hence there is no koinonia ton genon[7] [which is to say, no koinonia ton ideon;[8] for the genos[9] is Aristotelian-Eudoxian, and among kinds or species there indeed is koinonia; which is why there can be no knowledge of these gene, that is to say of sensible kinds or species].

There is also an ad hominem argument in the *Soph<ist>*.

The Stranger says two or three times that without koinonia, it is impossible to understand the "essence" of the Sophist. So that the world of ideas has to be set in motion in order to understand the Sophist?! That is a typically Homeric-Heraclitean ∼ "Protagorean" attitude: a goddess is supposed to tell of a man's anger! De facto there simply is no knowledge of the Sophist because he has no [eternal] essence (is, after all, but a Proteus!): one can only have an opinion (right or wrong) about the Sophist. That is indicated by the following, among other things, that (at the end of the *Statesman*) Socrates thanks the Stranger not for the "pathbreaking discovery" of the koinonia, but solely for the good (= correct = resembling) portraits (= images) of the Sophist and of the Statesman (who themselves are only "images").

That an unwitting half-Hegelian like N. Hartmann waxes enthusiastic for koinonia (Platos Logik des Seins)[10]—is only "natural." But how can you in the same breath fight Hegel and regard koinonia as true—that I really do not understand.

But I believe that a re-reading of the *Soph<ist>/States<man>* would persuade you. If only by the way the Stranger is introduced in them by Plato.

1. The Stranger, like "Pythodorus," is a disciple of Parmenides and of Zeno ("Zeno" = betrayer = Sophist) (216a).
2. He is introduced as a "Philosopher." But . . . by Theodorus. Now, in the *Theatetus* Theodorus did not understand irony, and he accepted at face value the caricature Socrates sketched (in connection with

"Thales"); what is more, he recognized himself in that "portrait"! But in fact it was the portrait of a < "learned man" or> "scholar" = a Sophist. Thus, if for Theod< orus > the Stranger is a "Philosopher," then for us (and "in himself") he is a Sophist. More precisely: "a man of theoretical learning." (In fact: Eudoxus.)

3. Socrates's reaction to Theodorus's introduction of the Stranger is typically ironic (216a/b), and reproduces Socrates's usual ironic exaggeration when he deals with famous Sophists. Moreover, Socrates defines the Stranger as an "adversary": "to survey and refute, he, the divine refuter, the poor reasoners we are" (216,b). The irony is here manifest. Whereupon the Stranger is introduced (by Theodorus) as a kind of parrot: "he admits having heard as many lectures as he could, and not to have forgotten them" (217b, in fine). De facto this means: Eudoxus has not invented anything new; he only repeats the basic doctrines of "Zeno" = "Heracliteanism" = Megera; yet he is so unphilosophical as to carry this doctrine ad absurdum, without even noticing that he does so; in the Sophist Plato does nothing else than to spell out these absurd consequences implicit in the Eudoxian theory: namely, the koinonia doctrine.

Finally, the Stranger's ¹¹behavior¹¹ (= Method) is shown as typically sophistic: "with a docile and accommodating partner (such as, for example, Thaetetus, and "learned" people in general), the easiest [!] way is with an interlocutor. Failing which, it is better to argue by oneself alone." (217c/d)

But as I said, the koinonia problem is too fundamental to admit of being settled by correspondence.

To be sure, the diairesis problem is just as fundamental (and corresponds to the first), but here your answer seems to me to rest on a misunderstanding. I expressed myself badly. Admittedly Plato denies the possibility of wisdom = absolute [discursive!] knowledge, whereas Aristotle allows this possibility. But the question I had in view is a different one. Since Kant we know that the "categories" (= divisions of being) may be valid for the "things-in-themselves" (= ideas, in Platonic terminology), but cannot be applied to the things-in-themselves (by men). In other words, what is at issue is the ontological structure as such. That is what Plato and Aristotle quarrel about (i.e. in the Soph< ist > -States < man >). In formal logical terms, the quarrel can be defined in the following way, that Aristotle speaks about contraries (with mesotes¹²), whereas Plato has contradictories (without mesotes) in view (cp. especially 257b in fine). The Aristotelian theory (contraries + mesotes), effectively denies the radical difference between good and evil (= not

-good) (cp. 258a: "hence the non-just must also be placed <u>on the same</u> <u>level</u> as the just"). That is the real reason for rejecting this "Aristotelian" method of division (which is illustrated <u>ironically</u> by means of concrete examples in the *Sophist-Statesman* in order to show that it leads to a mixing of the kinds, namely not of the next (proximate) kind [the only ones about which Aristotle, quite sensibly, speaks], but of the "higher" kinds, as far as good-evil).

<u>Thus</u>: there are <u>two</u> differences between Plato and Aristotle. Namely:

1. Both agree in saying that <u>for us</u> (pros hemos) all that is possible (or at least <u>discursively</u> possible), is an "induction" (from "below" to "above"), whereas "in itself" (physei[13]) the order is "deductive" (from "above" to "below"). But according to Plato there is a <u>break</u> in the induction pros hemos[14] (because of the aoristos dyas[15]): the One (= agathon[16]) reveals itself (if at all) not in the logos[17] (discursively) but in ecstasy (silently); but from <u>silence</u>, anything, that is to say nothing, can be "deduced." According to Aristotle (who replaces the dyad by the ether, that is to say who interprets the kosmos noetos[18] as Uranus) there is no break, and it is possible <u>for us</u> to return to the sensory "manifold" "deductively" after we have inductively ascended to the One (= Nous[19]), Thus: <u>discursive</u> wisdom or system as absolute knowledge (to speak with Hegel). [Only with this difference, that "reality"[20] is not, as it is in Hegel, completed[21] (human) history, but eternal revolution of the heavenly bodies ("the logos become flesh" = planetary sphere and <u>not</u> an "earthly phenomenon," for example, man)].

2. Independently of knowledge for us, there is a difference in their conception of the <u>in itself</u> (and in my letter I spoke exclusively about <u>that</u> difference. According to Plato, there is

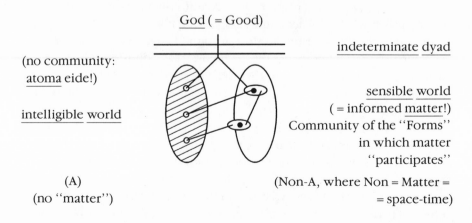

God (= Good)

indeterminate dyad

(no community: atoma eide!)

intelligible world

sensible world (= informed matter!) Community of the "Forms" in which matter "participates"

(A)
(no "matter")

(Non-A, where Non = Matter = = space-time)

<u>That is to say:</u>

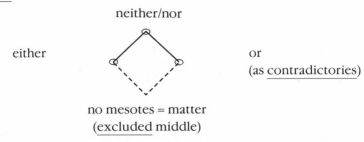

neither/nor

either   or
                                              (as <u>contradictories</u>)

no mesotes = matter
(<u>excluded middle</u>)

Whereas according to Aristotle

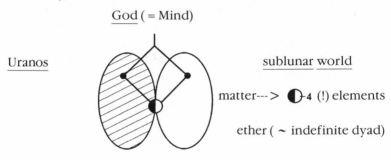

<u>God</u> (= Mind)

Uranos   sublunar <u>world</u>

matter---> ◖-4 (!) elements

ether (∼ indefinite dyad)

But that is to say:

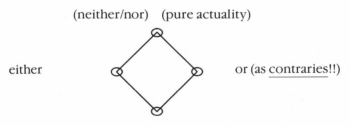

(neither/nor)   (pure actuality)

either   or (as <u>contraries</u>!!)

as well as = mesotes = potentiality = matter

In terms of method, this means that according to Plato: the positive
(= atomos eidos[22]) gets increasingly circumscribed by successive <u>contra</u>-
ditions, without a "definition" ever being reached; <u>according to Aristotle</u>:
one looks for the <u>contrary</u>, in the process finds 2 + 1, the third as
mesotes, and by this method all three are <u>defined</u>.

So that according to Aristotle one has

that is to say not 2 but (at least) 3. But the mesotos is "manifold." So that one really has

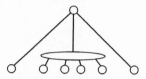

The number of these "intermediates" is determined in a <u>purely</u> empirical fashion since they are natural kinds (cp. *Parts of Animals* I—the polemic against the Plat<onic> diairesis[23]).

[I believe that *Nic<omachean> Eth<ics>* 1094b 25; 1095a 32; 1098a 27 is not only directed against Plato <u>in general</u>, but specifically against his diaeresis, which admittedly distinguishes very precisely between A and non-A, but leaves the classification of the mesotes[24] more or less "indeterminate."]

I also do not put much stock in the historical tradition. Still, it seems to me incredible that, as you assume, Plato should <u>not</u> have taken diairesis seriously, but should have been <u>serious</u> about koinonia,[25] whereas[26] Aristotle <u>never</u> so much as mentions koinonia but frequently speaks about Plat<onic> diairesis and criticizes it, and when he does so, he manifestly has <u>my</u> scheme in view.

I guess that that is the most essential. However, I do want briefly to speak to the other points in your letter.

1. You reprove me for separating the *Tim<aeus>-Crit<ias>* from the Rep<ublic> and in that connection you say that "Cephalus" represents a mixture between the Republic and . . . the Parm<enides>. I don't understand what you mean by that.

For me, the Rep<ublic> ~ Summa Theologica, and the Parmenides ---> Philebus ~ S<umma> contra Gentiles (in 7 Books). To be sure, "Cephalus" is a link between the two: in the Rep<ublic>, Ceph<alus> = head of a "Civil" (not a <u>philosophical</u>) family; in the Parm<enides>, Ceph<alus> (= Plato) = head of a philosophical "family" (= Academy). In <u>both</u> cases, the "sons" (in the Parm<enides>: Aristotle) are "corrupted" by the Sophists. The Tim<aeus>-Crit<ias> are not related to the Rep<ublic> directly but indirectly, through the Parm<enides> + Th<eatetus> ---> Soph<ist> ---> States<man>. In fact, the summary at the beginning of the Tim<aeus> is a summary of the *States<man>*, and not of the Rep < ublic > . (This last point has long been known, and it has led to the absurd hypothesis of a proto-Republic, as if a Plat < onic > dialogue could be assembled from disparate pieces!)

2. My interpretation proceeded on your own method: I was looking for a way to distinguish the positive from the negative (either evil = not-good, or good = not-evil) and reread the Sophist; whereupon I noticed the ironical character of the divisions; this led me to the States < man > ; then back to the Th < eatetus > ; then to the Parm < enides > ; and only then to the Tim < aeus > / Crit < ias > because of the summary at the beginning. Then the Phil < ebus > proved to be the "crown" of the whole: beatitude as neither-nor, and the "mixture" (= as well as = koinonia) as "sophistry."

The Proteptic us, Diogenes Laertius, etc., came much later (when I read Jäger's *Aristotle*, and I do not even regard them as confirmations; now, I do not want to be in the position of saying: "Arist < otle > misunderstood Plato!" [Although he sometimes consciously falsified him, but always in such a way that the letter of the Aristot < elian > text is correct: "In the Tim < aeus > , Plato," can also mean: the "Timaeus" Plato made up (for polemical purposes); but a reader can also take the Tim < aeus > at face value.

3. I never said that Aristotle invented the criticism of the theory of ideas. But Arist < otle > 's presence shows that he made this criticism his own (and it is certain that he did, since it reappears in the *Met < aphysics >* .) Now Pl < ato > could ignore the Megeran criticism of the theory of ideas; he had to respond to its being taken up by his own disciples, by Aristotle among others (the "gentiles" are not "pagans" but "heretics"!); and also to the presumed "correction" of the theory of ideas by Eudoxus (which is philosophical nonsense: ideas without chorismos[27] simply are not ideas in the Plat < onic > sense).

4. I agree with your interpretation of the basic difference between Pl < ato > and Arist < otle > (in the sense of what I have said above on this subject). Certainly, both assume noetic heterogenity. But they conceive of the structure of this "multiplicity" entirely differently (diairesis ≠ definition by prox < imate > genus).

For Plato the ground of the multiplicity of the ideas is not spatial, but the dyad as such; hence the ideas are immovable (for Plato: motion = not-rest, i.e., rest = positive, mot < tion > = privation. In Arist < otle > this ground is aether, hence spatio-temporal, which is why the ideas = planets move (albeit in an circle). Aristotle is thus a philosophically not

absurd theorist of Eudoxism (for in heaven there is no koinonia of the
planets; the planets are "atomic," like the ideas; they form a "hierarchy,"
as a series of <u>ordinal</u> numbers, namely the "lengths" of the radii; and
nevertheless . . . the planets move and are <u>causes</u> of the sub-lunar world,
which is just what the unmoving ideas are <u>not</u>).

5. I never denied that Theat < etus > is intellectually "superior" to
Theodorus. And the Stranger = Eudoxus is even more "superior" (intellectually). But <u>none</u> of them is a philosopher, and the Eudoxian "theory
of ideas" is <u>not</u> a <u>philo < sophical ></u> theory. But <u>morally</u> the order is re-
versed: Theod < orus > is quite "decent"; Th < eatetus >—so-so; the
"second Socr < ates > " (= Arist < otle >)—a "tyrant"; and the Stranger
(= Eudoxus) a murderer!

"Not worthwhile in your age, Socrates" etc. means: Eudoxus can
"save" Platonism by bringing the doctrine of ideas in line with "the results of modern science." But Plato is too old to understand it (besides
being too religious-poetic). This theme of age (= anachronism) recurs
time and again in the septet.

[Be that as it may, Theatetus is nevertheless depicted as <u>philosophi-
cally</u> "dumb" and a "chatter-box" ("amateur-philosopher" in the manner of Einstein).

<u>For example</u>: < Sophist > 262a in fine: "<u>The Str < anger ></u> : Hence names
alone, said one after the other, no more make up speech, than do verbs
unaccompanied by names. Theat < etus > : I didn't know that."[28] [!!!]
< [> In other words: he is incapable of distinguishing between sensible
(philo < sophical >) discourse and pseudo-scientific chattering in the
manner of Eudoxus.]

If the Aristotelian mesotos[29] is not a < form of > moral <u>relativism</u>,
then I don't know what the word (relativism) means. After all, it is
nothing else than the biological optimum. Admittedly there are only <u>two</u>
contraries; however the point is that <u>both</u> are "bad" (≠ optimum, and instead, either ex < cess > or defect); but the "good" mesotos is an "indeterminate many," depending on the . . . mode of life:
A function of age, gender, race, even—of the political constitution!

6. I, too, believe that Klazomenae is intended to bring Anaxagoras to
mind. But approximately as follows: Aristotle (in the Met < aphysics >)
criticizes Anax < agoras > for not having made use of Nous[30] as (final)
cause; he directs the same criticism at Plato (the ideas are not causes); in
the Phaedo Plato says the same thing, through clearly ironically (by mak-

ing fun of teleology [say of Diogenes of Ap<ollonia>'s]: "The earth is the center of the cosmos only because it is better for it to be there!" etc.); "our Klazom<enae>" in the *Parm<enides>* would then mean: "we" (= Acad<emy>) by no means want to lower the ideas to the level of (efficient) causes of phenomena, as do those [for instance Eudoxus] who place the ideas in things; hence Xenophanes ---> Parmenides ---> Anaxagoras ---> Socrates ---> Plato, and not (Homer --->) Heraclitus ---> Diogenes ---> Eudoxus ---> Aristotle.

Parm<enides>'s "warning" to Socr<ates> not to disdain worms and dust is, in my opinion, ironic: that is the criticism directed at Plato by the "learned" (besides, Socrates is by no means "persuaded" by Parmenides's remark). It seems to me altogether impossible to assume (Platonic!) ideas of worms and dust: there are no ideas of the negative (the idea is A, and non-A is no idea; more precisely: as non-A it "participates" in the idea of A, but as non-A it is only a function of the aoristos dyas[31]; worm and dust are "privations" of the "complete" animal and the "complete" mineral. That seems to me to be a basic principle of Platonism, in contrast to Aristotelianism, for which worm and dust are "between" A and non-A (mesotes!).

As regards the soul, I understand it approximately as follows: soul = A (idea); body = non-A (matter <---dyad); non(non-A) = A [solely on the basis of diairesis, without koinonia!]; that is to say: only when the body is "negated" does the soul become "pure" idea, and only man can "negate" his body (on the basis of diairesis without koinonia, which precisely allows the body to be understood as non-A, where the Non, which appears as space-time, is derived from the non-existing dyad.) In practical terms that means: one should abandon the polis, practice dialectic in the Academy, live accordingly, and one may then perhaps as a (for an instant) "pure idea" coincide (for an instant) with the One-Good.

In short, Plotinus is a genuine Platonist, and the "astrolatry" of the *Tim-<aeus>*, *Laws* X, *Epinomis* is either purely ironical, or forged (by the Eudoxian Speusippus), or . . . preached to the "people" for reasons of state.

7. Yes: diairesis is intended to show the hierarchy of the ideas which, inasmuch as they form a hierarchy, can be represented by (ordinal) numbers. But it is very difficult to do so, perhaps it is impossible to do so de facto (as long as one remains in the Non-). However, the divisions of the *Soph<ist>-States<man>* are Aristotelian, and have nothing in common with Platonic diairesis, precisely because they do not lead to hierarchy, but assume a juxtaposition of the species <or kinds>.

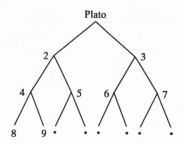

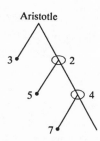

(also no difference between left/right, straight/crooked, or ideas/world).

8. The <u>entire</u> difference between Plato and Aristotle rests on the discovery of de facto <u>biological</u> cycles (🜚): (<u>man</u> begets <u>man</u> [and not dogs]). The cycle of biological species is <u>eternal</u>; hence it is knowable; hence there is no need of the ideas in order to ground knowledge (very clear in *Metaphysics* ⋀ , 3 (in fine)). Instead of the ideas, there are "forms" of the biological cycles; this "form" is the <u>cause</u> (entelechy) of the biological (cyclical) process; hence they are <u>in</u> space and <u>in</u> time although <u>eternal</u> (and they are <u>eternal</u> because eternity itself, that is to say Nous-Theos[32] as first (unmoved) mover, makes <u>time</u> itself cyclical (cp. *Physics* VIII), which is why the spatio-temporal processes are also cyclical. <u>Thus</u>: Platonic ideo-logy becomes Aristotelian etio-logy = bio-logy = astro-logy (for the cyclical biological "law" is <u>objectively</u> <u>actual</u>[33] as heavenly spheres [dis-order = inclined ecliptic]): there is a science of the phenomena, but it is purely "astrological" [<u>that</u> is the result of Aristotle's so-called "good sense" and "realism," in contrast to the "poet" and "mystic" Plato!!]

I am afraid that this letter will not clarify the issue, but only confuse it further. It would naturally be so much better to be able to <u>talk</u> about all this. But when? And where?

Incidentally, I have read your Jerusalem lecture.[34] Surely the best thing I have read of yours: extremely clear, dense, and brilliant. But . . . to speak about "the Moderns" without mentioning Hegel and Marx . . . ?! Up to Rousseau everything moves along very well, but then there is a gap, and we come to . . . Max Weber and Oppenheimer! That is to say to end-less, that is to say <u>senseless</u> so-called "history" (without "Napoleon"). It is naturally not difficult to show the absurdity of such a "philosophy." But what about a certain Hegel, who spoke of the <u>end-state</u> and <u>absolute</u> knowledge, and the people called Marx, etc., who actualize it? Is the silence about these people intended to be "pedagogic" (or <u>dema</u>-gogic?

since you are addressing an audience of grown-ups)? Or is the sacred soil responsible for that?

Otherwise, I am much better, and I am glad to hear that you, too, are better.

Well—I hope we will still be able to see and speak with one another.

With warmest greetings

your

Kojève

P.S. Enclosed a copy of a Note for my "book" that will not be published![35]

—————————

THE UNIVERSITY OF CHICAGO
Chicago 37, Illinois
Department of Political Science

Sept. 11, 1957

M. Alexandre Kojève
15 Bd. Stalingrad
Vanves (Seine)
France
Dear Mr. Kojéve:

It was only last week that I could read your typewritten statement and your letter. I had had a minor illness, no real vacation and I'm feeling very tired. My general reaction to your statements is that we are poles apart. The root of the question is I suppose the same as it always was, that you are convinced of the truth of Hegel (Marx) and I am not. You have never given me an answer to my questions: a) was Nietzsche not right in describing the Hegelian-Marxian end as "the last man"? and b) what would you put into the place of Hegel's philosophy of nature? I am under the impression that you read Plato from your Hegelian point of view without sufficiently waiting for what would reveal itself as Plato's view by simply listening to Plato and strictly adhering to his suggestions. You take for granted that the "ideas" are "concepts" and that Plato is exclusively concerned with the "ideas" and not with the "soul". Hence you are certain that there cannot be ideas of the "sensible species". Without a previous solution of the question "of which things are there ideas and of which things are there no ideas" there cannot be a fruitful discussion of the community of ideas. Your whole interpretation appears to me schematic and arbitrary. Apart from the dialogues you use the Aristotelian reports. The Aristotelian reports are of course most competent but they do not answer the question of how definitely or how seriously Plato asserted the things Aristotle says he asserted. (Incidentally, precisely Aristotle's report should induce one to ascribe to Plato the assertion that there are "ideas of the sensible species".) I am not satisfied that there are Platonic dialogues devoted to criticism of Aristotle and that the dialogues devoted to the criticism of Aristotle are the seven mentioned by you. In particular I regard it as impossible to divorce the *Timaeus* and the *Critias* from the *Republic* as you do.

I see only two points in your exposition regarding which we can at least begin to have a conversation. The two points are the Eleatic Stranger and the *Critias*.

I am absolutely certain that the stranger is not a parrot and that you misinterpret completely his introduction by Theodorus and Socrates' welcoming speech. On the other hand I believe that you are right in saying that there is something wrong about his assertion concerning the community of rest (ideas) and motion (non-ideas). This does not prove however that he lacks comprehension, for every Platonic dialogue is based on the deliberate disregard of something crucially important, and what is right for the Platonic Socrates is right also for the Platonic Eleatic Stranger. Briefly, the separateness of the ideas makes it impossible to understand the whole which consists of onta and gignomena[1]; it makes it impossible to understand the soul (and therefore the philosopher who can only be understood in contradistinction to the non-philosopher). In order to overcome the separateness the stranger assimilates onta and gignomena (motion and rest) and he expresses this thought most radically by defining being as acting and suffering which (acting and suffering) as far as I understand Plato cannot be said of the ideas; the stranger wrongly but not ignorantly abstracts from the radical difference betwen onta and gignomena. Instead of assimilating onta and gignomena one must seek for the <u>bond</u> between them, but the thesis of the stranger is superior to the mere chorismos-thesis <separateness-thesis> because it is based on an awareness of the fundamental inadequacy of the bare separateness thesis. I suspect that the *Timaeus* in its doctrine of the soul brings out the "bond" solution to the problem—at the price of abstracting from something else of utmost importance. (What that something else is I do not yet know.) The mere fact that the Stranger is the murderer of Parmenides shows that he is not a parrot. Cf. also the Beauty of the non-corrected Eleatic thesis: "there is only the One" and the philosopher-sophist-statesman are three, whereas I believe the Eleatic thesis as corrected by the stranger is to the effect "the one consists of many" and "philosopher-sophist-statesman" is One.

Regarding the *Critias* I make this suggestion: The *Republic* deals with the "city in speech", the *Timaeus* with the "cosmos in deed" and the *Critias* with the "city in deed": the cosmos in speech is missing ("the fourth is missing"): the promise of Hermocrates' speech conceals the not-promised but required speech by Plato himself. The city in deed is necessarily inferior to the city in speech—it is necessarily "diluted", the good is identified with the ancestral (therefore the best city in speech is necessarily Athenian; the *Critias* shows that the best city abounds not only in virtue but in gold as well). The city in deed must be the city in motion and motion means war. The biggest war of historical Athens was the Sicilian expedition and this was an unjust war and it ended in a defeat. The ideal war of "old Athens" must therefore be a just war (a war of defence) with a super Sicily (the biggest island in the farthest West) ending in an Athenian victory. The description of the most glorious Athenian deed cannot be given by an Athenian for reasons of propriety (see the much more limited praise of Athens given by the stranger Aspasia in the *Menexenus*). Now, the victory of Athens over "Sicily" has of course also a transpolitical meaning as you will be the first to admit (Hermocrates was the chief man responsible for Athens' defeat in the Sicilian expedition; Timaeus comes from southern Italy which is almost Sicily; Elea is in southern Italy; and last but not least the Cephalus of the *Republic* and his family stem from the same region). One must also not forget the invasion of Athens by Parmenides in the *Parmenides*. In brief Sicily, "the West", tries to conquer Athens but is defeated by Athens. This, if I understand you correctly, is exactly what you say, but this victory of Athens over Sicily is asserted by Critias, a somewhat dubious figure, and Plato prevents him from telling his story. It seems to me that the incomplete character of the *Critias* means exactly this: the victory of Athens over Sicily is a half-victory and therefore also a half-defeat. You will disagree with my final conclusion but it is obvious that you can use all my other statements regarding the *Critias* very well for your purposes. Yet this statement could not have been arrived at except by adhering to the unambiguous Platonic suggestion that the *Timaeus* and *Critias* belong with the *Republic* and this proves that one must stick much more closely than you do to the obvious données platoniques. (Critias is a competitor of Alcibiades and Alcibiades is the instigator of the Sicilian expedition.)

I hope that you continue to be in good health. I expect to have finished my study on Machiavelli by the end of this year.

Yours

LS

––––––––––

Geneva, 10.24.57.

My dear friends,

Truth to tell, I have absolutely nothing to tell you. Which is to say that regarding A <. . .> and myself everything is going well. I am in Geneva, where I expect to spend 5–6 weeks: Common Market meetings.

At the margins of "great politics," I granted myself a most restful [1]working party,[1] which allows me to read and write while meetings are in session: specifically this letter.

Enclosed a slip with three books. I would be most grateful if you could have them sent to me (in Vanves). I have read the Rosán book about Proclus recommended by Hering. Not very "profound," but very clear and apparently accurate. A useful book.

But it also contains the "biography" of Pr<oclus> by "Marinus"! Without commentary and taken 100% seriously. Now, in fact, and as I had assumed after reading the *vita Isidori*, this "Marinus" is clearly nothing but a pseudonym of my friend Damascius, and the so-called "biography" nothing but a shameless mockery of its hero. It is written in the style of the *vita*.

If you want to be amused, I greatly recommend that you read this "Marinus" in Rosán, *Proclus* (N.Y. 49). It takes up only 22 pages. But as I suspect that you will not choose to read them, I will copy a few particularly tasty passages.

III. . . . Every one of these [physical virtues] was naturally present in our blessed philosopher from birth, and their traces could be seen clearly even in that external oyster-like shell of his . . . He was so beautiful that, although all his pictures are excellent, none of the painters was able completely to capture his likeness, that all remained far behind in the imitation of his true form . . . [In this connection Rosán points out in a note: A protrait-bust has been found . . . It is one-third broken and has a peculiarly hooked nose"].

IV. . . . It is astonishing that those basic qualities of the soul, which he had spontaneously and innately, were the same parts of virtue that Plato considered to be the elements of a philosophical character . . .

IX. . . . He learned Aristotelian philosophy under Olympiodorus . . . Now Olympiodorus was known as an able speaker, but because of the ease and rapidity with which he spoke, only a few of his hearers could understand him . . .

. . . The logical writings of Arist., which are difficult to understand for those who read them, he [Proclus] nevertheless easily learned by heart, and at a single reading . . .

XIII. Within less than two years, Syrianus [one of the < . . . > of the *Vita Isidori*] read with him all the writings of Arist < otle > in logic, ethics, politics, physics and even theology. And after going through these sufficiently as if they were preparatory rites or lesser mysteries, he led him, systematically and not, as the [Chaldean] Oracle says "by enormous steps", up to the greater mysteries of Plato, and revealed their truly divine visions to the untainted eyes of his soul and the pure gaze of his mind. And Proclus, on his own part, by constant practice and attention, both day and night, and by writing down everything that was said in the form of a summary with his own opinions produced in a short time so much that by the age of 28 he has written his *Comm < mentary> on the Timaeus* as well as many other commentaries, all finely done and full of learning. Such an occupation improved his character even more, because he added knowledge to his moral virtues.

XIV. He also acquired the political virtues from the writings of Ar < istotle's> *Polit < ics>* and from the *Laws* and the *Rep < ublic>* of Plato. So that even in this no one might say he was concerned with words alone and not with deeds; since his preoccupation with higher things prevented him from taking part in political affairs himself, he persuaded the pious Archiadas to do this, by teaching him the political virtues . . .

XV. . . . Proclus showed that he possessed a Herculean courage even in politics. . . . And when his enemies, like a horde of giant vultures, tried to put him on trial [or perhaps: annoyed him excessively], he left Athens in obedience to the Revolution of the Whole,[2] and travelled to Asia. Actually this was all for the best, for his guardian Spirit really provided him with this pretext for the journey so that he might be initiated into the ancient rites that were still perserved there . . . Acting and living in this fashion, he passed even more unnoticed than the Pythagoreans [Epicureans??], who firmly obeyed that command of their master to "live unnoticed" [lathé biosas]. But he spent only one[3] year in Lydia and returned to Athens by the Providence of the Goddess of philosophy. This was the manner in which Proclus gradually obtained his courage . . .

XVI. . . . He was an excellent judge in every field. And whenever he found someone who was not taking his own work seriously, he severely censured him. It was this that made him appear very quick-tempered and quite emulous [cf. IV . . .: he appeared to us as to be by nature modest . . .], because he wanted and was able to judge everything correctly. He was indeed emulous, but emulous only in respect to virtue and goodness; perhaps nothing great among human beings could be done without this kind of motivation. I also admit that he was quick-tempered. Nevertheless[4] he was mild at the same time, for he calmed down easily and quickly, becoming as soft as wax within a moment;—one minute he would be scolding someone and the next minute because of his sympathetic nature he would be helping him . . .

XVII. I am glad that this sympathetic nature of his has come to my mind, for I believe that no other person can be said have been as sympathetic as he. Because he never desired a wife or children, although he had received many offers of marriage from noble and wealthy families, he was free of experience of having his own family, . . .

XVIII. . . . We now come to his purifying virtues which are quite different from social virtues. . . . . . But the purifying virtues are superior to these. . . . . . The philosopher Proclus practiced these purifying virtues throughout his philosophical career, ... He always did that which was conducive to separating the soul, and whether in the night-time or daytime, he would pray against evil demons, bathe himself, and use other methods of purification, both Orphic and Chaldean, such as immersing himself in the sea resolutely every month, or even twice or three times a month. And he did all this not only in the prime of his life, but even in his later years he religiously performed these customary actions.

XX. . . . He was indifferent in this way not only to physical pain, but even more so to external evils, whether ordinary or extraordinary. Whenever these occurred he would always say; "that's[5] the way things are; that's the way they usually are". Which seemed to me to be a maxim that deserved to be memorized and which sufficiently proved the greatness of the philosopher's soul. As to anger, he tried to repress it as much as he could . . . [cf. above XVI, in fine].

XXII. . . . he arrived at higher[6] virtues . . . which could no longer be called phronesis in the human sense but rather sophia or even some more reverent name. While he was absorbed with this, Proclus learned with ease all of Greek and non-Greek theology and also that truth that[7] had been hidden in the form of myths; he explained all these in a very enthusiastic manner . . . He went through all the writings of previous authors and whatever he found that was fruitful he would select and combine . . . In his lectures he was able to discuss each doctrine sensibly and he mentioned all of them in his writings. He had an unbounded love of work: sometimes he would teach five or more classes a day, write on the average about 700 lines of prose [Chrysippus, who was notoriously prolific, was said to write 300 lines], visit with other philosophers and then in the evening give lectures that were not based on any text; in addition to all this he would sleeplessly worship the gods every night and bow in prayer to the sun when it arose, at midday and when it set.

XXIII. Proclus himself was the originator of many previously unknown doctrines in natural, intellectual and even more divine subjects. He was the first to claim that there was a genus of souls who were able to perceive many Ideas at one time and who occupied a middle position between the Nous which knows everything at once . . . and those souls who can concentrate upon only one Idea at a time. Anyone who wishes to, may learn of his many other innovations by going through his works, which I cannot do now, since it would prolong this biography too greatly to mention all of them. But whoever does read his works will agree that what I have just said is true . . .

XXVI. . . . . . it was by means of these divine oracles that Proclus reached those highest virtues of the human soul which the inspired Iamblichus has excellently called "theurgic". For gathering the interpretations of previous philosophers together with proper judgment by a great deal of labour for five whole years [contra: "less than two years" for "all the writings of Arist < otle >." (cp. XIII above)], he brought together all the rest of the Chaldean literature and the most important commentaries on these divinely-given Oracles. In regard to this he had the following wonderful dream: the great Plutarch [Syriannus's teacher] appeared to him and foretold that he would live for as many years as there were four-page sheets in his works on the oracles; afterwards he counted these and found that there were 70. That the dream had been divine was proved by the close of his life. For[8] although he really lived, as was said before, for 75 years, during the last five years he was no longer strong . . . To be sure, he still prayed, even in this condition, composed hymns . . . but he did everything in accordance with this weakened condition so that he marvelled whenever he thought of the dream and constantly said: "I have really lived for only 70 years [?!].[9]

[compare with III: . . . Fourthly he had health . . . And he was gifted with this virtue from infancy so highly, that he was able to say that his body had been ill only two or three times in a long life of altogether 75 (sic!) years. The final proof of this, to which I myself can testify, was that he did not even recognize in his last illness what kind of suffering had befallen him, so rarely had he experienced pain.—compare XXXII:[10] . . . He had been afraid when he was in the prime of his life that the arthritis of his father might attack him also . . . And it was not without reason that he feared this, because, as I should have said before, he was indeed suffering pain of this kind.].

XXVIII. . . . . Proclus proceeded step by step; first he was cleansed by the Chaldean purification; then he held converse, as he himself mentions in one of his works, with the luminous [!] apparitions of Hecate which he conjured up himself; then he caused rain-falls by correctly moving the wryneckbird wheel,[11] by this means he saved Athens from a severe drought. He proposed means to prevent earthquakes; he tested the divinatory power of the tripod; and even wrote verses about his own destiny . . .

XXXIII. But if I wanted to tell everything about him, such as his friendship with Pan, the son of Hermes, and the great kindness and aid which he received from this god in Athens, or if I related the good fortune that he obtained from the Mother of the Gods to whom he always prayed and in whom he greatly rejoiced, I would probably seem to some readers simply to be prattling and to others to be saying the incredible. For the many great things which this Goddess did for him and said to him almost daily were so numerous and so unusual to be written about, that I no longer remember them very clearly. But if anyone wishes to know more about his affinity with the Goddess, let him read his book on the Mother of the

Gods [otherwise unknown!], for it will be seen how he reveals the whole theology of this Goddess[12] with divine inspiration and explains philosophically what is symbolically done or mythically said of her and Attis, so that no one need any longer be disturbed by hearing the seemingly absurd wails[13] and other things that are secretly said at her ceremonies. [Compare with Julian's equally ironic speech about the Mother of the Gods].

[These citations might suffice to elucidate the somewhat enigmatic meaning of the following passage from the Preface of the "Biography":]

I. . . . I was afraid lest, in the words of Ibycus, I might win the esteem of men by sinning, not against the gods, as he said, but against a wise man [sc. Proclus], especially since it would not have been right that I alone of all his friends should keep silent and should not, on the contrary, make every effort to tell the truth about him, in spite of the fact that of all men I was under the greatest obligation to speak out openly. Perhaps, in fact, I might not have even won men's esteem, because they would not have attributed to modesty my refusal to undertake this task but to mental laziness or even a worse fault of soul. For all these reasons, therefore, I felt myself compelled to set forth at least some of the countless superior accomplishments of the philosopher Proclus and some of the things that have been truly reported about him.

[All in all: amicus Plato . . .]

But isn't the irony unmistakable?

After you have read this letter, could you send it to Strauss in my name. I have spoken to him about Julian, Damascius, and "Sallustius." This "Marius" will complete the picture!

As ever yours,

K.

Geneva, 11.5.57

Dear Mr. Strauss,

Please excuse that I only now answer your letter of 9.11. But various things have interfered. I am here in Geneva (GATT meeting) and will probably stay here until the end of the month.

To the issue:

I fully agree with you that a "general" discussion of Plato does not make much sense. The only really sensible thing to do would be to read the 7 dialogues together.

But for my part, the whole thing did not in any way arise from preconceived "general" views. On the contrary, rather by accident, I came across some passages from the *Sophist* that seemed to me "senseless" or sounded "ironic." Thereupon I read the other 6 dialogues, in which I found many similar passages. All this then led to a comprehensive interpretation that in itself made sense and, in my opinion, is also historically possible (but very much astonished me!). In my first (long) letter in this connection I cited many of these passages (without copying them), and briefly interpreted the whole thing. What I really expected from you was that you would take a specific stand on everyone of the passages in question. Well, time did not allow you (as you yourself have told me) to look up the passages themselves. Thus you answer only with "general" considerations about Plato, and the entire discussion gets sidetracked.

I can only hope that when you are done with your Machiavelli you will have the time and the inclination to answer my first letter concretely (assuming that Klein has not lost it in the meantime [which would be a great pity, as it is my only writing dealing with the issue]). I attach particular importance to the first part of the *Parmenides* (up to the so-called "dialectic").

So far I am acquainted with only one concrete stand on your part: that regarding the Eleatic Stranger.

Now, here I can really not understand why you refuse to see the ironical element in the depiction of the Stranger. Socrates's reaction is, after all, exactly the same as his reaction to Protagoras, Euthydemus, etc.: ironically exaggerating admiration of the "divine wisdom" of a sophist.

Finally and in conclusion, the following may surely not be ignored:

1° The depiction of the "philosopher" in the *Thaet<etus>* is manifestly ironic;

2° Theodorus does not see the irony, takes the depiction seriously and recognizes himself in it [in which he is again right];

3° The Stranger is introduced [in the *Soph<ist>*] by this Theodorus, as a philosopher.

4° That is to say: in the eyes of Theodorus, the Stranger corresponds to the depiction of the "philosopher" in the *Thaet<etus>*; hence in Plato's eyes, the Stranger is a "sophist"; more precisely, a "modern [= post-socratic] sophist, that is to say, a scholar [natural-scientific with "philosophical" pretensions; I say, Plato has the "Pythodorus" of the *Parm<enides>* in mind [for me "Pythod<orus>" = Theodor<us> + Thaetetus + Eudoxus; that is to say, in the *Sophist*: Stranger = Eudoxus].

Here, then, is a concrete difference in our interpretations of Plato. But here, too, the question can probably be resolved only by a comprehensive interpretation of all relevant passages in the [7] dialogues.

In the meantime I have read [Apud Rosán, Proclus, N.Y.] the supposed "biography" of Proclus by the so-called "Marianus." When I read the *vita Isidori*, I suspected that this "Marianus" was nothing but an alias for Damascius and that the "biography" might in fact be an "ironic" parody. Reading this "biogr<aphy>" has fully confirmed it [here I did indeed have a preconceived opinion!] The "biogra<phy>" is a duplicate of the *vita Isidori*.

I have copied some passages from it and sent them to Koyŕe with the request that he forward the letter to you.

All this is interesting because Damascius emigrated to Persia and could have begun an oral tradition there that extends up to Farabi.

I have tried in vain to get Bloom to read the *vita Isidori* [Isi-dor or Pytho-dor]. But he is busy with an Othello interpretation where he appears as Yahwe and Iago as Christ . . .[1]

I have not yet begun my Julian-essay (for your Festschrift), but I hope
to be able to write it in Geneva. Perhaps with a short footnote about
"Sallustius"—Damascius—"Marinus." But I would have liked first to
know what you think about these texts. But that will hardly be possible.

With heartiest cordial greetings.

Your Kojève

———————

Paris 5.15.58

Dear Mr. Strauss,

Many thanks for sending me your *Farabi*. I have just read it. It is
"first-class."[1]

As you know, I am now more or less of the same opinion as Farabi.
Only, for me F<arabi>'s "Socrates" is the historical Plato himself. Either
the *Laws* are intended by Plato as Farabi understands them, or they are
forgeries (by Philippos of Opus and Speusippus) (or: Books I–IX [in particular IX] forged, and X–XII re-written). Plato's real opinion is found in
the *Rep<ublic>* + *Statesman* + (*Tim<aeus>* + *Kritias*) + *Philebus*.
They deal exclusively with the "Academy," that is to say, with life together [2]in view of wisdom,[2] or philo-sophizing. This "Academy" ought
to be a "monastery," that is to say, "separated" (chorismo) from the
"world." The "lawgiver" is the Kephalos, the Head of the Academy[3]: he
ought to be "sole ruler" and not bound by any "laws" (= prejudices).
Etc. However: the "common" reader knows nothing of the Academy and
thinks exclusively of the polis. Read that way, the *Republic* and the
States<man> are deliberately "absurd": in the *Republic* the cynic-
sophistic "communism" (including the ridiculous "community of
women"), and in the *States<man>*----sophistic "tyranny." The entirely
serious polemic (against Euclid—Eudoxus—Aristotle) revolves around
the "politeia" inside the Academy; that is to say: 1) either dialectics
(= genuine diairesis without "koinonia" [atomos eidos], or "logic" + "science"; 2) either "the good life" through the living model (paradigma) of
the "leader," or—"study."

This genuinely platonic conception was tried ("monks") for a thousand years (by both Christians and Muslims), and degenerated into
Bayle's Republic of Letters which remains "alive" to this day. Betrayal of

the Intellectuals).⁴ Genuine politicians (statesmen) were always opposed to this (as Julian already was): namely, what Plato may really have meant was of no concern to them, and what they (mis)understood of Plato was naturally "utopian" (because it could only be carried out by a "super-human" tyranny). That is how it stood until Hegel-Marx: for they did not want either to destroy the Academy (= "monasteries") or to render them inactive and ineffectual, but wanted on the contrary to transform them into a "polis." For Hegel/Marx (but by no means for Plato), the philosophers ought indeed (and hence can) become "Kings" (Napoleon—mine) [naturally not the other way around, which would be "utopian"; whereas the phil< osopher's> becoming king is not at all utopian—insofar as this "becoming" is a revolution]. [Something like this is perhaps also what Machiavelli had in view.]

As for "the art of writing," it is possible that Farabi goes back to a tradition (oral?), namely to Damascius's teaching in Persia. He stayed there for only two years, but that might have been enough. Damascius himself goes back to Julianus. [In the *Vita Procli*, "Marianus "quotes almost literally from Julian's Speeches, and in the *vita Isidori* echoes of Julian can also be found.] And Julian was not alone (even disregarding his friend Sallustius). The entire so-called "Vespasian School" thought as he did. It is not a "school," and certainly not "mystical" or "neo-platonic," but rather "epicurean" or democritian. So was Julian, but as Emperor or "civil servant" he deliberately opposed the "epicureanism" ("gardens") of those "intellectuals" (cp. his speech to [= against] Themistius). That is perfectly evident in Eunapius's *Vita Soph.*⁶ (although Eunapius himself did not understand it): especially clearly in connection with Julian's greeting of Maximus (a typical "adventurer"). If you have the time, you must read Eunapius!

With best greetings,

Your Kojève

P.S. By the way, Julian was of the opinion (as were Dam< ascius > and Farabi) that Plato thought exactly as they did, and only never said so openly.

Paris 2.17.59.

Dear Mr. Strauss,

Many thanks for the new book.[1] Although I know the lectures, the book seems to have come out very differently. I will certainly read it.

Please excuse me for thanking you only now. But I was travelling: India, Siam, then Geneva. As a civil servant, naturally.

I would like to hear what you think of my Julianus,[2] in which I publicly appear as a faithful Strauss-disciple.

If you now have more time we might perhaps also resume our Plato dialogue. Klein naturally did not react at all. And you yourself did not have the time to check the passages I cited.

In any event I would like it if I could have my first (long) Plato letter back. It must at present be with Klein. It is the only piece I have written on the question.

I keep hoping I can go to the U.S. But I am now so "European" that it is not altogether easy.

It appears that Gallimard (NRF) intends to have my posthumous works typed up: in exchange for the right to publish some parts post mortem. The latter is a matter of indifference to me. But as soon as I have a typescript, I will send it to you, for your judgment. Besides, Bloom has probably spoken to you about it.

With best greetings,

Your Kojève

_____

Paris, 4.6.61

Dear Mr. Strauss,

We have not written to each other for an eternity. I don't even know who first did not answer.

The last thing I had from you was your Machiavelli.[1] I am not sure I wrote you about it. It seems to me that I did.

In any event, the book is first class. I am naturally not in agreement with the conclusion suggested at the end. But that is not important.

According to Hegel (Ph < enomenology > of M < ind >, propaganda in the modern sense was not discovered until the Enlightenment. According to you, it was discovered by Machiavelli. You appear to be right. But Hegel is also right, in the sense that mass-propaganda in the modern sense developed only in the 18th century. However, Machiavelli is also right (at least according to your interpretation), when he says that the "modern" system of propaganda is specifically Christian..

In the meantime I have completed my *Ancient Philosophy*. Over 1000 pages. Taubes[2] has had them photocopied. In my view it is by no means "ready for publication." But if Queneau insists, I will not refuse. (To refuse would, in this case, also amount to taking onself seriously!)

Bloom is hard at work on his translation[3] and I hardly see him. On the other hand, I frequently talk with Rosen,[4] whom I rather like. He seems to me to be more serious than Bloom.

In terms of health, I am quite well. My official work is very interesting and productive.

I would enjoy hearing from you.

With most cordial greetings,

Your Kojève

THE UNIVERSITY OF CHICAGO
Chicago 37, Illinois
Department of Political Science

January 30, 1962

M. Alexandre Kojève
13 Bd. du Lycee
Vanves (Seine) France

Dear M. Kojève:

I write to you today at the request of Gadamer. He is very anxious that you should come to the opening meeting of the International Hegel Association which will take place at the end of July in Heidelberg and that you should give there a lecture. I suppose he wants you to present your overall interpretation of Hegel. I am sure it would be for the common good if you would give that lecture. Be so good as to let me know at your earliest convenience what you plan to do, so that I can inform Gadamer. The only reason why he did not write to you directly was that he thought that a letter from me to you might be more effective.

How far advanced is your work? I am preparing a small book to be called "The City and Man," three lectures, one on the *Politics*, one on the *Republic* and one on Thucydides. My German book on Spinoza is in the process of being translated into English; I plan to write a very long preface to it containing my autobiography.

Hoping to hear from you soon.

As ever yours,

Leo Strauss

LS:ef
enclosure

THE UNIVERSITY OF CHICAGO
Chicago 37, Illinois
Department of Political Science

March 27, 1962

M. Alexandre Kojève
13 Bd. du Lycée
Vanves (Seine) France

Dear M. Kojève:

On January 30 I wrote to you as follows:

"I write to you today at the request of Gadamer. He is very anxious that you should come to the opening meeting of the International Hegel Association which will take place at the end of July in Heidelberg and that you should give there a lecture. I suppose he wants you to present your overall interpretation of Hegel. I am sure it would be for the common good if you would give that lecture. Be so good as to let me know at your earliest convenience what you plan to do, so that I can inform Gadamer. The only reason why he did not write to you directly was that he thought that a letter from me to you might be more effective.

How far advanced is your work? I am preparing a small book to be called "The City and Man," three lectures, one on the *Politics*, one on the *Republic* and one on Thucydides. My German book on Spinoza is in the process of being translated into English; I plan to write a very long preface to it containing my autobiography.

Hoping to hear from you soon."

Inasmuch as I have not received a reply would you please give this your earliest attention.

As ever yours,

Leo Strauss

LS:ef

3.29.62

Dear Mr. Strauss,

Please excuse me for not yet having answered your first letter. Oddly enough, I was planning to do so today, before I received the second letter.

Well, the reason is that I could not decide to say no, although I had no desire to accept the invitation.

The older I get, the less interested I am in so-called philosophical discussions. Except for yourself and Klein I have not yet found anybody from whom I could learn something. If you or Klein or both of you were to go to Heidelberg, I would naturally also come. But otherwise. . . .

It is really a matter of utter indifference to me what the philosophical gentlemen think or say about Hegel.

A few days ago I gave a lecture on dialectics at the Collège Philosophique of Jean Wahl[1] who had been asking me to do so for over five years. It was terrible. More than 300 very young people came, the room had to be changed, and nevertheless people sat on the floor. When one thinks that this happens only for lectures by Sartre! And that when I first spoke at the Ecole barely a dozen people were in attendance! But the worst was that all these youths set down everything I said. I tried to be as paradoxical and shocking as possible. But no one became indignant, no one thought of protesting. Everything was quietly written down. I had the impression of having become a kind of Heinrich Rickert.[2] In other words, an "old gent." The public, on the other hand, was typically Saint Germain and Café Flore (I spoke at a short—at most 100 meters— distance from it). So that at times I felt like some famous twist-teacher. . . .

All this in order to tell you that I am becoming more and more "platonic." One should address the few, not the many. One should speak and write as little as possible. Unfortunately my *Essay at a Reasoned History of Pagan Philosophy* is to be published, and it comprises more than 1000 (sic) pages!

With very best greetings,

Your

Kojève

P.S. Why do you never come to Europe?

THE UNIVERSITY OF CHICAGO
Chicago 37, Illinois
Department of Political Science

May 29, 1962

M. Alexandre Kojève
15, Boulevard du Lycée
Vanves (Seine)
France

Dear M. Kojève:

I thank you for your letter of March 29. I informed Gadamer immediately. I understand your judgment on this kind of meetings and I am in the habit of acting on the same judgment. Your experience with the philosophic seminar of Wahl does not surprise me. If one wants to see young people who are not mentally in their seventies, one has to come to Chicago. Would it be at all possible for you to spend some time with us, assuming that the money could be raised?

I am looking forward with the utmost interest to your history of pagan philosophy. I am glad to see that, as is indicated by the adjective, you have returned to the faith of your fathers. I myself have written a fairly long chapter on Plato (but only on his political philosophy) for a history of political philosophy which I am editing. My present preoccupation is with my old book on Spinoza which has been translated into English and for which I am writing a new preface,[1] intended to bridge the gulf between 1930 Germany and 1962 U.S.A. It comes as close to an autobiography as is possible within the bounds of propriety. In addition I am preparing for publication three lectures on the city and man, dealing with the *Politics*, the *Republic* and Thucydides. Only after these things have been finished will I be able to begin with my real work, an interpretation of Aristophanes.

Klein claims to have finished his book on the *Meno*—only three more months for checking on the footnotes—but since he has said more or less the same three years ago I believe I shall have to wait another lustrum for its appearance.

Hoping to hear from you soon.

As ever yours,

Leo Strauss

THE UNIVERSITY OF CHICAGO
Chicago 37, Illinois
Department of Political Science

Ocotber 4, 1962

M. Alexandre Kojève
13 Bd. du Lycée
Vanves (Seine), France

Dear Mr. Kojève:

I am very sorry that it took me so long to reply to your letter of July 17. I was very glad to hear that you might be willing to pay us a visit here in Chicago. It is not impossible that we can arrange it financially in 1963, perhaps in the early months of that year. But in order to convince the authorities, I would have to know for how long a period you would be able to come; for a week, a month, a quarter (i.e., two months) or any other period. I must know this very soon, a brief postcard would be sufficient.

I am very anxious to see the second edition of your book especially the supplement on Japan.

With kindest regards.

As ever yours,

Leo Strauss

LS:ef

————————

THE UNIVERSITY OF CHICAGO
Chicago 37, Illinois
Department of Political Science

November 16, 1962

M. Alexandre Kojève
13 Bd. du Lycée
Vanves (Seine)
France

Dear M. Kojève:

I believe that a month's stay here would be perfectly agreeable to the authorities here. Unfortunately, the months June–September would be the worst from our point of view. What about April, or say April 10–May 10? Be so good as to let me know as soon as possible.

What you say about my preface to my book on Spinoza is not entirely new to me. I think I have taken into consideration your objection, whereas you have not taken into consideration the point which I make. Perhaps we can clear up this difficulty when you come here.

With kindest regards.

As ever yours,

Leo Strauss

THE UNIVERSITY OF CHICAGO
Chicago 37, Illinois
Department of Political Science

January 25, 1963

M. Alexandre Kojève
13 Bd. du Lycée
Vanves (Seine), France

Dear M. Kojève:

I am sorry that it took me such a long time to reply to your letter. There are all kinds of administrative difficulties, to say nothing of my own work. I eventually succeeded in talking to the individual who is in charge of the lectures such as those which I hope you will give. They are having a meeting next week; for one reason or the other he insists on corresponding directly with you. So I expect that you will hear from him within the next two weeks.

I am now writing the third and last chapter of a short book to be entitled *The City and Man* (Aristotle's politics; Plato's Republic; Thucydides). Around Easter Pines' new translation of Maimonides' *Guide* with a rather long introduction by me[1] as well as < a > *History of Political Philosophy*[2] written by my former students, and, last but not least, the English version of Gallimard's *On Tyranny* will be out. You may have heard that Bloom has succeeded in becoming a member of the Political Science profession.

With kindest regards.

As ever yours

Leo Strauss

Ls:ef

June 3, 1965

Dear Mr. Kojèvnikoff,

Thank you so much for your letter. I have told Cropsey that you did not get a copy of the Festschrift. He is certain that the publisher sent you one. Perhaps you can check once more at home.

I very much regretted that you could not make a side-trip to Chicago. As for myself, I hardly travel any more. I experience considerable discomfort ever since my circulation has stopped functioning properly. In any case, Gildin, who has evidently sat at your feet with open ears and open mouth, has given a detailed report on your political views. I was pleased to see that you are just as critical of U.S. liberals as I am. It did not surprise me, because I know there is reason, and that you are reasonable.

I almost came to Europe this Spring: I had accepted an invitation from Hamburg for the 1965 S<ummer> S<emester>, but then had to cancel it for reasons of health. I should have liked to see with my own eyes how things are developing in Germany. From intelligent young Germans I got the impression that the development exhibits a certain parallelism to 1830 and ff: a turning away from German speculation (in the twentieth century, away from Heidegger) toward Western positivism (that is to say, American social science).

I did not get your Koyré essay. Please do send it to me. Or do you mean your contribution to the *Mélanges Koyré*.[1] That one I did indeed get; it arrived together with your letter.

I was unable to write to Mrs. Koyré. That is very bad. I trust that she will forgive me.

As for your contribution to my Festschrift, I had been acquainted with it for a long time, since you had sent me the manuscript. I was very gratified, since it shows that persecution and the art of writing are not some fancy. (Incidentally, a young American—Hathaway—is currently working on the pseudo-Dyonisius from your point of view.[2] I have referred him to your observations regarding the neo-Platonists.)

I have just finished dictating a book, *Socrates and Aristophanes*.[3] I believe that it will elicit an occasional smile from you, and not only because of Aristophanes' jokes and of my Victorian paraphrases of them. If all goes well, I will then turn to Lucretius.

Did you get my *The City and Man*[4]? And what do you say about Klein's *Meno*?[5]

Cordially as ever,

Your

Leo Strauss

Editorial Notes

Strauss to Kojève, 6 December 1932

A postcard, written in German; two holes punched in along one edge, with a view to filing the card in a binder.

Strauss to Kojève, 13 December 1932

A postcard, written in French; holes punched in.

Strauss to Kojève, 17 December 1932

Written in German. The original is lost. The transcription is based on a photocopy.

Strauss to Kojève, from 47 Montague Street, London

A postcard, written in English, probably in early 1933. The original is lost. The transcription is based on a photocopy of poor quality that shaved off some letters at the right-hand edge of several lines of the text. Additional text was lost because of the holes punched into the card.

Strauss to Kojève, 16 January 1934

Written in English. The original is lost. The transcription is based on a photocopy of poor quality.

1. Jacob Klein (1899–1978), Strauss's and Kojève's life-long friend, took his doctorate in Marburg under Nicolai Hartmann.

2. Hans-Georg Gadamer (1900–), long-time professor of philosophy at Heidelberg University, best known for his *Wahrheit und Methode* (1960; tr. *Truth and Method*, 1975). The "Correspondence Concerning *Wahrheit und Methode*" between Strauss and Gadamer has been published in *The Independent Journal of Philosophy* (1978), 2:5–12. See also: "Recollections of Leo Strauss: An Interview with Hans-Georg Gadamer," *The Newsletter*, Politics Department, University of Dallas, Spring 1978, 2: 4–7; and Ernest L. Fortin, "Gadamer on Strauss: An Interview," *Interpretation* (1984), 12: 1–14.

Gadamer, Strauss and Kojève met in Paris in Spring 1933. The Gadamer *alias*, "Moldauer," seems to have been a private joke between Strauss and Kojève.

315

3. Heidegger's May 1933 Address upon assuming the Rectorship of Freiburg University a few months after the National Socialists' seizure of power. It has been translated and annotated by K. Harries under the title "The Self-Assertion of the German University," in *The Review of Metaphysics*, (1985), *38*: 470–480; page 474 of the translation corresponds to the page of the original publication to which Strauss refers.

4. Paul Ludwig Landsberg (1901–1944), studied with Husserl and Scheler; he was dismissed from his teaching position at the University of Bonn in 1933; he had by then published *Pascals Berufung* (Bonn, 1929), *Die Welt des Mittelalters und wir* (Bonn 1922) and *Wesen und Bedeutung der platonischen Akademie* (Bonn 1933); by the time his *Einführung in die philosophische Anthropologie* came out (Frankfurt a/M, 1934), he had moved to France, where he published in the review *Esprit*, and was politically active. In 1943 he was arrested by the Gestapo in Pau. He died a year later in the Oranienburg Concentration Camp.

5. Alexandre Koyré (Rostov-on-Don 1892–Paris 1964), the distinguished historian of philosophy and of science; he had gone to study with Husserl and Hilbert in Germany around 1910; fought in the French army in World War I, and settled in France, where he taught at the École Pratique des Hautes Études.

Strauss to Kojève, from 2 Elsworthy Road, London

Written in German, probably February or March 1934. The original is lost. The printed text is based on a transcription.

1. Julius Guttmann (1880–1950), best known for his *Die Philosophie des Judentums*, Munich, 1933 (Engl. tr. 1964); between 1922 and 1934 he was Director of the Akademie für die Wissenschaft des Judentums, in Berlin. Strauss was associated with that Institute from 1925 to 1932. His "The Quarrel between the Ancients and the Moderns in the Philosophy of Judaism," subtitled "Remarks on Julius Guttmann's *Philosophy of Judaism*," stands as the opening essay to his first volume of collected essays, *Philosophie und Gesetz*. Guttman became professor of Jewish Philosophy at the Hebrew University of Jerusalem in 1934.

Strauss to Kojève, 9 April, 1934

Written in German. The printed text is based on a poor photocopy of one side, and a transcription of the other side of a lost original into which holes had again been punched for filing purposes.

1. Dr. Zbigniew Lubienski, *Die Grundlagen des ethisch-politischen Systems von Hobbes*, Ernst Reinhardt, Munich, 1932.

2. Ferdinand Tönnies, *Thomas Hobbes Leben und Lehre*, Fromann, Stuttgart, 1886; 3rd enlarged ed., 1925.

3. "A recent and very competent writer (L Strauss in *Recherches philosophiques*, II, 610) has said that Hobbes was the true founder of liberalism (in the continental sense), that his absolutism was liberalism in the making, and that both the critics and the opponents of any thoroughgoing liberalism should go back to Hobbes." John Laird, *Hobbes*, Benn, London 1934, p. 312, n.1. Laird's reference is to Strauss's "Quelques remarques sur la science politique de Hobbes: à propos du livre rècent de M. Lubienski," *Recherches philosophiques*, (1933), 2: 609–622.

4. Strauss's stepson.

5. Strauss had addressed this letter to Monsieur Alexandre <sic> 15 bd. du

Lycèe, Vanves (Seine). It was returned—Retour à l'envoyeur—to 2 Elsworthy Rd., London N.S.3 with the handwritten note that the addressee is "inconnu au 15 Bd. du Lycèe." Thereupon Strauss wrote, in English, on the back of the envelope: "I am so sorry—but why did the post not find you? To speak like an Englishman (Englishmen, you remember, like jokes about death, as they are most original people)—are you dead or buried? The College of Arms decided the question concerning the Essays-Ms in the favorable sense: i.e. the Essays must be the earliest writing of Hobbes." He then re-mailed the letter in a correctly addressed envelope.

Kojève to Strauss, 1 May 1934

Written in German.

1. Serge Stavisky had started as a pretty criminal, but soon managed a series of major financial swindles with the complicity of persons in the highest reaches of French finance, politics and the police. When his house of cards collapsed, the police found him dead under suspicious circumstances and before he could implicate anyone. Nevertheless, the ensuing scandal brought down a government, caused riots in Paris in January 1934, and set off a wave of intense xenophobia. The repercussions of the "affaire Stavisky" continued to be felt for some time to come at all levels of French political life.

2. Jacob Gordin (St. Petersburg ca. 1896–Paris 1947); was later associated with the Institut des Langues Orientales. He came to be viewed as one of the most influential figures in the postwar renewal of Jewish studies in the French-speaking world.

3. Fritz Heinemann (1889–1970), student of Hermann Cohen, Professor at the University of Frankfurt a/M until forced to leave in 1933; he subsequently taught at Oxford. His *Die Philosophie im XX. Jahrhundert* (Stuttgart, 1959) contains brief allusions to Kojève and to Strauss.

Abel Rey (1873–1940), historian and philosopher of science. In 1932 Kojéve submitted a thesis on "L'idée du déterminisme dans la physique classique et dans la physique moderne" to him, with a view to obtaining a doctorat ès lettres. It has been edited by Dominique Auffret, and published by Le livre de poche, Paris, 1990.

4. Georges Gurvitch (St. Petersburg 1894–Paris 1966), had emigrated to France after completing his studies in Germany. His *Les tendances actuelles de la philosophie allemande: E. Husserl, M. Scheler, E. Lask, M. Heidegger* (Vrin, 1930), was based on a course of lectures he delivered at the Sorbonne in the preceding year. Later he became best known as a sociologist. During World War II he taught at the Graduate Faculty of the New School for Social Research in New York. From 1948 until the time of his death he taught at the Sorbonne. At the time of this letter of Kojève's, the phenomenologist Aron Gurwitsch (Vilna 1901–New York 1973) was also living in Paris.

Strauss to Kojève, 3 June 1934

Written in German. The original is lost. The transcription is based on a defective photocopy.

1. *Mitleben.*

Strauss Kojève, 9 May 1935

Written in German.

1. Jacob Klein, "Die griechische Logistik und die Entstehung der Algebra," *Quellen und Studien zur Geschichte der Mathematik, Astronomie und Physik*, Abteilung B:

Studien, vol. 3, fasc. 1 (Berlin, 1934), pp. 18–105 (Part I); fasc. 2 (1936), pp. 122–235 (Part II); translated by Eva Brann under the title *Greek Mathematical Thought and the Origin of Algebra*, The M.I.T. Press, 1968.

2. *Philosophie und Gesetz. Beiträge zum Verständnis Maimunis und seiner Vorläufer*, Schocken, Berlin, 1935; translated by Fred Baumann as *Philosophy and Law, Essays Toward the Understanding of Maimonides and his Predecessors*, The Jewish Publication Society of America, Philadelphia, 1987.

Kojève to Strauss, 2 November 1936

Written in German.

1. *The Political Philosophy of Hobbes: Its Basis and Its Genesis*, tr. Elsa M. Sinclair, foreword Ernest Barker; Oxford: Clarendon Press, 1936.

2. *vorgegebene Gegebenheiten*.

3. *aufgegebene* Werte.

Kojève to Strauss, 22 June 1946

Written in German.

1. "Farabi's *Plato*," Louis Ginzberg Jubilee Volume, New York: Academy for Jewish Research, 1945, pp. 357–393; reprinted in abbreviated and modified form as the "Introduction" to *Persecution and the Art of Writing*, The Free Press of Glencoe, 1952.

2. Raymond Queneau (1903–1976), the witty, inventive, and prolific writer, and editor at Gallimard.

3. Eric Weil (1904–1977) wrote his dissertation under Ernst Cassirer, as had Strauss. In 1933 he settled in Paris, where he attended Kojève's seminar. After the War he taught at the École Pratique des Hautes Études, and susbequently at the Universities of Lille and of Nice.

4. Klein came to America in 1938, and soon after his arrival began teaching at St. John's College in Annapolis. He served as Dean of the College from 1949 to 1958.

Kojève to Strauss, 8 April 1947

Written in German.

1. Most probably "The Law of Reason in the *Kuzari*," *Proceedings of the American Academy for Jewish Research* (1943), *13*, pp. 47–96; reprinted in *Persecution and the Art of Writing*, The Free Press, 1952, pp. 95–141; and "On Classical Political Philosophy," *Social Research* (1945), *12*, pp. 98–117; reprinted in *What is Political Philosophy?* The Free Press, 1959, pp. 78–94.

2. Alexandere Koyré, *Discovering Plato*, Columbia University Press, 1945.

3. *Logique de la philosophie*, Paris, 1950, which was Weil's *thèse principale*. His *thèse complémentaire* was a short but useful book on *Hégel et l'état*. While these works were heavily under the influence of Kojève's Hegelianism, Weil's later works became increasingly neo-Kantian.

Strauss to Kojève, 22 August 1948

Typewritten in German.

1. Foreword by Alvin Johnson; Political Science Classics, New York, 1948.

2. *Introduction à la lecture de Hegel*, Paris, Gallimard, 1947.

3. "the rational animal."

4. Nietzsche, *Thus Spake Zarathustra*, Zarathustra's Prologue, section 5.

Strauss to Kojève, 6 December 1948
   Typewritten in English.

Strauss to Kojève, 13 May 1949
   Written in German.
   1. Kojève's *Esquisse d'une phénoménologie du droit* was initially written during the War, in 1943; it was published posthumously by Gallimard, in 1982.

Kojève to Strauss, 26 May 1949
   Written in German.

Strauss to Kojève, 27 June 1949
   Written in German.
   1. Soma sēma; Greek pun: "the body is a tomb"; see Plato, *Gorgias*, 493a 3, *Cratylus* 400c
   2. "The happiness of contemplation is really available only from time to time, so says the philosopher." The reference is to Aristotle, *Metaphysics*, XII, 7, 1072b 25.

Kojève to Strauss, 15 August 1949
   Written in German.

Strauss to Kojève, 4 September 1949
   Written in German.
   1. In English in the text.
   2. Karl Jaspers, *Vom Ursprung und Ziel der Geschichte*, Artemis-Verlag, Zürich, 1949.

Kojève to Strauss, 10 October 1949
   Written in German.

Strauss to Kojève, 14 October 1949
   Written in German.
   1. In English in the text.

Kojève to Strauss, 26 December 1949
   Written in German.

Strauss to Kojève, 18 January 1950
   Written in German.
   1. peri tōn megistōn te kai kalliston; "about the greatest and the fairest things."

Strauss to Kojève, 24 March 1950
   Written in German.

Kojève to Strauss, 9 April 1950
   Written in German.

Strauss to Kojève, 26 June 1950
   Written in German.
   1. "about the principles (as well as about the beginning);" in Greek letters in the text.

Strauss to Kojève, 28 July 1950
 Written in German.

Strauss to Kojève, 5 August 1950
 Written in German.

Strauss to Kojève, 14 September 1950
 Written in German.

Kojève to Strauss, 19 September 1950
 Written in German.
 1. Torquemada (1420–1498), chief of the Spanish Inquisition; F. E. Dzerzhinski (1877–1926) organized the Soviet Secret Police (Cheka, later OGPU, then NKVD, and now KGB) on Lenin's instructions. Both Torquemada and Dzerzhinski were notorious for their inhuman cruelty.
 2. The reference appears to be to the paragraph on pp. 188f. above.
 3. The letter breaks off at this point; at least one sheet is missing.

Strauss to Kojève, 28 September 1950
 Written in German.

Strauss to Kojève, 19 January, 1951
 Written in German.
 1. Bertrand de Jouvenel (1903–1987), political journalist and author of works in political theory; regarding his career see Zeev Sternhell, *Neither Right nor Left*, University of California Press, 1986, *passim*.

Strauss to Kojève, 22 February 1951
 Typewritten in English.

Strauss to Kojève, 17 July 1952
 Written in German.
 1. *Persecution and the Art of Writing* (The Free Press, 1952), was reviewed by Yvon Belaval under the title "Pour une sociologie de la philosophie," in *Critique*, October 1953, *68/69*: 853–866; Strauss comments on Belaval's review as well as on a review by George H. Sabine in "On a Forgotten Kind of Writing," *Chicago Review*, 1954, *8*: 64–75, reprinted in *Independent Journal of Philosophy*, 1978, *2*: 27–31.
 2. A. Kojève, "Les Romans de la Sagesse," *Critique*, May 1952, *8*: 387–397.

Kojève to Strauss, 11 August 1952
 Written in German.
 1. Probably "On Collingwood's Philosophy of History," *The Review of Metaphysics* (1952), *5*: 559–586.

Kojève to Strauss, 29 October 1953
 Written in German.
 1. Presumably *Natural Right and History*, University of Chicago Press, 1953.
 2. King Ahab covets the vineyard of his neighbor Naboth who refuses to give it up to the king because "[t]he Lord forbid it me that I should give the inheritance of my fathers unto thee. ." *I Kings* 21:1–3, cited in epigraph to *Natural Right and History*.

The sequel of the story of Ahab and Naboth bears directly on the point here at issue between Strauss and Kojève.

3. Massen*dressur* und Volks*hygiene*.

Strauss to Kojève, 28 April 1954

Typewritten in English.

1. *De la tyrannie, par Leo Strauss; traduit de l'anglais par Hélène Kern, Précédé de Hiéron, de Xénophon, et suivi de Tyrannie et Sagesse par Alexandre Kojève*. Les Essays LXIX, Gallimard, Paris, 1954.

2. Karl Löwith (1897–1973), student of Husserl's and Heidegger's, taught at Marburg until 1934, when he was forced out of the University. He spent two years in Rome on a Rockefeller Fellowship, went on to teach at Sendai University in Japan, the Hartford (CT) Seminary, the Graduate Faculty of the New School for Social Research, and in 1952 he accepted a Professorship at Heidelberg University. His extensive writings, primarily on Hegel, Nietzsche and Heidegger, have been collected in a nine-volume *Sämmtliche Schriften* (J. B. Metzler, Stuttgart, 1981–1988). His correspondence with Strauss appears in *The Independent Journal of Philosophy*, (1983), 4: 107–108; (1988), 5/6: 177–191. The remarkable memoir which he wrote in 1940, *Mein Leben in Deutschland vor und nach 1933. Ein Bericht*, was discovered and published posthumously (Metzler, 1986).

Strauss to Kojève, 4 June 1956

Dictated in English.

1. Allan Bloom (1930–   ), currently Professor, Committee on Social Thought, The University of Chicago; author of *The Closing of the American Mind*, Simon and Schuster, 1987.

2. Shlomo Pines (Paris 1908–1989), historian of philosophy and of science, Professor at the Hebrew University of Jerusalem; (*Collected Works*, 2 vols., The Magnes Press, Jerusalem, 1979). Pines and Strauss collaborated on an edition of Maimonides's *Guide of the Perplexed* (see the letter of 25 January 1963). See also Shlomo Pines, "On Leo Strauss," (translated from the Hebrew by A. L. Motzkin), *The Independent Journal of Philosophy* (1988), 5/6: 169–171.

3. Prolegomena to any future chutzpa that might present itself as absolute knowledge.

Kojève to Strauss, 8 June 1956

Written in German.

1. Hilail Gildin (1929–   ), currently Professor of Philosophy, Queens College; founding editor of *Interpretation*, editor of *Political Philosophy, Six Essays by Leo Strauss*, Pegasus, 1975; author of *Rousseau's Social Contract, The Design of the Argument*, The University of Chicago Press, 1983.

Kojève to Strauss, 11 April 1957

Written in German; the quotations from Sallustius are in French.

1. "On the *Euthyphron*," published in Leo Strauss, *The Rebirth of Classical Political Rationalism*, Thomas Pangle, ed., The University of Chicago Press, 1989, pp. 187–206.

2. Division.

3. By Xenophon; see Strauss "The Spirit of Sparta or the Taste of Xenophon," *Social Research* (1939); *6*: 502–536.

4. The passage in parentheses is a later addition.

5. In English in the text.

6. *The Life of the Philosopher Isodorus*, restored <translated and elucidated> by Asmus, Leipzig, Meiner, 1911.

7. The last of the normal letter-size sheets, on which this long letter is written, ends here. It may be that the remainder of the letter is lost. However, a loose and otherwise unidentified half-sheet in the folder that holds this correspondence would seem to belong here, and is therefore printed as the conclusion of the present letter.

Strauss to Kojève, 22 April 1957

Typewritten in English.

1. Physis, "nature."

Strauss to Kojève, 28 May 1957

Written in English. Transcribed from a typescript in the Chicago Strauss Archive.

1. opinion

2. moderate, fitting, proper.

3. crossed out; the penciled substitution is illegible.

Kojève to Strauss, 1 July 1957

Written in German.

1. community of the kinds or species

2. community

3. Zeit = voll-*endete* Geshichte; Wissen = er-innerte [vollendete] Geschichte.

4. god-good

5. Sinn

6. separateness

7. community of the kinds or species

8. community of the ideas

9. kind or species

10. Giessen, 1909.

11. In English in the text.

12. the mean; or: the intermediate

13. by nature

14. for us

15. indeterminate dyad

16. good

17. speech, reason

18. intelligible universe

19. mind

20. or: actuality; Wirklichkeit

21. or: fulfilled; voll-endet

22. indivisible idea

23. division

24. mean

25. community

26. reading: woge < ge > n
27. separation
28. Kojève cites the French translation by Auguste Diès in Platon, *Oeuvres compètes*, Société d'édition "Les Belles Lettres," Paris 1925.
29. mean
30. mind
31. indeterminate dyad
32. mind-god
33. wirklich
34. "What is Political Philosophy?", delivered in 1954 and 1955 as the Judah L. Magnes Lectures at the Hebrew University; revised version published as the title essay of *What is Political Philosophy? and Other Studies*, The Free Press of Glencoe, 1959.
35. The "Note" is a photocopy of a 20-page French typescript with some inked-in corrections, entitled: "*Platon*—Critique d'Aristote," and inscribed:

Amicus Plato . . .

Kojève
10/VII 57.

We have not included it in this translation of the correspondence because Kojève very fully summarized its contents in the Plato interpretation of his letter of 11 April 1957, and in the present letter. A somewhat revised and expanded version of this Note eventually appeared in Kojève's posthumously published *Essai d'une histoire raisonnée de la philosophie païenne, volume II, Platon-Aristote* (Paris, 1972), pp. 364–378.

Strauss to Kojève, 11 September 1957

Typewritten in English.
1. beings and becomings

Kojève to Koyré, 24 October 1957

This letter, addressed to Mr. and Mrs. Koyré, ends with Kojève's request that they send it on to Strauss. It is written in French, but the extensive citations are in English.
1. In English in the text.
2. In Rosán: " . . . to the Almighty (lit.: the revolution of the whole), . . ."
3. Rosán: a
4. Rosán: quick-tempered; nevertheless
5. Rosán: say "That's
6. Rosán: at the higher
7. Rosán: which
8. Rosán: life, for
9. Rosán: Underlined by Kojève.
10. read: XXXI
11. See Rosán's note 19, page 29.
12. Rosán: goddess
13. Underlined by Kojève.

Kojève to Strauss, 5 November 1957

Written in German.
1. "Cosmopolitan Man and the Political Community: *Othello*," *The American*

Political Science Review, 1960, 54:129–157; reprinted in Allan Bloom with Harry V. Jaffa, *Shakespeare's Politics*, Basic Books, 1964, pp. 35–74.

Kojève to Strauss, 15 May 1958
Written in German.
1. Probably "How Farabi read Plato's *Laws*," *Mélanges Louis Massignon*, vol. III, Damascus, 1957; reprinted in *What is Political Philosophy? and Other studies*, the Free Press, 1959, pp. 134–154.
2. In English in the text.
3. In English in the text.
4. In English in the text.
5. Julien Benda, *La trahison des clercs*, Paris, Grasset, 1927; translated by R. Aldington as *Betrayal of the Intellectuals*, Wm. Murrow, NY, 1928.
6. *Lives of the Philosophers and of the Sophists*.

Kojève to Strauss, 17 February 1959
Written in German.
1. Probably *What is Political Philosophy? and Other Studies*, The Free Press, Glencoe, IL, 1959.
2. "The Emperor Julian and his Art of Writing" (translated by James H. Nichols, Jr.), in J. Cropsey ed., *Ancients and Moderns, Essays in the Tradition of Political Philosophy in Honor of Leo Strauss*, Basic Books, Inc., New York, 1964; pp. 95–113.

Kojève to Strauss, 6 April 1961
Written in German.
1. *Thoughts on Machiavelli*, The Free Press of Glencoe, 1958.
2. Jacob Taubes (Vienna 1923–Berlin 1987), author of *Abendländische Eschatologie* (1946), had held Visiting appointments at Harvard and Columbia Universities; in 1961 he became Visiting Professor, and in 1965 Professor of Jewish Studies and Hermeneutics at the Free University of Berlin. He tells of a meeting in Berlin in 1967 between Kojève and the leaders of the student rebellion, at which Kojève told "Dutschke & Co." "that the most important thing they could and should do, is . . . to study Greek." It was not what they had expected to hear; nor is it what they did. *Ad Carl Schmitt. Gegenstrebige Fügung*, Merve Verlag (Berlin, 1987), p.24 (I am indebted for this reference to Professor Lutz Niethammer; see also his *Posthistoire: Ist die Geschichte zu Ende?* [Rowohlt, Hamburg, 1989, p. 81, n. 21)].
3. Of Plato's *Republic*, published by Basic Books, New York, 1968.
4. Stanley Rosen (1929–   ), currently Evan Pugh Professor of Philosophy, Pennsylvania State University; author of significant works on Plato, Hegel, and contemporary philosophy; he discusses the debate between Strauss and Kojève in *Hermeneutics as Politics* (Oxford University Press, 1987), chapter 3.

Strauss to Kojève, 30 January 1962
Typewritten in English.

Strauss to Kojève, 27 March 1962
Typewritten in English.

Kojève to Strauss, 29 March 1962
Written in German.

1. Jean Wahl (1888–1974), Professor of Philosophy at the Sorbonne, he was among the first to introduce "existentialist" thought to France with such works as *Le malheur de la conscience dans la philosophie de Hegel* (1929), and *Études Kirkegaardiennes* (1938). The Collège Philosophique which he organized in the late 1940s provided a lively public forum outside the University for lectures and discussions by an unusually wide variety of distinguished French and foreign speakers.

2. Heinrich Rickert (1863–1936), neo-Kantian of the so-called Baden school, he was the very embodiment of professorial philosophy. He taught at Heidelberg for many years, and Kojève had studied with him there.

Strauss to Kojève, 29 May 1962

Typewritten in English.

1. "Preface to the English Translation" of *Spinoza's Critique of Religion*, tr., E. M. Sinclair, Schocken Books, New York, 1965, pp. 1–31; reprinted as "Preface to Spinoza's Critique of Religion," in *Liberalism Ancient and Modern*, Basic Books, New York, 1968, ch. 9, pp. 224–259.

Strauss to Kojève, 4 October 1962

Typewritten in English.

Strauss to Kojève, 16 November 1962

Typewritten in English.

Strauss to Kojève, 25 January 1963

Typewritten in English.

1. The University of Chicago Press, 1963.

2. Co-edited by Joseph Cropsey, Rand McNally & Co., Chicago, 1963.

Strauss to Kojève , 3 June 1965

Written in German.

1. "L'origine chrétienne de la science moderne," *Mélanges Alexandre Koyré*, vol. II, pp. 295–306; Paris, 1964.

2. Ronald F. Hathaway, "Pseudo-Dyonisius and the Problem of the Sources in the *Periphyseon* of John Scotus Errigena," Brandeis University Dissertation.

3. Basic Books, N.Y., 1966.

4. Rand McNally, Chicago, 1964.

5. *A Commentary on Plato's Meno*, The University of North Carolina Press, 1965.

Name Index

Subject Index

333